PLATONIC QUESTIONS

The double herm of Socrates and Plato in the Ambulacro of the Vatican.

Diskin Clay

PLATONIC QUESTIONS

Dialogues with the Silent Philosopher

The Pennsylvania State University Press
University Park, Pennsylvania

Library of Congress Cataloging-in-Publication Data

Clay, Diskin.
    Platonic questions : dialogues with the silent philosopher / Diskin Clay.
      p.   cm.
    Includes bibliographical references (p.   ) and indexes.
    ISBN 0-271-02043-1 (cloth : alk. paper)
    ISBN 0-271-02044-X (pbk. : alk. paper)
    1. Plato. Dialogues.—I. Title
    B395 .C57 2000
    184—dc21

                                                            99-056918

Frontispiece: Photos of the double herm of Socrates and Plato are from Georg Lippold,
Die Skulpturen des Vaticansichen Museums (Berlin, 1956), 3:2.

For Charles Kahn, ἐριήρει ἑταίρῳ

CONTENTS

PROLOGUE

Platonic Questions: Dialogues with the Silent Philosopher is meant as a companion and guide to the reader who has begun to read the dialogues of Plato and is left with the fascination and perplexities that a first reading of Plato provokes. The sources of Plato's fascination are vivid and evident. In reading his dialogues, we seem to return to Athens as it was during the lifetime of Socrates, a lifetime that coincided with the decades of Athens' greatest literature and art. There we sit silently as the audience of conversations between Socrates and his contemporaries. In many cases, we are given a precise setting for these conversations, both in place and in time. Socrates and his contemporaries come alive as characters on Plato's page. They are as carefully drawn as their counterparts on the stage of the Theater of Dionysos. And, as in the case of Attic tragedy, action described is as powerful as action seen.

It is only when these prose dramas end that perplexity sets in. We realize that these are philosophical dramas and that, in the case of Socrates and his interlocutors, real lives are at stake. The topics of these overheard conversations canvass the issues that engage us as we think about the choices we must make in life: the virtues of the individual, the virtues of society, and the virtues of the universe, which can appear unrelated to the virtues of individuals and their societies.

The Platonic dialogues are driven by questions, but Plato does not leave us with any great confidence that there are ready or stable answers to the questions Socrates asks and his surrogates of the later dialogues attempt to answer. The shorter dialogues, which are conversations on the virtues (*Charmides, Laches, Euthyphro,* the first book of the *Republic*), offer no clear conception of the principles of virtuous conduct: self-restraint, courage, piety, and justice. Neither Socrates nor his interlocutors seem satisfied with the definitions of these virtues that emerge in the course of the conversation. All we really learn is that at the end of the conversation Socrates' companions are no longer comfortable with conceptions that had once seemed self-evident to them.

Even more perplexing is our failure as readers to discover a source of authority within the Platonic dialogues. We look for the voice of authority and attend to Socrates with particular attention—and perhaps some reverence. But Socrates' habit of asking, rather than answering, questions and his urbane, self-assured manner of professing ignorance and playing the part of the eager pupil make us look elsewhere. We look beyond the drama of Socrates' conversations to their author, and we encounter, from the *Apology* to the *Laws*, silence. Plato's silence is like the silence of Sophocles. Sophocles does not speak in his tragedies; Plato does not speak in his dialogues. If Sophocles speaks at all, it is through his tragedies, not in them. Plato speaks in none of his dialogues. In the Platonic dialogues we do not know what Plato said.

As for his dialogues, they do not seem to speak directly to one another. In no dialogue is an argument made to depend on an argument already made in an earlier dialogue. By Plato's choice of the form of the dramatic dialogue, no speaker in any of his dialogues can refer back to a written dialogue. And Plato, who appears in none of his dialogues, can never say, as does Aristotle in the *Metaphysics*, "[W]e have proved these points in our Physics" (*Metaphysics* 12.1073a32, referring to *Physics* 8.8–9). No speaker refers back to an earlier dialogue in which he did not take part, although some dialogues contain references to earlier and unrecorded conversations between Socrates and his interlocutors. Disconcertingly, in the Platonic dialogues "the sun is new every day."

Another order of perplexity arises as the reader reflects on dialogues just read and confronts the meaning of their settings. These settings pose an enigma for readers who come to Plato with the experience of reading later philosophical texts. We ask: What is the purpose of the elaborate settings with which Plato invests the arguments of his dialogues? In four cases (*Phaedo, Symposium, Parmenides, Theaetetus*), one dialogue is recalled within the frame of another. In some narrated dialogues (*Charmides, Republic*), Socrates evokes the scene that provides the background to one of his conversations. Even in a dramatic dialogue like the *Phaedrus*, Socrates and Phaedrus reveal the setting for their conversation on the outskirts of Athens, at high noon, in the heat of high summer. We ask: What do these details contribute to the argument of the dialogue? Can we discard this "scenery" as we read on in search of a philosophical argument?

Two anecdotes concerning ancient readers of Plato ask to be repeated here. According to the first, after reading the *Gorgias*, a Corinthian farmer left his fields and vines for Athens and Plato's Academy; according to the second, after reading the *Republic*, a woman by the name of Axiothea left Arcadia for Athens and entered the Academy disguised as a man. As are all such anecdotes, these are emblematic. They convey the range of the appeal of Plato's dialogues among his contemporaries as the dialogues circulated outside Athens; they also convey the belief that contact with the author of these dialogues in the Academy would supply whatever was found wanting in his written dialogues. This is what moved the Corinthian and the Arcadian to cross the Gulf of Corinth for Athens. In Athens and Plato's Academy, his reader could enter into an actual conversation with the silent philosopher.

We are now separated from Plato by a gulf of 2,400 years. That distance is even greater because Plato has been so transformed in an unbroken posthumous life of assimilation and criticism that he now seems near and familiar. But "Plato" is a manner of speaking. Plato is read now both as a contemporary philosopher and as an Athenian dramatic poet. Perhaps Plato himself is responsible for this schism. In the *Republic* (3.392C), Socrates made the distinction between content (*logos*), or argument, and style (*lexis*). From the fourth century B.C. to the present, Plato's dialogues have been read either for their content or for their style. In the case of no other philosopher have voice and mind, language and thought, been so organically connected as with Plato, and in none have form and content been so traumatically severed. In the second edition of the *Oxford Classical Dictionary* (of 1970), the entry "Plato" was handled by two authors, with very different interests. One, by Richard Robinson, is devoted to the argumentation of Plato's dialogues; the other, by another distinguished Oxford scholar, J. D. Denniston, is devoted to Plato's style. Plato's style receives one numbered section to philosophy's fifteen. (Now, in the third edition of the *Oxford Classical Dictionary* [1996], the article on Plato by Julia Annas has no mention of Plato's style.)

A passage in Cicero's early dialogue *On the Orator* seems to articulate this disjunction between an appreciation of Plato's style and that of his thought. The statesman and orator Lucius Crassus is speaking. His subject is the split in oratory that Socrates brought about in the late fifth century. His complaint is that Socrates was responsible for "this severing, as it were, of tongue and heart (we would say mind). It is discordant, harmful, regrettable. Its result is that one set of teachers instruct us in eloquence; another in thought" (*On the Orator* 3.61). The odd feature of this judgment is that Cicero's Socrates is Plato's Socrates and that Crassus found the origins of this sundering of the whole body of philosophy in the dialogues of Plato. Socrates wrested the name of philosophy from the common understanding and practice of liberal studies "and in his own conversations sundered the art of thinking wisely and speaking with elegance. Plato has made his genius and varied conversations immortal to posterity in his own writings, for Socrates committed nothing to writing" (*On the Orator* 3.60). This is a distinctly Ciceronian manner of stating our problem as readers. But, where we now face the results of the severance of "tongue and heart" in the study of Plato and have two sets of professors, Cicero lamented that Socrates did not combine as a statesman both philosophy and oratory, as did Cicero himself.

A contemporary introduction to Plato must walk—in the words of the New England transcendentalist—on cloven hooves, placing weight both on the spirit and on the letter of Plato's dialogues. That is, in our context, on Plato's "philosophy" and on Plato's "poetry." My own inclination and training make me list on the side of the literary character of the Platonic dialogues. In addressing the "poetry" of the Platonic dialogues and the dialogue form, it is surely difficult to satisfy those philosophers who tend to look for consistency, coherence, and a system of logically related parts. In recent years, philosophical readers have been placing small slices of the Platonic dialogues under the microscope of logical analysis and disregarding the context from which these slices have been severed. The interest of present-day philosophy in making Plato its contemporary is a manifestation of the overwhelming authority of a philosopher who abjured authoritative modes of discourse but who, despite his failure to appear or to speak in any of his dialogues, has been recognized as the final authority for what his "spokesmen"—Socrates, the Eleatic Stranger, Timaeus, Critias, the Athenian Stranger—have to say.

This presentation of Plato divides into three chapters. The first, "Socrates," recognizes the importance of a philosopher whose life was centered in the city of Athens and spanned the period of its most dramatic development and equally dramatic decline (469–399 B.C.) but who never wrote a single word of philosophical discourse, to a younger philosopher who wrote in the decades of the city's attempt to reassert itself as a power in Greece and whose life spanned the period of the Peloponnesian War and the drab, belligerent, and repetitive first half of the fourth century (428–347 B.C.). But Plato, whose writing career might have begun with *The Apology of Socrates* in 399 and ended with the *Laws* at the end of his life, wrote as if the age in which he lived were that of Socrates. This at least is the great illusion of Plato's Socratic dialogues.

The second chapter, "Dialogue," presents the Greek literary genre developed to capture and transform the realities of Socrates' conversation, and the exploitation of this genre to its fullest realization by its greatest practitioner. Here we enter into the domain of Platonic "poetry," that is, the dialogue form he found already invented and developed to rival and replace the poetry of the polis, a public poetry that is subjected to stern criticism in the Platonic dialogues. Third and last comes "Dialectic," a chapter devoted to the major themes and modes of argument to be discovered in the Platonic dialogues. I have not rendered the forms of argumentation deployed in the dialogues in the quasi-formal notation of recent analytic philosophy, because I believe that this style, which is so characteristic of the linguistic and logical formalism of the age in which we now live and think, is not Platonic. It is not Platonic, because our modern abstractions tend to anesthetize us to Plato's moral, political, and metaphysical concerns. In place of "metaphysical" I might just as well say "theological." I have attempted throughout to place an appropriate stress on Plato's political philosophy, for it seems to me that here is the heart of his philosophy and his most abiding concern—in the long course of a writing career that stretches from the *Apology* to the *Laws*. It is a concern he has defined in its salient outlines and passed on to us.

Since I mean *Platonic Questions* as a guide to the reader new to the Platonic dialogues, I offer preliminary readings of a number of dialogues: the *Apology* (I § 5, "The Philosopher in Court"); the *Symposium* (I §§ 7–8, "Socrates *Hērōs*" and "Socrates Silenus"), the *Phaedrus* (II § 3, "Platonic Writing"), the *Republic* (III §§ 5–6, "The Sun, the Line, and the Cave," and "Kallipolis"), the *Timaeus* (III § 7, "The World of the Demiurge"), and the *Laws* (III § 8, "Magnesia").

When I speak of Plato's "Socratic" dialogues, I mean simply those dialogues in which Socrates is the dominant presence. This is universally true of the dialogues of examination and refutation (*elenchos*) placed in Plato's first period; it is also the case in many of the so-called middle dialogues (*Gorgias, Phaedo,* and *Republic*); in the cases of the *Phaedrus* and *Philebus*, Socrates remains the dominant presence in dialogues of Plato's third and last period. For the guidance of the reader, I have, in an appendix ("The Order of the Dialogues"), added some comments on attempts to order the dialogues in the sequence in which they were written.

As do all modern students of Plato, I cite his dialogues in the format of the edition of Henri Estienne (known as Henricus Stephanus, c. 1528/31–1598), who published his Plato in two folio volumes in Geneva in 1578. Stephanus divided each page into five segments and printed the Greek text with the longer Latin translation of Giovanni Serrano facing it, giving us *Apology* 3A for the beginning of the dialogues. (Volume 2 begins the numbering anew, so some dialogues have the same Stephanus page and column numbers.) Stephanus also included in his edition of the dialogues the pseudo-Platonic *Epinomis*, Plato's letters (some of which are later inventions; all of which have been disputed), the "Definitions" (derived mainly from moments of clarity when a definition is arrived at in the dialogues), and six dialogues of Platonic inspiration but uncertain authorship. Most of Stephanus' scheme for arranging the dialogues had already been devised in antiquity. The editor Thrasyllos (early first century A.D.) arranged Plato's works into groups of four dialogues after the model of the "tetralogy," or the group of four plays entered into competition in the dramatic festivals of Athens. The tragic tetralogy included three tragedies and one satyr play. The absurd result of Thrasyllos' application of this poetic model is that the *Phaedo*, the last dialogue of the first "tetralogy," and the collection of thirteen Platonic letters, which comes last in the last "tetralogy," figure in the final position of satyr plays.

Many of the dialogues Thrasyllos and Stephanus accepted as Platonic came under suspicion in the nineteenth and twentieth centuries. Some of these (e.g., the greater *Alcibiades* and the *Minos*) I mention in passing in this presentation. As it happens, I entertain the heretical belief that the greater *Alcibiades* is by Plato, and I believe that Plato was the author of Letter VII. (I doubt the authenticity of the *Minos*.) I know that I cannot convince the doubter, and, if these works are one day shown to be by a Platonist or by Plato, my arguments will not be disturbed.

All translations of Plato are my own. They are based on John Burnet's *Platonis Opera*, 5 vols., Oxford 1900–1907. I have reserved the footnotes for essential references to the text of Plato and other ancient writers; only occasionally will a modern writer be cited at the bottom of the page. In the endnote to each section I point the reader to recommended studies in English or English translation on the topics taken up in that section. Works that are there identified by short title and date are more fully described in the General Bibliography. The General Bibliography is designed to point the reader to further readings in English from what I consider the major presentations of the Platonic dialogues as a whole. Thus, the word "General." These works will, in turn, direct the reader to more specialized studies. I sometimes have to refer to standard editions of Greek works that have not been translated. When they become the focus of attention, I give essential Greek terms in Greek and in transliteration and then refer to them in transliterated form. The Greek is meant as a reminder of how different ἰδέα is from idea.

My policy for representing Greek names is simple and consistent, but it will give the appearance of inconsistency. I usually transliterate Greek names only if they have not been domesticated in English usage. Thus, Achilles and not Akhilleus. The exception is the names that figure as titles of the Platonic dialogues: thus Euthydemos for the young Athenian with whom Socrates speaks in Xenophon, *Memorabilia* 4.2; and Euthydemus, the sophist from Chios who spars with Socrates in the dialogue named after him. The names of Greeks who lived under Roman rule I give in their Roman form: Plotinus, not Plotinos.

ACKNOWLEDGMENTS

I began this work in the spring of 1983 with no inkling that it would develop into this book or that it would appear only with the new millennium. I could never have conceived of the project myself. The book began with an invitation from John Herington to write a small volume, gaudily entitled *Plato*, for his series introducing Classical authors to the general reading public, *Hermes Books*. *Plato* grew too long and philosophical for the series, and for its editor's exquisite literary taste. But it received a first and bracingly critical reading from John Herington and gradually transformed itself, out of the pure obstinacy of the author, into *Platonic Questions: Dialogues with the Silent Philosopher*.

In the summer of 1994, my colleague Michael Gillespie and I conducted a NEH summer seminar on Plato and the Polis at Duke University. Those demanding six weeks gave me the opportunity to present my thinking on the problems of reading Platonic dialogues and interpreting Platonic political philosophy to a group of inspiring teachers, to whom I owe a debt of gratitude, as I do to Michael Gillespie for a decade of dialogues on Plato.

I also owe a deep debt of gratitude to Charles Griswold, who at a critical stage convinced Sandy Thatcher at Penn State University Press that this book, which could please neither classicist or philosopher, was worth serious consideration. I thank my editor for his serene confidence in that book. Andrea Purvis read the manuscript with exacting care in the summer of 1999; she reintroduced me to the stern Muse of Logographic Necessity and, at a crucial final phase, helped prepare the indices.

My copyeditor, Keith Monley, further chastened my style and helped me to clarify my argument and the formalities of its presentation. Charles Kahn read the book with the sharpness of a philosopher and the rigor of a literary critic. He is the friend with whom I began to discuss these matters in the early fall of 1960, when at the beginning of a year in Greece we walked from the Marmaria to Delphi. I dedicate this book to him for his friendship, companionship, and inspiration.

ABBREVIATIONS AND SOURCES OF CITATIONS

Alcinous   *Alcinous: The Handbook of Platonism.* Edited by John Dillon. Oxford, 1993.

Aristotle   *The Complete Works of Aristotle.* Revised Oxford Translation. 2 vols. Edited by Jonathan Barnes. Princeton, 1984. *Aristotelis Fragmenta Selecta.* Edited by W. D. Ross. Oxford, 1955.

DK   *Die Fragmente der Vorsokratiker.* 3 vols. Edited by H. Diels and W. Kranz. 10th ed. Berlin, 1961.

DL   Diogenes Laertius. *Lives of the Philosophers.* Available in English translation of R.D. Hicks. 2 vols. Loeb Classical Library. Cambridge, Mass., and London, 1925.

Doxographers   *Doxographi Graeci.* Edited by Hermann Diels. Berlin, 1887. (Reprint, Berlin 1965.)

HGP   W.K.C. Guthrie. *A History of Greek Philosophy.* 6 vols. Cambridge, 1962–81.

Kahn   *The Art and Thought of Heraclitus: An Edition of the Fragments with a Translation and Commentary.* Edited by Charles H. Kahn. Cambridge, 1979.

Kraut   R. Kraut, ed. *The Cambridge Companion to Plato.* Cambridge, 1992.

KRS   *The Presocratic Philosophers: A Critical History and Selection of Texts.* 2d ed. Edited by G.S. Kirk, D.S. Raven, and M. Schofield. Cambridge, 1983.

Maximus of Tyre   *Maximus Tyrius: Philosophoumena-*ΔΙΑΛΕΞΕΙΣ. Edited by G.L. Koniaris. Berlin and New York, 1995.

Olympiodorus   *In Platonis Alcibiadem: Commentary on the First Alcibiades of Plato.* Edited by L. G. Westerink. Amsterdam, 1956.

PHerc.   *Papyrus Herculanensis.*

Philodemus of Gadara   *Filodemo, Storia dei filosofi: Platone e l'Academia* (PHerc. 1021 e 164). Edited by Tiziano Dorandi. La Scuola di Epicuro 12. Naples, 1991.

Plato   Paul Friedländer. *Plato: An Introduction.* Translated by Hans Meyerhoff. 3 vols. New York, 1958–69.

Platonica   Alice Swift Riginos. *Platonica: The Anecdotes Concerning the Life and Writings of Plato.* Columbia Studies in the Classical Tradition 3. Leiden, 1976.

PMG *Poetae Melici Graeci.* Edited by Denys Page. Oxford, 1962.

Proclus *In Platonis Rem Publicam Commentarii.* 2 vols. Edited by W. Kroll. Leipzig, 1899–1901.
Procli Diadochi in Platonis Timaeum Commentarii. 2 vols. Edited by E. Diehl. Leipzig, 1903.

TGF A. Nauck, *Tragicorum Graecorum Fragmenta.* Edited by A. Nauck. 2d ed. Leipzig, 1889.

SSR *Socratis et Socraticorum Reliquiae.* Edited by G. Giannantoni. 4 vols. Naples, 1990.

West *Iambi et Elegi Graeci.* Edited by Martin L. West. 2 vols. 2d ed. Oxford, 1992.

CHRONOLOGICAL TABLE

Names in bold type figure in the Platonic dialogues or letters.

469 B.C.	Birth of **Socrates**, son of Sophroniskos and Phainarete, of the deme of Alopeke, in Athens.
432	Athens campaigns against **Amphipolis** and **Potidaea** in northern Greece.
431–404	Peloponnesian War.
430	**Pericles** delivers the funeral speech recognized by the *Menexenos*.
429	Death of **Pericles**.
428	Birth of **Plato** (Aristokles), youngest son of **Ariston** and Perictione on 6 Thargelion (September) on Aegina.
427	**Gorgias** of Leontini in Sicily arrives in Athens. In the last decades of the century, the "sophists" **Protagoras** of Abdera, **Hippias** of Elis, **Prodicus** of Keos, and **Evenos** of Paros are all active in Athens.
424	The Athenians retreat from the sanctuary of Apollo (**Delion**) in Boeotia.
423	**Aristophanes** enters the first version of his *Clouds* in the contest of the City Dionysia (March).
421	Peace of **Nicias**; suspension of the war between Athens and Sparta.
418	Death of **Laches**.
416	Victory of **Agathon** in the tragic competition.
415	Spring: the Athenian fleet sails for Sicily, shortly after the mutilation of the statues of Hermes (herms) and the profanation of the Eleusinian mysteries in which **Alcibiades** was implicated. Decree of exile enacted while **Alcibiades** is in Sicily.
414	Death of **Lamachos** in Sicily.
413	Destruction of the Athenian forces in Syracuse. Death of **Nicias**.
408	Return of **Alcibiades** to Athens; **Euripides** leaves Athens for Thessaly.
406	Naval battle off Arginousai. The commanders of the victorious Athenian fleet are illegally condemned to death as a group for failing to recover their dead. **Socrates** opposes the motion.
405	Final defeat of Athens and her fleet at Aigispotamoi. Murder of **Alcibiades** in Phrygia.

404–403 The "Thirty," including **Critias** and **Charmides**, take control of Athens in an oligarchic revolution, supported by a Spartan garrison under the command of Lysander. Judicial murders of **Polemarchos** and **Leon** of Salamis. **Socrates** comes into conflict with the Thirty.

403 Defeat of the Thirty by democratic exiles. **Critias** killed. Amnesty decreed for political crimes committed during this period.

399 Trial and execution of **Socrates**. **Plato** and other Socratics leave Athens for Megara and other parts.

386 The Peace of the Spartan general Antalcidas, or the "King's Peace," giving Artaxerxes II control of the Greek cities of Asia Minor and proclaiming the autonomy of the cities of mainland Greece. This leads to the dismemberment of **Mantinea** by Sparta.

387 **Plato** visits the court of Syracuse for the first time. Here he meets **Dionysios I**, his brother-in-law **Dion**, his son **Dionysios**. On the way, he meets the philosopher **Archytas** of Tarentum.

c. 387 On his return to Athens, **Plato** founds an association of philosophers on the grounds sacred to the local hero Hēkadēmos (the Academy). Sometime after, the *Republic* is published.

384 Aristotle and Demosthenes born.

367 Death of **Dionysios I** and accession of **Dionysios II**. **Dion** persuades **Plato** to make a second trip to Syracuse.
At some date before 356, **Dionysios II** persuades **Plato** to make a third trip to Syracuse.

356 **Dion** takes control of Syracuse from **Dionysios II**.

354 Murder of **Dion** by Kalippos, an associate of the Academy.

348/347 **Plato** dies in Athens, leaving his *Laws* apparently unfinished. Philip of Opus provides a continuation in his *Epinomis*, or *On Philosophy*. Plato's nephew, **Speusippos**, becomes head of the Academy.

338 Philip II of Macedon defeats the combined armies of Thebes and Athens at Chaeronea in Boeotia and gains control of the Greek mainland, putting an end to Athenian autonomy.

335 Aristotle establishes his independent school in the Lyceum (the Peripatos).

323 Death of Alexander.

322 Aristotle leaves Athens. Death of Aristotle; suicide of Demosthenes.

A.D. c. 50–
c.120 Plutarch of Chaeronea, Platonist, biographer, and essayist. Revived the dialogue form in his *On Socrates' Daimonion* and *Dialogue on Love;* devoted a number of his essays to the explication of problems of Platonic philosophy.

Second
through sixth
centuries

The development of Middle Platonism (c. 80–220) and Neoplatonism and the elaboration of introductions to the Platonic dialogues by Alkinoos (active in 149–57), Apuleius of Madaura (c. 123–205), and then a series of commentaries on the individual dialogues by Olympiodorus of Alexandria (second half of sixth century, *Gorgias, Phaedo*), Proclus of Lycia (410–85, *First Alcibiades, Cratylus, Parmenides, Republic, Timaeus*); Hermeias of Alexandria (middle of the fifth century, *Phaedrus*), Damascius of Athens (c. 458–533, *Philebus*).

270   Death of the Neoplatonic philosopher Plotinus.

529   Date the emperor Justinian closes the Academy and the schools of philosophy in Athens.

1499   Death of Marsilio Ficino, principal force of the "Academy" founded in Florence.

1578   Publication of Stephanus' *Platonis Opera*.

Three Texts

1.) SOCRATES: If someone were to put a question to one of them [Pericles or another eloquent speaker], they would behave like a book and could neither make an answer nor ask a question themselves. And if someone in their audience were to ask a small question about something they had said, they would respond like a bronze vessel that has been struck and boom out a long echo and would continue sounding until someone clapped his hand on them. The orators behave in just the same way: ask them a question on a small point, and they resound with the drone of a long, interminable answer.

—*Protagoras* 329A–B

2.) SOCRATES: This, Phaedrus, is, I think, the strange feature of writing and one that makes it truly analogous to painting. The products of painting stand before us as if they were living and breathing. But, if someone puts a question to them, they maintain a solemn silence. So too do words [once written]. You would think that they possessed intelligence and had something to say. But if a reader wants to understand the meaning of what they say, they always signify one and the same thing. And every utterance, once set down in writing, begins to circulate everywhere and reaches people of discrimination as well as people who have no business reading it. It does not understand to whom it should speak and with whom it should remain silent. If it is given offense and is unjustly abused, this written utterance is in constant need of its father to come to its aid. By itself it is incapable of either protecting itself or coming to its own aid.

—*Phaedrus* 275D–E

3.) KLEINIAS: Let me ask you, Stranger: Shall we be patient with ourselves as we speak at such great length about drunkenness and music and poetry, but become impatient when we speak of the gods and like subjects? There is a great resource for legislation that has been intelligently accomplished. This is the fact that the commands of the law, once they have been set in writing, stand stock still and can give an account of themselves for all of time. There is no reason for alarm if, at first recitation, they are difficult. They are at hand and available, even for the person who is a slow learner, to return to. Even if they are long—but beneficial—he can return to them again and again. There is no justification whatsoever—nor in my opinion does it seem pious—for each one of us to fail to come to the aid of these writings to the extent of his abilities.

—*Laws* 10.890E–891A

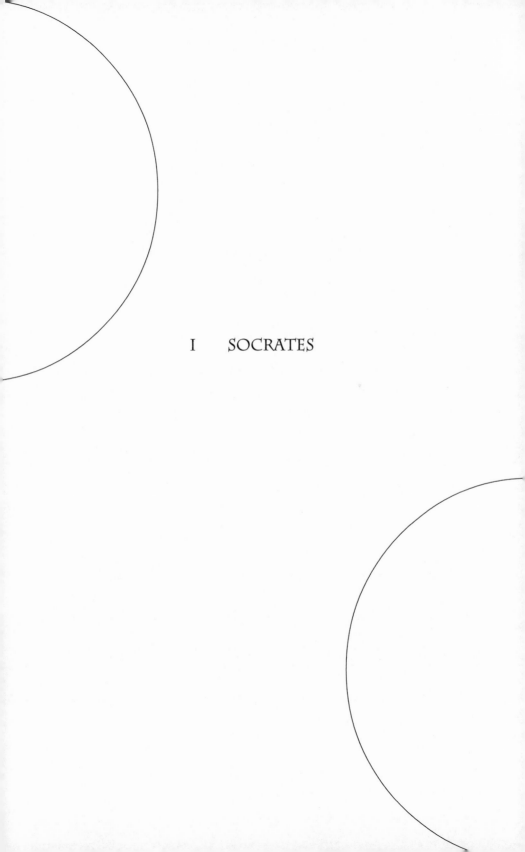

I   SOCRATES

Let us begin with the beginnings of some of Plato's dialogues and the immediate observation that they are dramatic and that, like the tragic poet, Plato nowhere speaks in his own voice:

EUTHYPHRO:

Socrates, what has happened to induce you to leave your familiar Lyceum and come spend your time at the King's Stoa? It can't be that you have a case at law to take up with the king Archon, which is what brings me here.

SOCRATES:

Well, Euthyphro, the Athenians don't call this a case at law, but a public indictment. (*Euthyphro* 2A)

SOCRATES TO HIS JURY:

Men of Athens, I do not know what impression my accusers have made on you. But what they said was so convincing that, to speak for myself, they nearly made me forget who I am. Yet, I must say that nothing they have said is true. (*Apology* 17A)

SOCRATES TO AN AUDIENCE UNKNOWN:

I made the trip down to the Peiraeus yesterday in the company of Glaukon, the son of Ariston. I wanted to offer my prayer to the goddess, and I also wanted to observe how they would conduct the festival, since they were celebrating it for the first time. (*Republic* 1.327A)

And let us turn to Plato's beginnings. According to one of the anecdotes in the ancient legend of his life, Plato began his literary career as an aspiring tragic poet. The story runs that, at the age of twenty, Plato planned to enter his plays in the tragic competitions of Athens, but became a pupil of Socrates and burned his plays.[1] Socrates was not the austere and fanatical Savonarola of Florence, who turned the young Pico della Mirandola from philosophy; he turned Plato to another form of dramatic literature, the philosophical dialogue. The transition from tragedy to the philosophical dialogue seems natural to us, but no Greek poet made this transition before Plato. Plato is now so well known to us as the most brilliant exponent of the philosophical dialogue that we tend to forget his beginnings, but, before he achieved his lasting fame, Plato was simply a "Socratic"—and only one of the many companions and imitators of Socrates known as *Sokratikoi*.

The three dialogues that open this essay are all familiar. The *Euthyphro*, *Apology*, and *Republic* are perhaps the Platonic dialogues most often read today. Socrates speaks in all three of them, and even the novice reader will recognize them as Platonic. In them Plato keeps an absolute silence. Yet, at the moment of Socrates' death in 399 B.C. and for a generation after, Plato was by no means the best known of the Socratics who wrote Socratic dialogues. He follows as last in Diogenes Laertius' history of the Socratics.[2] But Plato was a presence in Socratic circles. He was present in the court in which Socrates was tried for impiety, and Socrates could point him out to his jurors as one of the young Athenians whose character he had not corrupted. He asks Plato's older brother, Adeimantos, to attest to the truth of what he says: "And here is Adeimantos, the son of Ariston, whose brother Plato you can see here."[3] Plato, who was twenty-eight when Socrates stood trial, is named with three other young Athenians who were attached to Socrates (Theodotos, Theages, and Apollodoros) and accorded no pride of place, even in his own dialogue. He is conspicuously absent from the group of friends that gathered in Socrates' cell at the day of his execution. These names are not

1. DL 3.5. In his explanation of why Socrates exiles Homer from his ideal city and regards the tragic poet as "thrice removed from reality" (*Republic* 10.597E), Proclus tells a very similar story: "[Plato] seems to be contriving nothing else in these remarks than what Socrates recommended. When Socrates first met him, Plato was preparing for a career as a tragic poet. Socrates showed him that tragedy was of no good for human beings, and turned him away from this sort of imitation, and in a way [he turned him] to compose those illustrious Socratic discourses in which he revealed that tragedy was neither educational nor beneficial, but stands at three removes from reality." *In Platonis Rem Publicam Commentarii* (Leipzig, 1899), I.205.4–10 Kroll.

2. DL 2.48–144 is devoted to the Socratics, beginning with Xenophon, and all of book 3 to Plato.

3. *Apology* 34A. He is also named as one of the four Athenians willing to pay a sum of thirty minas as an alternative to the death penalty; *Apology* 38B.

well known today, but in antiquity some were famous as Socratics and even represented in a painting of the death of Socrates.[4] According to Plato's *Phaedo* and its narrator, Phaedo of Elis, present at Socrates' last day were Apollodoros, Crito and his son Kritoboulos, Hermogenes, Epigenes, Aischines, Antisthenes, Ktesippos, Menexenus, and still other Athenians. But Phaedo, who is our authority, adds: "Plato, I think, was ill."[5] Counting Simmias, Kebes, and Phaidondas of Thebes, Eukleides and Terpsion of Megara, and the Athenian Kleombrotos, who was with Antisthenes on the island of Aegina when Socrates died, Plato is simply one of a large group of Socratics, eighteen of whom are named by Phaedo in his account of Socrates' last day. But Phaedo's "Plato, I think, was ill" makes it clear that Plato could be expected in prison among the close companions of Socrates.

Years later Xenophon composed two versions of his defense of Socrates: the *Apology* (in imitation of Plato's *Apology of Socrates*) and what purports to be his own *Recollections of Socrates.*[6] In Xenophon's *Recollections*, Plato does not even figure in the list of Socrates' "true associates."[7] Xenophon names Crito, Chairephon, Chairekrates, Hermogenes, Simmias, Kebes, Phaidondas. Plato seems to reciprocate for this glaring omission of the name "Plato" among the "true associates" of Socrates. It is nowhere said in the *Phaedo* that "Xenophon, I think, was in Asia Minor with the remnants of the army of Cyrus," as in fact he was.

In the memory of the early fourth century and the changing circles of the Socratics, the name of Plato does not stand out conspicuously—even in his own modest presentation of himself in his dialogues. But Plato was a Socratic, and at the moment of Socrates' death, one of many. Without Socrates, there could have been no Plato. In retrospect and from the vantage of Plato's later career and Socrates' posthumous life in Plato's Socratic dialogues, it is fair to say too that without Plato there could have been no Socrates. For better or worse, our Socrates is Plato's Socrates. We have lost most of the dialogues of the earlier Socratics, in part, perhaps, because of Plato's sheer brilliance, and Xenophon, who was Plato's senior and who knew Socrates well, has come to be obscured by Plato's brilliance.

4. To judge from Lucian's biographical sketch, *On the Death of Peregrinus* 37.

5. *Phaedo* 59B. These names and the names that follow are significant in the Platonic dialogues. Phaedo, Crito, and Menexenus give their names to Platonic dialogues. Apollodoros is the narrator of the *Symposium*; Hermogenes speaks in the *Cratylus*. The Thebans Simmias and Kebes speak in the *Phaedo*; and the Megarians Eukleides and Terpsion speak in the frame dialogue of the *Theaetetus*.

6. In *Memorabilia* 1.1–2.

7. *Memorabilia* 1.2.48.

In a later age, Plato came to be considered one of the "major" Socratics, even as Socrates had become Platonic and was known as a philosopher mainly, if not exclusively, from the Platonic dialogues. But if we exert an effort of imagination and return to the moment (perhaps immediately after Socrates' death and with the *Apology*) when Plato began to write his Socratic dialogues, we can determine, with some surprise, that Plato was not the first to write Socratic dialogues and was far from alone in writing dramatic dialogues with Socrates as their protagonist. Many of the Socratics who are known to us imitated Socrates in that they did not write. Some of these, like Apollodoros and Chairephon, imitated Socrates in their dress and behavior, if in little else. Many of his more literate companions imitated Socrates in another sense: they composed dialogues that tacitly or explicitly claimed to be the records of his conversations. The first of the authors of *Sokratikoi logoi*—or the records of Socrates' conversations—were the comic poets who introduced Socrates to the theater of Dionysos in the first decade of Plato's life. The best known of these was Aristophanes, whose *Clouds* was produced in the spring of 423, when Socrates was forty-five and Plato not yet five years old. There were other "Socratic" comedies associated with the names Ameipsias and Eupolis, of which we have only tantalizing fragments.

Of the literary Socratics, some were well known in antiquity; some are mere names to us now. A review of them will help us recover the literary context in which Plato began to write his Socratic dialogues, which he continued to write as late as the *Philebus*. Some of their names are still familiar; the fact that so many are not is a silent testimonial to Plato's success in eclipsing the first generation of writers attracted to the enigmatic figure of Socrates. None, so far as we know, was a poet. Xenophon was slightly Plato's senior. Like Plato (who was present at Socrates' trial), Xenophon (who was not) wrote an *Apology* (relying on the report of Hermogenes); also a *Symposium*; a dialogue between Socrates and Crito's son, Kritoboulos, on household management (the *Oeconomicus*); and the brief Socratic dialogues collected and "recollected" in the four books of the *Memorabilia*. Before Xenophon, both Antisthenes and Aischines wrote Socratic dialogues. For Aischines we have titles and fragments. They place Socrates in the brilliant age of an Athens whose power was still intact. Diogenes Laertius lists a *Kallias* (the wealthy Athenian in whose house Plato's *Protagoras* is set), an *Aspasia* (the companion and mistress of Pericles, to whom the funeral speech in Plato's *Menexenus* is attributed), and an *Alcibiades* (a favorite topic of the literary Socratics), whose opening has been preserved. To Antisthenes are attributed titles that seem plausible for Socratic dialogues: an *Aspasia*, an *Alcibiades*, and a *Menexenus*. And there is the dialogue with the obscene pun on Plato's name, *Satho* (Pecker). Phaedo is credited with a *Zopyros* (a known associate of Socrates) and a *Simon*. Simon, a cobbler whose shop excavators believe they have unearthed in the ancient marketplace of Athens, is said to have recorded Socrates' conversations in a book that bore the nickname *Cobbler's Talk* (or perhaps *Conversations at the Cobbler's Shop*). There is a tradition that holds Simon to have been the first to set Socrates' conversations in dialogue form.[8] This tradition is likely a fiction, but, like all such fictions, it conveys an ancient literary judgment on the character of the dialogues that in a later age were thought to come from Socrates' lifetime. The first Socratic dialogues were taken to be the vivid and faithful records of his actual conversations. As for the other companions of Socrates on his last day, Eukleides of Megara, whom Plato introduces as the authority for his *Theaetetus*, is credited with six dialogues, including an *Aischines*, *Crito*, and *Alcibiades*; and to Crito, Simmias, and Kebes are attributed still other dialogues.

Finally, we come to the writer who seems to be the youngest of this group of Socratics who composed Socratic dialogues, Plato, the son of Ariston. Plato not only wrote the dialogues to be presented in this book; his name and fame attracted into the ancient editions of his dialogues other dialogues by unknown hands, known in Greek as Plato's "bastard" or spurious dialogues, which is, in its way, a compliment, since Plato fathered these imitations too. Nowadays, they are hardly read, but they illustrate antiquity's enduring fascination with Socrates and his conversations, and the power of the Platonic dialogues to produce imitations of Plato's *mimēsis* of Socrates. In all of these spurious dialogues, Socrates appears as the central character. As we shall see (in II § 7), all of Plato's dialogues are not "Socratic." In his last dialogue, the *Laws*, Socrates is not even present.

It is significant for our appreciation of the Socratics that, even when their dialogues were not the records of Socrates' conversations, they continued to write in the literary form that was invented to capture—or transform—the fleeting reality of Socrates' conversations and was congenial to the political culture of Athens, where public debate in the assembly decided public policy. And even when Socrates withdraws from the Platonic dialogues, as he does in the case of the *Sophist*, *Statesman*, *Timaeus*, and *Critias*, and even when he disappears completely from Plato's last dialogue, the *Laws*, Plato continues to

8. DL 2.123.

write in dialogue form, as did Aristotle at the beginning of his career in a clearly declared emulation of Plato.

Plato's dialogues have so eclipsed the Socratic dialogues of his predecessors and contemporaries that we are now hardly in a position to form a firm judgment of the character of the work of the eclipsed Socratics or of the origins of the Socratic dialogue. Because of this, we are hardly in a position to recover the character of the "historical" Socrates. Nietzsche put our quandary in the form of an epigram that takes its shape from the Homeric description of the chimera—"A lion in front, a snake behind, in the middle a goat": "Plato in front, Plato behind, in the middle a chimera."[9]

In his literary and philosophical portrait of Socrates, Plato was a Socratic like no other. Aischines—now reduced to the status of one of the "minor" Socratics but an author who was admired in antiquity for both grace of style and accuracy of detail—provides us with a telling contrast. Among Aischines' dialogues is the *Alcibiades* (already mentioned), in which Socrates is portrayed as narrating a conversation he had with the brilliant aristocrat who so fascinated the Socratics, just as he fascinated and at the same time repelled Athens. Aischines' dialogue opens with Socrates addressing an unknown audience: "We were seated on the seats of the Lyceum where the officials conduct the contest."[10] Such an overture is perfectly familiar to the reader of Plato. The *Lysis*, for example, is set near this gymnasium. Yet his *Charmides* is still more revealing of Plato's art, for it involves a setting not only in place, as was the case with Aischines' *Alcibiades*, but in time.

The *Charmides* opens with Socrates narrating a conversation to an unknown companion:

> The evening before, we had returned from the campaign at Potidaea. And with joy in my heart after so long an absence I returned to my familiar haunts. I entered the wrestling school of Taureas—the one located just opposite the precinct of the queen—and there I discovered quite a crowd. Some were unknown to me, but most were my acquaintances. And, when they saw me appear with no warning, they all got up from where they were seated to greet me right away. And Chairephon, being the impulsive person he is, sprang up from the crowd and ran up to me. Taking me by the hand, he said, "Socrates, how did you escape from the battle with your life?"[11]

9. *Beyond Good and Evil,* §190, in imitation of *Iliad* 6.181.
10. Aischines, *Alcibiades, SSR* VI.A.43 (vol. 2, p. 605).
11. *Charmides* 153A–B.

We do not have enough of Aischines' *Alcibiades* to make a precise comparison possible, but let us venture a rough one. Both dialogues open dramatically with Socrates as narrator speaking to an unidentified companion; both dialogues describe their settings; both settings seem to be places where we would expect to find Socrates and the young men who were his companions. But Plato, who might at first seem to be following Aischines, parts company with him and, so far as we can tell, with other Socratics in his precise description of the time (morning), place (a wrestling school just opposite the precinct of the queen), and historical context (just after the Athenian campaign against Potidaea in 432). And, what is more, we have Plato's subtle characterization of Socrates: his pleasure in returning to Athens and familiar pursuits after distinguishing himself in battle.[12] We have as well a characterization of both Chairephon's actions—"he sprang up from the crowd and ran up to me"—and the nature they reveal—"being the impulsive person he is."

Chairephon's question to Socrates concerns the battle at Potidaea; but Socrates is more concerned with the state of philosophy in the city he has been away from during the campaign. As he turns the conversation to the young Charmides and the somewhat older Critias, a new dimension enters our dialogue: the tacit contrast and connection between the Socratic virtue of courage and the virtue examined in the *Charmides*—prudent self-restraint (σωφροσύνη, *sōphrosynē*).

As we come to consider the dramatic settings of the Platonic dialogues and the dialogue form itself, we will return to still other contrasts between Plato and the other Socratics who wrote Socratic dialogues. But we can anticipate. Plato began his literary career as a poet and, in a sense that will be defined and illustrated, continued his career as the tragic and comic poet of the philosophical life. If, in the context of Socrates' life and the fifth century, Plato must be seen as a Socratic, and a "minor" Socratic at that, in the context of the fourth century and the last fifty years of his life, Plato emerges as the philosopher who transformed the Socratic dialogue into an unsurpassed vehicle for philosophical inquiry. In this context, he can be seen as parting company with the distinguished group of Socrates' contemporaries and eclipsing them by the brilliance of his own portraits of the master. But Plato's portraits of Socrates invite more than the careful attention of the historian of Socrates' life or the keen pleasure of Plato's reader at the illusion of their likeness to

---

12. Alcibiades mentions Socrates' service at Potidaea in his speech in praise of Socrates; *Symposium* 220D; see I §8 ("Socrates Silenus").

the object of their imitation. Plato's Socratic dialogues call for and provoke thought not only about the philosophical questions they address but about the form of the Platonic dialogue itself.

If Plato was hardly the first Socratic to write a Socratic dialogue, he was, so far as we can now determine, the first to invest his dialogues in recognizable historical settings—which means that his Socratic dialogues, with their carefully elaborated dramatic settings, display the distinctive irony of the tragic poet. None of the characters on Plato's distant stage—not even Socrates—is aware of the full meaning of his words and actions. But Plato's audience in the fourth century is well aware of the shape of Socrates' life and the careers of his contemporaries. Like the tragic poet, Plato is concerned not only with the words spoken and arguments made but the record of significant action. These actions tend to be lost sight of in philosophical readings of the Platonic dialogues, but, if Plato, like nature, does nothing without purpose, they must have their significance.[13] Indeed, to some of his contemporaries, what Socrates did was as interesting as what Socrates said.[14]

If the historical context of Socrates' conversations is important to a reading of the Platonic dialogues, so is action and gesture. Plato was not alone in attending to dramatic gestures. It is clear from the reports concerning Aischines' *Alcibiades* that his Socrates described Alcibiades as putting his head on his knees and breaking into tears in utter discouragement with the realization that he could never rival Themistocles.[15] In Plato's Socratic dialogues, gestures—that is, reports of "things done"—seem to have a deeper significance. In the *Phaedo*, for example, Socrates rubs his legs and experiences a strange mixture of pleasure and pain. Thereby, he initiates the dialectic of opposites (sleeping and waking, life and death) that will inform the arguments of the dialogue to follow.[16] In the *Symposium*, the comic poet Aristophanes is assailed by an attack of hiccoughs, and, as a consequence, his speech on love is postponed and brought into direct association with that of the tragic poet, Agathon. By the original plan of the speeches, Aristophanes should have spoken before the doctor, Eryximachos.[17] And, in this same dia-

---

13. For the Aristotelian aphorism and its application to the Platonic dialogues by the principle of "logographic necessity," see II §3 ("Platonic Writing").

14. Accordingly, Phaedo relates not only what Socrates said on his last day but what he did; *Phaedo* 58C. Socrates' conversations and activities are of equal interest to his chronicler, Apollodoros; *Symposium* 172C.

15. Aischines, *Alcibiades*, SSR VI.A.51 (vol. 2, p. 609).

16. *Phaedo* 60B.

17. *Symposium* 185C.

logue, the drunken Alcibiades, who had burst into the banquet room with a crown for the victorious Agathon, crowns Socrates as well.[18] We will weigh the meaning of these gestures as we contemplate Plato's portrait of Socrates as the demigod Eros, and Alcibiades' comparison of Socrates to a silenus (I §§ 7–8, "Socrates Eros" and "Socrates Silenus").

One last example—among many possible examples—of significant action in the Platonic dialogues comes from the *Phaedrus*, a dialogue Plato is careful to set in time (late summer, at noon) and place (in the Attic countryside, on the grass of the banks of the Ilissos, under a plane tree). After Socrates has spoken his piece in praise of the nonlover and is preparing to return to Athens, Phaedrus notices that the sun is standing at midday. If the reader asks why Plato has Phaedrus notice the time of day, the significance of this dramatic detail becomes clear: it is precisely at this demonic hour, when gods appear to men and Pan makes his sudden epiphany, that Socrates decides to remain on the banks of the Ilissos and begin his inspired speech in praise of love as a kind of divine madness.[19]

Plato is dramatic in still another respect. Like the dramatist, he never speaks in his own person. Nor does he intrude himself into his dialogues, as does Xenophon, who figures as a character in some of the dialogues of the *Memorabilia* or introduces a Socratic dialogue with the claim: "I once heard Socrates speaking on the topic of friendship."[20] What this means is that as readers of the Platonic dialogues we are engaged in a dialogue with a silent philosopher who never spoke in his own person or with the authority of his own voice.

There might be still another point of contrast that distinguishes Plato from the Socratics who wrote Socratic dialogues. Plato is aware, and seems alone in being aware, of the difficulties of capturing the spoken word in the fixity of the written word, or the reality of the Forms (εἴδη, *eidē*) that both inform the world of sense experience and make it intelligible, and of attempting to imitate as an artist the character (ἦθος, *ēthos*) that is the object of his imitation. These are all questions to which we will return in Chapter II.

In the Ambulacro of the Vatican, there is a double herm of Socrates and Plato. The reader of Plato's Socratic dialogues faces Socrates head-on; from this point of view, the features of Plato are invisible. Plato was born in Athens on the seventh day of the Attic month of Thargelion (our September)—a

18. *Symposium* 213D.
19. *Phaedrus* 242A.
20. *Memorabilia* 2.4.1.

day sacred to Apollo—in 428 and died in Athens in 347. Socrates was born in Athens in 469 on the sixth day of Thargelion—a day sacred to Artemis and on which the Athenians maintained ritual purity; he was put to death in 399. Socrates was intimately and inextricably engaged in the life of his city and century and knew its politicians, poets, tanners, and cobblers. Except for the campaigns in which he served during the first stage of the Peloponnesian War (at Amphipolis and Potidaea in 432, and at the Delion in Boeotia in 424), he never left Athens. In Athens he was a figure familiar to the audience of the comic performances at the festivals of Dionysos and known to the great foreign sophists (professors) who visited Athens to display their forensic skills and attract many of the same wealthy young men who were also attracted to the Athenian "sophist," Socrates. These foreign sophists were Gorgias of Leontini in Sicily, Protagoras of Abdera, Hippias of Elis, and Prodikos of Keos. At the end of his life and at the end of the Peloponnesian War, Socrates opposed the tyranny of Charmides and Critias, two of the thirty oligarchs who had seized control of Athens in 404 and who had been his young friends at the beginning of the war. We meet them as young men in the *Charmides*, when Socrates has just returned from Potidaea. And we meet Critias again in the *Critias*. Socrates' association with these men was remembered when he was brought to trial for impiety and corrupting the youth of Athens in 399.

Plato was one of the young men Socrates might have "corrupted." He left Athens for neighboring Megara after Socrates' execution. Plato lived the greater part of his adult life in the fourth century, and became deeply involved not in the politics of Athens but of the court of Dionysios I and Dionysios II in Syracuse from his first visit there (in 387) until his hopes for a Syracuse governed by a philosopher king collapsed with the death of Dion in 354. Yet in his literary imagination and in his philosophical concerns, he seems to have lived the life of Socrates in the fifth century and in Athens. This was a vicarious and distant life. But as a literary Socratic, Plato has left us with so vivid a *mimēsis* of Socrates and his age that, in the grim half century that followed the defeat of Athens and in the nearly fifty years in which he wrote dialogues, he has left us with the illusion that he lived his life in the Athens in which Socrates lived and died. As readers, we live in the fifth century and are contemporaries of Socrates, not of Plato.

ENDNOTE: For Plato as a companion of Socrates, see the fine study of George Grote, *Plato and the Other Companions of Socrates* (1875). More recent studies of the Socratics are contained in the collection of essays *The Socratic Movement*, edited by Paul A. Vander Waerdt (1994); in this collection, I treat the dialogues of the Socratics as a literary movement ("The Origins of the Socratic Dialogue"). Charles Kahn has a parallel treatment of Plato as a Socratic in *Plato and the Socratic Dialogue* (1997). The fragments of the Socratics except Xenophon and Plato are collected in Gabriele Giannantoni, *Socratis et Socraticorum Reliquiae* (1990).

Plato never broke his self-imposed silence as a philosopher, but he did speak of himself toward the end of his life. He speaks of himself in a letter written in 354 to the friends and associates of his close friend Dion of Syracuse, who had been killed in attempting to take the city from Dionysios II. In many ways this letter can be read as "The Apology of Plato":[1]

> When I was a young man, I had the experience of many men of my age: I thought that, if I could have my wish and soon gain my independence, I would immediately enter political life. And some of the developments in politics turned out in my favor. Since many abominated the kind of government that was then in power, a revolution in government came about, and fifty-one citizens took charge of the new constitution. There were eleven in the city and ten in the port of Peiraeus—in control of the market and the other institutions of the city and port; and of the entire body thirty were given absolute powers. Some of these happened to be relatives and acquaintances of mine. And they immediately invited me to join them, arguing that their program was made for me. Because I was young, there was nothing unusual in my reaction to them: I believed that they would bring the city over from an unjust to a just mode of living and would administer it with justice.
>
> Since this was my belief, I watched closely to see what they would do. And in a short time I saw these men reveal our former constitution by contrast as an age of gold. One of the worst actions I witnessed was that they sent for Socrates, an older friend of mine, whom I would not hesitate to call the justest man of that time, to join others and go and forcefully bring a certain citizen to be executed, so that, willing or not,

1. Letter VII 324B–325A.

he would be implicated in their actions. But he refused to obey them and risked the greatest danger rather than become a partner to their unholy crimes. When I witnessed this and other actions equally serious, I became disgusted, and I withdrew myself from the evils of that period.

Plato begins his life and apology at the point when his early and youthful enthusiasm for the oligarchic regime of the Thirty in Athens (404–403) gave way to bitter disillusionment. The biographer can take Plato's life from the execution of Socrates in 399 into the new century: following Plato to his self-imposed "exile" in neighboring Megara with Eukleides and still other associates of Socrates; perhaps to the coast of North Africa and Egypt, if the ancient biographical tradition can be relied on; surely to Tarentum on the coast of Italy; and finally to Sicily and Syracuse in 387, when he was about forty. This history will return him to Athens, where Plato seems to have established an association of philosophers in an institution that came to be known as the Academy, from the name of a local hero (Hēkadēmos) whose cult was situated on its grounds. It will take him back to Sicily in 367 at the age of sixty, perhaps two decades after he had begun to make his argument for the philosopher king in the *Republic*, which probably took years in the writing. In Syracuse, the accession of Dionysios II to the tyranny of his father put Plato's philosophy—and his friendship with Dionysios' uncle Dion—to a severe test: "that I would not appear in my own eyes to be pure theory and nothing more."[2] Plato's sense of obligation—both to his friend and pupil Dion of Syracuse and to his own philosophy—compelled him to return to the court of Dionysios II for a third and last time, only see his hopes for a philosophical regime in Syracuse frustrated. For a time he was confined to a guest house in the gardens of Dionysios' fortified palace.

This path into the fourth century is the path of the historian who is compelled to follow Plato's life through the thirteen letters attributed to him, the historians of Sicily, Plutarch's *Life of Dion*, and the rich biographical tradition that grew up around him in antiquity. In Athens, where he remained for the rest of his life among associates of the caliber of his nephew Speusippos, Aristotle, and Eudoxos of Knidos, Plato learned of Dion's seizure of power in 357 and how he perished in the dangerous tides of civil war in 354. It was in Athens and the Academy that he finished his *Laws*, the last statement of his political philosophy. This dialogue was set not in Athens but in Crete, far from the brutal testing grounds of Athens and Syracuse.

2. Letter VII 328C.

The first stage of Plato's political career came to an abrupt end with the disastrous regime of the "Thirty Tyrants"; his final disaffection with the city of Athens came with the death of Socrates, "an older friend of mine, whom I would not hesitate to call the justest man of that time."[3] From that point, Plato's political activity shifted to Sicily, where, after three trips to the courts of two tyrants, it ended painfully and vicariously with the murder of Dion by Plato's fellow Athenian and associate in the Academy, Kalippos. Both deaths required apologies. Plato wrote the first in his *Apology of Socrates*, and at the very end of his career, when he was working on his last political dialogue, the *Laws*, he composed the second apology in his long letter to the party and family of Dion (Letter VII). It seems incredible that these are the historical circumstances in which the Platonic dialogues were written, for the dialogues, with the exception of the *Laws*, seem to belong to Athens and another age. In none of them do we hear the voice of Plato, their author, speaking to us from the next century.

There is reason to think that Plato's career as a writer of Socratic dialogues began with his *Apology of Socrates* immediately after the death of Socrates. When we can locate ourselves in the dramatic settings of the Platonic dialogues, we find ourselves in the better times of the last three decades of the fifth century—an age, in the words of Letter VII, that had come to seem "golden"—golden not only in relation to the reign of terror of the Thirty but in relation to the nostalgic retrospection of the fourth century. If the reader considers the historical settings visible in the background of Plato's Socratic dialogues, an unexpected pattern of some clarity begins to emerge. For some of the Socratic dialogues no distinct historical setting can be clearly made out: Socrates is present in them, and usually at their center, engaged in conversation with boys or men younger than himself. The *Lysis*, the *Cratylus*, and the *Phaedrus*, for example, are not provided with a definite historical setting. In all of these dialogues we are recognizably in Athens or—in the unique case of the *Phaedrus*—in Attica. But other Socratic dialogues are more circumstantial and, taken as a whole, can be located in Athens during the period of the Peloponnesian War. The great and puzzling exception is the *Parmenides*, a dialogue now placed late in the middle phase of Plato's career and well into the fourth century in the date of its composition. In it, Socrates is introduced as "very young" and Parmenides as quite old.[4]

---

3. In the words of Letter VII 324E.
4. *Parmenides* 127C; for the setting, see I §3 ("Portrait Frames") and III §4 ("Thinking About Ideas").

To review the Socratic dialogues that are set in the first three decades of Plato's life and the last three decades of Socrates' is to gain a view of the context in which Plato invested his artistic and philosophical re-creations of Socrates' conversations and at the same time a better appreciation of his skill as a dramatist. We have seen that the *Charmides* is set just after the Athenian campaign at Potidaea in 432. The *Republic* is set at the moment when the cult of the Thracian goddess Bendis was introduced to the Peiraeus around 430, and in it Plato evokes a world that will soon change forever. The setting of the dialogues is the Peiraeus, the seat of Athenian naval power and home to the wealthy foreigners active there. One of them, Polemarchos, will be put to death by the Thirty, and another, his brother Lysias, will prosecute one of the Thirty (Eratosthenes) for the murder of his brother. The *Laches*, Plato's dialogue on courage, looks directly back to the Athenian retreat from Delion (the sanctuary of Apollo at modern Dilesi) in Boeotia in 424, during the first phase of the Peloponnesian War. Plato is precise and allows us to be precise about the occasion for the *Symposium*: the victory of the tragic poet Agathon at the dramatic festival of the spring of 416. In this dialogue, Alcibiades recalls two of the campaigns in which he had come to admire Socrates' courage and hardiness: the retreat from the Delion and the campaign against the city of Potidaea in the winter of 432–431. The *Ion* seems to be set before the revolt of Ephesos from the Athenian empire in 412. The period imagined for the *Gorgias* is elastic. Gorgias first visited Athens in 427, but a small detail places the dramatic date of the dialogue much later: in the course of this long and bitter conversation with Gorgias' associate, Kallikles, Socrates mentions his own service on the Athenian Council in 406 and his ignorance, as a member of its executive board, of how to put a motion to the vote.[5] The vote was on whether to condemn the Athenian captains victorious at the naval battle off Arginousai as a group for their failure to retrieve their dead. There is in fact no consistent chronological setting of the *Gorgias* in time, but Socrates' reference to the battle off Arginousai takes us closer to the defeat of Athens. We are now nearing the end of the Peloponnesian War and the decisive naval battle off Aigispotamoi on the Hellespont in 405. In 405, Plato was twenty-two.

The other dialogues to which Plato gives some historical definition cluster around the period at the end of Socrates' life and his trial and execution for impiety—precisely the period when Plato, as a young man, would have

5. *Gorgias* 473E.

known Socrates best. The *Euthydemus* belongs to the last years of Socrates' life. Here, Socrates is described as an old man, and Alcibiades (who was murdered in 404) is glimpsed as a figure from an already distant past.[6] The dramatic setting of the *Meno* can be dated to the winter of 402. In Socrates' ominous conversation with Anytos, one of his accusers in 399, the shadow of Socrates' death is cast over the dialogue.[7] This same shadow falls over the conversation of the *Theaetetus*, in which a "digression" is devoted to the fate of the philosopher in a popular court.[8] This interlude in the inquiry into what constitutes knowledge points directly to the end of the dialogue, when Socrates makes his exit to appear before the king Archon to answer to the charge of impiety brought against him by Anytos, Meletos, and Lykon.[9] We are clearly in the year 399. The *Sophist* and *Statesman* follow as the next two dialogues of this "trilogy." Last in this review of the chronology of the settings Plato provided for his dialogues comes the "tetralogy" (the first of Thrasyllos' tetralogies), which opens with the *Euthyphro* and the encounter between Socrates and the pious Euthyphro at the King's Stoa, continues in the *Apology* and *Crito*, and concludes in the *Phaedo*—a sequence sometimes entitled *The Last Days of Socrates*.

This brief history of the discernible dramatic settings of the dialogues is wildly different from any modern reconstruction of the sequence in which Plato actually composed his dialogues.[10] He did not write the programmatic sequence *Euthyphro*, *Apology*, *Crito*, and *Phaedo* in that order. But the dramatic settings in which he invests Socrates' conversations illustrate one of the most arresting features of his Socratic dialogues: when Plato casts them in recognizable historical settings, these settings are virtually limited to Athens in the last three decades of the fifth century. Socrates is central to all of them. A number of these settings can be seen to cluster around the period just before Socrates' trial and execution. Thus, the dialogues Plato has been careful to set in a historical context occupy roughly the first thirty years of Plato's life, and they take on a more definite and significant historical shape around the period of Plato's young adulthood, the period in which he had come to know Socrates, "an older friend of mine."

The following story is told in Xenophon's *Memorabilia*:[11] Critias, Plato's

---

6. *Euthydemus* 272B and 293B; 275A.
7. *Meno* 94E. For this shadow, see I §4 ("The Shadow of Death").
8. *Theaetetus* 172A–174B.
9. *Theaetetus* 210B.
10. See "Appendix: The Order of the Dialogues."
11. 1.2.31–33.

uncle and the most interesting and notorious of the Thirty Tyrants, issued an edict against the teaching of rhetoric; under its cover he intended to silence Socrates. When Socrates interrogated Critias and his colleague Charikles about the scope of the edict, he soon managed to extort from them their real intention. Socrates was to speak to no Athenian under the age of thirty. This episode can be read as a kind of parable. In the Platonic dialogues, Socrates' conversations with young Athenians and visiting sophists are mainly set in the first thirty years of Plato's life. When Plato reached the age of thirty, Socrates could no longer speak to him, but Plato could speak for Socrates.

In Plato's *Apology*, Socrates has arrived at that time of life when, in the face of death, men become prophetic. The prophecy he utters in court is this:

> Immediately after my death a punishment will befall you, much worse, I swear by Zeus, than the punishment of death you are now inflicting on me. You have brought about my death in the fancy that you will be free of having to give an account of your lives. But, I say, the result will be just the opposite. There will be more people in the future to bring you to account. Up until now, I have restrained them and you have not noticed them. But they will be harsher on you because they are younger, and you will feel even more resentment.[12]

This passage is almost certainly a prophecy of the dialogues Plato began to write immediately after Socrates' death. With his *Apology of Socrates*, Plato began to preserve and to transform—by the act of interpretation that is essential to *mimēsis*—Socrates' words, for his own century and then for every successive generation. He has done so with such brilliance that his dialogues leave us with the lasting and vivid impression that they are an immediate reflection of Athens and the last decades of her power and brilliance in the fifth century. But he wrote them all, from *Apology* to *Laws*, in the first half of the fourth century. That we tend to forget this is a tribute to Plato's powers as a mimetic and dramatic poet.[13]

We end this survey of the dramatic settings of the Platonic dialogues with a story. It comes from a Platonist. Plutarch tells it in his *Life of Gaius Marius*, who at the moment of his death regretted that he had not accomplished all that he had set out to do in life. Plutarch was struck by the differ-

---

12. *Apology* 39C–D.
13. David Hume captures our situation as readers neatly: "[T]he author is entirely lost in dramatic compositions, and the spectator supposes himself to be really at the actions represented"; *An Inquiry Concerning Human Understanding*, ed. Charles W. Hendel (New York 1955), 37.

ence of Plato's attitude as his life drew to a close: "Plato, approaching the moment of his death, celebrated his *daimōn* and fortune: he reckoned first that he was born a human and not a beast, which by its nature does not share in reason; then that he was born a Greek and not a barbarian; and, in addition to these blessings, that he happened to be born in the age of Socrates."[14]

ENDNOTE: This section is not meant to be biographical, either for Socrates or for Plato. Those interested in the ancient traditions out of which our modern accounts of Socrates and Plato are constructed should begin with Diogenes Laertius (2.1–47 for Socrates; 3 for Plato). For the life of Plato, Letter VII and Plutarch's *Life of Dion* (which depends on it) are also recommended. An excellent presentation of the Platonic letters is Glenn Morrow's *Plato's Epistles* (1962). W.K.C. Guthrie's treatment of Socrates in *HGP* 3 (1971) has been published separately. The anecdotes concerning Plato are collected in *Platonica* (1976). Gilbert Ryle has produced an engaging, entertaining, and in some respects unbelievable account of Plato's career in *Plato's Progress* (1966).

14. *Life of Gaius Marius*, 46.1; *Platonica*, Anecdote 21 (p. 58).

Phaedo

If Plato produces the illusion that his intellectual life remained fixed with Socrates in the fifth century, he also reminds us that his dialogues speak to another age—his own. The other Socratics evoked the memory of Socrates by bringing him into contact with the large and varied cast of his contemporaries. Plato did more. He not only provided his dialogues with recognizable historical settings, he also fashioned frame dialogues for the canvas of his dialogues that belong to another age. These outer dialogues too are part of the full picture of the Platonic dialogues they frame. Like Raphael in his *Scuola di Atene* in the Stanza della Segnatura of the Vatican, Plato is capable of depicting himself and his contemporaries at the edges of his own School of Athens. The *Phaedo* presents the first example of a frame that is not contemporary with its canvas and includes a figure not present in the canvas. Echekrates of Phlius speaks for his unnamed companions:

ECHEKRATES:
Tell me, Phaedo, what were the circumstances of his death? What was said and what was done, and which of his close associates were present? Or did the authorities refuse to allow them to be with him? Did he die alone, without friends?

PHAEDO:
Not at all. A number of his friends were there and in fact a good many.

ECHEKRATES:
Well then, tell us the story as clearly as you can, if you would, unless you do not now have the time.

PHAEDO:

I have the time, and I will try to give you the full story. You know, to recall Socrates—both when I speak of him himself and when I listen to others speak of him—always gives me the greatest pleasure.

ECHEKRATES:

That is excellent, Phaedo. Those who will hear you speak will share that pleasure too. Now do your best to give the entire story as exactly as possible.[1]

The dramatic setting of the *Phaedo* is the state prison in Athens on the day of Socrates' execution. But Plato's portrait of Socrates on his last day— like that of the Jacques-Louis David canvas in the Metropolitan Museum of Art—has a frame that is newer than its canvas. Although the dramatic account of Socrates' last hours with his family and friends rivets our attention, the frame in which it is so carefully set attracts our attention too, once we have read the dialogue. Its frame is not contemporary, and it places us at a distance from the scene of Socrates' last day in Athens. We discover ourselves in the small city of Phlius, in the Peloponnesus west of Corinth, some time after Socrates' death. Someone had arrived there from Athens and brought news of Socrates' trial, but concerning Socrates' death only the report that he drank the hemlock has reached Phlius. Phaedo's assurance that Socrates did not die alone is our assurance that some memory of his last day will survive. Echekrates is familiar with Socrates and the character of Apollodoros, who was overcome by grief when the moment for Socrates' execution arrived.[2] But, as a foreigner, he does not know of the religious taboo that delayed Socrates' execution during the festival of Delian Apollo, when ritual purity had to be preserved.[3]

Phaedo, who was present in Athens at Socrates' death, can explain to his audience in Phlius the reasons for the stay of his execution. Clearly, the frame dialogue in Phlius portrays the devotion to the memory of Socrates that Phaedo shares with Echekrates and his fellow citizens. His pleasure is all the more intense because of the pain of recalling Socrates' last conversation. The combination of pleasure and pain and the emotional logic by which one succeeds another is, in fact, one of the themes of this conversation. We dis-

1. *Phaedo* 58C–D.
2. *Phaedo* 59A and 117D. In the *Symposium* (173D), Apollodoros is called "emotional."
3. *Phaedo* 58A–D.

cover another interesting feature of the frame Plato created for the *Phaedo*: the faint signature of the missing artist. Plato, Phaedo tells us, was not present in the prison; he was ill.[4] But Plato is the artist who created both the canvas and the frame of the *Phaedo*. The frame dialogue in Phlius has a dramatic immediacy, whereas the dialogue in Athens is mediated and set at a distance by Phaedo, the narrator.

What then is the function of this frame? It is not unique to the *Phaedo*; three other Socratic dialogues have similar frames: the *Theaetetus*, the *Symposium*, and the *Parmenides*. Before turning to these in search of an answer to our question, two observations seem right for the frame dialogue of the *Phaedo*: first, it commemorates, as nothing else could, the fascination that Socrates held for his contemporaries not only in Athens but in the small and distant city of Phlius. Second, in fashioning this frame dialogue, which is not contemporary with its canvas, Plato has directly associated the memory of Socrates with another age—his own. Yet he has also associated this memory with Phlius and not with Athens, where the philosopher was put to death.

Theaetetus

The frame dialogue of the *Theaetetus* seems similar to that of the *Phaedo*. The central conversation of the *Theaetetus* is set in Athens shortly before Socrates' trial, but the frame dialogue is set in neighboring Megara perhaps thirty years later (perhaps just after the Corinthian campaign of 369). The speakers of this dialogue are the Megarians Eukleides and Terpsion, who are brought together by the news that Theaetetus, once a companion of Socrates, has been seriously wounded and is being carried through Megarian territory to Athens. Theaetetus' bravery in battle reminds Eukleides, who went out to meet him, of Socrates' prediction, years before, that young Theaetetus would distinguish himself. And this prediction brings to mind the conversation, held years earlier, that brought together Socrates, the mathematician Theodoros, who was visiting Athens from Cyrene, and the young Athenian Theaetetus. Their long conversation had been preserved by Eukleides in a book. Eukleides himself was not present, and his knowledge of this conversation depends entirely on Socrates:

> As soon as I returned, I immediately jotted down my notes on the conversation, and later, when I had the time, I began to write it out, as I

4. *Phaedo* 59D.

recalled it. And, whenever I went to Athens, I asked Socrates to fill in the details I could not remember. When I returned here, I would make my revisions. And so I have written down just about the entire conversation.[5]

The book Eukleides asks his slave to read is remarkable. Unlike the conversations recalled in the other frame dialogues, it dispenses with the reminders of Socrates' narrative—"and I said" and "he agreed."[6] The contrast with the style of the *Symposium*, with its narrator repeating "and he [Aristodemos] said that he [one of the speakers] said," is striking. In the *Theaetetus*, the editorial suppression of narrative links creates the illusion of dramatic immediacy. Unlike the *Phaedo*, the *Theaetetus* seems to be acted in Athens and not recalled at another time in another place. What Eukleides wanted to avoid, evidently, was his literary chore as Socrates' Boswell. But Plato wanted to give this—one of Socrates' last conversations—an immediacy in another time and place. And, as we shall see (in II § 4, "Mimesis"), Plato also chose the most vivid, and dangerous, form of narrative, the "mimetic" or dramatic, in which the reader is forced to take the part of—and impersonate—Socrates, Theodoros, and Theaetetus. The subject of the *Theaetetus* grows out of the question Socrates puts to Theaetetus: What is knowledge, or "Is learning becoming wiser about what one learns?"[7] This question is not irrelevant to the frame dialogue in Megara; knowledge cannot, as Theaetetus first proposes, be limited to sensation, for one form of knowledge is memory.[8] The "memory" of the conversation of the *Theaetetus* is, of course, Plato's invention. But the recollection of Socrates' conversations offers an analogue to the doctrine, set out at length in the *Phaedo*, that knowledge is recollection (see III § 4, "Thinking About Ideas").

In presenting this distant conversation from the very end of Socrates' life as if it were contemporary, and in removing Socrates' narrative links as he reported it to Eukleides, Plato has both preserved a memorial of Socrates' fascination to his own age and rendered it as immediate as the vivid sensation of hearing a voice from the past audible in Megara, perhaps thirty years after Socrates pronounced his last words: "We owe a cock to Asclepius, Crito. [Friends] do not neglect to pay my debt."[9] But the very care to guarantee the

5. *Theaetetus* 143A.
6. *Theaetetus* 143C.
7. *Theaetetus* 145D.
8. *Theaetetus* 163D.
9. *Phaedo* 118A.

"historicity" of this conversation of the young Theaetetus and the older Socrates points to its character as a philosophical fiction. Eukleides' book, which his slave reads, is in fact Plato's *Theaetetus*. One can also say of the settings of the *Phaedo* and *Theaetetus* that they reflect an alienation from the state that put Socrates to death. Set in Phlius and Megara, the conversations recalling Socrates' last days in Athens belong to cities more devoted to Socrates than was Athens. We recall that after Socrates' execution Plato and other companions of Socrates left Athens for Megara.[10]

Parmenides

At the opening of the *Parmenides*, we hear Kephalos, a philosopher from Klazomenai in Asia Minor, addressing an unidentified audience and relating the events of a recent trip to Athens, where he happened to find Plato's brothers, Adeimantos and Glaukon, in the Agora. He and his companions from Klazomenai are looking for Plato's older, half brother, Antiphon. They have heard that Antiphon can repeat the conversation between Socrates and Parmenides, who had come to Athens from Elea in southern Italy years before for the great festival of the Panathenaia.

As Kephalos discovers, Antiphon was not himself present at this momentous meeting; he learned of it from Pythodoros, a companion of Zeno (himself a companion of Parmenides), who was there.[11] Kephalos finds Antiphon in a smith's shop, having a bridle repaired. Despite his evident reluctance, Antiphon summons up the conversation, which he himself has heard at second hand, and repeats it verbatim to Kephalos, who repeats it, in an equally incredible feat of memory, to his unknown audience—and to us. Thus, we are made to stand at three removes from the reality of the dialogue between Socrates and Parmenides. Even at this distance, we confront the intense interest, throughout the Greek world, in Socrates and his conversations, especially since this conversation is with the "pre-Socratic" Parmenides and his companion Zeno. Kephalos' concern for recovering the words of this conversation can stand as an emblem for the concern of many outside the group of "Socratics" for preserving Socrates' memory, for he not only listens to Antiphon's narrative, he relates it to others in his turn. He begins his narration: "Once we had arrived in Athens from our home in Klazomenai, we met Adeimantos

10. According to DL 2.106 and 3.6.
11. *Parmenides* 126A–127D.

and Glaukon in the Agora."[12] He seems to be speaking to people back home on his return to Klazomenai. Again, Athens does not seem to be the center of interest in Socrates' conversations, but we come to realize that Plato wrote the *Parmenides* and the other dialogues whose frames are set outside of Athens in Athens and that his Academy, with its precinct of the Muses (*Mouseion*), had become the place where Socrates' memory was preserved.

The frame dialogue of the *Parmenides* reveals the delicate signature of the silent artist who kept himself at a distance from his dialogues—in this case at a great distance. Plato's signature can be found in the mention of his half brother, Antiphon. We have heard Socrates name Plato's older brother Adeimantos in the *Apology*,[13] and Adeimantos and Glaukon are Socrates' main interlocutors in the *Republic*. In the *Parmenides* we meet Adeimantos, Glaukon, and Antiphon, whose early interest in Socrates and philosophy had given way to the properly aristocratic interest in horses.[14] Plato's passion for philosophy lasted a lifetime and led him to compose the *Parmenides*. Plato is the only brother not named in the frame dialogue of the *Parmenides*, but he is inevitably recalled by the mention of his three brothers.

Plato was a mimetic artist who was acutely aware of the meaning of the historical settings he elaborated for his Socratic dialogues; he was also aware of the distance between himself, as well as his reader, and the object of his imitation. In insisting on the anachronism of a meeting between the young Socrates and the ancient Parmenides, he is also drawing attention, I think, to his own philosophical fiction.[15]

Perhaps we can now go beyond our initial observations on the frame dialogue of the *Phaedo* and suggest that the significance of the four frame dialogues among his others is ambiguous: Plato both attaches his fifth-century canvas to its later frame and at the same time reminds us that the frame and its canvas are not contemporary; between his narrators and Socrates, between himself and Socrates, and between his readers and Socrates, Plato indicates a distance that can only be closed by a philosophical fiction.

---

12. *Parmenides* 126A.

13. *Apology* 34A.

14. *Parmenides* 127A.

15. We are given the same signal in the *Timaeus* in the circumstantial guarantee of the historicity of Plato's account of the war between Atlantis and prehistoric Athens. Here Critias (the "tyrant" of 404–403) insists on his youth (he was just ten at the time) and the advanced years of his grandfather Critias ("nearly ninety"), who related to him an account, derived from Dropides, a relative of Solon, of Solon's epic of Atlantis. *Timaeus* 20D–21D.

Symposium

The frame dialogues give the impression of historical accuracy and present themselves as the scrupulous record of the sources of our knowledge of past events. In them we encounter the sources and guarantors of our knowledge of Socrates: Phaedo for Socrates' last day; Eukleides (and Socrates) for Socrates' conversation with Theaetetus; Pythodoros, Antiphon, and Kephalos for Socrates' meeting with Parmenides. In the case of the *Symposium*, our authorities for what was said and done at the tragic poet Agathon's victory celebration are Apollodoros, Aristodemos, and Socrates himself. But, when the curtain closes, we realize that it is Plato himself who is the ultimate authority for the Socratic dialogues that are his creations. In attributing his dialogues to others, Plato is imitating Socrates, who liked to claim (in the words of the heroine of Euripides' philosophical drama, *Melanippe the Philosopher*), "[T]he tale I tell is not my own."[16] To attribute them to others and to Socrates himself is to create the impression of history rather than artifice. But, in the case of the *Symposium*, Plato has also introduced in his frame dialogue figures whom we should now describe (following Wayne Booth) as "unreliable narrators."[17] A mere description of the links of memory that preserve the speeches and events of the banquet at Agathon's is baffling because of its sheer complexity and apparent lack of motivation. What is the reader to make of it?

The frame dialogue of the *Symposium* opens with Apollodoros, Socrates' self-appointed Boswell, responding to the inquiries of an unidentified audience: "Speaking for myself, I am well prepared to answer your question. . . . I make it my business to know what Socrates says and does every day."[18] As it happens, Apollodoros, on his way from Phaleron to Athens, had just been asked about this banquet by an acquaintance named Glaukon. Apollodoros' sources of information about this historical event are two: Aristodemos and Socrates himself. This schematic representation of the sources of our knowledge of what happened one evening in the spring of 416 reflects the tenuousness of our knowledge of it. The broken lines represent the gaps in the transmission of what was said and done (Fig. 1).

Two unreliable narrators make our knowledge of Agathon's victory celebration elliptical: the first is Aristodemos, Socrates' companion at the ban-

---

16. *TGF*, frag. 484. Socrates repeats this apology in *Apology* 20E, when he defers to the authority of Apollo. In *Symposium* 177A, Eryximachos invokes it when he defers to the authority of Phaedrus.
17. Booth 1983, chap. 12.
18. *Symposium* 172A and 172C.

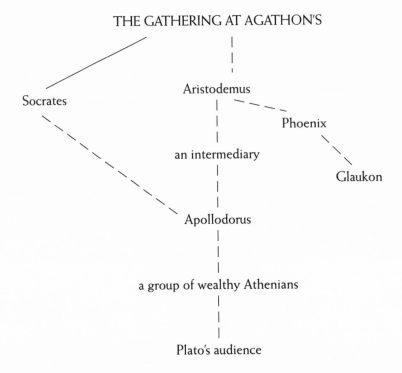

THE GATHERING AT AGATHON'S

FIG. 1   The Banquet at Agathon's: The Genealogy of Knowledge

quet, who did not remember the speeches of some of Agathon's guests or what Socrates had to say to Agathon and Aristophanes at the end of the evening;[19] the second is Apollodoros, who heard of what had happened at Agathon's from Aristodemos and liked to repeat what he had heard. He also checked some details with Socrates, but he did not have the wit to ask Socrates to fill in the gaps of Aristodemos' account.[20] Aristodemos fell asleep toward the end of the party and could not recall just how Socrates managed to convince the tragic poet Agathon and the comic poet Aristophanes that one and the same poet could write both tragedy and comedy.

In 416, the date of Agathon's victory in the tragic competitions, Apollodoros was only a child and Plato was just over ten. The author of the *Symposium* did not supply all of the speeches that were part of Agathon's banquet. He seems thereby to be making a distinction between Agathon's banquet,

19. *Symposium* 180C and 223B–D.
20. *Symposium* 173B.

whose historicity seems guaranteed by the fact that some part of our record of it has been lost, and his own *Symposium*, which possesses exquisite artistry disguised by the appearance of the elided and the accidental. As readers, we should not ourselves neglect Plato's care in characterizing the two figures who are so important to his frame dialogue: Aristodemos, the barefooted and passionate admirer and imitator of Socrates, who possessed none of his stamina or powers of memory and, apparently, did not speak himself; and Apollodoros, nicknamed "softy,"[21] who attributes Socratic ignorance to everyone he comes into contact with, including himself and his anonymous audience.[22] What Plato seems to be suggesting by adding these details to the frame dialogue of the *Symposium* is the possibility that the memory of Socrates cannot be independent of the character of his memorialist and that even the brilliant portrait of Socrates at Agathon's is not complete. Thus, Plato's reader is invited to fill in what is missing—and particularly the argument "lost" from the end of the *Symposium*. In an age when no tragic poet wrote comedies and no comic poet wrote tragedies, can there be a poet who can combine the talents of both in a single art? The answer to this question might be expressed in a single word: Plato. We shall soon test the possibility that Plato is the tragic and comic poet glimpsed as a dreamlike figure at the end of his *Symposium* (see I § 7, "Socrates Eros").

ENDNOTE: There has been no full study of the four frame dialogues discussed here. I have made a beginning in "Plato's First Words," in *Beginnings in Greek Literature* (1992), 113–29. David Halperin has written what I regard as the best essay on the frame dialogue of the *Symposium*, "Plato and the Erotics of Narrativity," in Klagge and Smith 1992, 93–129. Mitchell H. Miller Jr. gives serious consideration to the frame dialogue of the *Parmenides* in *Plato's Parmenides: The Conversion of the Soul* (1986), chap. 1.

---

21. *Symposium* 173D.
22. *Symposium* 172A–173B.

Plato places us readers at a distance from Socrates in yet another way, even as he creates a Socrates who seems immediately present to us. Behind the brilliant foreground of Socrates' conversations, Plato has—with all the artistry of a tragic poet treating a plot well known to his audience—created a dark and somber background. In Greek, the past was conceived of as clearly projected in front of the individual; the future was regarded as what lies behind us (*eis topisthen*). In Plato's dialogues, Socrates has his future dimly illuminated behind him, and his fate, as adumbrated by an author who began his career as a tragic poet, gives the Platonic dialogues a depth we do not find in the works of the other *Sokratikoi*. Before we read the dialogue in which Socrates defends his life at the risk of his life (see I § 5, "The Philosopher in Court"), we should come to terms with the dramatic irony that is so arresting a feature of Plato's Socratic dialogues. It is a theme we will return to when we consider the dialogue form itself (see II § 2, "Socratic Irony").

If Socratic irony can be seen as a manner of self-deprecation before someone who is credited with being superior to the modest and doubting Socrates, Platonic irony can be seen as a manifestation of the superior knowledge of the dramatist. It requires, as did Attic tragedy, a knowing audience. This irony forces us to return to our initial characterization of Plato as a Socratic who, unlike the other Socratics, invested his dialogues with a meaningful historical background (see I § 2, "Dramatic Settings") and to face the paradox of Jorge Luis Borges' parable of *Pierre Mesnard: Author of Don Quixote*: Does the text of Cervantes' *Don Quixote*, published at the beginning of the seventeenth century (1602), have the same meaning as the exactly equivalent chapters of Pierre Mesnard's *Don Quixote*, written in the early twentieth century? Or can

Mesnard's *Don Quixote* be read as "verbally identical, but . . . almost infinitely richer?"[1]

This paradox can be recast in terms of the Socratic dialogue: Aischines' *Alcibiades* and Plato's *First Alcibiades* and *Symposium* would be very different works if they were written before Alcibiades' demonic career had played itself out in 404. Indeed, any dialogue involving Alcibiades as a character and written after the night of the profanation of the mysteries in March 415 and the sailing of the Athenian fleet that summer to Sicily—that is, after the dramatic date of Plato's *Symposium*—would be a very different work. The *First Alcibiades* provides an elegant example of Plato's dramatic irony. It concludes with a promise of the young Alcibiades (who is twenty, which puts the dramatic date of the dialogue at 431) to Socrates: from that day on he will exert himself in the pursuit of justice. To this, Socrates responds:

> I would have you spend your entire life in this pursuit. But I have a premonition. It is not because I am not confident in your character, but because I fear that the power of our city will prove stronger than I and stronger than you.[2]

Socrates was prophetic in his premonition, but at the dramatic date of the dialogue the precise shape of his own destiny in Athens or that of Alcibiades had not yet been drawn. In the Platonic dialogues, Platonic irony is superior to Socratic irony; it invests the conversations of Socrates with a significance they could not have possessed either for him or for his companions. Both Socratic and Platonic irony are, however, a manifestation of the gap between appearance and reality. These forms of irony are not symptomatic of a benign world in which appearances disclose reality and in which humans can read the invisible in the face of the visible. Both depend fundamentally on the presence of a silent observer in the audience, who sits in a position to see the dim shape of reality—both historical and philosophical—behind the façade of appearances. The difference between the two forms of irony is that Socrates does not sit in Plato's audience. In Plato, the historical settings of his Socratic dialogues and the words and actions of the actors in them have a deeper meaning. They must be understood not only as they seem to be captured in the dramatic moment of a recorded conversation; they must be understood in retrospect.

It is principally Socrates over whom the long dark shadow of Plato's

---

1. Borges 1962, 52.
2. *First Alcibiades* 135E.

dramatic irony falls. The memory of Socrates' trial and execution by the state of Athens casts its shadow over Socrates in the Platonic dialogues from the *Euthyphro* to the *Statesman*. This shadow is darker and more ominous in some dialogues than in others. When it passes over a dialogue, it emerges in a context in which the world of the philosopher and the political opinions of the polis in which he lives are set in sharp contrast, as it does in the *Gorgias*, *Meno, Republic, Theaetetus*, and as late as the *Statesman*.[3]

Republic

Take first the most poignant example. In the *Republic*, the meaning of Socrates' parable of the cave in book 7 is transformed by a single question. Socrates, in order to illustrate to Glaukon "our education or lack of it," has described a cave in which prisoners are bound and forced to sit facing the shadows playing over a back wall.[4] Behind them unseen puppeteers project images and voices onto the wall of the cave, and these images represent the only reality the cave dwellers know. But what, Socrates asks, if one of the prisoners were to escape into the light of day and were one day to return to the cave?[5]

SOCRATES:
If a prisoner were to descend into the cave again and take his old seat, would his eyes not be flooded suddenly with darkness as he suddenly arrived there from the light of the sun?

GLAUKON:
Indeed, they would.

SOCRATES:
And if he had to enter into a contest with those who had remained prisoners there in identifying the shadows of the cave, when his eyes were dimmed and before they could grow accustomed to the darkness, and it took him a long time to adjust his eyes, would he not provoke howls of laughter? And would they not say of him that he had climbed upward only to return with his eyes ruined and that it was not even worth the attempt to make the ascent. And, if the prisoners could lay their hands on the

3. *Statesman* 299B.
4. *Republic* 7.514A. For the other side of the analogy of the cave and the divided line, see III §5 ("The Sun, the Line, and the Cave") and Figure 2.
5. *Republic* 7.516E–517A.

person who attempted to release them from their bonds and to lead them upward and could put him to death, would they not put him to death?

GLAUKON:

They certainly would!

The Athenians certainly did when they put Socrates to death.

Meno

The *Meno* also contains a premonition and a reminder of Socrates' death and the fate of the man "who was the best of all those we knew at that time and by far the wisest and most just"—in the words of *Phaedo*, which come very close to the words of Plato himself.[6] We have noticed the dramatic date of the *Meno*: 402, only three years before Socrates' trial. In the *Meno*, Anytos, who was later to step forward as one of Socrates' three accusers, warns Socrates to be careful: "Perhaps in some other city it is easier to harm men than to help them, but in Athens doing harm takes no effort!"[7]

Gorgias

The shadow of death is also cast over a dialogue that evokes the spectacle of the philosopher in a democratic court, the *Gorgias*. The *Gorgias* is an intensely bitter dialogue; it is also "tragic," as is no other Platonic dialogue, in that it dramatizes the conflict between the philosopher and politician, which Euripides had first staged in the *Antiope* through its contest (*agon*) between the brothers Amphion and Zethos over their ways of life. The *Gorgias* is named after Gorgias of Leontini and concentrates on the power of rhetoric and its ally public opinion. It dramatizes, as the *Apology* had not, the powerlessness of the philosopher in court. In this dialogue, Socrates plays the part of the musical brother, Amphion, whose music built the walls of Thebes, and Kallikles, an Athenian aristocrat and associate of Gorgias, the part of the political brother, Zethos in Euripides' play.[8]

In Socrates' view, the rhetor is the teacher of what is just and unjust in

6. *Phaedo* 118A; Letter VII 324E.

7. *Meno* 94E.

8. The reader of the *Gorgias* can gain some sense of the character of Euripides' *Antiope* from the papyrus fragments translated in *Select Papyri* III (*Literary Papyri: Poetry*), ed. D. L. Page (Cambridge, Mass., and London, 1962), 60–71.

cities: in its legal assemblies and other meetings "he can only persuade. But I do not suppose that he could possibly instruct such a great crowd in such great matters in so short a time."[9] Kallikles agrees. On trial, Socrates had about forty minutes measured by the waterclock in which to persuade a jury of some 501 of his fellow citizens that he was not guilty of the charges brought against him and to give an account of his life as a philosopher. From the vantage of the demagogue, the philosopher is helpless in court.[10] But perhaps in another court and in another world it is Kallikles who will stand before another judge: "[W]hen he takes hold of you, and leads you away, you will be as tongue-tied and as giddy in that place as I am here."[11] There is an irony in all of this, since Socrates was anything but tongue-tied and giddy on the day of his trial. Then, at least in Plato's *Apology of Socrates*, he spoke in his "accustomed manner" of interrogation,[12] but he also employed all the rhetorical commonplaces of the Athenian courts.[13]

Theaetetus

The *Theaetetus* is still another dialogue on which the shadow of Socrates' trial and execution falls. Its dramatic setting is the year 399, and it ends, as we have seen, with Socrates leaving his companions to answer the charges of Meletos at the offices of the king Archon. Socrates' description of the abstracted and defenseless philosopher in the *Theaetetus* is grotesquely inaccurate as a self-portrait. In this dialogue, Socrates repeats Kallikles' (and Zethos') claim that those who have passed their lives as philosophers put on a ridiculous show when they have to speak in the courts:

> They don't know the way to the market or the council chamber or to any other place of assembly in their city. The laws that are proclaimed publicly or inscribed on stone they neither see nor hear. They never even dream of taking part in party politics, with its passionate factions, or joining in gatherings, dinners, and revels with flute girls. . . . In reality, only the philosopher's body dwells in the city and resides there. His mind deems all these concerns as trifling and meaningless, and, in its contempt for them, it takes wing and flies, in Pindar's phrase, "beneath

9. *Gorgias* 455A; cf. *Apology* 37A.
10. *Gorgias* 484C–E and 508D.
11. *Gorgias* 527A. This is part of the transcendental meditation opposing "here" and "there" in the *Gorgias*, *Phaedo*, and *Republic* and explored in II §8 ("The Open Dialogue").
12. *Apology* 17D–18A.
13. *Apology* 17C; see I §5 ("The Philosopher in Court").

the earth," as it measures surfaces, and to "the heavens above," as it studies the stars.[14]

There is something comic about Socrates' philosopher in the *Theaetetus*; he is a caricature—the philosopher "Socrates" we find suspended in a basket in Aristophanes' *Clouds*. This is the "Socrates" of Socrates' "first accusers," the comic poets, whose farcical charge is that "Socrates has committed a crime in his meddlesome inquiries into the realm beneath the earth and the realm of heavens."[15] In the *Apology*, Socrates can assure his jury: "You have seen all this yourselves in Aristophanes' comedy, where you witnessed 'Socrates' being carried about, saying that he treads upon air and talking a lot of similar nonsense."[16]

According to one tale, foreigners in Aristophanes' audience at the City Dionysia of 423 asked, "Who is this Socrates?" In response, Socrates simply stood up during the performance of the *Clouds*, as if to say *this* is Socrates, not the "Socrates" you see on stage.[17] Aristophanes' "Socrates" is simply the polis-eye's view of the philosopher. As we shall see, this point of view is described by Socrates himself in the *Sophist*.[18]

The charges of Socrates' second accusers were far more serious, not because they were far different from the first but because they were made in 399 during the crisis of Athens' "failure of nerve" after her defeat at Aigispota-moi and the Spartan occupation of Athens and the Peiraeus; they were not made in the freedom of a dramatic festival of Dionysos but before 501 paid jurymen. The courtroom drama of the *Apology* helps us understand the moments in the Platonic dialogues when the shadow of Socrates' death passes over the scene. This is the moment to which they all lead and from which they all radiate.

All these moments of tragic irony have a context and echo the dramatic moments of Plato's *Apology* when Socrates has to quiet the jury he has provoked by his claim to some kind of superiority. Latent in the *Republic*, *Meno*, *Gorgias*, and *Theaetetus* is the contrast between the knowledge of the philosopher and the political opinions of his city.[19] In the *Republic*, these opinions of

14. *Theaetetus* 173C–E, quoting Pindar, frag. 302 Bowra.
15. *Apology* 19B.
16. *Apology* 19C. Socrates in court is presented in I §5 ("The Philosopher in Court").
17. The anecdote is retailed in Aelian, *Varia Historia* 2.13 (p. 24) Dilts.
18. *Sophist* 216C–D, a passage read in I §6 ("Socrates *Hērōs*").
19. The same contrast is to be found in *Phaedo* 118A and Letter VII 324E.

the city are represented as (in Francis Bacon's phrase) the "idols of the cave."[20] In the *Theaetetus*, the "digression" on the philosopher in court is introduced by Socrates' application of Protagoras' dictum "Man is the measure of all things" to the opinions of states and their transient and corporate conceptions of what is just and unjust.[21] Socrates' cartoon of the philosopher answers to the city's opinion of the philosopher. But in this dialogue the philosopher's opinion of the city and its courts is also expressed quite forcefully. In the courts citizens

> speak forever under pressure—for the waterclock urges them on—and they cannot choose the topics they want to speak of. The accuser stands opposite wielding the power of compulsion and the indictment that is read out to the jury and circumscribes the subjects the defendant can address. The arguments in court always concern some fellow slave and are addressed to a seated slavemaster, who holds some written affidavit in his hand. These contests never turn on an issue that involves someone else, but they touch the defendant himself, and often the race is a race for his life.[22]

In the *Theaetetus*, the "digression" on the philosopher in court is not a digression, for the problem of distinguishing knowledge from opinion arises in its political guise in the popular courts of democratic Athens and specifically in the case of Socrates' defense before a popular jury. At the end of this dialogue, Socrates must appear before the king Archon at the King's Stoa to answer Meletos' indictment against him; and from there he must go on to stand trial for his life. Socrates says no more than: "Now I have an appointment at the King's Stoa to respond to the indictment Meletos has drawn up against me."[23] Plato's readers know what this will mean.

ENDNOTE: Suggestions for further reading on Socratic and Platonic irony can be found in the Endnote to the essay on Socratic irony (II § 2). Andrea Nightingale has written a revealing study of Euripides' *Antiope* as the background to Plato's *Gorgias*, "Plato's *Gorgias* and Euripides' *Antiope*: A Study in

---

20. Bacon owes his term to Plato. It is developed in *The New Organon* (1620), bk. 1, xxxix and xlii; see III §5 ("The Sun, the Line, and the Cave").

21. *Theaetetus* 172A; DK 80 B 1 (from the *Theaetetus*).

22. *Theaetetus* 172D–E.

23. *Theaetetus* 210D.

Generic Transformation" (1992). This essay is preliminary to her larger study "Use and Abuse of Athenian Tragedy," in *Genres in Dialogue* (1995), 60–92. A reading of Sophocles' *Oedipus* that stresses dramatic irony as the product of the gap between appearance and reality is Karl Reinhard's classic *Sophocles* (1979), a study from which the reader of Plato can profit.

We reach, inevitably, the solid object that has cast its shadow over the Platonic dialogues, the trial and execution of Socrates, and Plato's *Apology of Socrates* (a title that will now be shortened to the *Apology*). At the very beginning of his defense, Socrates gives offense to his jurors. When he first addresses them, he does not call them judges, *dikastai*, he calls them rather "men of Athens."[1] In Athens, juror and judge were one, and the *dikastēs* was a citizen sworn to determine where justice δίϰη, *dikē*) lay. The significance of this form of address is apparent only later in the *Apology*, at the moment when Socrates calls those who had voted to acquit him "gentlemen, judges," and enters into a "dialogue" with this minority on the meaning of his conviction and death, "for in calling you judges, I would be choosing the proper name."[2]

Plato's *Apology* is the best known of his dialogues and generally is the Platonic dialogue first read. But it has two peculiarities: it is not exactly the speech Socrates made in his own defense, and it is not strictly a dialogue. The fact that another *Apology* has come down to us among the Socratic works of Xenophon may also unsettle the historian of the historical Socrates, for Xenophon's *Apology* is remarkably different from Plato's, in part because it is motivated by Xenophon's concern to explain, as "others"—including Plato— had not, Socrates' arrogant and uncompromising manner of speaking (his *megalēgoria*).[3] Plato would seem to have a claim on the truth that Xenophon

---

1. *Apology* 17A.
2. *Apology* 40A.
3. Xenophon, *Apology* 1.1. The reference to Socrates' uncompromising manner of speaking, or "big talking," is justified by what Socrates says to his jury in Plato's *Apology* 20E. I take Xenophon's plural in "Others have written about this matter and all have touched on his uncompromising manner of speaking" as the "evasive plural" characteristic of Greek polemical writing and a reference to Plato.

did not; he was actually present at Socrates' trial, and Socrates points him out when he calls attention to "Plato here";[4] Xenophon was not. His knowledge of Socrates' trial depended on an associate of Socrates by the name of Hermogenes (a speaker in Plato's *Cratylus* and one of the Socratics with Socrates on his last day). Xenophon's *Apology* contains only two passages that purport to be direct quotations of what Socrates said.[5]

Because Plato was present at Socrates' trial, his *Apology* has been taken as the most historical of the Platonic dialogues and a more accurate witness to Socrates' trial than Xenophon's secondhand *Apology*. And it has been plausibly argued that Plato could not have misrepresented what Socrates actually said, because there were so many others present at the trial to confound him if he did. This must be true in the sense that his intention was not to misrepresent Socrates or his defense (*apologia* in Greek); but it is also true that the intention of the *Apology* is to represent or re-present Socrates. This intention seems to be recognized by Diogenes Laertius in his *Lives of the Philosophers* when he says that in his first "tetralogy" (*Euthyphro, Apology, Crito,* and *Phaedo*) Plato intended to "give a demonstration of what the life of the philosopher is like."[6]

Although Plato was in the audience at Socrates' trial, he could not have been present at Crito's private conversation with Socrates; he was not in the prison during Socrates' last conversation, and it is unlikely that he overheard Socrates' conversation with the fanatically pious Euthyphro, whom Socrates encountered at the King's Stoa. Another record we possess of the charges against Socrates does not correspond word for word with Socrates' statement of them in the *Apology*. Diogenes Laertius knew from Favorinus of Arles (second century A.D.) that there was a copy of the indictment against Socrates in the State Records Office (Metroon) of Athens. In this indictment the order of the charges against Socrates is the reverse of the order Socrates gives in the *Apology*.[7]

In a question where no certain knowledge is possible, it seems a fair assumption that in his *Apology* Plato represented the meaning of Socrates' defense as this had become apparent after his execution. In his actual, vanished words Socrates represented himself. Between the two representations there is a level of interpretation. Plato, whose *Apology* is an exquisite literary document, did not sit in the audience as a court stenographer. But after the

---

4. *Apology* 38B.
5. Xenophon, *Apology* 11–21 and 24–26.
6. DL 3.57.
7. Compare *Apology* 24B and DL 2.40.

verdict and Socrates' execution he had the time and motivation to reflect on what Socrates had said in his defense and the meaning of his life and death.

The word "apology" in the title *The Apology of Socrates* is misleading in English, for Socrates never "apologized" for his life; his ἀπολογία is his spirited and outlandish defense against the charges of his accusers. Plato's *Apology* is not the "apology" of Socrates as Socrates defended himself against the charges of his three accusers; it is rather Plato's considered defense of Socrates and his entire life. Nor does it constitute a defense of Socrates, like those we find in Xenophon: in the first two chapters of the *Memorabilia* (and indeed in the entire *Memorabilia*) and in his *Apology*. It is rather the literary and philosophical demonstration and justification of a certain kind of life. As for the *apologia* of—if not for—Socrates, it is said that the orator Lysias offered to compose for Socrates a speech in his defense. And Plato is said to have made an attempt to mount the speaker's platform and offer a speech in Socrates' defense—only to be shouted down by the court.[8] In late antiquity the pagan orator Libanius (fourth century A.D.) composed still another defense for Socrates. Unlike his many accomplished and eloquent defenders, Socrates is said to have been prevented from meditating a defense by his inner divine voice, or *daimonion*.[9]

Do we have Socrates' unpremeditated words in Plato's *Apology?* Any reader familiar with Greek rhetoric can attest that Socrates' opening words in Plato's *Apology* are both highly contrived and commonplace in the forensic rhetoric of the courts of Athens. Plato's Socrates begins by expressing his amazement that his accusers, who had just spoken, should have warned the jury he was a formidable speaker; he reminds them that at the age of seventy he has never yet mounted the speaker's platform in a court; and he protests, even as he employs the well-worn language of the courts: "[H]onestly, I am a stranger to the language people use in this place"; "If you hear me speaking in the same language I am accustomed to use in the market and at the tables of the bankers, where many of you have heard me speak, don't create an uproar in court because of this."[10]

Socrates' familiar language did create an uproar in the court. I count six interruptions.[11] There is no wonder why, in Plato's representation of the trial. Throughout his trial, Socrates provokes his jurors by asserting his superiority

8. DL 2.40–41.
9. Xenophon, *Apology* 4–5.
10. *Apology* 17D and 17C.
11. At *Apology* 20D and E, 21A, 27B, 30C, and 31E.

to other men and refusing to conform to the expectations of the court. The effect of Socrates' offensive language (*megalēgoria*) on the jury is evident in the uproar provoked by Socrates' account of his friend Chairephon's mission to Delphi to ask if there was anyone wiser than Socrates, to which question the god had responded enigmatically that—as Chairephon thought—"no one is wiser than Socrates," and by Socrates' justification of his own "mission" in Athens to "test" the truth of the god's assertion by attempting to discover an Athenian wiser than himself.[12]

The offense Socrates gave in court by his manner of speaking is something the two authors who report his speech agree on. Xenophon attempted to explain the motivation for Socrates' offensive tone by arguing that he was an old man and not only ready but eager for death. But Plato's *Apology*, rather than Xenophon's, conveys the tone that so annoyed Socrates' jury. In Plato, Socrates represents his "divine mission" and service to Apollo as his modest attempt to prove the god, who "cannot lie," false in his oracle that Socrates is the wisest of all humans.[13] This involves the vexation of Socrates' posing questions to his fellow citizens in the vain attempt to discover an Athenian wiser than he.[14] Unheard of in an Athenian court is the tactic of his first defense against Meletos' charges "that he corrupts the young, and does not believe in the gods of his city but introduces new and strange divinities": Socrates makes a comedy of them and diverts the attention of his jury to his "first accusers"—the comic poets. He formulates their indictment from Aristophanes' caricature of the sophist "Socrates" in the *Clouds*:

> Socrates has committed a crime in his meddlesome inquiries into the realm beneath the earth and the realm of heavens and by making the weaker case the stronger and teaching others to do the same.[15]

Those of his jury who were old enough to remember the City Dionysia of 423 would recognize the justice of this formulation. In the theater of Dionysos they could see Socrates suspended above the stage and addressing the stooped human figure of Strepsiades below as "gnat, thou creature of a day," and hear him proclaim, "I tread upon the air, and my mind encompasses

---

12. *Apology* 21A.

13. *Apology* 21A, an oracular response that provokes an uproar. Apollo's delicacy is conveyed by the words "No one is wiser than Socrates"—not that "Socrates is the wisest of all humans."

14. *Apology* 21B–24B. In proving Apollo truthful, Socrates also proves his fellow citizens ignorant.

15. *Apology* 19B.

the sun."[16] The clouds themselves are Socrates' new and strange divinities, and as for Zeus, he "doesn't even exist."[17] Socrates' disciples can be seen kneeling upon the ground with their rear ends facing the audience, "inquiring into what lies beneath the earth."[18] The central *agon*, or contest, of the play is between personifications of Wrong and Right.[19] And, of course, Aristophanes' "Socrates" is willing to corrupt the young—and even the wily old Strepsiades—by teaching them the useful lesson of how Wrong can defeat Right.

What Plato's Socrates has managed to accomplish by this extension of Meletos' indictment to the "comic poets" is to make a mockery of it and to introduce comedy into Socrates' contest for his life. The comic and playful character of Socrates' defense was recognized by some of Plato's readers in antiquity, but even a reader like the Stoic Epictetus could not have appreciated just how offensive this defense was—or would have been—to an Athenian popular court in 399.[20] Socrates both parodies and violates the conventions of forensic rhetoric. Speaking in his "accustomed manner" he turns his defense into a Socratic dialogue, in which he interrogates Apollo, the wealthy Kallias, and Meletos and is interrogated in turn by an anonymous member of his jury, who asks, "Well, what is it that you *do*?"[21] After his conviction, Socrates goes beyond the time allotted to him by the waterclock and enters into a "dialogue" with those who had voted to acquit him.[22] He summons as his "witnesses" "the god who has his oracle in Delphi," the members of his jury, and finally his own poverty.[23] As a counterproposal to Meletos' stipulation of the death penalty, Socrates reflects on what a poor man like himself would deserve from Athens and proposes free meals in the town hall.[24] And, equally shocking, he introduces animals into the judicial assembly with his talk of calves and foals, horses, asses, half-asses, and horseflies.

When it is time to question Meletos, as he had the right to, Socrates conducts a perfect Socratic interrogation:

16. *Clouds* 225.
17. *Clouds* 253 and 367.
18. *Clouds* 188.
19. *Clouds* 889–1111.
20. In one of the conversations recorded by Arrian of Nicomedia (*Discourses* 2.5.18–19), Epictetus invokes Socrates' playful interrogation of Meletos as an example of how the philosopher should play the game of life, with equal expertise and indifference. We will examine the passage he has in mind below.
21. *Apology* 20C.
22. *Apology* 39E.
23. *Apology* 20E and 31C.
24. *Apology* 36D, echoing in an artful (and I think Platonic) manner Xenophanes of Kolophon's lines on the deserts of wisdom, DK 21 B 2.

SOCRATES:

Come up here now, Meletos, and tell me this: Do you consider anything of more crucial importance than that the young should develop into the best men possible?

MELETOS:

Nothing at all.[25]

The courtroom examination that follows disguises serious Socratic concerns. If Meletos is right in his charge that Socrates corrupts the young of Athens, then the accused is making them worse and thereby harming himself by creating a harmful human environment for himself.[26] And, faithful to his conception that virtue is knowledge (and vice ignorance), Socrates holds up to Meletos a conception of punishment as instruction. If virtue is truly knowledge and vice ignorance, then the only appropriate punishment for vice is instruction—an argument that has a long career in the Platonic dialogues.[27]

But the Socratic questioning also has its comic side as Socrates turns to refute Meletos' charge that he does not worship or believe in the gods of his city but introduces "new and strange divinities." It is clear that Socrates' divine monitor, which repels him from action rather than propel him to action, his δαιμόνιον (*daimonion*), is the new and strange divinity Meletos has in mind.[28] This is the tangle that catches Meletos in a contradiction, for, as Socrates forces the very reluctant Meletos to agree, the belief in a *daimonion*, or something divine, entails a belief in *daimones*, or divinities. And, by Socrates' peculiar conception of *daimones*, a belief in divinities entails a belief in both gods and humans. This line of reasoning causes another uproar in the court,[29] but Socrates persists:

Now, again, if *daimones* are certain illegitimate children of the gods and of nymphs or of certain other women whose children they are said to be, what mortal could possibly believe in the existence of the children of the gods but not the gods? It would be equally absurd for a person to

25. *Apology* 24C–D.
26. *Apology* 24C–26A, anticipating Socrates' argument on the harm of injustice to oneself in *Republic* 1.335B.
27. *Apology* 26A, *Gorgias* 477A, *Republic* 1.337D–338B, *Critias* 106B; and see III §2 ("The Virtue of Knowledge").
28. *Apology* 31C, confirmed by Xenophon, *Apology* 12.
29. *Apology* 27B.

believe in the existence of the children of horses and asses—half-asses, that is—but to refuse to believe in horses and asses.[30]

He adds *hērōes* to his list of mixed breeds.

Here Socrates ends his refutation of Meletos and returns to his jury. Whether any member of this jury had the wit or the presence of mind to detect the proportional scheme hidden beneath the surface of this argument, we will never know, but one member of Socrates' audience had, and he either recorded it or invented it for his *Apology of Socrates*. Read sideways, Socrates' three-tiered proportional scheme reads:

Gods are to horses
as *daimones* (and *hērōes* and *hēmitheoi*) are to half-asses
as men are to asses.

The crucial middle term "half-asses" (*hēmionoi*) has its parallel in half-gods (*hēmitheoi*). It has so offended modern sensibilities that it does not appear in the Greek text of some editions of the *Apology* and is thus missing from some translations. This comedy is only one facet of Plato's *Apology*, just as the comic is only one side of Socrates' personality. "Comedy" in the sense of what is base and negligible is manifested in Socrates' representation of himself as a god-sent horsefly settling on the body politic of Athens:

If you were to put me to death, you would not easily find another creature like me. If I can speak plainly and in somewhat comic terms, it is as
if the god had fastened me on the city as on some large and thorough-
bred horse that is a little drowsy and sluggish because of its size and
needs to be aroused by a horsefly. I think the god has settled me on the
city as just such an insect, never ceasing the day long in rousing you,
exhorting you, and reproaching you, each and every one of you, as I
settle on every part of you.[31]

This comic mask appears for a last time in the *Apology* when Socrates contemplates the life he would lead in Hades, if the legends about Hades have any truth. Life there would not be very different from the life he has led in Athens:

Life there would be wonderful. I could meet Palamedes and Ajax, the
son of Telamon, and any of the other men of ancient times who died

30. *Apology* 27D–E; cf. Xenophon, *Apology* 4–5. It is in this passage that Epictetus discovered the model for how the philosopher should conduct himself in life (note 20 above).
31. *Apology* 30E.

because of an unjust verdict. And I could compare my experience with theirs, something I imagine would not be without its pleasure, and—the greatest bliss of all—live my life there as I do here, exploring and examining men to discover who is wise and who only fancies that he is wise but is not.[32]

With this passage open before him, Søren Kierkegaard wrote:

One cannot deny that Socrates becomes almost ludicrous with this zeal for spying on men, a zeal which allows him no peace even after death. And who can refrain from smiling when he visualizes those somber shades of the underworld with Socrates in their midst indefatigably examining them and showing them that they know nothing.[33]

In Hades, Socrates could also examine Odysseus, the false accuser of Palamedes and the Achaean warrior judged superior to Ajax in the contest for the arms of Achilles, just as Odysseus himself had questioned the shades in *Odyssey* 11. This spectacle of an Odyssean Socrates interrogating the shade of Odysseus gives a new meaning to the charge of the comic poets that Socrates commits the offense of meddlesome inquiry into the realm beneath the earth.

Every reader of the *Apology* will recognize the tragic and serious aspect of Socrates' defense, which displays the other side of Socrates' complex personality. This serious side is present throughout the *Apology*, either hidden under the smiling surface of Socrates' irony or revealed openly, as it is in the final words Socrates addresses to those of his jurors who had voted to acquit him. These parting words are the expression of his lifelong concern for the young men of Athens and their development into men of virtue. Now, at the end of his life, Socrates' concern is no longer for the wealthy and aristocratic young men we meet in the Platonic dialogues; it is directed toward the three sons of a poor father who will soon be orphans. To his accusers and the jurors who had voted to condemn him to death, Socrates says:

Even so, I have this request to make of them. Gentlemen, if my sons, once they are grown men, seem to you to be more concerned with money or anything other than virtue, punish them and cause them exactly the same distress that I caused you. And if they imagine that they amount to something when they in fact amount to nothing, reproach

---

32. *Apology* 41A–B.
33. Kierkegaard 1966, 77.

them, just as I have reproached you, because they are not thinking of the matters that should concern them and think that they are important people when they are inconsequential. If you do this, I—and my sons—will have received justice at your hands.

The time has come now for us to depart—I to go to my death and you to live your lives. Which of us goes to the better destiny is unclear to all save the god.[34]

The *Apology*, which begins with an address to "men of Athens," concludes with the words "the god."

ENDNOTE: Plato's *Apology of Socrates* has long served as the foundational document for the recovery of the historical Socrates. John Burnet, in his treatment of it in his excellent 1924 edition and commentary, *Plato's Euthyphro, Apology of Socrates, and Crito* (pages 63–66 especially), gives the powerful, if not entirely persuasive, reasons for regarding it as privileged among the Platonic dialogues as a source for our knowledge of Socrates. Recent studies of the trial and the dialogue (for it remains a dialogue, even as it is a forensic speech in form and occasion) accept Plato's *Apology* as historically accurate. These are the analysis of T. C. Brickhouse and N. D. Smith, *Socrates on Trial* (1988), and the impassioned defense of Athenian democracy by I. F. Stone, *The Trial of Socrates* (1988). Accounts of the trial that place it in a historical context are W. R. Connor, "The Other 399: Religion and the Trial of Socrates" (1991), and Mogens Herman Hansen, *The Trial of Socrates from the Athenian Point of View* (1995).

C.D.C. Reeve has produced an acute and philosophically rigorous analysis of Socrates' speech, *Socrates in the "Apology"* (1989). While professing agnosticism about the question of the historicity of the speech, he speaks of Socrates' self-interpretation as "the richest single self-portrait we have" (xii). Richard Kraut has produced a similarly acute study of the *Crito*, in *Crito, Socrates, and the State* (1984). He claims that Plato's portrait of Socrates in the early dialogues, and the *Crito* in particular, is essentially accurate (3 n.1). My own reading of Plato's *Apology* is that, as an apology *for* Socrates, it reveals Plato's retrospective interpretation of the meaning of Socrates' life. I argue for this

34. *Apology* 41E–42A, an injunction to the orphans of the war dead repeated in Plato's funeral oration, *Menexenus* 246B, where Socrates (rehearsing a speech of Pericles that Socrates claims was provided by Aspasia) says to the orphans of the war dead: "And I too exhort you, sons of courageous men, both on this occasion and in the future; whenever I meet one of you, I will call to mind whose sons you are and instill in you a desire to be as great as you can be."

interpretation of the dialogue in "Socrates' Mulishness and Heroism" (1972). Thomas G. West takes the same tack in *Plato's "Apology" of Socrates: An Interpretation, with a New Translation* (1979). A prudent summary of what one can claim were the views of the historical Socrates is given by W.K.C. Guthrie in *HGP* 3:323–484.

Destiny is equal for the warrior who hesitates and the warrior who fights
   fiercely.
We are all, coward and brave, held in a single honor.
He who does nothing dies as does he who does much.
—Achilles to Odysseus, *Iliad* 9.318–20

I don't care for your tall general,
with his long stride and long hair in locks
and beard well trimmed. Show me a stocky man,
bandy-legged, sure of foot, full of heart.
—Archilochos of Paros, frag. 114 West

These words of warriors and poets are relevant to the conception of heroism
that informs Plato's portraits of Socrates as a *hērōs* of the philosophical life,
for both Achilles and Archilochos reject a dominant conception of heroism,
as does Plato in representing Socrates as a *hērōs*.

The final words of the *Apology* point to one conception of Socratic philosophy. Socrates saw himself as a servant of the god Apollo. His claim to
the jury was that he had a religious obligation "to philosophize and to examine myself and others."[1] But what can this claim mean? Socrates' presentation
of himself forces us to recast the puzzled question of one of his judges, "What
is it that philosophers *do*?"[2] In response one can say that Plato's dialogues are
a lifelong response to the puzzlement of many Greeks over the question
What is it that philosophers do? Plato formulates his response in a number of

1. *Apology* 28E.
2. In the words of *Apology* 20C.

portraits of Socrates, or what the Greeks would call *eikones*, which reveal the novel in terms of familiar types and at the same time transform these cultural types into philosophical paradigms.

In one version, that of the *Apology* and *Phaedo*, Socrates is portrayed as a man of deep piety, devoted to the service of Apollo, the god of clarity; in other versions, including those of the *Apology* and *Symposium*, he is cast as a Homeric warrior (*hērōs*), like Heracles, Achilles, or Odysseus; in the *Gorgias*, he is given the role of the poet of Euripides' *Antiope* as he plays Amphion to Kallikles' political Zethos; in the argument of the *Symposium* as a whole, he is portrayed as a *daimōn*, the human embodiment of the god Eros; and in the comparisons made by Alcibiades in this same dialogue, he is represented as half human and half beast, a silenus and a satyr. In the *Theaetetus*, Socrates presents himself as the son of a midwife and as a midwife himself. The one term that does not serve as a basis of comparison for this odd life of relentless inquiry and examination is the term "philosopher." All of these other comparisons recognize the most glaring fact of Socrates' life in Athens: he is out of place (*atopos*). In order to "place" him and make him intelligible, Plato has adduced a great variety of paradigms from Greek culture and in so doing has transformed the terms of comparison and, with these, traditional Greek values.

When he concludes his giddy speech in praise of Socrates in the *Symposium*, Alcibiades reveals what it is about Socrates that renders inadequate the artful comparisons in which Plato invested the life of the philosopher:

> So far as other pursuits in life are concerned, a speaker might say as much concerning someone else. What deserves our admiration is that this man is like no other, either men of the past or our contemporaries. One could compare Brasidas and others to the character of Achilles, and the character of Pericles to the models of Nestor and Antenor, and there are others too [for whom such comparisons can be found]. And one could go on to discover terms of comparison for other men along these same lines. But in order to capture the character of this man in his outlandishness, both in his personal appearance and his talk—one could not readily come upon a comparison that comes close, either with men of the past or men of the present, unless he should choose the terms of my own comparison and liken him—in his appearance and in his talk—to no human being but to sileni and satyrs.[3]

3. *Symposium* 221C–D.

We shall see what Alcibiades meant by this claim when we examine his speech in the *Symposium* and Plato's likeness of Socrates to a silenus (see I § 8, "Socrates Silenus"). But we should keep Alcibiades' claim in mind as we consider the meaning of the variety of Plato's representations of Socrates. Socrates is unlike any human being who ever lived. In assessing the meaning of this bold claim, we should recall Alcibiades' word for his strangeness: he is—literally—out of place (ἄτοπος, *atopos*) and therefore difficult to place in the game of comparisons fashionable at that time.

What, then, does a philosopher do? Plato never wrote a dialogue on the philosopher. Yet he seems to have had the possibility of such a dialogue in mind when he announced the program of the three dialogues that were to follow the *Theaetetus*: the *Sophist*, the *Statesman*, and the unwritten *Philosopher* (a sequel that seems promised at the beginning of the *Sophist*). The *Sophist* continues the conversation of the *Theaetetus*, which had centered on the definition of knowledge. At the end of the *Theaetetus*, Socrates and his two companions, Theodoros and Theaetetus, have failed to agree on the meaning of the term, but they have agreed to meet on "the next day" to continue the discussion.

The next day brings a surprise. Theodoros and Theaetetus appear in the company of a visitor from the southern Italian city of Elea (modern Velia). Socrates greets him in Homeric and Hesiodic fashion as a god come to observe the disorders and lawfulness of mankind. Theodoros piously corrects Socrates by saying that it is his custom to refer to such beings as "godlike, but not as gods."[4] Socrates seems to approve of this distinction, yet he observes that it is difficult to distinguish this race of men from that of the gods, because, as these godlike strangers appear among men, they present a number of guises:

> Indeed, due to the ignorance of other men, these men appear in all manner of guises as they "roam through cities"—those of them who do not feign philosophy but who are true philosophers—looking from their heights down upon the life of men below them. To some they seem to be worthless, to others beyond any price. And sometimes they appear in the guise of statesmen and sometimes in the guise of sophists; and there are occasions when they can give the impression of being utterly insane. Now I would like to ask this visitor, if he is agreeable, what people from his part of the world think about these phenomena and what names they give them.[5]

4. *Sophist* 216B.
5. *Sophist* 216C–D.

Socrates' question leads to the *Sophist* and *Statesmen* and, by implication, to the unwritten *Philosopher*. In the *Sophist* and in the *Statesman* the method of division (διαίρεσις, *diairesis*) is employed to define the sophist and statesman by distinguishing him from other natural classes, or "families" (γένη, *genē*). But in the Platonic dialogues the implicit portrayal of the philosopher emerges not in a species or a class of human beings but in an individual, Socrates. Possibly it is because of his uniqueness—or outlandishness (*atopia*)—that in the *Statesman* and *Sophist* Socrates has nothing to contribute to the generic discussion of two of the three classes he identifies at the beginning of the *Sophist*. The stranger from Elea addresses Theaetetus in the *Sophist* and a young Socrates in the *Statesman*, both of whom resemble Socrates in one superficial respect: Theaetetus looks like him, and the young Socrates shares his name.[6] Yet Socrates would seem to belong to no *genus*, and in philosophical argumentation from Aristotle to Locke, Socrates was taken as the representative of the individual—a unique and therefore vivid example of personal identity. We find the outlandish (*atopos*) Socrates evoked by Aristotle in the *Topics* to illustrate the category of sameness or identity. It is merely an accident that the man who is now "seated" or "musical" happens to be Socrates. These are both accidental attributes and do not constitute the essential Socrates; Socrates is no accident but—in Aristotle's conception—a numerical unity, which guarantees his identity seated or performing on the lyre.[7] In Locke's *Essay Concerning Human Understanding* we meet Socrates once again as the salient example of the personal identity that derives from the identity and continuity of consciousness.[8]

The problem of the *Sophist* and *Statesman* is to place two recognizable types into classes, or, as the Greek would have it, families (*genē*). Socrates had spoken of the Eleatic Stranger as one class of divinity—a *daimōn* described by Homer as "roaming through cities." When Socrates alludes to Homer in this passage in the *Sophist*, he seems to be conflating two Homeric passages. The first is a passage in the *Odyssey* where Zeus is referred to as the protector of strangers;[9] the second is the episode in *Odyssey* 17 where one of the suitors

---

6. *Theaetetus* 143E (Theaetetus looks like Socrates) and *Statesman* 257D–258D (Socrates comments on the appearance of Theaetetus and the name of the young Socrates). In *Metaphysics* 7.11.1036ᵇ15, Aristotle mentions a young Socrates as arguing a version of the Platonic theory of ideas.

7. *Topics* 1.103ᵃ30.

8. *An Essay Concerning Human Understanding*, 4th edition (London, 1700), 2.27.19 (ed. Nidditch [Oxford, 1975] 342).

9. *Odyssey* 9.270–71.

applies this phrase to Odysseus disguised as a stranger. Perhaps he is some god descended from heaven: "The gods take on the appearance of men from other lands, and appear in all kinds of guises, visiting various cities and observing the injustice and lawfulness of men."[10] The divine concern for human justice is not the mark of the sophist, and in Plato's *Statesman* it is not the obvious character of the statesman, who is described both as a shepherd and as a weaver. But in Athens justice was the very human concern of Socrates. Plato was well aware that the Homeric conception of strangers as gods in disguise was to be found in Hesiod as well, in his myth of the ages or races (*genē*) of mankind. In the *Works and Days* the first generation of men was golden and not divine but godlike. When the men of this race died, they became *daimones*, "good men, living upon the earth, the guardians of mortal men. In a garment of mist, they roam over the earth and watch over righteousness and wicked deeds."[11]

As Plato understood him, Socrates did not belong to the race of ordinary men. In some of the Socratic dialogues he is represented as a *hērōs;* in one dialogue, the *Symposium*, he is portrayed as a great *daimōn*. As *hērōs* and *daimōn*, Plato's Socrates occupied a place in the middle range of a hierarchy that has four terms and is consistently evoked from the *Apology* to the *Laws*. These four terms are, in descending order: gods, *daimones*, *hērōes*, men. We have already noticed the comic potentials of this paradigm as they are exploited in the *Apology* (see I § 5, "The Philosopher in Court"). In the *Laws*, the visitor from Athens organizes his elaborate provisions for the cults of the new city of Cretan Magnesia in exactly this order and includes human beings (*anthrō- poi*) in his provisions for the family cult of ancestors and even living parents.[12]

In the *Cratylus*, Plato's little-read dialogue on the rightness of names, Socrates demonstrates by very elastic etymologies how the names of "what always exists and exists in the nature of things" are established to express certain fundamental realities. He gives four examples of such names; they must be given in his Greek: θεοί (*theoi*), δαίμονες (*daimones*), ἥρωες (*hērōes*), ἄνθρωποι (*anthrōpoi*).[13] Socrates' etymological speculations might seem to fit well with Voltaire's definition of an etymologist as someone who pays little attention to consonants and none to vowels. But there is a serious issue in Socrates' wordplay that is relevant to his portraits of himself—and, indeed,

10. *Odyssey* 17.484–87.
11. *Works and Days* 254–55.
12. *Laws* 4.717A–B.
13. *Cratylus* 397C–399D.

his theology. The Greek word for gods (*theoi*) is revealed as latently expressing Plato's conception of the real gods as astral divinities, for these gods "run" their course in the heavens (from the Greek verb *thein*). Next in order come *daimones*. Socrates cites Hesiod's lines on the race of gold to reveal their character.[14] They are "pure, virtuous, the protectors of mortal men," and their name derives from the root *da, "to know, perceive." *Hērōes* follow, whose name Socrates derives, by generously embracing a number of etymologies, from the noun ἔρως (*erōs*, "passionate desire") and verbs meaning "to speak" and "to ask questions" (*eirein* and *erōtân*). In their origins, *hērōes* are part divine, for they spring from the love of a god and a mortal; they are also "wise, skilled speakers, and dialecticians."[15] Last come men, who are named *anthrōpoi* from the distinguishing human trait of standing upright and looking upward at the heavens (*anathrein* and *opōpen*).[16]

We are reminded of one of Meletos' charges against Socrates: he refuses to worship the gods worshiped by the city of Athens and introduces new and strange divinities (*daimonia*). Socrates did possess his own inner voice (*daimonion*); but it was Plato who is open to such a charge, for in his dialogues he introduced to Athens and the Greek-speaking world a new kind of *daimōn* and a new kind of *hērōs* in Socrates. Socrates was not as comforting to the citizens of Athens and the visiting foreigners as the protecting *hērōes* of Athenian and Greek cult, but Plato made his life and calling comprehensible by connecting him with higher powers from another world. By these comparisons he also estranged Socrates from the very human world of the city of Athens.

Plato's first representation of Socrates as a *hērōs* is the presentation of Socrates himself in the *Apology*. In his defense before the Athenian jury, he compares himself to Heracles, then to Achilles, and finally to Palamedes and Ajax, who died because of an "unjust verdict." In this play of heroic paradigms, the comparison to Heracles is latent in Socrates' words to his jury: "Now I must represent my wanderings to you as those of someone undergoing many labors."[17] His word "labors" (*ponoi*) points unmistakably to the labors of the *hērōs*, half human and half divine, whose toil and endurance had made him a paradigm of the power of civilization. Heracles served the tyrant Eurys-

<hr>

14. *Works and Days* 121–23.
15. *Cratylus* 398D. For their origins, compare *Apology* 27D (see I §5, "The Philosopher in Court") for Socrates' distinctive genealogy of *daimones*.
16. *Cratylus* 399C.
17. *Apology* 22A.

theus; Socrates, the oracle of Apollo. Socrates also compares his firm resolve to serve Apollo—even in the face of death—to Achilles' decision to avenge Patroclus, even after Achilles' divine mother warns, "After Hector your fate awaits you."[18] Finally, Socrates compares himself to two of the "demigods who died at Troy"—Ajax and Palamedes. Both died because of an unjust verdict. Socrates' comparison casts Meletos in the role of Odysseus, who encompassed the death of both Palamedes and indirectly Ajax. Significantly, the controversy between Ajax and Odysseus was over the arms of Achilles and, it would seem, the coveted title "best of the Achaeans" indirectly awarded to Achilles in *Iliad* 2.768 and implicit in the quarrel between Achilles and Odysseus mentioned in *Odyssey* 8.73–82. It is to this title that the philosopher now lays claim.

We will never know if Socrates made all of these comparisons as he spoke in his own defense. In Xenophon's *Apology*, Socrates concludes by comparing himself to Palamedes, whom Odysseus had falsely accused of treason out of vindictiveness and who was put to death by the Greek army at Troy.[19] Such comparisons to figures from the heroic past were common in the age of Socrates and Plato.[20] But in some way Socrates can be compared to Odysseus, the hero of eloquence and guile. Alcibiades tacitly makes such a comparison in his praise of Socrates' endurance in the *Symposium*.[21] In his speech in praise of Socrates, Alcibiades praises his courage in the campaigns of Potidaea and at the Delion in Boeotia. Alcibiades confesses that in this last rout of the Athenian forces the Athenian generals awarded the prize of bravery to himself, even though Socrates had saved him and his armor. Alcibiades' word for this prize is *aristeia*, a term familiar from the Homeric contest over the title "best of the Achaeans."[22] The Athenian generals were moved by Alcibiades'

18. *Iliad* 18.96, quoted by Socrates in *Apology* 28C.

19. Xenophon, *Apology* 26. Palamedes enjoyed a vogue during Plato's youth. Gorgias wrote an epideictic speech in his defense, and his pupil, the orator Alkidamas, produced a speech of Odysseus, "Against Palamedes." Euripides produced a *Palamedes* in the dramatic festivals of 415. Diogenes Laertius quotes three lyric lines from Euripides' play, claiming that they convey Euripides' reproach to the Athenians for the murder of Socrates; DL 2.44. Euripides was long dead when the Athenians executed Socrates, but the lines from his *Palamedes* were obviously applied to the judicial murder of Socrates and to the Athenians: "You have killed, Danaans; you have killed the all-wise nightingale of the Muses, who has done no harm"; *TGF*, frag. **588**.

20. We find them in *Phaedrus* 261B–C and in Alcibiades' speech in praise of Socrates in the *Symposium*, for which, see I §8 ("Socrates Silenus").

21. 220C, a quotation from *Odyssey* 4.242, Helen's words describing Odysseus' bravery in Troy. Alcibiades also compares him to Ajax in his invulnerability to money, "more than Ajax to steel"; *Symposium* 219E.

22. *Symposium* 219E–220E.

position in society, and Socrates joined them in urging that Alcibiades be awarded the prize.

Then, in the retreat from the Delion, Socrates faced the enemy on foot while Alcibiades withdrew on horseback. This sight of Socrates deliberately and fiercely facing his enemies as he retreated, inspires Alcibiades with a line from Aristophanes' *Clouds:* "He made his way there as he does here in Athens, swaggering from side to side, with his eyes shifting from one side to the other."[23] Alcibiades is adapting the *Clouds'* address to Socrates: "We would pay heed to you, because you swagger as you walk the streets and cast your eyes from side to side; unshod, you bear up under many trials and assume a haughty mien as you turn your eyes to us."[24] Alcibiades does not cite this last line explicitly. It could bear citation to illustrate Socrates' endurance during the winter campaign in Potidaea, when he went out barefoot in the frost, and his strange endurance during the summer, when he stood stock-still, from one morning to the next, meditating on some problem and, as the sun arose on the next day, made his prayer to it and walked off.[25]

This is a new form of heroism, one forecast by the warrior and lyric poet Archilochos of Paros:

> *I don't care for your tall general,*
> *with his long stride and long hair in locks*
> *and beard well trimmed. Show me a stocky man,*
> *bandy-legged, sure of foot, full of heart.*[26]

His terms are just right for the contrast between Alcibiades and Socrates.

The *Hippias Minor* is devoted to the question Who is the best model for conduct, Achilles or Odysseus? The issue that pits the virtues of straightforward courage in battle against guile and deception is never quite settled in this conversation. But in the Socratic dialogues of Plato we discover a new conception of heroism and a new paradigm for imitation in Socrates, who incorporates both the antithetical qualities of the two rivals.[27]

In one of his animal parables, Archilochos also wrote: "The fox knows many a trick, the hedgehog one single truth."[28] This antithetical comparison

23. *Symposium* 221A–C.
24. *Clouds* 363–64.
25. *Symposium* 220A–D.
26. Frag. 114 West.
27. We return to this dialogue and this question in II §5 ("Plato and the Poets").
28. Frag. 201 West.

has sometimes been applied to the very different characters of Odysseus and Ajax, the two claimants for the armor of the best of the Achaeans. Perhaps the parable should be extended to Socrates, son of Sophroniskos and Phainarete, of the deme Alopeke (named after the skin of a fox). The son of a man whose name means "a little wise" and a woman whose name means "she who makes virtue appear" is both a hedgehog and a fox in that he combines the antithetical qualities of Odysseus and Ajax. He is a hedgehog in his single-minded devotion to a life of questioning the opinions of his fellow men and in his physical courage and stamina, and a fox in his apparently disingenuous claim to ignorance, in his adaptability to his interlocutors, and in the yarns he spins throughout the Platonic dialogues. But if Socrates in the Platonic dialogues can challenge almost every Greek paradigm of heroism, Plato can claim a still higher status for him—that of "a great *daimōn*"—and a lower status as well—that of a silenus or satyr. We can now turn to the dialogue in which Plato presents his brilliant portrait of Socrates as the "great *daimōn*" Eros. Alcibiades confirms its details by his outlandish comparisons of Socrates to a silenus and satyr.

ENDNOTE: For the heroic paradigms that lie behind these comparisons, there are a number of excellent studies to recommend: Gregory Nagy, *The Best of the Achaeans: Concepts of the Hero in Archaic Greek Poetry* (1979) is the first; then, for Achilles, Seth L. Schein, *The Mortal Hero: An Introduction to Homer's "Iliad"* (1984); for Odysseus, W. B. Stanford, *The Ulysses Theme: A Study in the Adaptability of a Traditional Hero* (1963), and Jenny Strauss Clay, *The Wrath of Athena: Gods and Men in the Odyssey* (1983), 96–111. For Socrates as a Homeric *hērōs*, there is Clay, "Socrates' Mulishness and Heroism" (1972); for Socrates as a tragic hero, there is T. H. Irwin, "Socrates and the Tragic Hero" (1988).

If in the *Apology* Socrates defines himself as a hero in the mold of Heracles or Achilles or Palamedes or Ajax, he also recasts that mold and re-forms the terms of comparison as he casts the *hērōes* of epic in his own image. Heracles' labors become the philosophical quest of testing the meaning of an oracle of Apollo; Achilles' readiness to face death to avenge his friend Patroclus becomes the strict obedience of a demigod to a divine command to expose human ignorance; and the two trials held by the Achaean army in assembly are recast as the Athenian judicial assembly that finds Socrates guilty as charged. These all entail self-representations.

Likenesses

But Socrates can reach lower, as can his interlocutors, in his search for comparisons. In the *Theaetetus*, in a passage we shall examine later, Socrates describes himself in much humbler and decidedly unheroic terms as a midwife.[1] This is the last of his self-presentations. In Plato's Socratic dialogues others see Socrates differently. Meno, in the *Meno*, compares him to the flat electric ray that numbs its prey;[2] far from enlightening his associates or delivering them of knowledge, he fills them with numbing perplexity. Meno's comparison is not the only low and comic comparison a companion of Socrates invents for Socrates in the Platonic dialogues. In an elaborate play of "likenesses," or similitudes (εἰχόνες, *eikones*), Alcibiades compares Socrates to the statue of a silenus, to a satyr, and the satyr Marsyas in particular.[3] Homeric

---

1. In *Theaetetus* 148E–151D, a passage read in III §1 ("The Socratic *Elenchos*").
2. *Meno* 80A.
3. *Symposium* 215A–B, comparisons examined in I §8 ("Socrates Silenus").

hērōs, male midwife to young men, an electric eel, a silenus, a satyr, Marsyas—all of these comparisons register the fact of Socrates' "outlandishness" (*atopia*) and taken together illustrate the range of comparisons required to capture Socrates' "outlandishness."

In Greek, the word for such similes is *eikones*—"likenesses," "images," or, in the essays in portraiture of Lucian and of the Philostrati, "portraits." The attempt to cast a simile in order to capture just the right image for a person is *apeikasia*. Another likeness of Socrates is developed with elaborate care by Plato himself in a dialogue devoted to praise of the god Eros. It is the most carefully developed and significant of all such "icons" of Socrates in the dialogues. The argument of the *Symposium* begins with the attempt of the guests at the house of the tragic poet Agathon to offer an adequate praise of Eros, the neglected god of passionate desire. We first hear six speeches in praise of Eros: by Phaedrus, who suggested the topic, Pausanias, Eryximachos, Aristophanes, Agathon, and Socrates; and then—unexpectedly—we hear a speech in praise not of Eros but of Socrates, by Alcibiades, who disrupts the sober celebration of Agathon's victory just after Socrates has finished speaking. When the last speech of the *Symposium* has been delivered, what is revealed by a retrospective reading of the seven speeches of the dialogue taken together as a single speech is not an encomium of the god Eros but a likeness offered by Plato in praise of Socrates.

Speeches in Dialogue

The *Symposium* is a dialogue only in its interludes and in Socrates' rehearsal of his conversations with Diotima. Yet the seven speeches offered by Agathon's guests enter into a kind of dialogue—a dialogue recognized by Aristophanes when he declares that something of what Socrates had just said about Eros reminded him of his own speech[4] and by the fact that Alcibiades' unruly praise of Socrates participates fully in the themes of the other speeches of the *Symposium*, even though he was not present to hear these earlier speeches. The speeches of the *Symposium* substitute for the previous evening's drinking, song, and music in celebration of Agathon's victory in the tragic competitions. Socrates had avoided that celebration because, as we are told, he "feared the crowd."[5] So we avoid the company of actors, Agathon's chorus, and representatives from Agathon's tribe and the state of Athens. The day

4. *Symposium* 212C.
5. *Symposium* 174A.

before, Agathon had been victorious "before more than thirty thousand Greeks."[6] Today the company is small and more intimate, and there are intimations of the erotic relations that bind some of its members, just as there are bonds of affinity among the speeches. This particular celebration is meant for a happy few. The intimate setting of Agathon's banquet reminds us of how difficult it is for the tragedian to present a character like Socrates on stage, "before a motley group of people assembled in a theater"—a "character, intelligent and calm, that remains always true to itself."[7]

The declared object of the speeches delivered at Agathon's banquet is praise of Eros; the ultimate subject of Plato's *Symposium* is an erotic Socrates. Aristodemos, who accompanied Socrates to the banquet uninvited, recalls seven of the speeches given after the banquet. The first four are delivered by Phaedrus, "father" of the evening's entertainment, who praises Eros as the oldest of the gods; Pausanias, who distinguishes between a heavenly and earthly Eros; Eryximachos, for whom *erōs* is the cosmic principle combining opposites in a healthy harmony; and Aristophanes, whose place had been taken by Eryximachos until he could recover from a fit of hiccoughs and who speaks of the "healing" of our primordial nature, which has been sundered. Agathon, the triumphant tragic poet, then delivers a virtuoso eulogy of Eros in florid terms worthy of the poet of the *Antheus* (Flower man), the title of one of his lost plays. Socrates, who occupied the last place on the banquet couches, next to Agathon, since he arrived late, speaks sixth. He does not invent a speech himself, but recalls what a woman by the name of Diotima told him when he was a young man. We will return to this speech when we begin to consider the theory of Ideas.[8]

But Socrates' is not the concluding speech of Plato's *Symposium*. The final speech of the evening belongs to Alcibiades, whose drunken epiphany disrupts the orderly and sober entertainment. After he has usurped the place of Phaedrus as "father" of the evening's entertainment and appointed himself master of the revels, he proposes to praise Socrates by means of likenesses.

Significant Action

Plato's *Symposium* is, then, composed of speeches. But, since it is narrated at three removes (see Fig. 1) by a narrator who is concerned with preserving

6. *Symposium* 175E.
7. As Socrates puts the matter in *Republic* 10.604E.
8. III §4 ("Thinking About Ideas").

the memory not only of what Socrates says but what he *does*,[9] there is more to the *Symposium* than mere speech. There is significant action even before Socrates arrives at Agathon's house. When he first encounters Aristodemos, Apollodoros' source for his narrative, Socrates is bathed and wearing an elegant pair of sandals.[10] This is an eloquent Platonic gesture: usually Socrates goes about unbathed and barefoot, but today he has "become fair"—"to go to the home of the fair"—that is, to the house of Agathon, whose name, as Socrates recalls, suggests the fair and noble (*agathos*). But something odd happens as Aristodemos and Socrates make their way to Agathon's: Aristodemos is forced to leave Socrates behind, lost in thought in a neighbor's doorway.[11] Strange doings. Another piece of stage action is Aristophanes' violent attack of hiccoughs, which forces him to speak out of turn and after the doctor Eryximachos. As a result of this apparent accident, the speech of the comic poet is brought into direct association with the speech of the tragic poet. This has, as we will come to appreciate, a bearing on the pairing of the tragic and the comic poets in the last conversation of the dialogue.

Another significant and dramatic gesture is Alcibiades' sudden and boisterous entry into the banquet room, which providentially coincides with the conclusion of Socrates' speech. When he sees Socrates, Alcibiades accuses him of lying in ambush for him, and, in an impulsive gesture, he removes some of the strands from the garland he had placed on Agathon's head and places them on the head of Socrates—"this wonderful head."[12] As Helen Bacon (1959) saw, this drunken gesture is the dialogue's tacit verdict in the contest between Agathon and Socrates over *sophia*—a word that can mean wisdom or the poet's skill. Earlier in the dialogue, Agathon had promised that Dionysos would judge their respective claims to *sophia*.[13] Last, there is the dim concluding scene of the dialogue, where we find Socrates drinking with Agathon and Aristophanes and forcing two very confused and weary poets to agree to his paradoxical proposition that a single poet can compose both comedy and tragedy. Aristophanes falls asleep first; then Agathon. Victorious, Socrates leaves the comic and the tragic poets fast asleep at dawn and departs with Aristodemos for a gymnasium, where he spends the day like any other and returns home only at evening.[14]

9. *Symposium* 172C.
10. *Symposium* 174A.
11. *Symposium* 175A.
12. *Symposium* 213E.
13. *Symposium* 175E.
14. *Symposium* 223D. We will return to this dim and enigmatic scene when we consider the theme of Platonic poetry (II §6), since one interpretation of this concluding episode is that it reflects Plato's conception of himself as a tragic and comic poet in his representation (*mimēsis*) of Socrates.

Eros

None of the speeches and none of these dramatic gestures would suggest, if read in isolation, that the object of the *Symposium* is anything other than the praise of Eros begun with Phaedrus' speech. But, taken together, they constitute the most brilliant literary portrait of antiquity. All of the accidents at Agathon's banquet can be seen as deliberate and meditated in the plan of Plato's *Symposium*. All that appears as an accident in the speeches and action of the dialogue can be explained by the principle of "logographic necessity," which Socrates lays down in the *Phaedrus*. By this principle every part of a written composition has some function in an organic whole.[15] By a delicate irony, which is both Socratic and Platonic, Socrates is not allowed to praise himself. When the time comes for Socrates to offer his praise of Eros, he does not himself praise Eros, but recalls what a wise woman from Mantinea once taught him about love in a number of conversations.

According to Diotima, Eros is not the oldest and most honorable of the gods, as Phaedrus had first argued, nor is he fair and wise, as Agathon had argued. Rather, he is a "great *daimōn*" intermediary between gods and men, and the means of human communication with the gods and of divine communication with men.[16] Diotima gives a genealogy of Eros that contradicts both Greek mythology and Pausanias' claim that there are in fact two Erotes, the sons of the heavenly and the younger Aphrodites. Rather, Eros is the son of Invention (Poros) and Poverty (Penia). He takes after both of his parents:

> First of all, he is forever poor, and far from being tender and fair, as most men believe him to be, he is hard and tough. He has no sandals or home, but keeps to the ground and has no bed, sleeps in doorways and on the roadways in the open air. In this he is the son of his mother and dwells always in need. But, favoring his father, he is always plotting for the fair and noble and is courageous, filled with initiative, intense, a redoubtable hunter, who always has some new stratagem in mind; he has a passion for and is productive of wisdom, and, as he pursues philosophy throughout his life, he is a dread enchanter, a doctor skilled in drugs, and a sophist.[17]

Socrates' speech anticipates Alcibiades' and responds to much that has been said by the first five speakers at Agathon's symposium. It is confirmed as

---

15. The principle is examined in II §3 ("Platonic Writing").
16. *Symposium* 202D.
17. *Symposium* 203C–D.

a portrait of Socrates as Eros by what Alcibiades goes on to say about Socrates. These two final speeches of the dialogue—Diotima's exchange with Socrates on the subject of Eros and Alcibiades' outrageous praise of Socrates—allow us to understand the motivation of many of the seemingly accidental gestures of the dialogue: Socrates' bath and the sandals he rarely wears;[18] the fact that he has "become fair" to join Agathon; his trance in a neighbor's doorway, which echoes the episode Alcibiades relates about how he spent an entire day and night lost in thought and out in the open air during the Athenian campaign in northern Greece; or went about barefoot in winter; and the courage he displayed during the Athenian retreat from the Delion.[19] Eros has become Socrates, and Socrates Eros.

Diotima has developed the conception of Eros as a great *daimōn* who moves restlessly between the levels not only of gods and men but of knowledge and ignorance. Eros is a constantly stimulated and eternally frustrated desire (*erōs*) for wisdom, which explains and justifies Socrates' claim that he is ignorant in everything but love.[20] His questions to Agathon in the interlude following Agathon's brilliant display of rhetoric in praise of an Eros that is young, beautiful, and delicate prepares for the moment in the dialogue when the discussion will be deflected from the god Eros to *erōs*, passionate desire.

Socrates innocently asks the tragic poet if Eros is the desire of something or of nothing.[21] This odd question leads to another conception of Eros as *erōs*, or the desire for something lacking in the subject who feels the desire. The genitive case in the phrase "desire of something" is in Greek an "objective genitive" indicating the source or object of desire and not a genitive indicating a relation, such as that of father and son. Demoted from mythology to psychology, from divinity to human desire (*erōs*), this new understanding of desire leads directly to the conception of philosophy that Diotima expounds to Socrates. In Greek, the word *philosophia* compounds two elements: *sophia* (wisdom), the object of the desire and the passion described by the Greek verb *philein*, to like or be fond of. Thus, Eros is the personification of this

---

18. *Symposium* 174A.

19. *Symposium* 220A–C (Potidaea in summer of 332), 219E (Potidaea in winter), and 220D (Delion in summer of 424). One ancient reader and self-professed philosopher recognized the Platonic portrait of Socrates as Eros. This was Maximus of Tyre, who lays out its essential lineaments in his speech on Socrates' erotic art, *Philosophoumena* XVIII (p. 223) Koniaris.

20. *Symposium* 177D and *Meno* 76C; revealing of Socrates' experience of passion is his reaction to the young Charmides that Socrates reports in *Charmides* 155C–E.

21. *Symposium* 199D.

human passion (*erōs*) for something lacking. It is the passion of the philosopher:

> The case is this: No god is a philosopher or desires to become wise, for he *is* wise. Nor, if anyone is wise, can he be a philosopher. Likewise, the ignorant are not philosophers either—they do not even want to become wise.[22]

Socrates Eros is the distant focus of all seven speeches of the *Symposium*. He binds their separate details into the recognizable physiognomy of the mature Platonic portrait of the ugly, barefoot, tough "older friend" whom Plato had known when he was a young man in Athens and who had turned him from tragic poetry to the anonymous drama of the philosophical dialogue. The end of the *Symposium* suggests that Socrates' influence on Plato the writer was not entirely apotropaic; he did not finally persuade Plato to abandon tragedy altogether, but he turned him to a distinct genre of dramatic composition that seemed the antithesis of tragedy—comedy. The final episode of the *Symposium* intimates as much. Here we glimpse Socrates arguing indefatigably with Agathon and Aristophanes that the poet "who has the skill of the tragic poet is also a comic poet."[23] Any accurate representation of Socrates would seem to require the arts of both the tragic and the comic poets, for, like Eros, he moves restlessly between the high and the low as he binds heaven and earth. Socrates' range at its highest is apparent from the moments of rapture both Aristodemos and Alcibiades describe and from Diotima's description of how the soul mounts from the sensible and individual to its vision of Beauty itself.[24] Alcibiades captures the comic side of Socrates Eros when he portrays him as a silenus and says of the themes of his conversations that they would seem "utterly ridiculous" to most casual listeners.[25] When he first discovers Socrates reclining next to Agathon, he is surprised by the association and asks why he is not reclining next to Aristophanes "or some other clown."[26]

---

22. *Symposium* 204A. This definition of the philosopher is arrived at early in the *Lysis* (218A), where Socrates, who has spoken for the desire for the Good, says to Lysis: "For these reasons we would say that those who are already wise no longer desire wisdom [his verb is *philosophein*], whether these are gods or humans."

23. *Symposium* 223C.

24. *Symposium* 209E–212A, a passage translated and discussed in III §4 ("Thinking About Ideas").

25. *Symposium* 221E.

26. *Symposium* 213C.

Alcibiades offers three very similar likenesses of Socrates to the guests at Agathon's second evening of triumphant banqueting: he can be compared to silenus, satyr, and Marsyas. These we will consider in the essay that concludes this chapter on Plato's Socrates (I § 8). Alcibiades might have devised still another "icon" of Socrates, one even more outrageous than the witty comparisons that were designed to rile Socrates. According to Plutarch, Alcibiades' luxurious and unconventional manner of life shocked many of his contemporaries. He was overfond of wine and sex, and, unlike Socrates on campaign, he would not endure hardship but slept on a hammock, rather than on ship's benches, when at sea. He carried a shield of gold and ivory. On it he devised an emblem unlike anything ever depicted on an Athenian shield: the figure of Eros, about to hurl a thunderbolt.[27] One wonders if Socrates saved this shield on the retreat from the Delion.[28] Gold and ivory are the materials of Pheidias' statue of Athena in the Parthenon; bronze and hide were the materials of the Athenian citizen's shield. More outrageous still is Eros with Zeus's thunderbolt, an image stolen, it seems, from the shield of Athena Parthenos on the Acropolis, on which Zeus is painted in his struggle with the giants.[29] Could Alcibiades, who had once fallen so completely under the spell of the erotic Socrates, have devised this shield as a tribute to Socrates Eros? If so, Plato's is the second portrait of Socrates as Eros.

ENDNOTE: The suggestion that the Eros on the shield of Alcibiades was an emblem of Socrates is urged, elegantly and briefly, by Peter H. von Blanckenhagen in "The Shield of Alcibiades" (1964). Von Blanckenhagen returned to the *Symposium* and its significant gestures in "Stage and Actors in Plato's *Symposium*" (1992). In his essay on the *Symposium* in *Plato* (1969), 3:3–34, Paul Friedländer is sensitive to the argument and significant detail of its seven speeches, but does not dwell on the end of the dialogue. Helen Bacon has written a perceptive literary study of the *Symposium* in "Socrates Crowned" (1959). For the problem of the tragic and comic poet at the end of the *Symposium*, see the Endnote to II § 6 ("Platonic Poetry"). Charles Kahn has returned us to Aischines' appreciation of the protreptic and educational impact of Socratic *erōs* in "Aeschines on Socratic Eros" (1994).

---

27. *Life of Alcibiades* 16.
28. *Symposium* 220E.
29. This gigantomachy is recalled by Aristophanes in *Symposium* 190C.

The race of worthless Satyrs,
no one can cope with them.
—Hesiod, frag. 123 Merkelbach and West

Any visitor to Athens who sits in the theater of Dionysos will notice the marble figures of two crouching sileni, who have been removed from a theatrical monument and pressed into service to support the stage platform about them. This "stage" does not belong to the fifth century or to the fourth. It is not in fact a stage, but a speaker's platform—the so-called *bēma* of Phaidros. It was assembled out of a variety of older monuments of the second century A.D. The sileni incorporated into this new platform are hauntingly familiar: they have pointed ears, balding high-domed foreheads, widely spaced and somewhat bulging eyes, and impressive bellies that swell with the strain of the weight they carry. They are bearded and have thick lips. If they seem familiar, it is because they look like Socrates. Ultimately, Plato is responsible for the appearance of these sileni.

The portraiture of Socrates in bronze began shortly after Socrates' execution. According to a tradition known to Diogenes Laertius, "The Athenians immediately repented and closed their training grounds and gymnasia. Socrates' other accusers they exiled; Meletos they condemned to death. But Socrates they honored with a bronze statue [εἰκών, *eikōn*], which they set up in the Hall of Processions. This was the work of Lysippos."[1] If the word "immediately" also refers to the commission of a statue by Lysippos, this report cannot be true. Lysippos' Socrates in bronze is dated to six or seven decades

1. DL 2.43.

after Socrates' death. But the report prompts a question: How would a sculptor best known for his freestanding statues of gods (including Eros), of his powerful contemporaries (including Alexander of Macedon), and of successful athletes have recovered the appearance of a figure he had never seen?

By the middle of the fourth century, at about the time of Plato's death, Lysippos would have had at least one source of inspiration for a retrospective portrait statue of Socrates. This is Plato's *Symposium*. Socrates' striking appearance attracted the attention of those who had the opportunity to view him, and from younger contemporaries we have three records of what he looked like. The earliest of these is that of Aristophanes in the *Clouds*, where the chorus of Clouds express their admiration for their devotee, Socrates. The passage is now familiar, but in the context of Plato's portraits of Socrates it bears repetition: "We would pay heed to you, because you swagger as you walk the streets and cast your eyes from side to side; unshod, you bear up under many trials and assume a haughty mien as you turn your eyes to us."[2]

Then there is the description by Plato. In the speech spontaneously delivered by the Dionysiac Alcibiades in his *Symposium*, Plato gives us a brilliant word picture of Socrates as a silenus and a satyr. We have seen Alcibiades burst in on the drinking party Agathon held to celebrate his tragic victory, just after Socrates had delivered his speech in praise of Eros. Instead of praising Eros, as had the other members of the company, Alcibiades gets it into his head to praise Socrates by means of likenesses (*eikones*). The first comparison he offers his distinguished companions is that of Socrates as a silenus: "I say that he looks remarkably like a silenus, one of those sileni you can see seated in the shops of the sculptors that the artists make holding pipes and oboes."[3] Archaeology has not retrieved what Alcibiades had in mind. He invites Socrates to contradict him if this comparison is not just. Socrates holds his peace. Nor does he protest when Alcibiades pointedly applies Aristophanes' description of him to his behavior eight years earlier in the Athenian retreat from the sanctuary of Apollo in Boeotia.[4]

Alcibiades' comparison of Socrates to a silenus and a satyr and his talk of the bacchic madness and ecstasy Socrates inspires in his closest companions[5] is right for the occasion of a symposium, whose equipment of mixing kraters and drinking cups was decorated with exquisite scenes of Dionysos, satyrs,

2. *Clouds* 361–63.
3. *Symposium* 215A.
4. *Symposium* 221B.
5. *Symposium* 218B.

and maenads; and it is right for Aristophanes, who might not have had to go to the trouble of having a portrait mask of Socrates made for the production of his *Clouds*. Socrates bore the features of a comic character, and indeed of the satyrs of satyr plays, and his character in the *Clouds* may have worn a standard satyr mask.[6] Xenophon recognized the justness of Alcibiades' likeness of Socrates in his own *Symposium*, where he stages a beauty contest between Socrates and the young Kritoboulos. Socrates had challenged Crito's handsome son, and the young man replies in mock indignation that, if he were uglier than Socrates, "I would be the ugliest of all the sileni in the satyr plays." Xenophon adds, "Socrates just happened to look like a silenus."[7]

In this unequal beauty contest Socrates calls attention to his prominent eyes, snub nose, and wide flared nostrils. Kritoboulus in turn draws attention to Socrates' thick lips, which prompts Socrates to compare himself to the offspring of river nymphs, "who are goddesses," the sileni.[8] Socrates' bulging eyes and snub nose are noticed in the *Theaetetus* as well.[9]

According to Cicero, the Persian physiognomist Zopyros read a sensuous nature in Socrates' distinctive features.[10] Although Socrates' actual physiognomy might have been expressive of an inner, erotic nature, he was not entirely responsible for the way his appearance was imagined after his death. In his verbal portrait of Socrates as a silenus and a satyr, Plato was responsible for the way in which Socrates was *seen* in antiquity. Yet, in the case of no other ancient philosopher does outer appearance so stridently belie inner reality. And this is precisely the point of Alcibiades' comparison: "These statues of sileni, when you open them up, are seen to hold within statues of gods. And I say that he resembles the satyr Marsyas. That you bear a resemblance to these creatures—so far as appearances go—I do not imagine you yourself would dispute."[11]

It is significant that no human being can provide Alcibiades with an adequate term of comparison. As we have seen (I § 7), at the end of his inspired speech in praise of Socrates, Alcibiades confesses that Socrates' outlandishness is such that no ancient hero, like Achilles, can afford a term of comparison. Brasidas could be compared to Achilles and Pericles to Nestor

---

6. This is the elegant suggestion of K. J. Dover (1967, 28).
7. Xenophon, *Symposium* 4.19.
8. Xenophon, *Symposium* 5.7.
9. *Theaetetus* 143E.
10. *On Fate* 5.
11. *Symposium* 215B.

or Antenor; but no human can be compared to Socrates.[12] Alcibiades has subtly shifted the rules of the game he is playing; Socrates has become the model for comparison. The earlier comparison with Marsyas is genial, as is the game of inventing comparisons. Like sileni, this satyr exists to confound categories of Greek thinking. He is neither man nor beast, and as such he is disturbing both to gods and to men. But sileni and this satyr are the only creatures that can serve as terms of comparison.

Socrates' reaction to Alcibiades' speech and the comparisons he offers is to call it a "satyr or silenus play."[13] The oddity about the satyr play is that it was the final play, following three tragedies, entered into competition at the festivals of Dionysos. Socrates is reacting to what he understands as the erotic motives of Alcibiades and to the lowering of the serious level of the six earlier speeches to these crude and frank comparisons, with all their erotic suggestions. Could Plato have really intended to praise Socrates by portraying him not only as a *hērōs* and as Eros but as a silenus and a satyr? The serious philosopher could well complain that the real Socrates "was to this as Hyperion to a Satyr" (the words of Hamlet on the relation between his father and uncle).

Both sileni and satyrs are combinations of the animal (either horse or goat) and the human. In Greek vase painting of the sixth and fifth centuries, satyrs were shown with unruly full beards, horse tails, pointed ears, sensuous mouths, snub noses, and an erect penis, usually directed at another companion of Dionysos and usually at a maenad. Like Socrates' *hērōes* in the *Apology* and like Diotima's Eros, these creatures are mixed breeds, or "in between." In their lower reaches sileni and satyrs are feral and, for the Greeks, embody lust and the violation of civilized propriety. They dwell in the country, not the city, and they invade the city only during the dramatic festivals of Dionysos, when they form the choruses for the last play of the tragic "tetralogy," the satyr play. These considerations help us to appreciate what Alcibiades has in mind when he speaks of Socrates' "outlandishness" (*atopia*). In terms of Athens and its civic assemblies, Socrates Silenus must seem out of place.

But, in the civic context of the dramatic festivals of Dionysos and the late-night revel that is the occasion for Plato's *Symposium*, Socrates is in congenial company. Alcibiades affirms the justness of his comparison of Socrates to a satyr when he calls Socrates "outrageous" (*hybristēs*).[14] His word has many con-

12. *Symposium* 221C.
13. *Symposium* 222D.
14. *Symposium* 215B.

notations in Greek. It can describe anyone who has transgressed social bounds, and it possesses a clear sexual connotation. This sexual connotation is recognized precisely to be rejected when the still youthful Alcibiades tells how Socrates "outraged" his beauty by rebuffing the suggestion of a sexual relation.[15] Appearances in the case of this silenus and Marsyas are belied by an inner reality, as Socrates, in the uncanny combination of his outward appearance and inner self-control, affronts the conventions of the aristocratic segment of Athenian society. Yet both comparisons suggest, as do the other Platonic likenesses of Socrates, the fact that Socrates is a mix. To look at him, he seems half human and half beast; but open him up, and images of the gods appear.

These images of divinities are Socrates' words and the subjects of his conversations. These too seem strange, but underneath their surface they are not what they seem. Alcibiades prepares for this extension of his comparison by elaborating on the ways in which Socrates resembles the satyr Marsyas. Marsyas is an enchanting flute player, and Socrates' words are like his music in their enchantment. The "flute" (aulos, or oboe) was a wind instrument of extraordinary potency for the Greeks. An expert aulētēs added so much to the performance of a tragedy that the best performers were assigned to the three competing tragic poets by lot. The music of the flute accompanied the festivals of Dionysos and the mysteries at Eleusis, and not surprisingly Alcibiades turns to the language of Dionysiac frenzy and mystic possession to convey the effects of Socrates' words upon him and upon others who hear him speak or even hear reports of what he says.[16]

What is perplexing about Alcibiades' Dionysiac speech in praise of Socrates is that everyone in the company at Agathon's could appreciate the justness of his *likeness* of Socrates to a silenus or the satyr Marsyas; yet his description of Socrates' words remains tantalizingly vague. We know the impact of Socrates' conversations on the soul of Alcibiades—they cause him shame and make him despise his former life and infect him with a wound more painful than a snakebite.[17] But what does Socrates say? Alcibiades finally describes no more than the impression Socratic conversations first made on others and gives only a hint of the words themselves:

> His words too are very much like those figures of sileni that can be opened. I mean, if some one is willing to listen to Socrates' conversation, it would appear perfectly ridiculous at first. On the outside what he says

15. *Symposium* 219C.
16. *Symposium* 215D.
17. *Symposium* 215C–216C; 217E–218A.

seems to wrap itself up in queer words and phrases, just like the hide of an outrageous satyr. He is forever talking of pack asses and tinkers and cobblers and tanners and always seems to be saying the same things by means of the same illustrations. As a result, any dolt who has not heard him talk before would simply laugh at what he says.[18]

There is a serious point to these comic illustrations, and we have seen the point of Socrates' talk of asses and half-asses at his trial (I § 5, "The Philosopher in Court"). We will better understand his interest in craftsmen—in particular, the cobblers who work from patterns—when we come to consider Plato's theory of Ideas (III § 4, "Thinking About Ideas"). These members of the working poor in Athenian society had at least the considerable virtue of their know-how.

Another creature resembling Marsyas did in fact possess something like divine wisdom. This was Silenus himself. Silenus was captured by King Midas, who wanted access to his more-than-human knowledge. In one of his early dialogues, Aristotle recalled Silenus' Delphic response to Midas' question: "What is meetest and best for mankind?" "You, you creature that lives for a day, it is better never to have been born or, once born, to pass through the gates of Hades as soon as possible."[19] This is wisdom from another world, and Socrates seems to repeat it in Plato's *Phaedo* as he conveys his parting words to Evenos of Paros: "If you are truly wise, you will follow me as soon as you can."[20]

The comparisons Alcibiades chooses to describe Socrates point to the difficulty of any attempt to approximate the reality of Socrates by means of comparisons. As we have noticed, his noun *eikōn* corresponds to the verbal noun *apeikasia*, or the making of comparisons. In attempting to penetrate to the reality underlying Socrates' appearance and conversations, as these are recorded in the Platonic dialogues, we stand at the bottom of the line Socrates produces at the end of book 6 of the *Republic* to illustrate the relation of appearance to reality. The bottom of the line occupies the lowest level of reality and is occupied by *eikones*, reflections and images. The gap between appearance and reality opens as a problem for the reader of Plato's "Socratic" dialogues, that is, the dialogues in which Socrates plays a major role.

18. *Symposium* 221D–222A.

19. *Eudemus*, the dialogue written in provocative imitation of Plato's *Phaedo*, frag. 6 Ross. Aristotle's near contemporary, the historian Theopompos of Chios, attributes to captive Silenus a divine knowledge of the world that lies beyond the ken of human beings. The report of this comes from Aelian in *Historical Miscellany* 3.18 Dilts.

20. *Phaedo* 61C–D.

Let me anticipate a fuller presentation of the divided line.[21] In the *Republic*, Socrates produces a line divided into two unequal sections to illustrate to Glaukon the distinction between the objects of the senses and the objects of the mind, between appearance and reality. We are now concerned with only the lowest section as we assess Plato's icons of Socrates. The level on which we encounter Socrates in the Platonic dialogues is at the very bottom of the divided line along which Socrates apportions degrees of reality. The initial and unequal section of this line is repeated proportionally in two further segments. The two segments that stand for the world as it appears represent objects and their reflections. As examples of these reflections Socrates instances likenesses, shadows, and reflections on water or smooth hard surfaces. Socrates' word *eikones* reminds us of Alcibiades' attempt to capture Socrates' reality "by means of likenesses." Like Alcibiades' *eikones* of Socrates as silenus and satyr, Plato's sustained *mimēsis* of Socrates and his conversations occupies the bottom segment of the divided line and, in the language of book 10 of the *Republic*, places us at "three removes from reality."[22] But, as we shall see, the movement from level to level on the divided line is transitive; that is, the lowest level is intelligible only in terms of the next and implies the next. Shadows imply an object casting then; icons imply an original.

Alcibiades' icons of Socrates carry a warning for Plato's reader. Plato, in the vehicle he chose to convey his philosophy, was not and could not be a systematic philosopher. Systems were for another age and for philosophers who believed not only that knowledge was within their grasp but that it could be communicated to others once grasped. Plato did not share their optimism about the possibility of the communication of knowledge, but he was so successful as a literary artist and the maker of images that his dialogues leave us with the impression that, if we know nothing else about the Platonic dialogues, we know Socrates at least. Unlike Alcibiades, who was Socrates' contemporary and who actually saw Socrates and heard his conversations, we cannot judge Plato's original. Our difficulty is compounded by two features of Plato's Socrates and the Platonic dialogues themselves. The first is the Socratic irony that Alcibiades recalls in the *Symposium*: "He is perpetually in ignorance and knows nothing . . . and he spends his whole life pretending he does not know and

---

21. *Republic* 6.509D–510A, III §5 ("The Sun, the Line, and the Cave"), and Figure 2 (page 233 below).

22. In the Greek idiom of *Republic* 10.602C. In English idiom, we stand at two removes from reality.

toying with mankind."[23] This Socratic "irony" justifies Alcibiades' confession that "none of us really knows Socrates."[24] And then there is Platonic irony, which, in the revealing retrospective vision of the tragic poet, makes us realize that, even at his most playful, the Platonic Socrates could not fully appreciate the meaning of his own words and that Socrates' claim to ignorance is in some sense justified: Socrates did not fully understand Socrates.

There is one last difficulty in addressing the meaning of Socrates in the Platonic dialogues and the issues raised by the Platonic dialogues themselves. Does any reader of the Platonic dialogues really know Plato? How are we as readers to penetrate the surface of Socrates' conversations, and the conversations in which he himself is silent (or, as in the *Laws*, absent), to discover Plato's meaning? In many of the dialogues, Socrates is voluble; but in all of his dialogues, from the *Apology* to the *Laws*, Plato maintains an unbroken silence. Which means that we as readers of the dialogues must engage in a dialogue with a silent philosopher.

ENDNOTE: The standard work on Greek portraits and portraiture is G.M.A. Richter, *The Portraits of the Greeks* (1965), abridged and revised by R.R.R. Smith (1984). The portraiture of Socrates is treated in Richter 1965, I.109–19, and 1984, 198–204. It is instructive to compare the iconography of Socrates with that of the long-haired and stunningly beautiful Alcibiades; Richter 1965, I.105–6, and 1984, 81–83. The reader interested in Plato's verbal portraits of Socrates should study Paul Zanker's *Mask of Socrates: The Image of the Intellectual in Antiquity* (1995), not only for its brief treatment of the portraits of Socrates (57–62) but for the evolution of the portraiture of the "intellectual" in antiquity. The iconography and civic meaning of satyrs are well treated by François Lissarrague, "Why Satyrs Are Good to Represent," in *Nothing to Do with Dionysos? Athenian Drama in Its Social Context*, ed. Winkler and Zeitlin (1986), 228–36. Martha Nussbaum's treatment of Alcibiades' speech, in *The Fragility of Goodness: Luck and Ethics in Greek Tragedy and Philosophy* (1986), 165–99, is a wedge that opens her reading of the *Symposium* as a whole. Important for the relation between Socrates and Alcibiades, which cost Socrates so much ill will in 399, is Michael Gagarin's "Socrates' *Hybris* and Alcibiades' Failure" (1977).

The reader interested in the career of Alcibiades should turn first to Plutarch's *Life of Alcibiades* and then to Thucydides, *The Peloponnesian War* 5–8, and Xenophon, *Hellenica* 1.

23. *Symposium* 216E.
24. *Symposium* 216C.

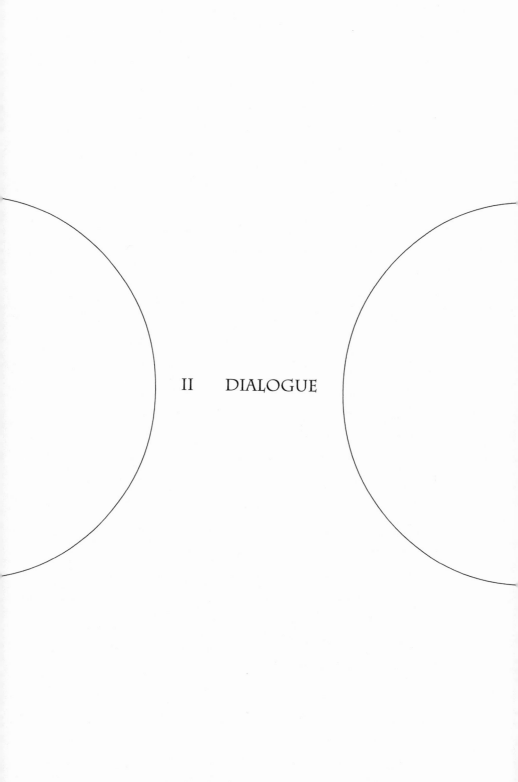

II   DIALOGUE

Dialogos

The term "Platonic" is habitually associated with the words love (*erōs*) and idea (*idea/eidos*); the term "Socratic" is habitually associated with the word "dialogue" διάλογος, *dialogos*). Aristotle knew of a number of authors of "Socratic conversations" (*Sokratikoi logoi*),[1] but we are not as privileged as was he. We have some fragments of the Socratic dialogues of Aischines and other Socratics whose works we have reviewed (I § 1, "Plato the Socratic"). And we have the Socratic dialogues of Xenophon. But it is Plato who has fixed our conception of the Socratic dialogue. *Dialogos* is a noun derived from the verb *dialegomai*, which means to become involved in a conversation with another. The force of the middle, rather than the active (*dialego*), voice is precisely involvement. In Greek, one can make an argument (*logous poiō*, active voice), or one can become involved in an argument (*logous poioumai*, middle voice), whose outcome the participant is involved in. The Socratic form of dialogue was not simply conversation with an interlocutor: notoriously, it involved questions and answers involving people who had a stake in the discussion, and throughout antiquity the rudimentary definition of dialogue was simply "question and answer."[2] In the Socratic dialogues of Plato, it is usually, but not always, Socrates who is the questioner.

The dialogue now seems unremarkable and uninteresting as a form of

---

1. *Poetics* 2.1447ᵇ11.
2. Defined more elaborately in Diogenes Laertius: "A dialogue is discourse composed of question and answer concerning some philosophical or political subject, with the appropriate rendition of the character of the actors involved" (DL 3.48). The element of question and answer also figures prominently in the treatment of the dialogue form in the *Anonymous Prolegomena* to Plato; see the Endnote to this section.

philosophical discourse. It is familiar to philosophers from Plato and Cicero to Berkeley and Hume, but it is not now a vehicle for philosophy. It is a faded form of discourse. In the fifth century B.C., as the living dialogue was practiced in Athens by Socrates, and even in the fourth century, as it was imitated and elevated into a Panhellenic literary and philosophical genre by Plato and Xenophon, the early Aristotle and Herakleides of Pontos, there were powerful and long-sanctioned alternatives for philosophical writing. Plato had a choice among many competing forms of philosophy. First was the hierophantic language of the pre-Socratic philosophers, some of whom wrote poetry; then there was a secular form of philosophical discourse—the epideictic speeches of the "sophists" who were Socrates', and Plato's, contemporaries. It is against these two paradigms of discourse that the Platonic dialogue can be best understood.

The Masters of Truth

The pre-Socratic philosophers of the sixth and fifth centuries were both poets and the first authors of prose treatises (*syggramata*). There can be no greater contrast with Plato's manner of writing in his Socratic dialogues than the opening of a book Socrates had read and that was on sale in the Athenian Agora (or market): the treatise of Anaxagoras.[3] Anaxagoras of Klazomenai was the contemporary of Socrates and Pericles and a formidable intellectual presence in Athens. Like Socrates, he was accused of impiety. He provides one of our earliest specimens of Greek prose. It begins:

> All things were together, infinite in their number and smallness. For the small was infinite as well. And, since all were together, no thing was distinct because of its smallness. For *aither* and air, both heavy and pure, suppressed them all, and both were without bound. For these are the greatest components in the sum of things, both in number and in magnitude.[4]

Anaxagoras gives us no indication of the audience he is addressing, who he is, or by what authority he says what he says.

Three earlier philosophers stand out in the form of their philosophical

---

3. Socrates, who doubts that knowledge of the heavens and the regions beneath the earth is possible for humans, mentions the book of Anaxagoras as readily available in the Agora of Athens, and finally expresses his own disappointment in the high hopes Anaxagoras' Mind (*Nous*) had inspired in him: *Apology* 26D–E and *Phaedo* 97C–99D.

4. Anaxagoras, *On Nature*, DK 59 B 1 (= KRS 467).

rhetoric. Heraclitus of Ephesos, Parmenides of Elea (in southern Italy), and Empedocles of Akragas (in Sicily). They can be called masters of the truth.[5] Heraclitus, who deposited his book in the temple of Artemis in his native Ephesos, addresses no audience in particular and assumes a voice of transcendental and Delphic authority. At the beginning of his book he claims that his discourse (*logos*) is the same as the eternal principle of Intelligibility (*Logos*), which human beings fail to comprehend.[6] Parmenides' wrote hexameter poetry and thereby arrogated to himself the authority of the epic. The rhetoric of his *On Nature* is complex, as is the structure of the poem, with its proem and very dissimilar arguments on the Way of Truth and the Way of Opinion. In the proem to *On Nature* the poet, who does not identify himself, narrates a voyage he took through the Gates of Day and Night into the light and an encounter with a divinity (*daimōn*), whose discourse to him he gives directly. His speech is for all but the first twenty-three lines of his poem divine. Empedocles too wrote in hexameter verse. In his *On Nature*, Empedocles addressed an individual (Pausanias); in his *Purifications* he addressed the citizens of Akragas. In both of these poems (if they are, indeed, separate poems), Empedocles emerges as a figure of divine authority, an authority granted by the Muses in *On Nature* and by his experience of transmigration in *Purifications*.[7] In the declarations of Heraclitus' *logos*, Parmenides' *daimōn*, and the divine Empedocles there can be no question and answer. The contrast with the Platonic dialogues is immediately evident: the Parmenides of Plato's *Parmenides* is an acute questioner, and his questions, beginning with his inquiry about Socrates' belief in certain "forms" (*eidē*),[8] drive the dialogue. In the *Sophist*, Socrates recalls this (fictive) conversation of years past and says that the conversation took "the form of questioning."[9]

Heraclitus, Parmenides, and Empedocles are all recognized in the Platonic dialogues. Their manner of writing affords a striking initial contrast to the style of the *Sokratikoi logoi* and the Platonic dialogues. Two of these

---

5. From the Marcel Detienne title *Les maîtres de la vérité dans la Grèce archaïque* (1967, translation 1996). His subtle analysis of poets' self-representation as masters of the truth can be applied to the pre-Socratic philosophers, whom he also studies.

6. DK 22 B 1 (= KRS 194), translated and discussed more fully below.

7. He addresses the Muses as goddesses in DK 31 B 3.1–7 and B 131. In the *Purifications* he addresses the citizens of Akragas, calling himself "a god immortal and mortal no longer" (DK 31 B 112.4 = KRS 399) and proclaims, "I have once already been a young man and a young woman, a bush, a bird, and a mute, leaping fish" (DK 31 B 117 = KRS 417).

8. *Parmenides* 130E–131A.

9. *Sophist* 217C–D.

philosophers are now regarded as philosophical poets. Parmenides and Empedocles adopt the dactylic hexameter, the verse form not only of Homer and Hesiod but of the early Delphic oracles, and they deliver truth as if from an oracle. They all recognize a great abyss between the divine truth of which they are hierophants and the pitiful knowledge and capacities of human beings. Heraclitus, a philosopher Plato understood well (despite Socrates' playful caricatures of his thought in the *Sophist*), wrote in prose, but his style also has striking affinities with the language of the Delphic oracle. We have seen that Heraclitus' book begins abruptly with his arrogation of understanding to himself. He makes no distinction between the *Logos*, or principle of intelligibility he lays out, and his own *logos*, or account of reality: "But of the account I give here, humans prove forever uncomprehending, both before they have heard it and once they have heard it for the first time."[10] Few books in antiquity began with an adversarial "But," expressed by the contrasting particle *de*. Heraclitus' beginning registers his uncompromising opposition to the accounts of other men. Heraclitus' *logos* is not a dialogue. He asks no questions and, like the god who has his oracle in Delphi, "neither speaks nor conceals his meaning, but he gives indications."[11] Such is the authority of his *logos* that he does not identify himself.

The goddess who addresses Parmenides and then mankind in Parmenides' poem *On Nature* speaks of humans as helpless and "carried along, at once deaf and dumb, lost in amazement, a tribe of no judgment."[12] She adopts the contempt for the larger audience she addresses that we find in the Muses, who address Hesiod in the *Theogony*: "Shepherds who know only the mountains, your life is your bellies; you are poor excuses for human beings."[13] The mode of address of Parmenides' goddess, when she addresses the figure of the poet, is imperative not interrogative. She is the *daimōn* who guides all things, just as her authority guides—and compels—Parmenides' reader. Empedocles followed Parmenides in his choice of the hexameter, and in his *Purifications* he speaks to his fellow citizens as if he were a god: "[F]riends, you who inhabit the great city on the yellow river Akragas, who have your minds fixed on noble actions, havens of respect to visitors, with no experience of evil, I greet you. For you I am a god immortal, a mortal no longer."[14] In the poem usually

---

10. DK 22 B 1 (= KRS 194 = 1 Kahn), a sentence we can be sure was the beginning of Heraclitus' book.

11. As Heraclitus seems to describe his own style in language echoed by Socrates in *Apology* 20E–21B; DK 22 B 93 (= KRS 244 = XXXIII Kahn).

12. DK 28 B 6.6–7 (= KRS 293).

13. *Theogony* 26.

14. DK 31 B 112.1–4 (= KRS 399).

entitled *On Nature* but perhaps continuous with the *Purifications*, Empedocles' mode of speech is that of a hierophant. The moods of the verb are declarative and imperative, and the rare question is the rhetorical means to excluding any alternative explanation.[15]

These pre-Socratics were prior to Socrates and "pre-Socratic" in two senses: they were interested in the origins, logic, and processes of the world; and on these matters they spoke with an authority that Socrates never claimed to have. They were also pre-Socratic in their mode of communication. In their transcendental authority they did not recognize the possibility of dialogue—or of irony, either Socratic or dramatic.

Sophistic Rhetoric

In antiquity, the discovery of the dialogue as a philosophical form was sometimes attributed to Zeno of Elea, the associate of Parmenides with whom Socrates speaks in Plato's *Parmenides*. This claim, often repeated, originates in Aristotle's statements that Empedocles was the inventor of rhetoric and Zeno the inventor of dialectic.[16] Dialectic derives from the same verb as *dialogue*, *dialegesthai*. The kind of conversation originally envisaged by dialectic involved asking and answering questions.[17] But it came to involve the making of distinctions by way of answering questions. In his *Sophistical Refutations*,[18] Aristotle seems to have in mind Zeno's skill in distinguishing the many possible senses of a word when he discusses the problem of whether arguments are directed against words or thoughts. Dialectic, conceived of as the art of drawing distinctions in argument, can involve conversation. But it differs from the Socratic dialogue (as we know it from Plato) in that Socrates engages in conversations with real Greeks in well-determined situations, which reveal the nonphilosophical and human contexts out of which philosophical questions arise. Socrates' questions have a purpose that transcends mere refutation.

A work of the end of the fifth century or the very beginning of the fourth has acquired the title *Dialexeis* or *Dissoi Logoi*—either "Dialectics" or "Arguments For and Against." Let us call it *Double Arguments*. This treatise was written when the Athenian defeat at Aigispotamoi was still a recent memory.

---

15. As are the questions in DK 31 B 14 and B 17.32–33 (= KRS 349).
16. In the dialogues, the *Sophist* (Empedocles, DL 8.2.57 = frag. 1 Ross) and *On Poets* (Zeno, DL 3.48 = frag. 3 Ross).
17. Cf. *Cratylus* 390C.
18. 10.170ᵇ19 = DK 29 A 14.

It is of great interest as a treatise the young Plato or aging Socrates might have been familiar with. Oddly, it is written in the Doric dialect, and it seems to be inspired by works like Protagoras' notorious book *Antilogiai*, or Counterarguments. This puerile handbook interests us now only because it takes up many of the "dialectical" arguments to be discovered in Plato's early dialogues, particularly the question whether wisdom and virtue are teachable (see III § 2, "The Virtue of Knowledge"). It gives us a caricature of what sophistical culture was like at the end of Socrates' life and the beginning of Plato's writing career.

Our author begins with the question whether virtue can be taught and then turns to the arguments advanced against the traditional notion that virtue can indeed be inculcated in and transmitted to the young. Against these arguments (for example, "If you transmit something to another, it is no longer in your possession") our author advances his own countervailing arguments. There are no questions in this odd primer of argumentation, only arguments put forward to be challenged by the counterarguments of our author. Our author believes that one virtue—or skill—is teachable: a student of this kind of rhetoric can learn to *argue* in a short space of time. His word is *dialegesthai*, the same verb from which the noun *dialogos* derives.[19] By this he does not mean to enter into a conversation, or to seek for truth by a method of question and answer, or to be personally engaged in the outcome of an argument; he means the ability to refute one's opponent. This kind of argumentation, so influential in the democratic culture of Athens in the last three decades of the fifth century, also gives us a notion of a kind of "dialectic" recognized in the Platonic dialogues and occasionally imitated (as it is in the case of the sharp and puerile debates of the *Euthydemus*).

A passage from Plato's *Republic* makes explicit the issues involved in the choice of the Socratic dialogue over eristic (or competitive argumentation). Socrates is attempting to persuade his companion Glaukon that some women can serve in the guardian class of his ideal state. Socrates, Glaukon, and his brother Adeimantos had agreed that each individual is equipped by nature to pursue a single task. But, an opponent might point out, men and women are of different natures. Socrates anticipates this facile objection: to fail to distinguish the distinct meanings of the word "nature" (φύσις, *physis*) is to fall into the trap of contradiction (*antilogia*). Such an objection depends on a superficial conception of "nature." To fail to make necessary and natural dis-

---

19. *Double Arguments* (*Dissoi Logoi*), DK 90 §8.

tinctions is to debate, not to philosophize.[20] Socrates illustrates his point by staging a mock debate between himself, Glaukon, and an anonymous wit, giving us one illustration among many in the Platonic dialogues of the modes of argumentation available both to Socrates at the end of the fifth century and to Plato at the beginning of the fourth.

Plato's choice of the dialogue form was the commitment of a lifetime. In making it he recognized and rejected other forms of philosophical and public discourse. In his early dialogues, Plato makes it clear through Socrates what some of his alternatives were. One is the unbroken speech, in which a speaker puts his oratorical skills on display before a captive (and sometimes paying) audience, which cannot interrupt to object or to ask for clarification. This is the second sophistic paradigm we shall consider. In the *Protagoras*, the sophist Hippias of Elis contrasts Socrates' excessively curt and precise form of discourse with Protagoras' speechifying, which he compares to a ship in full sail scudding across the open sea out of sight of land.[21]

This characterization puts the contrast in vivid terms. In Plato's Socratic dialogues, it is Socrates who assumes the role of the questioner; his contributions to the conversation are often but not always brief and choppy. This procedure gives the appearance that Socrates is ignorant on some point and that his interlocutor is in the superior position of being able to enlighten him. Indeed, if this interlocutor is one of the "sophists" who visited Athens and came into contact with Socrates in the last decades of the fifth century, he is given a long speech to testify to his "authority." In the *Gorgias*, the great orator from Leontini in Sicily, who is reported to have given his long display speech before the dialogue begins, challenges his Athenian audience to pose any question that comes to mind.[22] The question, put by Chairephon, a follower of Socrates, to Polos, a follower of Gorgias, is: "What name shall we give him by virtue of the art he professes?"[23] This is a Socratic question, and at the beginning of the *Gorgias* Chairephon and Polos act as understudies for Socrates and Gorgias. Polos answers Chairephon's question with a short incomprehensible answer.[24] But neither Polos nor Gorgias are comfortable with a simple answer, although both have the ability to respond in monosyl-

---

20. *Republic* 5.454A.

21. *Protagoras* 338A.

22. *Gorgias* 447C. This moment is defined as the beginning of rhetoric and the "first sophistic" by the historian of the "second sophistic," Philostratus of Lemnos, *Lives of the Sophists* 1.1 (482) and 1.9 (492).

23. *Gorgias* 448C.

24. *Gorgias* 448C.

lables if forced to. In the choice between dialogue and oration, the sophists of the Platonic dialogues are more comfortable with orations, which are to be followed only by applause, not questions. In his own century, Plato chose the philosophical dialogue; his contemporary and rival Isocrates chose the oration.

In Plato, Socrates sometimes speaks of his aversion to speaking before large groups. His jury (of 501) is the largest group he has ever addressed.[25] His explanation for this aversion is that a divine voice keeps him away from the arena of the city and confines him to the more intimate association with individual citizens.[26] In particular, he (or the philosopher) will not confront the deafening hubbub of the political assemblies of Athens, where the rocks of the Pnyx echo the roar of the crowds, or the vast audience of the theater of Dionysos.[27] Socrates also refused to address an unknown and anonymous group of readers. He never put his conversations in writing in order to gain a wider and more permanent audience for his incessant questioning, for perfectly good reasons. His mode of pursuing wisdom was to pursue his fellow citizens and visitors to Athens with questions.

Isocrates, Equal of Socrates

Plato wrote most of his dialogues as representations of Socrates engaged in conversation in well-defined settings and with companions who were well known in his own time and are still known to the historical record, in part thanks to Plato. His audience was not a replica of Socrates'. He addressed the individual reader, who would read his dialogues aloud, alone or in a small group, and presumably Plato's dialogues were performed in the Academy. It is a pity that they are now read silently. He did become directly involved in the political life of Athens: "I became disgusted, and I withdrew from the evils of that period."[28] Plato also withdrew from one of the modes of philosophy, and especially political philosophy, open to him in the first half of the fourth century—the epideictic speech delivered not to the political assemblies of Athens but to an audience of readers. The political pamphlet, which sometimes took the form of an epideictic speech delivered at a festival, is a

---

25. *Apology* 17D.
26. *Apology* 31D.
27. *Republic* 6.492B–C and *Symposium* 175E.
28. A phrase we have already seen in Letter VII 325A; see I §2 ("Dramatic Settings").

genre of writing we know best from Plato's older contemporary Isocrates of Athens (436–338).

Isocrates is our last term of comparison. A comparison with Plato is particularly revealing, since the long career of Isocrates allows us to gain a retrospective view of Plato's choice of the dialogue form. Isocrates was an orator who claimed to be both a sophist (of the second generation) and a philosopher. He often had Plato in the sights of his criticism of "eristic" sophists (as he calls them), but he never mentions Plato by name. He himself is glimpsed at least twice in the dialogues of Plato: He is named in the *Phaedrus*, where he is called Socrates' "companion." At the end of the dialogue, Socrates prophesies that in time Isocrates will prove to be superior to his contemporaries in his command of language and might even rise to higher endeavors: "There is . . . some philosophy native to the mind of this man."[29] Then he is glimpsed in the *Euthydemus* as occupying the no-man's-land between philosophy and political life.[30]

Isocrates did not take part in the political life of Athens, but he claimed to be an educator and philosopher. His orations *Against the Sophists* (written when he entered his career, perhaps about 390) and *Antidosis* (written at the end of his career) trumpet his rhetorical and political philosophy with great fanfare and occasional blasts at his rivals and Plato. No doubt he was provoked. The language he employs to announce his qualities as an orator are parodied in Plato's *Gorgias*.[31] His *Antidosis* (or speech arguing for an exchange of property to avoid the expense of a contribution to a state service) is in fact Isocrates' *Apology*, written at the age eighty-two (in 354–353) and provocatively designed to rival Plato's *Apology*. For all its deliberate and grand gestures of imitation, the long pamphlet Isocrates composed in defense of his long career as a teacher of rhetoric is strikingly unlike Plato's *Apology*. It is, to begin with, a speech that is to be read from a written text, like Lysias' speech in the *Phaedrus*.[32] Of the Platonic dialogues only one, the *Theaetetus*, is presented as a text for reading. There is no dialogue in this long imitation of Plato's *Apology*, and, as we have seen, there is a great deal of dialogue in the *Apology* (see I § 5, "The Philosopher in Court"). Isocrates does, indeed, use the verb *dialegesthai*, but, unlike Socrates, he does not engage in questioning his imagined audience of jurors or one of his accusers. Isocrates reports two

29. *Phaedrus* 279A.
30. *Euthydemus* 305C.
31. *Gorgias* 463A, almost certainly aimed at in Isocrates' *Against the Sophists* §16.
32. *Phaedrus* 230E–234C; *Antidosis* §1.

conversations, one with his famous pupil Timotheos (son of Konon), who dedicated a bronze statue to his master, and the other with one of his advisors.[33] In neither case is the other side of the conversation reported.

Unlike the occasion of any Platonic dialogue, the occasion of this speech is an avowed fiction. In this, at least, Isocrates is original. In response to an earlier trial that had made him painfully aware of the resentment the Athenian jury felt against him, he defends his career and his educational philosophy by inventing a trial and an accuser: one Lysimachos has come forward to accuse him of corrupting the young pupils who come to him. For this crime Lysimachos has proposed the death penalty.

In making his defense, Isocrates reviews the forms of literature open to eloquence: there are the varieties of verse forms adopted by the poets, and there are the varieties of prose, including philosophy, oratory, and history. His own choice for his *Antidosis* is the public, poetic, and Panhellenic pamphlet, and what he calls the type of prose "dealing with questions and answers." He calls the practitioners of the dialogue form *antilogikoi*, or "contradiction mongers," after the title of Protagoras' treatise *Antilogiai*.[34] Plato is, doubtless, one of the quibblers hiding under the label "contradiction mongers." Isocrates reveals to us just what, in his own century, fed and renewed Plato's resentment against the sophists of the first generation; he also shows us, through the tribute of his imitation, the rhetorical powers of what might have been Plato's first dialogue. The *Antidosis* imitates Plato's *Apology* in almost everything, except that it is a monotonous monologue addressed to an imaginary audience. Despite the fact that their names have been confused in the treatise on the lives of the ten orators attributed to Plutarch, Isocrates is not equal to Socrates.[35]

Even when he had withdrawn from the centers of Athenian public life, Isocrates presented his political and "philosophical" writings to his reading public behind the thin façade of a dramatic public address—an *Antidosis*, an *Areopagitikos*, a *Panegyrikos*, a speech *On the Peace*, and finally a *Panathenaikos*. All have public occasions as their hypotheses and a Panhellenic readership as

33. *Antidosis* §§133–37 and §§142–49.
34. *Antidosis* §§45–47.
35. Both the names Socrates and Isocrates have been proposed as supplements to the papyrus of Philodemus' history of Plato and the Academy, *Filodemo, Storia dei filosofi: Platone e l'Academia*, PHerc. 1021 II.13–14, p. 128 Dorandi. Socrates' rival, Isocrates, was much concerned with his image and its posterity, as clear from *Antidosis* §6; cf. §137. His pupil Timotheos commissioned a statue for him; [Plutarch], *Lives of the Ten Orators, Moralia* 838D.

their actual aim. A speech Isocrates never delivered before a political assembly begins: "All who have in the past mounted this platform . . ."[36]

Plato, by contrast, chose a very different manner of presentation. He mounted no speaker's platform. The audience of his dialogues is never represented as an Athenian political assembly, except the funeral oration cobbled together by Socrates in the *Menexenus*. Only once, in the *Apology*, is a Platonic dialogue directed to a judicial assembly. Unlike Isocrates, Plato never spoke in his own person. Unlike Isocrates, Plato did not address his contemporaries directly. He produced for his public the representation of figures from another age engaged in conversation and sometimes in fierce debate. In his early and middle dialogues, it is Socrates who is at the center of the conversation, either as this conversation is presented immediately and dramatically or as it is represented in narrative. Only in the later dialogues does Socrates eventually withdraw to the sidelines, as he does in the *Sophist, Statesman, Timaeus,* and *Critias,* or disappear from view, as he does in the *Laws.*

Questions move all of Plato's dialogues—from the earliest to the latest. A question is at the heart of the *Apology*: "What can Apollo mean by his oracle that no human is wiser than Socrates?"[37] The long conversation of the *Laws* begins with a question of the Athenian Stranger to the Cretan Kleinias and the Spartan Megillos: "Was it a god, strangers, or some mortal, who is responsible for the arrangement of your laws?"[38] But most of the questions asked in the dialogues come from Socrates, and almost all emerge from contexts that have on their surface nothing to do with philosophy. The massive project of Plato's *Republic,* for example, is deeply embedded and concealed in Socrates' innocent question to his wealthy and aged host, Kephalos: "What is the greatest enjoyment your great wealth provides you with?"[39] Kephalos' response—being able to pay his debts both to men and to gods before he dies—leads directly to the question of the nature of justice and to the vision of the afterlife Socrates discloses in the myth of Er at the end of the dialogue.

Plato's dialogues renounce the very paradigms of authority claimed by the pre-Socratics and by the "sophists" who were Socrates' contemporaries. They also renounce the rhetorical inventions of the "sophists" who were Plato's contemporaries, although Plato is quite capable of imitating both the first and second generation of sophists. In the case of the *Phaedrus,* Plato is so

---

36. *On the Peace* §1.
37. *Apology* 21B.
38. *Laws* 1.624A.
39. *Republic* 1.330D.

adept at imitating the rhetorical style of Lysias that the written speech attributed to Lysias is included in some editions of Lysias' works.[40]

The primitive definition of dialogue as "questions and answers" brings us to the question of authority and, in conclusion, back to the fifth century. The Platonic dialogues do not resemble any available genre of Greek philosophical literature. They resemble neither the prose or poetry of the pre-Socratics nor the speeches of the sophists. In their representation of a contemporary figure engaged in question and answer and debate, they resemble Attic comedy as it discovered its subject in the notorious Athenian sophist Socrates. But in a number of striking respects, they resemble tragedy—a genre characterized by incessant questioning, informed by dramatic irony, and centered on the struggle of the debates (*agōnes*) that engage its characters. Tragedy too is a genre of Greek poetry in which the author never speaks in his own person. Our difficulties in interpreting the Platonic dialogues resemble our difficulties in interpreting tragedy. Just as the chorus in tragedy is often taken to be the tragedian's spokesmen, Socrates is often taken to be Plato's spokesman. But in the Platonic dialogues, as in tragedy, the author only speaks through the many characters of the dialogue, their dialectical relationships, and the dialogue interpreted as a whole. Even when Socrates dominates a conversation, as he does in virtually every one of Plato's Socratic dialogues, it is not clear if Socrates is to have the last word, especially in the dialogues in which the search for a definition is frustrated, the so-called aporetic dialogues. And, more fundamentally, it is not at all clear if we can take Plato at Socrates' word.

As a philosophical form, the Platonic dialogues are frustrating for many reasons. They lack a center of authority for what is said, and their author nowhere speaks in his own voice; questions are left flapping in listless suspense, to the reader's intense frustration; the level of acuity and intelligence of many of the interlocutors within the dialogues is low, and their contributions to the philosophical dimensions of a conversation are often minimal expressions of assent or incomprehension. They are not as sharp as Plato's modern readers in spotting fallacy; and, then, the Platonic dialogues have the remarkable property of refusing to connect explicitly one with another and to support one another in a progress of philosophy. All of these frustrations

---

40. In *Phaedrus* 230E–234C. This speech can be found in the Hude's Oxford Classical Text *Lysiae Orationes* (Oxford, 1912), no. 35.

are protreptic to another form of dialogue—the outer dialogue between Plato and his reader.[41]

ENDNOTE: In antiquity, the reader of Plato was well prepared for reading the dialogues by a series of introductions. The task of interpretation was made easy. Answers to the reader's questions were provided not at the end of the book but in the introduction that prepared for reading the dialogues. In his commentary on the *First Alcibiades*, Olympiodorus of Alexandria (sixth century A.D.) reveals that this dialogue was designed by Plato himself as an introduction to his other dialogues. This is available in the translation of William O'Neill, *Proclus Diadochus: Alcibiades 1* (1985). We have translations to the anonymous prolegomena and Albinus (now recognized as Alcinous) by L. G. Westerink, *Anonymous Prolegomena to Platonic Philosophy* (1962), and John Dillon, *Alcinous: The Handbook of Platonism* (1993). These academic introductions all reflect on Plato's choice of the dialogue form. Of modern introductions, the most stimulating to a nondogmatic reading of the dialogues are Paul Friedländer, *Plato* (1958), vol. 1, chap. 8; R. B. Rutherford, *The Art of Plato* (1995), chap. 1; and Charles Kahn, *Plato and the Socratic Dialogue* (1997), chap. 1. The late dialogues present in an acute form the problem of the relation between the dialogue form and philosophical argument. Responses to this general problem are given in the essays edited by Christopher Gill and M. M. McCabe, *Form and Argument in Late Plato* (1998), especially Michael Frede, "The Literary Form of the *Sophist*" (chap. 5), and Christopher Gill, "Afterword: Dialectic and the Dialogue Form in Late Plato" (chap. 10).

Another approach to the Platonic dialogues is taken by Leo Strauss, *The City and Man* (1964), chap. 2 ("On Plato's *Republic*"), and by Jacob Klein in the "Introductory Remarks" to his *Commentary on Plato's "Meno"* (1965). The fundamental question of why Plato chose the dialogue form is asked and intelligently pursued by Charles L. Griswold Jr., "Plato's Metaphilosophy: Why Plato Wrote Dialogues" (1988). All three interpreters stress Plato's anonymity and the interpretative problems this poses for the reader.

For rhetoric of "the masters of truth," M. Detienne's study by that title is crucial (original 1967, translation 1996). The rhetoric and logic of the sophists are well treated by George B. Kerferd, *The Sophistic Movement* (1981), especially chap. 6 ("Dialectic, Antilogic and Eristic"); Friedrich Solmsen, *Intellectual*

41. A dialogue examined in II §8 ("The Open Dialogue").

Experiments of the Greek Enlightenment (1972), chaps. 1 ("Argumentation") and 2 ("Persuasion"); and, for the individual sophists and the intellectual preoccupations of the sophistic movement, W.K.C. Guthrie's *HGP* 3, *The Sophists* (1971) is a guide.

Andrea Nightingale has an excellent treatment of Plato and Isocrates in *Genres in Dialogue* (1995), chap. 1, which pertinently reminds us that Plato had contemporaries in the fourth century. The title of her book is inspired by the theory of the dialogue and the novel elaborated by Michail M. Bakhtin; four of his essays on the "dialogic imagination" are translated in *The Dialogic Imagination* (1981).

Translations of what remains of the first generation of the sophists are to be found in Rosamund Kent Sprague, ed., *The Older Sophists* (1972).

Postscript: Two recent assessments of the interpretative questions taken up in this section are Hayden Ausland, "On Reading Plato Mimetically" (1997), and Charles Griswold, "E Pluribus Unum? On the Platonic Corpus" (1999).

On the face of it, Socratic irony is easily described as it is exhibited in the Socratic dialogues of Plato. For some of Socrates' associates, irony is Socrates' self-deprecation interpreted as a form of insincerity. But irony is a word so often invoked in interpretations of the Platonic dialogues that it is worth our while to understand it and its motivation in both its Socratic and in its Platonic manifestations. Perhaps the most striking case of Socratic irony occurs early on in Socrates' defense against the charge of impiety. His first set of accusers, the comic poets of Athens, do not take Socrates to be ironic or a person who deprecates his own knowledge or abilities, since their charge is precisely that "Socrates is a wise man who frets about the world above his head and has inquired into the realm below the earth and makes the weaker case the stronger."[1] If the comic poets have misrepresented Socrates as a sophist and a "pre-Socratic," what, a juror might ask, has laid Socrates open to the charges of his present accusers? "For no other reason than for a kind of wisdom," Socrates responds. "The tale I tell is not my own. . . ."[2] In answering his own question, Socrates tells the strange tale that has Apollo as its author, "the god, the god of Delphi." As we have seen (I § 5, "The Philosopher in Court"), Socrates' close associate Chairephon is indirectly responsible for this tale. Chairephon went to Delphi and asked the oracle if there was anyone wiser than Socrates. The response of Apollo was that there was none.[3]

Socrates' tale of how he gained his reputation for being a nonconformist can be taken as "ironic" in one of two senses and from one of two points of view: either he is insincere and, as a consequence, boastful and conceited; or

1. *Apology* 18B.
2. *Apology* 20C.
3. *Apology* 20E–21A; see I §5 ("The Philosopher in Court").

he can be taken as sincere and as truly doubtful of his own knowledge. And, indeed, *eirōneia,* or self-deprecation, can be interpreted in one of two ways: either as concealed arrogance or as true modesty. Even true modesty is not always an appealing trait. Aristotle sets *eirōneia* at one extreme against the other extreme of *alazoneia* (or boastfulness) in his study of character types in the *Nicomachean Ethics.*[4] What makes Socrates' tale of Chairephon's visit to Delphi seem "ironic" or insincere to most of the audience at his trial is the interpretation Socrates puts upon it: "What can the god mean, and what is the solution to his riddle?" With this question his mission to test the truth of the oracle begins as he sets out to look for Athenians who are wiser than he—evidently to prove the god wrong. Socrates' wisdom, as he discovers to his own satisfaction and to the intense chagrin of the people he interrogates, consists in this: "I seem to be wiser . . . in this small point—that I do not fancy that I know what I do not know." Socrates finally arrives at the conclusion that it must be for this reason alone that Apollo chose Socrates as an example, hinting in his riddling manner: "Mere humans, he is the wisest among you; who, like Socrates, knows that in truth he amounts to nothing when it comes to wisdom."[5]

We can disengage some important lessons from this apology and parable. Socratic irony is ambiguous, depending on the point of view from which it is interpreted. Many of his interlocutors in the Platonic dialogues, as well as the majority of the jury before which he made his defense, took his irony as insincere and, indeed, as an offensive assertion of superiority. As we shall see when we come to consider the evaluation of Socrates' self-deprecation by foreigners—that is, by the sophists he encounters—there was a very strong suspicion abroad that Socrates was an *eirōn,* or dissembler, in his phony insistence on adopting the seemingly inferior role of the questioner in need of enlightenment. In the view of those he annoyed, Socrates knew the answers to his questions, and his questions were designed to expose the pretensions and ignorance of his unwilling victims.

But there is another point of view shared by Socrates and the Delphic oracle that contemplates his irony from higher ground and sees it as sincere. If Socrates is wise by contrast with his fellow human beings, his wisdom resides in his knowledge of his ignorance. From this point of view, Socratic irony has still another dimension. This dimension has more to do with the

---

4. *Nicomachean Ethics* 4.7. This sketch leads to Theophrastos' sketch of the character of the *eirōn* in *Characters* 1.

5. *Apology* 21D and 23B.

rhetoric of philosophical inquiry than with either Socrates' arrogance or modesty. In Plato's *Apology* and throughout the Socratic dialogues, Socratic irony makes the questions with which Socrates is engaged seem impersonal. What Socratic irony is meant to foster is the search for enlightenment free from both the entanglements of pride and the authority of a dominating philosophical personality in possession of the truth. In the *Apology*, Socrates makes what could have been an unbroken oration into a dialogue by giving voice to the question of an anonymous juror. He invokes not his own authority but that of Apollo, and he represents Apollo as putting a riddle to him. Socrates' language in describing Apollo loses its precise significance in translation, but in Greek he is clearly deferring to the authority of Euripides and Heraclitus. "The tale I tell is not my own" alludes to a speech in Euripides' *Melanippe the Philosopher*. In Euripides' then notorious play, this wise woman was forced to make her own apology, which she begins with the words "The tale I tell is not my own." In his description of Apollo and his oracle at Delphi, "the god, the god in Delphi," Socrates evokes Heraclitus' description of Apollo's riddling style: "The Lord, whose oracle is the oracle in Delphi, neither speaks out nor hides his meaning, but gives indications."[6]

Socratic irony, then, possesses both a fundamental ambiguity and a philosophical function. In terms of its ambiguity, there are two levels from which it can be interpreted. There is first the lower point of view of the polis and the sophists, from which the true modesty and self-deprecation of the philosopher seem insincere and offensive. The other point of view is gained, not by looking up to the philosopher in order to look down on him, but by looking up to a reality that transcends the human. From this vantage, a gap opens up between two modes of knowledge, the human and the divine, and between two realms, that of things as they appear to be and that of things as they are—the appearances by which men live and the reality that lies beyond their ken.

Irony is a term common in the characterization of both Socrates and Plato, but *eirōneia* as a noun is used only once in the Platonic dialogues. It is pronounced in the *Republic* by Thrasymachos of Chalkedon. He casts it into Socrates' face because he has become impatient with Socrates, who has confessed to Polemarchos, the son of his host, Kephalos, that he is unable to discover what justice really is. Socrates defers to Thrasymachos:

6. *Apology* 19E and Heraclitus, DK 22 B 93 (= KRS **244** = **XXXIII** Kahn).

I think we cannot [discover what justice is]. And since we cannot, it is more appropriate for you clever people to pity us than to be annoyed with us. When he heard this, [Thrasymachos] broke into a cackle and said with elaborate sarcasm: "By great Heracles! Here we have that familiar pretense (*eirōneia*) of Socrates. I knew it was coming and made a prediction to this company here—you would refuse to answer questions, but would keep up your pretense of ignorance and perform contortions not to have to answer a question, if someone were to ask you one."[7]

Thrasymachos reads two things into Socrates' gentle treatment of Polemarchos: an annoying pretense to ignorance and a tactic of avoiding commitments while forcing others to make them. Thrasymachos' attitude is understandable. He regards discussion as debate and truth as victory in debate, and, as it turns out in this dialogue at least, he is right that Socrates actually knows what justice is: it is "doing one's proper task."[8] Whatever context this definition has and whatever difficulties it entails, it is clear from the conduct of the dialogue that, without an initial confession of ignorance and a motivating philosophical doubt, the common search that leads to agreement on this conception of justice would have been impossible. Thrasymachos supposes that his own definition of justice ("the interest of the stronger") is potent enough to stop all further conversation.[9] There is nothing ironic about Thrasymachos; he says exactly what he thinks. But there is nothing philosophical about the absolute authority he arrogates to himself in debate.

Socrates' irony is noticed by another sophist, and, indeed, the verb *eirōneuesthai* is concentrated in dialogues in which Socrates confronts sophists or which deal with sophists. In the *Gorgias*, Gorgias' Athenian companion Kallikles takes the conversation with Socrates over from Gorgias and Gorgias' understudy, Polos. When Socrates treats Kallikles as a teacher whose school he is eager to enter, Kallikles responds appropriately: "You can't be serious" (or, in Greek, "you are being ironic").[10] Kallikles had been provoked by Socrates' heaping unmeaning compliments on him such as "wisest of men," "divine being." In two other dialogues, Socrates pretends to enter the schools of other sophists, that of the great Hippias of Elis in the *Hippias Maior* and that

7. *Republic* 1.336E–337A.
8. *Republic* 2.370A and 4.433A.
9. *Republic* 1.338C.
10. *Gorgias* 489E.

of Dionysodoros in the *Euthydemus*.[11] In this latter dialogue, the "supremely wise" Dionysodoros treats Socrates with irony, or mock condescension, and he is repaid in kind by Socrates' insincere professions of respect. This bowing and scraping strikes the reader as significant only as the polite expression of the hostility between Socrates and the sophists, but the conclusion of Plato's *Sophist*—the dialogue to which all the early dialogues with sophists leads—makes it clearer what is at stake.

The *Sophist* is the sequel to the *Theaetetus* and is dedicated to discovering the essence of the sophist. It opens with the meeting promised at the end of the *Theaetetus*, but with an unexpected addition. A visitor from Elea accompanies Theaetetus and Theodoros for their appointment with Socrates. With the appearance of this unnamed visitor (the Eleatic Stranger), the previous day's conversation concerning the nature of knowledge turns to the attempt to distinguish three distinct types of knower—the sophist, the statesman, and the philosopher. On his first encounter with this visitor, Socrates suspects that he might be a divinity in disguise, "a god come to examine us."[12] Such beings are difficult to recognize; they can appear as sophists, statesmen, or madmen.

This scene is familiar to us (see I § 6, "Socrates *Hērōs*"). Its relevance to fuller understanding of Socratic irony is suggested by the gap between the shifting guises of the god as he is sighted in the cities of men and as he is seen from a higher vantage. To men, the philosopher might seem mad. This separation of points of view must explain why the term "irony" (in its verbal form) is stressed at the end of this dialogue more emphatically than in any other Platonic dialogue.[13] "Image" and "reality" are the terms that articulate the final stage in the search for the sophist that the visitor conducts with Theaetetus, while Socrates listens silently. At the conclusion of the dialogue, the visitor rehearses what had been said earlier about the sophist as a merchant of appearances and about his making of images and phantoms.

The art of making images divides into the production of true and accurate likenesses and that of false semblances.[14] It also divides into a series of disjunctive possibilities. The art can involve either divine or human productions. Human images in turn can either be accurate to their originals or distort them; and the human producer of the image can either know his model or be

---

11. *Hippias Maior* 291B; *Euthydemus* 302C.
12. *Sophist* 216A.
13. *Sophist* 264B–268D.
14. *Sophist* 264A–B.

ignorant of it. The final result of these divisions—the answer at the back of the book—is a definition of the sophist that has never gained currency in any dictionary, but it reads something like this in the language of the lexicographer:

> **Sophist, n:** a mortal adept at producing false semblances in the guise of arguments, who is confident that his product will not be detected as bogus, and who presents his product not to political assemblies but in the rapid give-and-take of debate.[15]

The interesting point is not this elaborate definition of the sophist but the virtual definition of irony implicit in one of the visitor's many divisions: his distinction between the knowledgeable and the ignorant makers of images. The word "ironic," or "insincere," describes the sophist's attitude toward both the image he produces and those who accept it as accurate to its original.[16] This description of the sophist's irony also seems to carry an implicit definition of the philosopher's irony. The art of imitation by which humans produce counterfeits of reality is contrasted with the human art of imitation that seeks reality "with knowledge."[17] We hear no more of this second art of image making in the dialogue, but the first division the Eleatic Stranger makes is between the art of someone who is sincere (in that he thinks he really knows the objects of his opinions) and that of someone who is not: "But, because he has been around the track in debate, the style of the second is one of worry and fear that he does not know what, in the eyes of others, he makes a pretense of knowing."[18] Such an image maker is "ironic," or insincere.

The Eleatic Stranger makes these elaborate distinctions in the presence of a silent Socrates, who, in his own testing of human opinions, knows that he has a perfect reason to be anxious and fearful that he does not know the reality pursued in his conversations. Socrates would perhaps answer to the visitor's description of a human who seeks to produce "with knowledge" a true representation of the objects his words would describe. This last qualification does not mean that Socrates knows reality as the god knows the model for his own products. But in the world of appearances, Socrates at least knows how to search for these divine models.

If we return to the beginning of the *Sophist*, we will see that we have

---

15. *Sophist* 268C–D.
16. *Sophist* 268C–D.
17. *Sophist* 267D–E.
18. *Sophist* 268A.

gained in retrospect perhaps an insight into the meaning of Socratic irony in the Platonic dialogues. It takes a philosopher to recognize a philosopher. Theodoros cannot agree with Socrates that their visitor from Italy is a god; it is better to call him "godlike." Socrates agrees. As for Socrates, he is more a *daimōn* out of Homer and Hesiod, "a god come to examine us." Such beings wander through the cities of men and assume many guises in the eyes of humans—sophists, statesmen, and madmen, the category that occupies the place of the missing philosopher.[19] From the earthbound point of view, Socrates' irony might seem insincere, but it is at least divine. It also introduces us to Plato's own manner of introducing his reader to philosophy and his own philosophy of transcendence.

ENDNOTE: The classical study of irony in its Greek meaning and context is that of J.A.K. Thomson, *Irony: An Historical Introduction* (1926). A much more complex study, which is as much concerned with nineteenth-century German philosophy as it is with Socrates as we find him in Plato and Xenophon, is Søren Kierkegaard's dissertation *The Concept of Irony with Constant Reference to Socrates* (1841, translated 1966). Kierkegaard himself was a master of irony, anonymity, and masks. Two recent presentations of Socratic irony are far divergent in their evaluation of the phenomenon in Plato: Paul Friedländer, *Plato* (1958), vol. 1, chap. 7 ("Irony"), and Gregory Vlastos, *Socrates: Ironist and Moral Philosopher* (1991), chap. 7. Where Friedländer sees Socratic and Platonic irony as metaphysical, Vlastos is practical, analytic, and sincere and focuses on Socratic, not on Platonic, irony.

---

19. We have reviewed this theme in I §6 ("Socrates *Hērōs*").

But if a man be thought secret, it inviteth discovery;
as the more close air sucketh in the more open.
—Francis Bacon, "On Simulation and Dissimulation"

Platonic Irony

In reading Plato, the disconcerting phenomenon of Socratic irony creates problems of interpretation. We can never be certain that Plato is serious in accepting Socrates' deprecation of his own wisdom. Socrates tells the brilliant and victorious tragedian Agathon: "My wisdom just might be something of no importance and open to question, as if it were a dream."[1] The challenge of coming into contact with Plato is more difficult than coming into contact with Plato's Socrates. If there is a Socratic irony in the Platonic dialogues, there is also a Platonic irony that stands above it and, when examined, begins to look like the mask behind the mask.

Plato's irony is double. If Socratic irony springs from Socrates' appreciation of the limits of human knowledge and the limits of philosophy itself, and if it appears as mock self-deprecation to those who do not share this appreciation, Platonic irony can be seen as both literary and philosophical. It is literary because it is the dramatic irony of the tragic poet, who can depend on his audience's knowledge of the stark and immutable outlines of his plot. As we have seen in contemplating the shadow of death that is cast over the Platonic dialogues, there are moments when Socrates and his interlocutors are not fully aware of the implications of their words (see I § 4, "The Shadow of Death"). Plato's readers are aware of the plot of Socrates' life and death;

1. *Symposium* 175E.

Socrates is not. Socrates' question to Glaukon in the *Republic* concerning the fate of the prisoner who would return to the cave—"Would they not put him to death?"[2]—is the Platonic equivalent of Oedipus' promise in Sophocles' *Oedipus the King* that he will discover the murderer of King Laios: "I will fight for the dead man as if he were my father."[3] As he speaks these confident words, Oedipus does not know that the dead man was his father or that he has murdered him, and Socrates could not know the precise shape of his own fate in the cave of Athens. The difference between the situation of Oedipus and that of Socrates is simply that Oedipus' ignorance encompasses the past, whereas Socrates is ignorant of his fate in democratic Athens.

As a result of Plato's choice of the form of a dramatic dialogue in which he never appears as a character and never speaks himself, either as actor or as author, the problems of interpreting a Platonic dialogue are at bottom the problems of interpreting a Sophoclean or Shakespearean tragedy. Plato speaks through his dialogue as a whole, not through any single character. Plato's choice of the form of philosophical expression that most resembles tragedy means we cannot view Socrates as Plato's "spokesman"—any more than we can take the chorus of a Sophoclean tragedy to be Sophocles' spokesman. Nor (as I will argue in III § 8, "Magnesia") can we see in the Athenian of the *Laws* a mask bearing the thinly disguised features of Plato himself. It is only with Aristotle and then Cicero that the author of a dialogue introduces himself as a speaker in that dialogue and arrogates to himself an authority Plato abjured.

In giving the speaking parts of his dialogues to others and allowing the characters of the age of Socrates to speak to his own age, Plato is following the inspiration of Socrates, who advances arguments by recalling the famous tag from Euripides' *Melanippe*: "The tale I tell is not my own."[4] Let us review the moments when Socrates—and thus Plato—defers to another the authority of what he says. In the *Apology* Socrates makes Apollo responsible for his claim to knowledge of his own ignorance.[5] In the *Charmides*, he attributes to a Thracian follower of Zalmoxis his theory of health as depending first on the state of a person's soul.[6] In the *Meno*, he attributes to certain "priests and priestesses" a theory of the soul's immortality and its recollection of its past experience.[7]

---

2. *Republic* 7.517A.
3. *Oedipus the King* 264–65.
4. *TGF*, frag. **484**; already familiar from the citations in II §2 ("Socratic Irony").
5. *Apology* 20E.
6. *Charmides* 156D–157C.
7. *Meno* 81A.

What he knows of love he claims he owes to a prophetess from Mantinea, Diotima;[8] The eschatological myth that concludes the *Republic* he gives to one Er, son of Armenios of Pamphylia.[9] Socrates' tendency, within the Socratic dialogues, to attribute his doctrines to others is a reflection of Plato's early and fundamental decision to attribute everything said, argued, and done in his dialogues to others.

Questions of Authority

There is still another doctrine that Socrates attributes to the authority of another. This is the parable he tells Phaedrus in the *Phaedrus* about the danger of the written word, both to its author and to the soul of its reader. It affords still another indication of Plato's reflection on the problem of writing dramatic dialogues, and we will examine it in this context. But Socrates' resort to the parable is also a reflection of Plato's reflections on the question of authority. Socrates illustrates the dangers of writing by telling of an encounter between Theuth, the inventor of writing, and Thamous, the king of upper Egypt.[10] Phaedrus, who knows Socrates well, responds to Socrates' habit of deference: "It is easy for you to make up Egyptian tales and tales from any other source."[11]

Socrates has a response, if not a justification for attributing his wisdom to others. He appeals to the tradition that the oaks of Dodona delivered the first oracles:

> Now the people of that age, since they were not sophisticated like you young men, were content in their simplicity to listen to "an oak and a rock," provided they told the truth. But who the speaker is and where he comes from seem to make a difference to you, since you do not consider only if what he says is true or not.[12]

Socrates has his own authority for saying this, for he is alluding to the proverb best known from Homer and Hesiod. He appeals to it in making his defense before his jury: he was not, he says, "born from an oak or a rock." He has a family, but he will not make a spectacle of them on stage to extort

---

8. *Symposium* 201D.
9. *Republic* 10.614B.
10. *Phaedrus* 274C.
11. *Phaedrus* 275B.
12. *Phaedrus* 275B–C.

pity.[13] This proverb has a sharp point in the *Phaedrus* and also a meaningful background in Greek poetry. In the *Odyssey*, Penelope invokes the proverb much as does Socrates in the *Apology*, when she questions her disguised husband, Odysseus: "So tell me about your family and where you come from, for I do not suppose you come from the proverbial oak or rock."[14] Some ancient interpreters explained the meaning of oak and rock by reference to the prophetic oaks of Dodona and the oracular rock of Delphi.

What this proverb means in context of the *Phaedrus* is that the authority, standing, or family of the person who makes an argument is of no consequence to philosophy. Author and authority are separated from the truth of a tradition, statement, or argument. And, in having Socrates take this position, Plato the aristocrat has Socrates depart radically from the norms of authority in his culture. We have seen how the Athenian generals awarded the prize for bravery to Alcibiades because of his "status."[15] What matters in philosophical discussion is not the social status of the speaker or writer but inquiry freed from the trammels of authority and received opinion.

Here, the contrast with the Pythagoreans of southern Italy is revealing. Like Socrates, Pythagoras did not commit himself to writing; his instruction was oral and confined to a group of intimates. But in striking contrast with Socrates, the followers of Pythagoras needed no more authority for a doctrine than the fact that Pythagoras had said it: αὐτὸς ἔφα, *ipse dixit*. For those who would follow the thinking of Socrates and of Plato in the Platonic dialogues, it is unwise to invoke the authority of Plato or Socrates, for despite the title of Paul Shorey's *What Plato Said*,[16] Plato said nothing in his dialogues, and Socrates, who does most of the speaking in the Socratic dialogues, attributes his wisdom either to others or stands as the authority for his own ignorance.

There are, though, figures of some authority in the Platonic dialogues, and on occasion Socrates is one of these. It is crucial to keep in mind that Socrates is not uniform as a character throughout the Socratic dialogues of Plato. A reader who wonders at this assertion should consider the three positive but very different versions of Socrates Plato presents in the *Republic*, the last third of the *Phaedrus*, and the *Philebus*. To his close companions Socrates is not as evasive as he is with others, and in the *Republic* he takes control of the conversation after the impasse reached at the end of book 1. In the *Phae-*

13. *Apology* 34D.
14. *Odyssey* 19.162–63.
15. *Symposium* 220E and I §6 ("Socrates *Hērōs*").
16. Shorey 1933.

drus, he and Phaedrus are alone, and Socrates, who professes the inspiration of the Attic countryside as he delivers his praise of the lover, needs no higher authority as he speaks on rhetoric.[17] In the *Philebus*, we find Socrates enamored with a new philosophical method of "division" and completely in control of the conversation with the younger men, Philebus and Protarchos.

Other figures of authority in the Platonic dialogues are the Eleatic Stranger in the *Sophist* and *Statesman*, dialogues whose positive results are qualified by the silent presence of Socrates; the aged Parmenides in the *Parmenides*; and Timaeus in the *Timaeus*, a dialogue that was taken in antiquity to be the single most dogmatic expression of Plato's own philosophy.[18] There is one "Egyptian tale" Socrates does not tell. This is the Egyptian tale of the war of the worlds of prehistoric Athens and Atlantis that Critias tells in the *Critias*. It has the great authority of Solon, whose own source for it was an Egyptian priest whom he had met during a visit to Sais and who knew of the prehistory of Athens from hieroglyphic records preserved in the precinct of Neith, Egyptian Athena. Solon's manuscript, translated into Greek from the Egyptian, had been preserved in Critias' family.[19] Plato's elaborate guarantees for the historicity of Critias' account simply serve to reveal that account as a philosophical fiction, representing the very beginning of Greek fiction. Plato's reader is left with the unsettling question, Do the dominant figures of his later dialogues possess the authority they assume?

A symptom of the authority assumed by speakers in Plato's later dialogues is an odd stylistic tic. An example of this tic, which every reader notices but none comments on, comes from early in the *Philebus*, as a coy and sometimes portentious Socrates suddenly tells Protarchos: "Now we will make this claim even more secure by our agreement." Since Protarchos has no idea what claim Socrates has in mind, he naturally asks: "Which claim do you mean?"[20] So would any reader. The portentious and riddling statement of something an interlocutor is unprepared to understand is a feature of many of the late dialogues, including the *Sophist* and *Statesman*; we find it as late as the *Laws*.[21] It seems to undercut the authority of the dominant speaker, since he is obviously failing to communicate his meaning. Finally, in his search for

---

17. *Phaedrus* 257B–274C, up to the point where he tells the tale of Theuth and Thamous.
18. Diogenes Laertius depends on it for his summary of Plato's "positive philosophy"; DL 3.67–77.
19. *Timaeus* 20D–25E.
20. *Philebus* 13B.
21. A striking late example among many, *Laws* 6.752B.

figures of authority within the Platonic dialogues, the reader comes upon the Athenian Stranger, who conducts the discussion of Plato's last and longest dialogue, the *Laws*. As we attempt to assess the project of this complex dialogue (see III § 8, "Magnesia"), we will see that it lacks a discussion of the Nocturnal Council, which is essential for the stability of the new state. There can, I think, be little doubt that Plato grew more dogmatic and less Socratic as he matured as a thinker and a writer, and even made Socrates more dogmatic. But as a philosopher he preserved his anonymity and detachment in the dialogue form to the end of his life and persistently posed for his reader the question of the authority of what is said in his written dialogues.

The Wisdom of Thamous

Yet Plato wrote and published dialogues under his own name. He wrote one dialogue in particular to expose the limitations, dangers—and potentialities—of the written word. This is his *Phaedrus*. The *Phaedrus* returns us to Socrates' Egyptian parable and the problem of Platonic writing. The dialogue begins with the chance encounter of Socrates and the young Phaedrus, who was on his way for a walk in the Attic countryside to memorize a clever speech of the orator Lysias—that is, to make the *logos* that belonged to another his own. He carried a papyrus roll of this novel speech in his left hand, hidden under his cloak. Long before Socrates' tale of the encounter of Theuth and Thamous, the initial encounter of Socrates and Phaedrus illustrates the dangers of writing. Lysias had delivered his erotic argument before a large group of admirers; but his authority over this speech ceased the moment he gave Phaedrus a written copy to carry away with him.[22] Phaedrus reads this speech to Socrates, and Socrates subjects it to harsh criticism after he has delivered two rival speeches himself.[23] Lysias is not on hand to defend his composition against Socrates' telling criticism that he began his speech with what should have been its conclusion.[24]

It was dangerous for Lysias to entrust the papyrus roll containing his speech to Phaedrus, for it fell into the hands of a severe critic. Lysias faces still another risk. This is the risk he—and by extension any writer—runs of being considered a *logographos*. The word means simply a writer of speeches (*logoi*). Its opprobrium is not evident to us; it is explained by the political

---

22. *Phaedrus* 227A–228E.
23. *Phaedrus* 262E.
24. *Phaedrus* 264A.

context of late-fifth- and early-fourth-century Athens, where the word describes the professionals—like Lysias and Isocrates—who wrote speeches for
others to deliver in court. Since Lysias was a resident alien, he could not
(with the exception of a single speech delivered when he was made a citizen)
speak in the courts and political assemblies of Athens. Lysias is first described
in the *Phaedrus* as "most formidable *in writing*."[25] The usual formula for praise
(or abuse) is "most formidable in speaking."[26] Lysias is an alien and in his
writing offers what can be termed an "alien discourse." Anyone in possession
of a written copy of his speech can pretend to address the object of his desire
as if he were not a lover: "You understand my situation, and you know that I
believe it will be in our interest if this comes about."[27] And anyone can subject
his speech to criticism. Removed from his written speech, Lysias could not
respond, except in writing, as became the fashion in the fourth century. Isocrates' disparaging remark on the theoreticians who compose "laws and consti-
tutions," in section 12 of his *Address to Philip*,[28] is a good example of a skirmish
of written words, made when Plato could no longer defend his *Republic* and
Laws.

These are some of the dangers of writing Socrates finally captures in the
parable of Theuth and Thamous. Clever Theuth presents a series of wonderful inventions to Thamous, king of Egyptian Thebes. He makes a grandiose
claim for the invention of writing: "This art, my Lord, will make the Egyptians
wiser and improve their memories; for I have discovered a formula for wisdom
and memory."[29] Other claims for the virtues of writing had been heard in
Athens as Greek culture was becoming more literate. Critias—or more likely
Euripides, in his *Sisyphos*—had spoken of writing (through a character in a
play) as the "safeguard of speech, discovered in Phoenicia."[30] Gorgias, in his
Defense of Palamedes (the Greek inventor of writing, who was unjustly accused
by Odysseus of receiving treasonable correspondence from Troy), boasted of
his long-dead client that he had invented "laws, the written guardians of

25. *Phaedrus* 228A.
26. "Formidable in speaking" is the charge made against Socrates by his accusers; *Apology* 17
A–B.
27. *Phaedrus* 230E.
28. Written to Philip of Macedon in 346, the year after Plato's death.
29. *Phaedrus* 274E.
30. Attributed to Critias in DK 88 B 2.10. There are strong arguments for assigning this fasci-
nating fragment to the Euripidean tetralogy, *Alexander, Trojan Women, Palamedes*, and its satyr play
Sisyphos, despite Nauck's rejection of the long citation from Sextus Empiricus (who attributes it to
Critias); *TGF*, p. 572.

justice, and writing, the tool of memory."[31] In 415 Euripides echoed Gorgias in his own *Palamedes* (followed by the satyr play *Sisyphos*) by having his doomed hero claim for his invention that it was a medicine (*pharmakon*) against forgetfulness.[32]

In Plato's *Phaedrus*, the Egyptian king Thamous declared against Theuth:

> My exceedingly inventive Theuth, it is for one person to discover the world of the arts, and it is for another to judge the portion of harm or benefit for those who will make use of these arts. You, now, the father of writing, have claimed for it just the opposite of what it can do. Writing will instill forgetfulness in the soul, because the power of memory will not be exercised as men rely on the drawing of characters that are not their own and come from without and that they do not themselves recall from within by themselves. What you have discovered is not a formula for memory but a prompt.[33]

Thamous understood the wisdom of Heraclitus, that the learning or hearing of many things does not make a man wise.[34] But we, as readers of Plato's written word, should note that Thamous does not claim that all wisdom is simply a matter of an individual's autonomous memory:

> Having heard many a thing *without being instructed*, men will fancy that they understand many things, but most of them will have no real understanding and will be tiresome to associate with, once they have acquired the appearance, rather than the reality, of wisdom.[35]

The harshest indictment against the written word is that it is secondary, alien, impersonal, and dead. It is like a painting. It looks alive, but keeps a solemn silence, and, if a question is put to it, it can only repeat itself. Then, if it gets loose, it can come into the wrong hands as it is taken up both by readers of discernment and those who have no business with it. It does not distinguish between those it should address and those before whom it should keep silent. Nor can it defend itself if reviled.[36] The relation between Socrates and Phaedrus represents, it would seem, the advantages of personal contact and the spoken word; that between Lysias and Socrates—and Lysias and

---

31. Gorgias, DK 82 B 11a30.
32. *TGF*, frag. 578.
33. *Phaedrus* 274E–275A.
34. Heraclitus, DK 22 B 40 (= KRS 255 = XVIII Kahn).
35. *Phaedrus* 275A–B.
36. The sum of *Phaedrus* 275D–E, a passage that repays careful reading.

Phaedrus as well—the limitations and dangers of the written word. Reduced to writing, "Lysias" can only repeat himself; he cannot defend himself against the criticisms of Socrates.[37] But, as he encounters Phaedrus, Socrates can delve into the life of his companion by asking, "Where, my dear Phaedrus, are you going, and where have you come from?"[38] Socrates speaks to a companion who is well known to him, as does Phaedrus.[39] And Phaedrus can question Socrates if he does not understand what he says.

But the contrast between the spoken and the written word, so vividly represented in the *Phaedrus*, is illusory. The dialogue of the *Phaedrus* itself is rendered in the written word, in external characters rather than the spoken word that issues from within the speaker's breast; it is copied onto lifeless papyrus or printed on lifeless paper. As some of its recent readers have dramatically shown, the text of the *Phaedrus* can be put to many uses. It can be made to serve as an ancient Greek parable for the deconstructionist. Read as this parable, the *Phaedrus* possesses no stability of intention, only the instability of shifting interpretations. And if asked questions, as it frequently is, it seems to repeat itself in solemn silence. Its author lacks all authority; its reader is the only authority for its interpretation. The paradox of the *Phaedrus* is that it appears to be a self-consuming artifact; and it seems to consume itself with voracious appetite as it advertises the dangers of the written word in the written word.

But the *Phaedrus* has a peculiarity. Unlike any other Platonic dialogue, it contains speeches that are subject to criticism and revision within the dialogue. First, there is the speech of Lysias, the so-called *Erotikos*; second comes Socrates' speech in the manner of Lysias, also in dispraise of the lover; last comes his unexpected "palinode" in praise of Eros.[40] In his discussion of rhetoric in the last part of the *Phaedrus*, Socrates returns to these speeches. Although he pairs his first speech with that of Lysias, it is clear that the two speeches are distinct in their character and capacity to develop under the pressure of criticism. Phaedrus is asked to read once again the speech of Lysias, now to examine the art with which it is composed. Lysias, as read by another, can only repeat himself, and his speech is shown once again by

37. As he does at *Phaedrus* 262E and 263E: "You understand my situation and you know that I believe that it will be in our interest if this comes about."
38. *Phaedrus* 227A.
39. As is clear from the exchanges at *Phaedrus* 228B and 236C.
40. *Phaedrus* 230E–234C (Lysias' speech), 237A–241D (Socrates' Lysianic speech), and 243E–257B (Socrates' "palinode").

Socrates to be a paltry production lacking any principle of organization. The situation with Socrates' two speeches is remarkably different. His first speech was already inspired (it begins with an invocation to the Muses), and it illustrates a form of erotic mania.[41] When Socrates returns to his treatment of *erōs* in his "palinode," it emerges that his first speech is capable of being radically revised and extended. In its careful divisions and distinctions it is shown to conform to the principle of "logographic necessity." This, I think, is the genius of the Platonic dialogues: they evade the limitation and repetition of writing by constantly recasting their *logoi* as these are shaped by new contexts and new points of view.

Logographic Necessity

The *Phaedrus*, like the *Ion*, the *Republic*, and the *Laws*, exhibits a submerged feature of all criticism of poetry and writing in the Platonic dialogues: all such criticism reflects on the Platonic dialogues as a form of communication; criticism forces the reader to reflect on the dialogues themselves.[42] It seems certain that in having Socrates proclaim in the *Phaedrus* the possibility of a truly philosophical rhetoric—a "leading of the soul through words"—Plato is writing a manifesto for his own mode of writing. His rhetoric is an art that exerts its power over his hearers (and readers) "not only in the courts and other popular assemblies but in private gatherings, and it is the same art in matters large and small. Its value, if it is rightly done, is no greater in serious matters than in things that are inconsequential."[43] This rhetoric would seem to have three conditions: a knowledge of the topics it addresses; a knowledge of the character, or soul, of the audience it addresses; and an obedience to "logographic necessity" (ἀνάγκη λογογραφική, *anankē logographikē*), according to which every form of discourse "should be structured like a living organism, having its own particular body, so that it lacks neither a head nor feet, but has a middle and extremities adjusted to one another and to the whole."[44]

It is easier to accept the principle of logographic necessity for a poem than for a work like the *Phaedrus*: the record of what appears to be a chance conversation. Much of the action of the *Phaedrus* seems accidental and unpremeditated: Socrates' chance meeting with Phaedrus outside the walls of Ath-

---

41. *Phaedrus* 262E–266C.
42. This is a principle of reading the Platonic criticism of poetry that we shall test again, in II §5 ("Plato and the Poets").
43. *Phaedrus* 261A.
44. *Phaedrus* 264C.

ens; his happening to notice an altar to Boreas; the chance that he ends his first speech at high noon[45] or concludes the dialogue with a prayer to Pan.[46] These details hardly seem planned or significant in the architecture of the dialogue as a whole.

In the case of the philosophy of the dialogue, it would seem that the internal coherence and rightness of Socrates' exposition of the themes of love and rhetoric are of more importance than the determination of how they articulate in an organic whole. As for the truth of what Socrates says about love and rhetoric, no reader can properly form a judgment unless he or she has already formed an opinion about these subjects that can be tested against what Socrates says. And then the requirement that the writer should understand the soul of the reader he will address seems frustrated by the well-attested fact that, once published, the *Phaedrus* has come into the hands of those who do not read Greek or read aloud and has reached places Plato had never heard of, in ages he could never envisage.

But Socrates' principle of logographic necessity—articulated only here in the *Phaedrus*—is of crucial importance in directing the reading of any Platonic dialogue. By this principle, not only do arguments possess meaning and integrity, so do the sequence and structure of what is said and done in a dialogue. The doctrine of logographic necessity, if observed by Plato's reader, deflects our attention momentarily away from what the characters in a dialogue say and toward the relation of individual speeches to the *logos* or meaning of the dialogue as a whole. And an assessment of the logographic necessity informing a Platonic dialogue can only come from a retrospective reading of that dialogue.

By the decree of logographic necessity we are encouraged to read a Platonic dialogue as if it constituted an organic whole and a whole in which every detail—even the most casual—has a function, which is to say, a meaning in the whole. It is tempting to adapt Aristotle's aphorism about nature to Plato and assert, as a hypothesis to be tested by careful reading, that "Plato does nothing in vain."[47] And it is useful to apply to the Platonic dialogues Aristotle's test for the relevance of the parts of a work of poetry to the whole:

45. *Phaedrus* 242A.
46. *Phaedrus* 279B–C.
47. An aphorism often invoked by Aristotle, most memorably in *On the Heavens* 1.3.271^{a}33: "God and nature do nothing to no purpose." In this same treatise (2.11.291^{b}13) he invokes this principle to explain why the heavenly bodies are spherical: "Nature does nothing without reason or without purpose."

remove a part of dubious relevance; if it does not affect the whole, it is not relevant to the whole.[48]

The accidental disruptions of the plan of the conversations of some of the Platonic dialogues encourage us to ask how the new subjects relate to the old and how a deeper foundation is disclosed by the disruption of a superficial plan. The reader of the *Symposium* is provoked to ask why Aristophanes is seized with the fit of hiccoughs that disrupts the orderly sequence of speeches moving around Agathon's banquet hall. The accident of Aristophanes' hiccoughs reveals the plan of Plato's *Symposium*; by displacing the speeches of Aristophanes and Eryximachos, Plato has placed the speeches of the comic poet, Aristophanes, and the tragic poet, Agathon, in significant juxtaposition. This significant pairing of poets tacitly prepares for the end of Agathon's symposium and the argument Socrates forces Agathon and Aristophanes to agree to.[49] In the case of the *Phaedrus*, the demonic world of Eros is disclosed by Socrates' decision to bring his speech in praise of the nonlover to an end at high noon.[50] What is the meaning of Phaedrus' noticing the time of day? "Don't go yet, Socrates, not until the heat passes. Or have you not noticed that the sun is just about standing at midday, the so-called standstill of the day?" In Greece, ancient and modern, noon is the witching hour; this is the time of day when divinities are afoot in the land. As we know from Theocritus,[51] it is the hour of Pan, to whom Socrates makes the prayer that brings the dialogue to a close. The invisible presence of this terrible and erotic god helps explain Socrates' "palinode" in praise of passionate desire (*erōs*).[52]

As a third illustration of what is to be gained by attending to the principle of logographic necessity and in anticipation of our reading of the *Republic* (see III § 6, "Kallipolis"), we should notice the significance of a whispered question at the beginning of book 5, when Polemarchos takes hold of Adeimantos' sleeve and asks: "Shall we let him [Socrates] get away with it?"[53] The philosophical foundation of the *Republic* is revealed at a moment when a conversation deemed complete at the end of book 4 is diverted into the storm of three "waves of paradox" by a whispered question concerning Socrates' assertion that the property of the guardian class of his state—including

---

48. Aristotle, *Poetics* 8.1451ª23–35.
49. *Symposium* 223C–D.
50. *Phaedrus* 242A.
51. Theocritus, *Idyll* 1.15–18.
52. *Phaedrus* 241D–257B.
53. *Republic* 5.449B.

women and children—should be held in common.[54] This question leads to the heart of the dialogue (books 5–7); without it, there would be no mention of the communism and potential equality of male and female guardians or of the necessity of a philosopher king. Here we can apply Aristotle's test of relevance and the principle of logographic necessity. The reader of the *Republic* is invited to assess the importance of books 5–7 by removing them from the *Republic* as a whole. And in a dialogue that has often been seen as the intended sequel of the *Republic*, the *Timaeus*, the reader is in fact invited to reassess the relevance and logographic necessity of Socrates' proposal that stirs up the third wave of the *Republic*,[55] as Socrates recalls a conversation like that of the *Republic* but with no mention of the philosopher king.[56]

The Platonic dialogues speak to their readers in their organization; and, unlike the written word in its repetitiveness, they are eloquent in provoking questions in their readers. An introduction to the reading of Plato cannot answer the questions provoked by the edict of logographic necessity, for there are no answers at the back of the book. But it can suggest that Plato chose the dialogue form—most familiar to his audience from tragedy and comedy—in order to enter into a conversation with his readers. The characters of the Platonic dialogues who enter into conversation with Socrates or his surrogates are all representatives of the range of Plato's intended readers. They represent as "readers of first intent" the souls Plato meant to move on the path of his *psychagōgia*. They quicken the dead form of the written word by asking questions. The answers to these questions are not always satisfactory, but the questions of the internal dialogue keep the conversation of the external dialogue alive. The very agreeableness of some of the interlocutors within the dialogues can provoke irritation and dissent in the reader.

There is no more powerful antidote to the common belief that Socratic dialogue is the give-and-take of powerful philosophical personalities than to excerpt the contribution of one of Socrates' interlocutors, that of Phaedrus in the *Phaedrus*. I choose a passage at random:

> What do you mean by this? I don't understand.
> What?
> Not as far as I am concerned.
> Right you are.

54. Adeimantos lets the suggestion pass without comment in *Republic* 4.424A; but Polemarchos forces him and Socrates to return to it in *Republic* 5.449A–C.
55. The philosopher king, or king become a philosopher; *Republic* 5.473C.
56. *Timaeus* 17A–19B.

Exactly so.
Right you are.[57]

But Socrates' arguments and the arguments of the other dominant personalities are adjusted to the souls (to use an unfashionable word) of the characters he speaks to, and the variety of characters who appear on the stage
of Plato's philosophical dramas gives us the best gauge of Plato's intended
readership. (They will soon pass in review: see II § 7, "Dramatis Personae.")

Even so, the written characters and the papyrus rolls in which the Platonic dialogues circulated do have their limitations. Plato's meditation on the
medium that set him apart from Socrates, who did not write philosophical
dialogues, surfaces in Letter VII when Plato mentions the pamphlets purport-
ing to give his conversations with Dionysios II of Syracuse. Plato's last written
thoughts about the problems of writing he set down when he wrote the
Phaedrus are now made in his own name, as he writes to the friends and
relations of Dion in 354, long after he had finished the *Phaedrus*. If the discovery of the truth is a matter to be seen and not spoken of, it is also the result
of dialogue with another inquirer and of a life of inquiry in a society of
philosophers:

> There is no writing of mine concerning these matters nor will there ever
> be. This is something that cannot be expressed in words, as can other
> branches of knowledge. It comes from an association that has lasted for
> a long time and a common life devoted to this very thing—suddenly,
> like the light flashing from a flame that has darted up, when it has been
> kindled in the soul and comes to feed on itself. Yet, I know this much:
> if these matters were to be spoken of or set down in writing, they would
> be best expressed by me.[58]

ENDNOTE: A daring hypothesis on the relation between the increase in literacy and Platonic philosophy is put forward by Eric Havelock in his modestly
entitled *Preface to Plato* (1963). He argues that in what might be called the
"Hermetic Galaxy" of literacy it was Plato's intent, by exploiting the written
word, to destroy the spell and mind-set of an earlier poetic and oral culture.
Paul Friedländer's refined treatment of the written word, in *Plato* (1958), vol.
1, chap. 5, now seems archaic. I recommend it. The *Phaedrus* is an invitation

---

57. *Phaedrus* 257E–258C; in III §1 ("The Socratic *Elenchos*"), I choose a similar passage in discuss-
ing the *Meno* 85C–D to illustrate one response to the Socratic *elenchos*.
58. Letter VII 341C–D.

to critical reflection on the fate of all writing and the instability of an author's meaning. The most influential critical sermon on this "pretext" is Jacques Derrida, "Plato's Pharmacy," in *Dissémination* (original 1972, translation 1981). His reading of the *Phaedrus* affords a vivid illustration of the risks an author faces when he lets go of his written word. In a sense, well illustrated by Stanley Fish (1972), the *Phaedrus*, is a "self-consuming artifact," but, more important, it is an example of a nonauthoritarian and open mode of discourse. The *Phaedrus* opens up the problem of interpreting Plato's written word both as it indicts the written word and as it poses fundamental problems of reading the Platonic dialogues. E. N. Tigerstedt's *Interpreting Plato* (1977), is an excellent brief guide to the history of interpreting the dialogues.

As for interpretations of the *Phaedrus* that place the myth of Theuth and Thamous in context, recommended are Charles L. Griswold Jr., *Self-Knowledge in Plato's Phaedrus* (1986); G.R.F. Ferrari, *Listening to the Cicadas: A Study of Plato's "Phaedrus"* (1987); and R. B. Rutherford, *The Art of Plato* (1995), chap. 9. Andrea Nightingale has skillfully addressed the significance of the speech of the absent Lysias in the *Phaedrus*, in *Genres in Dialogue* (1995), chap. 4 ("Alien and Authentic Discourse").

I stress the meaning of the setting of the *Phaedrus* in place and time, in "Socrates' Prayer to Pan" (1979).

Whoever does not cherish painting,
commits an unjustice against truth.
—Philostratus of Lemnos, *Imagines*

The title of Erich Auerbach's classic work is *Mimesis: The Representation of Reality in Western Literature*.[1] Auerbach found his starting point for his vast theme of the representation and interpretation of "reality" in Western literature in book 10 of Plato's *Republic*, in Socrates' final discussion of the problems of μίμησις (*mimēsis*), a word I have used before without apology. Here I will introduce it in Greek and transliteration, but leave the English equivalents "representation," "imitation," and "impersonation" to be explained. If we begin, as did Auerbach, at this starting point, we discover that book 10 of the *Republic* is a summit from which the contours of Plato's earlier discussions of painting and poetry can be seen to stand out in new clarity. It is a summit reached by an arduous climb and one not sighted in the discussions of poetry in books 2 and 3 and not yet visible at the end of book 9, when the project of the *Republic* seems complete. From this new vantage Plato invites us to reflect on Socrates' long discussion of poetry that had taken up so much of his discussion of the training of the new class of guardians who will protect his new city from threats from without and guarantee its harmony within. It is important to observe that when Socrates unexpectedly returns to the theme and problem of *mimēsis* in book 10, he no longer speaks of his guardians; he speaks rather of "we"—that is, himself, Glaukon, Adeimantos, and the rest of the company at the house of Kephalos.

1. Auerbach 1953, first published in German in 1946.

To understand the final and radical rejection of all mimetic poetry from Socrates' city and the new concept of *mimēsis* and reality that makes this possible, we should begin not on the summit of book 10 of the *Republic* but on the lower ground of Socrates' discussion of poetry and music in books 2 and 3.[2] This discussion is directed to Adeimantos (the more literary of Plato's older brothers), and it begins the treatment of the new guardian class of Socrates' new state with the consideration of stories that are lies. The discussion has two distinct stages: in the first, Socrates takes up the content (*logos*) of traditional poetry as it describes first gods and then *hērōes*;[3] in the second, he discusses the "style" (*lexis*) of traditional poetry as this poetry speaks of human beings.[4] Overt discussions of *mimēsis* as such are limited to books 3 and 10 of the *Republic*, but they can be found in other dialogues—most notably the *Sophist, Timaeus,* and *Critias.*

Mimēsis makes its appearance in the *Republic* as luxury invades the first and essential city Socrates is founding in theory. A more agreeable way of life than that of the farmers and artisans of Socrates' first city requires hunters. These are followed by a troupe of *mimētai*—painters, poets, rhapsodes, actors, and choreutai.[5] The grouping of the new classes that make their appearance in Socrates' city is significant, and the pairing of painters and poets is calculated. Greek painters rendered, in a conventional and indeed idealizing manner, humans both in implied action and in repose; they were called *zōgraphoi* in Greek, which means the painters of living creatures. Painters can be said to be imitators in that they copy or represent an external reality. The dramatic poets evoked by Socrates depend on another form of *mimēsis*—that of the mime (*mîmos*), in which an actor or the reader of a play mimics or impersonates a comic or tragic character or, as was the case with the Sicilian poet Sophron, a human type. The verb *mimeisthai*, to mimic or impersonate, is used in precisely this sense in the Homeric *Hymn to Delian Apollo*, in which the chorus of young women on Delos (Deliades) is described as "imitating":

> *In their hymns, they bring to mind men and women*
> *Of the past, and they charm the tribes of men.*
> *They know how to imitate the voices and accents of all men.*

2. *Republic* 2.376C–3.402A.
3. *Republic* 2.376C–3.392C.
4. *Republic* 3.392C–398B.
5. *Republic* 2.373B.

Anyone who heard them would say that he himself was speaking,
So close was their fair song to truth.[6]

The pleasure of the audience in recognizing the objects of the chorus' imitation was congenial to Aristotle's conception of *mimēsis*, for, as Aristotle viewed it, *mimēsis* is a form of learning in which an audience experiences pleasure in recognizing that this person in this play or painting is that person out there and that this is a copy of that original.[7] But in his discussion of *mimēsis* in the *Republic*, Socrates gives no indication that *mimēsis* as representation gives any such pleasure or that it has any cognitive value. *Mimēsis* as a representation of something out there is clearly Socrates' theme as he discusses the content of poetry: to say that a god can castrate or bind his father, as do Kronos and Zeus, or don a disguise, as do Hera and Zeus, or lie, as does Apollo about Achilles to his mother, Thetis, or grieve over the death of a mortal son, as does Zeus over Sarpedon, is to "lie."[8] That is, the imitations of Hesiod, Homer, and Aeschylus do not accurately represent their objects; they fail to produce true likenesses.

To this point, Socrates has only been concerned with content (*logos*). It is only when he shifts to the question of the style of poetry (*lexis*) in book 3 that *mimēsis* takes on another meaning.[9] The lesson in literary criticism Socrates offers Adeimantos presents many novelties and initiates a very long history. Socrates' general term for poetic speech is *diēgēsis*—a term we might best translate as "discourse" (*discours* in French), a word that is not quite domesticated in English. This he divides into three categories: simple (third-person narration), dramatic impersonation (*mimēsis*), and a mixed style that is at times narrative and at times dramatic. This last is the style of Homer, who speaks both as "himself" and as others: that is, both as narrator and as one of his characters. The illustration Socrates gives Adeimantos is the beginning of the *Iliad*, where Homer speaks as "himself" up to the point when he assumes the character of the aged priest Chryses and imitates his posture and voice as he says: "Sons of Atreus and you other Achaeans . . ."[10] We can now appreciate Socrates' words as we listen to the tapes of Derek Jacoby reading Robert Fagles' translation of the *Iliad* and hear Jacoby take the part of Homer and

6. *Hymn to Apollo* 160–63.
7. Οὗτος ἐκεῖνος, "This man is that man," as he puts it in *Poetics* 4.1448[b]17.
8. Consider Socrates' language in *Republic* 2.377E and 3.388C.
9. *Republic* 3.392C–398B.
10. *Iliad* 1.17–21.

then, adjusting his voice and intonation, the parts of the old priest, Agamemnon, Achilles, and Hera. All of tragedy—and all of comedy—is managed in Socrates' second style, that of *mimēsis* as impersonation. As Socrates describes the first style of narration, he also describes by implication the second: "If the poet were never to *conceal* himself, all his poetry would dispense with impersonation [*mimēsis*] and would stand as narration."[11] I place the word "conceal" in Italics because it points to the practice of the philosopher who conceals himself in all of his dialogues.

Mimēsis as impersonation represents a danger to a well-ordered city, for by impersonating vile and violent characters the actor or young pupil becomes assimilated to the kind of person whose character he assumes. An actor is "tainted" by the character he impersonates. And as in Shakespeare's *Sonnet* 111, the young reader and performer "becomes subdued to that which he works in, like the dyer's hand."[12] *Mimēsis* as impersonation helps explain the ethical motivation of Socrates' discussion of the style of poetry in book 3 of the *Republic*—as does the culture of the polis, for which "literature" was the public and dramatic performance of poetry. In the literate fourth century, even the written texts of Homer or Plato were read aloud. *Mimēsis* is potentially more dangerous in a culture of oral poetry like that of Athens than it is in a culture of books and solitary and silent readers, for it is performed and makes an actor of its reader. Remarkably, at the conclusion of their discussion of the style of poetry Adeimantos and Socrates come to prefer the kind of poetry that entails the danger of the dyer's hand. This is the style of the *Republic* itself, which, although it can be (and has been) classified as a "narrative dialogue," is performed by whoever reads it aloud and plays the part of Socrates and the other parts Socrates plays as an actor.[13]

Three genres of Greek poetry are described in this lesson in literary criticism: dithyramb is pure narration; comedy and tragedy are purely dramatic, or mimetic; and epic is a stylistically mixed genre. That which concerns Socrates most is the dramatic style. His immediate question is what kind of characters the young guardians of Kallipolis should impersonate as they are trained in the memorization and performance of poetry. The answer—"men who are brave, orderly and restrained, god-fearing, and free"[14]—

11. *Republic* 3.393C.
12. Shakespeare's metaphor is that of Plato's *Republic* 4.429D.
13. In view of Socrates' warnings about the dangers of dramatic poetry and impersonation, this conclusion of *Republic* 3.397D is surprising.
14. *Republic* 3.395C.

excludes almost all the poetry of a city like Athens. The more remote but pressing question is reserved for Plato's reader: What then is the style of the Platonic dialogue? It was, of course, a question asked by readers in antiquity, and Plato's dialogues came to be characterized as either "narrative" or "dramatic."[15] In his lectures on the *Republic*, the Neoplatonist Proclus classed the *Republic* itself as "mixed,"[16] since Socrates both narrates his conversation of yesterday as he supplies the narrative links "I said" and "he said" and dramatically renders his own words and those of the others.

But it is more accurate to Socrates' analysis of style to classify all Platonic dialogues as dramatic. Plato's reader takes the part of Socrates taking his own part and the roles of the others who speak. This is potentially the most dangerous style of poetry—or prose. But at the end of the conversation, the unalloyed imitator of a decent character is the type of poet—or prose writer—preferred by Adeimantos.[17] The reason for this preference is clear: depending on its model, such impersonation can involve a salutary emulation. But, as we shall see (II § 7, "Dramatis Personae"), Plato's dialogues are filled with characters who are not entirely admirable or worthy of emulation. Adeimantos' natural preference for the dramatic reflects the preference of an author who began his career as a tragic poet: as a mimetic artist himself, Plato is seriously concerned with types of character, character formation, and the ethical problems inherent in the portrayal—or making—of character (*ēthopoiïa*). His dialogues were not intended for the cloistered guardian caste of Kallipolis. They were meant primarily for the readers of Socrates' distempered city, Athens, who were themselves distempered. As we know from the history of Plato's Academy, they reached many other cities throughout the Greek world.

Third from the King

At the end of his discussion of style, Socrates turns to a discussion of music and then psychology, and the theme of poetry and its dangers recedes from view. Socrates returns quite unexpectedly to the question of poetry in the concluding book of the *Republic*, with no apparent motivation. He says merely that the earlier discussion of psychology (at the end of book 4) has justified

15. According to the traditions summed up in DL 3.50.

16. In his introduction to the dialogue, he reviews the three styles and classes the style of the *Republic* as "mixed"; *In Platonis Rem Publicam Commentarii*, I.14.15–15.19 Kroll.

17. *Republic* 3.397D.

their rejection of mimetic poetry.[18] He is now speaking to Glaukon. Adeimantos had long before opted for mimetic poetry representing a virtuous character. In his earlier discussion of the dangers of poetry to the future guardian Socrates seems to have been quite clear about what the noun *mimēsis* and the verb *mimeisthai* mean: roughly to represent a god or hero or, in the discussion of style, to impersonate, or play the part of, a human being. But now, at the end of the day, he confesses perplexity: "I myself am not sure that I quite comprehend the meaning of the term *mimēsis*."[19] Nor, it appears, have we as Plato's readers.

The deep motive for Socrates' new uncertainty is revealed as he argues that the objects represented by the mimetic artist stand, as he says, "third from the king and truth"—a phrase usually translated "at three removes from reality."[20] Such a claim could not have been made in the first discussion of poetry, absent a theory of "ideas" to establish some reality that transcends and informs the world of our senses. (This theory we will address in III § 4, "Thinking About Ideas.") The notorious example Socrates offers of an imitation that stands at three removes from this reality is a bed painted by a painter—not human beings in action, which was the usual subject for Greek poetry and painting.[21] Socrates' bed is designed to show why poetry, insofar as it is "mimetic," should not be admitted into his city.[22] The painting of a bed serves his purpose, as the painting of a hero or the tragic imitation of gods and humans in action could not, precisely because it shifts attention away from human action to human production—from *praxis* to *poiēsis* and from the objects of the mind to the objects of sight. His choice of bed allows him to penetrate from the appearance of a bed in a painting to the bed that is the painter's model, and from this bed to the pattern bed created, it would seem, by a divine craftsman.

In his final discussion of *mimēsis* Socrates proposes to proceed "along our usual line of inquiry" and to posit a single form under which are grouped all

18. *Republic* 10.595B.

19. *Republic* 10.597E.

20. *Republic* 10.597E. In English, which does not count inclusively, we would say "at two removes from the king." This distancing of the mimetic artist from the object of his representation had already been introduced in *Ion* 533C–E, in a passage we will take up in II §5 ("Plato and the Poets").

21. *Republic* 10.603C and Aristotle, *Poetics* 2.1448ᵃ1, 6.1449ᵇ31, and 22.1459ᵃ15. The tight focus on poetry as representing humans in action explains why Aristotle does not regard the poetry of Empedocles as poetry; *Poetics* 1.1447ᵇ16–20.

22. *Republic* 10.595A.

things designated by the same name. His examples are beds and tables. Both are manufactured objects (*skeuē*). Both are distinct from one another in their forms (*eidē*). Socrates then distinguishes three forms designated by the word "bed": that of the painter, that of the carpenter, and—last and sovereign—the form that provides the carpenter with the pattern for the bed he fashions. A novel conception of manufactured objects belongs to the philosophical center of the *Republic* and Socrates' illustration at the end of book 6 of the degrees of reality and clarity as these can be distributed along four segments of a divided line (see Fig. 2 on page 233). In the context of the question of the status of *mimēsis*, a crude sketch must serve.[23] Socrates is attempting, with Glaukon's help, to illustrate the gap between appearance and reality and the degrees of truth and reality that ascend from shadows and images to the highest objects of the intellect. As we have seen, he asks Glaukon to take a line that has already been divided into unequal sections. One section is occupied by the objects of thought; the other by things seen. These two sections are then divided into proportional segments to produce four divisions in all. Forms are the objects of thought at the highest segment; below them are their mental representations. Manufactured objects (such as beds) belong to the highest of the two segments of the visible; paintings of beds and what Socrates calls *eikones*, to the lowest.[24] This scheme yields the painter's bed as standing not at one but at two removes from reality, for, astonishingly, there exists a reality beyond the bed that the painter has taken as his model.

Socrates' bed does not belong in the city he had founded by the end of book 4. It belongs rather to the world of the mind of the philosopher. It is not a part of the furniture of a city intent on forming the character of its citizens. It is precisely for this reason that Socrates speaks of the effect of poetry on *himself* and leaves the guardians entirely out of account in his last discussion of poetry.[25] His bed leads to a radical degradation not only of all forms of mimetic poetry and all forms of *mimēsis* but of the products of human *poiēsis*, or making, such as beds and tables. The bed has its origin in a carpenter and in the pattern from which he works. His bed is the bed on which we sleep; another is the bed painted by the painter. But the real bed exists neither in pigment nor in wood; it exists as the pattern contemplated by the carpenter. Amazingly, Socrates asserts that this ideal bed was "wrought by god in

23. See the earlier discussion of the divided line in I §8 ("Socrates Silenus").
24. *Republic* 6.511C and 510A; see III §5 ("The Sun, the Line, and the Cave").
25. *Republic* 10.595B.

the nature of things."[26] And just as amazingly, his companion, Glaukon, agrees. Making and begetting are the two metaphors that inform the theory of Ideas. The philosophical metaphors of making and begetting help explain Socrates' verdict that the tragic poet and the painter stand "third," that is, in the third generation, from the king. In Greek, a poet or a tragic poet (*tragōdopoios*) is also a maker (*poiētēs*).

The philosophical problem posed by Socrates' three beds is that they cannot easily be reconciled with his statement of his "usual method." He has generated not a single form but three forms of beds under a single name; only one of these has the status of a Form. He has also invoked god as the creator of the blueprint of the Bed that exists "in the nature of things." A more serious difficulty is that he has assimilated the tragic poet's art, which represents humans in action, with the idealizing and static art of the painter. What form (*eidos*), one asks, is the pattern for Clytemnestra in Aeschylus' *Agamemnon*? Socrates' bed has also deflected our attention away from the distinctive character of Platonic *mimēsis*: the *mimēsis* of Plato's dialogues is fixed on the representation of character (*ēthos*), and the character of Socrates in particular. Unlike the bed, which serves as the painter's model, *ēthos* is not immediately present to Plato's mimetic art. Like the characters of Attic tragedy, Socrates exists in another and now distant age.

The Mimesis of *Ēthos*

Auerbach's starting point in book 10 of the *Republic* takes us finally and inadvertently to what is most important about Socrates' discussions of *mimēsis*. *Mimēsis* of character is, in fact, the theme to which Socrates reverts in his last discussion of poetry in the *Republic*. He returns to Homer, who had been at the center of his discussion of the content of poetry, and to the themes of virtue and vice. Claiming that Homer knows nothing of virtue but only its simulacrum (*eidōlon*), Socrates demotes him from the high position he enjoyed in Greek culture. He stands "third from the king," as does the painter. The honest carpenter stands closer to reality. Yet Homer holds up the possibility of a poet who can create virtuous men, found cities, and understand the meaning of virtue and vice. Despite all he has said against *mimēsis* in these final words on poetry, Socrates now speaks of a form of imitation that is not

26. *Republic* 10.597B. How strange this claim is can be gauged by contrasting it with the work of the Demiurge in the *Timaeus*, where beds and artifacts are not part of the divine program; III §7 ("The World of the Demiurge").

varied in its subject matter but represents "a character, intelligent and calm, . . . always true to itself." This character holds no appeal to the festival crowd, since the object of this *mimēsis* in a stable and temperate disposition is alien to it.[27] Plato, who criticizes poets, here seems to return to and reflect on his own project of writing philosophical dialogues in the "mimetic," or dramatic, style. His criticism of Greek poets is a form of self-examination in the sense that it prompts his readers to recognize the nature of his project in its own terms.

The word *mimēsis* and the verbs related to it have a range of meanings and applications in Plato: Auerbach's "representation of reality" is only one of them. Impersonation and emulation are other meanings of the term. In its manifold meanings *mimēsis* is a theme that runs from the *Apology*, where we find Socrates' young companions mimicking his style of examining others,[28] to the *Laws*, where the Athenian offers the dialogue of the *Laws* itself as a model for the education the Guardian of the *Laws* should provide the citizens of the new city of the Magnetes.[29] In one sense, the dialogues and writings of all the literary Socratics were prose imitations of Socrates; and for this reason Aristotle classed them with the Sicilian *mîmoi* of Sophron.[30]

As Plato understood it, the *mimēsis* of and by the philosopher is a kind of poetry that has its gaze fixed on an ideal and works in a medium other than words: it works on the soul as the individual who would become a citizen of the heavenly city of Socrates' discourse. This citizen must look up to the paradigm of an order laid up in heaven and make his own soul conform to it.[31]

It is no accident that precisely this reflection on the *mimēsis* of human life on a heavenly model leads Socrates to his final consideration of mimetic poetry in book 10 of the *Republic*. This kind of imitation—the working from a perfect model to form human materials—can equally describe the "poetry" of the lawgivers of Plato's Cretan city, who greet an itinerant troupe of tragic actors and send them away with these polite words: "Best of visitors, we ourselves are the creators of tragedy . . . tragedy in its best and fairest form. Our city has been founded as an imitation of the best and noblest life, and this is what we call that which is in reality the truest tragedy."[32] The Demiurge of the *Timaeus* is a mimetic artist working in still another medium as he

27. *Republic* 10.604E.
28. *Apology* 23C. We might say "aping"—a term that is perfectly Greek. The vulgar and virtuoso actor Kallippides was nicknamed "the ape"; Aristotle, *Poetics* 26.1461^{b}34–35.
29. *Laws* 7.811C–D; see II §6 ("Platonic Poetry").
30. *Poetics* 2.1447^{b}11.
31. *Republic* 9.592E.
32. *Laws* 7.817A–B, a passage we will return to in II §6 ("Platonic Poetry").

creates the universe and its soul with his eye fixed on perfect proportions and geometrical patterns (see III § 7, "The World of the Demiurge"). This properly philosophical conception of *mimēsis* is "thrice removed" from the reality of Socrates' bed and its painter.

Plato never worked in the medium of the political life of Athens or Syracuse, although there is abundant evidence that this "plastic god"[33] worked in the medium of the soul of his associates and readers. He worked mainly in the imitation of patterns, such as Socrates, Kallipolis, or Magnesia. This is why Plato's doctrine of *mimēsis* as "an imitation of reality" is as inadequate a description of his own practice as it is as a description of the art of Greek painters or tragic poets. The example Socrates produces of the consummate imitative artist is the great virtuoso and "sophist" who can "imitate" the universe simply by holding a mirror up to it. He not only produces a photographic copy of beds but in his way creates "all that grows upon the earth and all creatures, and himself along with all of this, and beyond all this he fashions the earth and heavens and gods and all the bodies in heaven and everything beneath the earth in Hades."[34] This wonderful wizard, who even produces a self-portrait, is none other than Plato.[35]

In the *Critias*, Critias recognizes the difficulty of his enterprise as be begins his description of the war between prehistoric Athens and Atlantis. He contrasts the license given the painter who depicts the bodies of the gods with the potential criticism that awaits the painter who would capture the familiar human form.[36] But here Critias' analogy with painting fails. For painting, no more than poetry, cannot capture the instant present or remote past of "men in action." Most forms of *mimēsis* in Greek are not mirrorlike; the painter and tragedian represent not what they see but what they think. Even an accurate representation (*eikōn*) of appearance can be profoundly false to reality. Alcibiades' icon of Socrates demonstrates the conflict between outer appearance and inner reality; this conflict holds not for Socrates' strikingly satyric physiognomy but for his words, which have to be opened up to reveal "images of virtue" (see I § 8, "Socrates Silenus").

Then, too, the Socrates or the Critias or the Alcibiades of the Platonic dialogues is not present to the mirror of the reflecting artist. The unknown author of Letter II, a Platonist with, I think, a refined appreciation of Plato's

---

33. The θεὸς πλάττων (*theos plattōn*) of Socrates' myth of the metals in *Republic* 3.415A.
34. *Republic* 10.596C.
35. We will examine his conception of his art more attentively in II §6 ("Platonic Poetry").
36. *Critias* 107B.

mimetic art, recognized that his Socrates was not a portrait of the "real" Socrates but a rendition of an ideal—a Socrates made "fair and young" and brought back to life again.[37] Sometimes the word fair (*kalos*) is translated (as it is by Glenn Morrow) as "idealized."[38] This is not unjust to the aspirations of Plato's mimetic art. In the very dialogue in which he holds up the painted bed of the painter for criticism, Socrates claims that in creating the model of a perfect city he is like the painter, attempting to capture the reality of the perfect and fairest human being and working from an ideal model (παρά-δειγμα, *paradeigma*).[39] He returns to the analogue of the painter as he describes the philosopher in book 6. The philosopher keeps his eye trained on the real, just as painters keep their eyes trained on their perfect models.[40] It is this paradigm of art that has had a decisive influence on the evaluation of art, especially the art of the Renaissance by the artists of the Renaissance.[41] It is a paradigm that Plato appreciated.

ENDNOTE: Erich Auerbach gave Plato's conception of mimēsis only a few pages in the epilogue to his *Mimesis: The Representation of Reality in Western Literature* (1953, 554–57). An enlightening introduction to the use of *mimēsis* and related words is given by Froma Zeitlin, "The Artful Eye: Vision and Spectacle in Euripidean Theater" (1994). Among recent studies of *mimēsis* in Plato are Eric Havelock, *Preface to Plato* (1963), 20–35; Alexander Nehamas, "Plato on Imitation and Poetry in *Republic* 10" (1982); and Catherine Osborne, "The Repudiation of Representation in Plato's *Republic* and Its Repercussions" (1987). A revealing analysis of the relation between the theory of Ideas and the renewed discussion of poetry in book 10 of the *Republic* is that of Charles Griswold, "The Ideas and the Criticism of Poetry in Plato's *Republic*, Book 10" (1981).

Stephen Halliwell presents a clear account of how Aristotle parts ways with one understanding of *mimēsis* in Plato, in *Aristotle's Poetics* (1986), 109–37. Aryeh Kosman very usefully returns the discussion of *mimēsis* to the concept of impersonation in "Acting: Drama as *Mimesis* of *Praxis*" (1992).

Two important contributions to the metaphysical conception of *mimēsis*

---

37. In the words of Letter II 314C.

38. Morrow 1962, 198: "There is no writing of Plato's, nor will there ever be; those that are now called so come from an idealized Socrates."

39. *Republic* 5.472C–D, as Socrates prepares for his third paradox of the necessity for the philosopher king. Paul Shorey (1930, 1.504) translates "the ideally perfect man."

40. *Republic* 6.480C–D.

41. In III §4 ("Thinking About Ideas") I return to the importance of this paradigm from art for the argument for Forms.

are Gregory Vlastos, "A Metaphysical Paradox," chap. 2 of *Platonic Studies*, 2d ed. (1981), and James A. Coulter, "Mimesis: Eicon and Symbol," in *The Literary Microcosm: Theories of Interpretation of the Later Neoplatonists* (1976), 32–72. An important contribution to the broad question of the status of *mimēsis* and painting in Plato is Eva C. Keuls, *Plato and Greek Painting* (1978).

The Ancient Quarrel

If Plato, who founded the Academy, cannot be held responsible for the pejorative sense of the word "academic," he can be held partly responsible for the pejorative sense of the word "poetic." His sustained criticism of the implicit claim poets made on knowledge was reflected back on himself, as he came to be seen as more a poet than a philosopher. We find this tendency to regard the Platonic dialogues as a form of poetry already in Aristotle, who described Plato's theory of Ideas as "metaphorical" rather than philosophical and characterized the Platonic dialogues as "midway between poetry and prose."[1] In later antiquity we know of treatises devoted to Plato's adaptation of Homeric language,[2] and the severe critic of sophistic rhetoric was himself the constant object of rhetorical criticism.[3] In the Renaissance, Plato's greatest offense was his exile of poetry from his ideal city, Kallipolis. Actually, the sentence of exile pronounced in book 10 of the *Republic* was not meant to be permanent; it could be lifted if Poetry found friends to defend her.[4]

In making the defense of Poetry, two poets noticed the paradox of a poet's exiling poetry from his commonwealth. In his *Defense of Poesie* (1595), Sir Philip Sidney said of Plato that "of all philosophers [Plato] is the most poetical." In his reluctance to attack Plato, he echoed Socrates in his profes-

---

1. *Metaphysics* 1.991^{a}20. Aristotle's assessment of the poetic character of the Platonic dialogues comes from his early dialogue *On Poets* (DL 3.37 = frag. 4 Ross).

2. Mentioned by the critic Longinus in the treatise *On the Sublime* 13.3.

3. One example is Dionysius of Halicarnassus, *Demosthenes* 2, citing the Socratic dialogues as models of the plain and even style—"with the exception of Plato"—and 6, speaking of Plato's "dithyrambic" style (evidently thinking of Socrates' inspired speech in the *Phaedrus*).

4. This proviso is clear from the language of Socrates in *Republic* 10.607A–E.

sions of respect for Homer.[5] The young Milton seized on the contradiction between Plato's theory of Forms and his practice of exiling the fictions of poetry and dismissed the Forms as poetic fables:

> But, you, everlasting glory of the rural Academy, if you first brought these monstrosities into the philosophic schools, you must surely now recall the poets, those exiles from your city, since you yourself are the greatest maker of fables, or else you, the founder, must go into exile.[6]

In the early nineteenth century the last of the Neoplatonists, Thomas Taylor, elaborated a lengthy defense of poetry to introduce his translation of Socrates' first indictment of poetry in books 2 and 3 of the *Republic* and to inoculate his reader against the virus of Socrates' charges.[7] The justice of the claim that Plato, who treated poetry so harshly, was himself a poet will be assessed in the next section (II § 6, "Platonic Poetry"). There is some justice in it, but as a refutation of the sustained Platonic indictment of poetry it is no more than an *ad hominem* argument.

The terms defining the "ancient quarrel" between poetry and philosophy are formulated by Socrates in *Republic* 10. They are appropriate to the argument of the *Republic* itself, but they are misleading when viewed in terms of the long-standing relationship, and in some cases identity, between Greek poetry and Greek philosophy. In his concluding reflections on the banishment of poetry from his new city, Socrates recalls that "there is an ancient quarrel between Philosophy and Poetry." He instances tags from five anonymous poems to prove his point. In the eyes of the poets, Philosophy is "a bitch snarling and barking at her master"; philosophers are dismissed as "great in the idle chatter of the ignorant," "a crowd of personalities of penetrating wisdom" who "tease out fine conundrums" and who "go hungry."[8] Socrates himself is living proof of the last charge, and it is likely that the last two squibs are comic. They come close to Aristophanes' cartoon of Socrates in the *Clouds*. The first tag is also likely to be comic. The Athenian of the *Laws* recalls it and identifies its target as the "pre-Socratic" thinkers, who, like An-

---

5. "But now indeed my burden is great, that Plato's name is laid upon me, whom, I must confess, of all the philosophers I have ever esteemed most worthy of reverence, and with good reason: since of all philosophers he is the most poetical"; *Miscellaneous Prose of Sir Philip Sidney*, ed. K. Duncan-Jones and J. Van Dorsten (Oxford, 1973), 107.

6. From his treatise *On the Platonic Idea as Aristotle Understood It* (of 1628–29), in *The Complete Poetical Works of John Milton*, ed. Douglas Bush (Boston, 1965), 58.

7. "An Apology for the Fables of Homer" (1804).

8. *Republic* 10.607B–C.

axagoras in the mid–fifth century, held that the heavenly bodies were not divine but merely fiery forms of matter, and so, like dogs, they bayed at the divine moon.[9] What is incongruous about Socrates' description of the ancient quarrel between Poetry and Philosophy is the fact that it is very one-sided. The attack comes entirely from the side of Poetry.

On the side of Philosophy, the quarrel with the poets has nothing to do with the fact that poets wrote in verse. Two of the pre-Socratic philosophers who attacked poets urged their criticism in verse. Of the hexameter poets Homer and Hesiod, Xenophanes said, in hexameters: "[T]hey attribute all acts that are a scandal among mankind to the gods: thievery, adultery, mutual deception."[10] Empedocles implicitly criticized the impiety of Homeric and Hesiodic traditions concerning the gods—again in hexameters.[11] In his Delphic prose Heraclitus criticized poets and writers of prose impartially. He dismissed Hesiod, Pythagoras, Xenophanes, and the early historian Hekataios, whose "knowledge of many things" (polymathīe) did not endow them with sense.[12] Like Plato, Heraclitus was keenly aware of the public character of ancient poetry and its dangers. In his view, Homer and Archilochos deserved to be "driven from the poetic contests of the city and beaten"— presumably with their own poet's staffs.[13] His concern was not with poetry but with morality. The same is true of Pindar's criticism of poets on the count of appropriateness and accuracy. He would not make of the gods cannibals who eat human flesh: "I stand apart."[14]

Socrates' Examination of the Poets

The quarrel between Poetry and Philosophy takes an unexpected turn at the beginning of the fourth century. According to Plato's Apology, Meletos brought charges against Socrates, "aggrieved on behalf of the poets."[15] Which of Socrates' crimes would have most offended the poets of Athens: corrupting the young or introducing new divinities? Aristophanes accused Socrates—if a comic poet can ever be said to accuse—of introducing new gods, the Clouds and the Vortex (Dinos), and of corrupting the young Pheidippides.

---

9. Laws 12.967C.
10. DK 21 B 11 (= KRS 166).
11. DK 31 B 3.1–8 and Purifications, DK 31 B 131.
12. DK 22 B 40 (= KRS 190 and 255 = XVIII Kahn).
13. DK 22 B 42 (= XXI Kahn).
14. Pindar, Olympian 1.52.
15. Apology 23E.

But the *Apology* itself gives us the real source of Meletos' resentment. As part of his divine mission, Socrates tested three classes of public figures in Athens in search of someone wiser than himself: the politicians, the poets, and the artisans. Σοφός (*sophos*) is the term on which the issue turns. As we have noted for the contest between Agathon and Socrates in the *Symposium* (I § 7, "Socrates Eros"), the Greek noun *sophia* can describe either the skill of a poet or the wisdom of a philosopher. But only in the lowest class of Athenian, which included neither poets nor philosophers, did Socrates discover any genuine know-how (*epistēmē*). His disappointment with the poets was profound. During his interrogation, he discovered that any amateur in his audience "could speak better about the subjects of their poetry" and that poets did not compose their poems out of any skill or wisdom (*sophia*), but thanks to the gift of divine inspiration.[16]

Socrates' principle of criticism is that poetry can and should be reduced to statements of the truth and their defense. This view of poetry reduces the poet's art to practical knowledge. Socrates' expectation is that if Hesiod could describe the parts of a plough in the *Works and Days*, or Homer the hanging of the suitors in the *Odyssey*, Hesiod was a wainwright and Homer a hangman. The reduction is from verse to prose, description to statement, *sophia* to *technē*. Socrates' assumptions concerning the expertise tacitly claimed by poets are not far from the views of poetry held by many Greeks in the fifth century. The poets who most concerned Socrates were the tragic and dithyrambic poets, who composed for performances in the great state festivals of Athens. Socrates examined their poems and asked them "what they meant."[17] In the case of the tragic poets, who never speak in their own voice, Socrates makes the simplistic assumption that poets speak through their characters and take responsibility for what their characters say. By this principle of reading, Plato could be held responsible for everything said in his dialogues; but Socrates' view does in fact reflect a prevalent assumption. Critias assumes that everything Archilochos says about himself is confessional.[18] In the *Republic*, Socrates assumes that the dithyrambic poet speaks as "himself," yet dithyrambic poets compose not for an actor but for a chorus.[19] Given the political nature of his service to Apollo, it is significant that Socrates questioned the poets

16. *Apology* 22B–C.
17. *Apology* 22B.
18. DK 88 B 44.
19. *Republic* 3.394C.

who were most in the public's eye and who competed in the festivals of Dionysos, "with more than thirty thousand Greeks as witnesses."[20]

Ion of Ephesos

In the *Apology*, the terms of the discussion of poetry have been intellectual and practical: Do the poets know what they are talking about? One professional Socrates encounters claims emphatically that they do. This is Ion of Ephesos, in the *Ion*. In this dialogue Ion has arrived in Athens, fresh from a victory in the dramatic recitations at Epidauros, to compete in the Athenian Panathenaia. Such itinerant performers are known as rhapsodes (*rhapsōidoi*); they "stitched together" and performed episodes from the Homeric epics. Socrates professes great admiration for Ion's splendid festival costume, displaying the kind of figure often illustrated in Greek vase painting.[21] His compliment disguises a veiled criticism that becomes apparent in the course of the dialogue (and in the *Republic*): the art of the rhapsode is like his robe, splendid but superficial. Strip him of his clothing and he will be found to lack a real understanding of the poetry he has memorized and performs with great dramatic effect. His understanding of Homer is external, like his robe. The significance of Socrates' compliment to Ion becomes clearer in book 10 of the *Republic*, where Socrates strips poets of the ornate mantle of their diction and meter and examines the "naked" truth of their prose statements.[22]

Ion claims to "understand" Homer and asserts that Homer himself understands the subjects of his epics. In Greek, the phrase "I understand Homer" (῞Ομηρον ἐπίσταμαι, *Homēron epistamai*) is ambiguous: it can mean that I can recite Homer from memory or that I understand the meaning of Homer's poetry. There is no question that Ion "understands" Homer in a practical way: he can recite him. But Socrates' question to Ion is whether he *understands* Homer. This question reverts to the question whether Homer understands, practically and with an expert's knowledge that parallels Ion's practical art, the subjects of his epics.

Socrates' examination of Ion exemplifies the main criticism Plato directs against poets and extends to their interpreters. The first line of attack is that of the *Apology*: poets must know what they describe. The second, directed

---

20. In the familiar words of Socrates in *Symposium* 175E.

21. *Ion* 530B–C. An illustration of a vase by the Kleophrades painter is to be found in John Herington's presentation of rhapsodic performance, *Poetry into Drama: Early Tragedy and the Greek Poetic Tradition* (1985), pl. I.

22. *Republic* 10.601B.

against the interpreter, is that only an expert can judge the poet's descriptions of an art. The principle of expertise imposes requirements on both the poet and his interpreter that no poet or critic can possibly satisfy.

Plato's interpreter is forced to ask in exasperation what is to be gained from Socrates' interview with Ion. Ion is not Homer. He is a rhapsode, who recites the poetry of Homer as a *hermēneus*—a human Hermes who carries messages across boundaries from a dead poet to his living audience. He is a medium, like Diotima's Eros. Socrates offers the magnet as an illustration of Ion's status as a medium and intermediary. Structurally, if not dynamically, his model of the magnet parallels his illustration of the bed in *Republic* 10 (see III § 4, "Thinking About Ideas"), for it places Ion's audience at a distance from the reality of his inspiration. In the *Ion*, the rhapsode's audience actually stands "at three removes" from the source of the poet's inspiration. The epic poet is purely passive, as Homer seems to admit when he invokes the Muse. Yet he exerts a power over his audience, as does one iron ring in a chain created by a magnet. The poet's magnet is his Muse. She inspires Homer, Homer inspires Ion, and Ion in turn inspires his audience: "All good epic poets recite all these fine poems not by any art but because they are inspired and possessed."[23] This is nearly a repetition of Socrates' diagnosis of poetry in the *Apology*,[24] except that here he draws out the full force of the Muses' magnetism, which renders Homer, Ion, and Ion's audience the passive and irrational respondents to a divine power. This divine power might or might not be irrational itself, and there are clear indications that the "passive" and inspired Ion is quite rationally aware of the effects of his performance on his audience.[25]

In his conversation with Ion, the first line of Socrates' attack is directed at Homer. As a poet, whose poetry is the product of inspiration and not art, Homer is required to understand the arts he describes in the *Iliad*. The test of poetry is its accuracy, and only the expert can judge its accuracy. If Homer describes Nestor giving advice to Antilochos on how to manage his chariot in the funeral games for Patroclus, Homer must be an expert charioteer himself.[26] By extension of this principle of expertise, only the charioteer can judge Homer's accuracy. What this means is that the poet is an expert in everything save the art of poetry and that the rhapsode and his audience can

---

23. *Ion* 533C–E.
24. *Apology* 22B.
25. *Ion* 535D–E.
26. *Ion* 537A–C; *Iliad* 23.306–46.

judge only as much of Homer's poetry as they can judge as professionals. The *Iliad*, then, is fractured into innumerable facets, any of which only the relevant expert can properly pronounce on. None of these results justifies Socrates' earlier claim that, "[i]n some sense, the art of poetry constitutes a whole."[27] To extend Socrates' principle of expertise to its conclusions: To have been able to describe in detail the making of a plough,[28] Hesiod must have been a wainwright, and his description can only be judged by a wainwright; and only the complete angler could pronounce on the rightness of Homer's simile likening the flight of Iris down to the sea goddess Thetis to the dropping of a weighted line.[29]

The severely limited and rigid terms of this kind of literary criticism exclude all the political and ethical issues of Homer's *Iliad* (and *Odyssey*), as well as any consideration of the logographic necessity or the artistry behind the organization of the Homeric epics. Ion has given agreeable assent to these propositions because, like the cobblers of the *Apology*, his possession of one art makes him think that he and Homer possess others.[30] But he is never quite persuaded by Socrates' arguments, and at the end of the dialogue he still maintains that the rhapsode is qualified to speak on all of Homer.[31] This last claim reminds us that the possibility of a unifying poetics is left unexplored. We will explore its possibilities when we come to the conversation Socrates had with Agathon and Aristophanes in the *Symposium*.

Hippias of Elis

The sophist Hippias was an occasional poet, but in the conversations of the two dialogues that bear his name, Socrates questions him not as a poet but as an expert on the subjects of poetry. In the *Hippias Minor* Hippias says: "Let's leave Homer, since it is quite impossible to tell what he had in mind when he composed [these verses]."[32] Here we have a conversation not with a performer of poetry but a critic. Hippias is forced into the role of Homer's professional exegete. In coping with Socrates' suggestion that the Homeric

---

27. *Ion* 532C.
28. As Hesiod does in *Works and Days* 420–36. No matter that he can preface his advice on seafaring by telling his brother Perses that he had only once been to sea; *Works and Days* 618–62.
29. *Ion* 538C–D; *Iliad* 24.80–82.
30. *Apology* 22C. In *Republic* 4.421A, Socrates contemplates with some alarm the prospect of cobblers leaving their lasts and entering a life of leisure and politics.
31. *Ion* 240D.
32. *Hippias Minor* 365C.

contrast between a truthful Achilles and a deceitful Odysseus excludes the possibility of a hero who can be both truthful and deceitful, Hippias fails to grasp the possibility of a whole that embraces both Achilles and Odysseus and the *Iliad* and *Odyssey*. And the possibility, present in the dialogue itself, that a philosopher like Socrates (or Plato) can employ deception in the service of the truth is entirely beyond his ken.

In his speech to Achilles, Odysseus does not lie to Achilles; he suppresses the conclusion of Agamemnon's speech, with its exhortation to Achilles to yield to the man of greater authority.[33] The possibility of an understanding of this Odyssean deception is apparently canceled by Homer's death. We can never recover what Homer really had in mind, which leaves the issue to the expert in Homeric poetry, Hippias. Before the dialogue began, Hippias had just delivered a speech on Homer. The question Socrates addresses to him is not new; it is a version of Homer's question in the Catalogue of Ships in the *Iliad*: "Who was the best of the Achaeans."[34] It arises from the judgment that the *Iliad* is a nobler—or fairer—poem than the *Odyssey* insofar as Achilles is a better man than Odysseus.[35] This verdict is strange to the modern reader. It confounds moral and aesthetic categories of judgment, as does the Greek adjective *kalos* itself. Hippias is unable to resist the weight of the conventional belief that lying is bad and truthfulness good, and he cannot conceive of the possibility that an intelligent person can combine both truthfulness and deceptiveness. In a larger and relevant sense, Hippias cannot see the possibility of a combination of opposites. In the contest for the title of the best of the Achaeans, Socrates awards the title to both Achilles and Odysseus.[36] In doing so, he points to the possibility of a more comprehensive poetics than that of Hippias. This inconclusive episode in early literary criticism points us back to Homer and the potential unity of two characters regarded as antithetical heroic types—the hedgehog and the fox (see I § 6, "Socrates *Hērōs*"). It also points us in the direction of Socrates, whose irony offers the appearance of deception. As it turns out, the ironic Socrates is a better judge of the moral and conceptual dimensions of Homeric poetry than the professional exegete Hippias.

33. *Iliad* 9.225–306 and 9.158–61.
34. *Iliad* 2.761.
35. *Hippias Minor* 363B.
36. *Hippias Minor* 370D–E.

Agathon and Aristophanes

In the titles of Plato's dialogues the names of sophists are prominent: Protagoras of Abdera, Gorgias of Leontini, Hippias of Elis, Euthydemos. No dialogue is named after a poet, but in a number of dialogues Socrates examines poets, both dead and living. In the *Protagoras*, Socrates offers a perverse interpretation of a poem by Simonides.[37]

We return to the possibility that the poet's art is "somehow a whole." What such a unified poetics might look like is suggested by the other Platonic dialogue in which Socrates questions a poet, the *Symposium*. The poet in question is Agathon, who held a banquet to celebrate his victory in the tragic competitions. We have noticed the contest between Agathon and Socrates over *sophia*—a word that can denote poetic skill, as it does in Solon and the *Apology*, or wisdom.[38] Another poet invited to the victory celebration, Aristophanes, had produced his *Clouds* seven years earlier. Of all the speeches of the *Symposium*, Aristophanes' parable of the primordial unity of what are now the two sundered halves of our sexual selves is the most brilliant, and he properly recognizes something of his own conception of Eros in the speech of Diotima.[39] This recognition is an indication not only of the potential unity of speeches of the *Symposium* but the potential unity of the arts of the tragic and the comic poets. Socrates questions his host, Agathon, and not his profound parodist, Aristophanes.

Agathon had delivered his speech in the prose poetry characteristic of Gorgias, and he had festooned it with many quotations from poetry.[40] Agathon's aretalogy of the young god Eros, despite its contrasts with the four speeches preceding, maintains the original conception of Eros as a god. Socrates demonstrates to Agathon that Eros read as *erōs*—or the desire for something lacking—cannot be a god, and that, as desire, Eros is lacking in all the qualities Agathon had so graciously attributed to him. The theology behind this argument incorporates the lesson Socrates had received from Diotima

---

37. *Protagoras* 339A–347A. This is his symposiastic poem for the dynast Skopas of Thessaly to be found in *PMG* 542—a fragment reconstructed in great part from Plato.

38. Solon proclaims his poetic skill as *sophia* in his "Hymn to the Muses," 13.52 West, as does Aeschylus in Aristophanes, *Frogs* 1515–19. We have seen (I §7, "Socrates Eros") that the term is crucial and ambiguous in the contest between Socrates and Agathon in *Symposium* 175C–D, a contest to be decided by Dionysos.

39. *Symposium* 212C.

40. *Symposium* 194E–197E.

(see I § 7, "Socrates Eros," and III § 3, "Eros and Psyche"): Eros is not a god but a great *daimōn*—an intermediary and Hermes-like divinity—that negotiates the straits between the human and the divine.[41] What this lesson given first by Diotima and then by Socrates means appears only in the dim concluding scene of the *Symposium*. At the end of the evening, Socrates forces the tragic poet Agathon and the comic poet Aristophanes to agree that, despite the strict segregation of their respective genres in the fifth century, "the same poet can possess the ability to compose comedy and tragedy, and, if he possesses the art of the tragic poet, he possesses the art of the comic poet as well."[42]

We cannot recover Socrates' arguments, but can we conjecture what they might have been? It is likely, I think, that he asserted that the art of poetry is a whole and that the poet capable of imitating the high and serious is also capable of imitating the low and ludicrous. There was no such Athenian dramatic poet in the fifth century. But early in the fourth century, Plato, who had begun his career as an aspiring tragic poet, turned to the Socratic dialogue. In the *Apology* we can see the early manifestations (assuming he began with that dialogue) of his tragic and comic bent (see I § 5, "The Philosopher in Court"). At some time after 385,[43] when he came to write the *Symposium*, Plato gives us clear intimations of his conception of himself as a tragic and comic poet. The young tragic poet had turned his talents to the imitation of Socrates and his conversations and a representation of the serious potentials hidden in the human comedy.

We have seen, as did Aristophanes long before us, that there is something comic about Socrates. In terms of the *Symposium*, Socrates, like Eros, was not fair. Indeed, Socrates looked like a silenus and satyr, and "became fair" and bathed and shod to attend Agathon's banquet.[44] Alcibiades expected to find him reclining next to the comic poet Aristophanes—"or some other clown." But he discovered him next to the handsomest man in the company, Agathon.[45] These gestures are not the gesticulations of a drunken man; they are eloquent and pointed. They point to Plato's conception of himself as the tragic and comic poet capable of uniting the high and the low in his represen-

---

41. *Symposium* 202E.
42. *Symposium* 223D.
43. This rare *terminus post quem* is established by Aristophanes' anachronistic reference to the breakup of the small cities that made up Mantinea after the King's Peace; *Symposium* 193A.
44. *Symposium* 174A.
45. *Symposium* 213C.

tation of Socrates. They also point to the new literary genre of Platonic "poetry."

ENDNOTE: The indictment of poetry throughout the dialogues reviewed here has produced the protests noted at the beginning of this essay as well as a long series of essays on "Plato and the Poets." Particularly recommended are Hans-Georg Gadamer, "Plato and the Poets" and "Plato's Educational State," in *Dialogue and Dialectic* (1980); Werner Jaeger's treatment of the *Republic* in *Paideia* (1945), 2:198–370; and Eric Havelock, "Plato on Poetry," in *Preface to Plato* (1963), chap. 1. All make it clear that in attacking poetry Plato is attacking the larger target of traditional education in the democratic polis. Other contributions are G.R.F. Ferrari's (1989) general treatment of "Plato and poetry" in the context of Greek literary criticism; Stanley Rosen, "The Quarrel Between Philosophy and Poetry," in *The Quarrel Between Philosophy and Poetry: Studies in Ancient Thought* (1988), chap. 1; and Penelope Murray's introduction to *Plato on Poetry* (1996).

Richard Patterson, "The Platonic Art of Comedy and Tragedy" (1982), helpfully introduces the *Philebus* into the theater of criticism. In her essay "Plato on Poetic Creativity," in *The Cambridge Companion to Plato,* ed. Kraut (1992), Elizabeth Asmis appropriately brings the sophists into the discussion. Iris Murdock, *The Fire and the Sun: Why Plato Banished the Artists* (1990), is a stimulating philosophical and literary discussion of the complex of problems involved in the "banishment" of poetry in the *Republic.* The studies and essays listed in the Endnotes to II § 4 ("Mimesis") and II § 6 ("Platonic Poetry") are also relevant to this discussion.

Almost all Plato's criticisms of poets and poetry are negative, if taken as judgments on the moral and cognitive status of poetry. But, if turned from poets and trained on the dialogues of Plato himself, his criticisms point to a positive assessment of the possibilities of poetry and seem to reflect Plato's conception of himself as a writer. There are a number of passages where the Platonic dialogue itself becomes visible in the discussion of poetry. Most impressive and delicate is the scene at the end of the *Symposium* (see II § 5, "Plato and the Poets"), which discloses Plato's presentation of himself as a poet who united the polar arts of the comic and the tragic poets precisely in his imitation of Socrates, the human embodiment of demonic and philosophic Eros.

As an intermediary between gods and men, Socratic Eros connected the high and the low and required of his imitator the encompassing art of both the comic and the tragic poets. Diotima's conception of poetry within the *Symposium* is crucial to an appreciation of Plato's conception of the character of his own dialogues, for Plato thought of his dialogues as incorporating and extending the conception of poetry as making (*poiēsis*). Diotima's discussion of *poiēsis* reflects Plato's own meditation on the art form he found already developing, and developed and perfected himself—that of the Socratic dialogue. Eros, if fully understood, is the desire to attain and possess its object—whatever that is—forever. Like the word *erōs*, which has been restricted to describe erotic passion, the term *poiēsis* is larger than the mere making of verse. Love is more than sexual desire; it is a larger desire to possess its object forever. And poetry is more than versifying; it is creating or making in general: "All of poetry, you see, is the cause for anything progressing from nonbeing into existence."[1] Traditional poetry is then just one kind of making. *Paidopoiia*, the making of children, is another; and the philosopher is capable of immortality by making his words survive not only in his children (Plato had no children) but in the souls of his companions—and readers.[2]

The term μουσική (*mousikē*), or the art of the Muses, receives the same kind of metaphorical extension in the *Phaedo*. Socrates' late attempts at poetry are a matter of interest to Kebes, who wonders why Socrates had begun to compose poetry only once he had entered prison. Socrates' explanation is that only in prison did he understand the meaning of a recurrent dream that, taking on a variety of shapes, appeared with the command "Socrates, make music, practice music." Earlier, Socrates had believed that philosophy was his appropriate form of devotion to the Muses, but in the confines of prison he wondered if his dream did not want to be taken literally—whether he should actually write poetry.[3] His first liberal conception of *mousikē* matches Diotima's comprehensive conception of poetry as making and production. Following the lines traced by these suggestions, it would seem that, in its productiveness, the Platonic dialogue is a form of poetry and that it matches Socrates' first conception of *mousikē* as philosophy. The difference is that Platonic *mousikē* is philosophy written as prose.

The conception of Platonic poetry is revealed in still other dialogues. The discussion of *mimēsis* in the *Republic* suggests that, if it is to be classed as a genre of poetry or discourse, the Platonic dialogue must be classed as dramatic. The readers of the *Sokratikoi logoi* and Plato's dialogues confronted something new in Greek poetry. If, in their perplexity, they were to ask what recognized form of Greek poetry presented contemporary characters involved in conversation and argument, the ready answer would have been Attic comedy. Like the characters of most of Attic comedy, Socrates himself comes from the lower classes of Athenian society, and he often provokes laughter. As the protagonist of the drama of the *Apology*, he drags the comic poets into court as his "first accusers" and speaks "in his accustomed manner" of undignified things not named in public assemblies: colts, calves, horses, half-asses, asses, and horseflies. Even in prison, on the day of his death, and in a dialogue sometimes described as a tragedy, Socrates provokes laughter,

---

1. Diotima to Socrates in *Symposium* 205B.
2. *Symposium* 209C–D.
3. *Phaedo* 60C–61B. We find the products of this inspiration in less than four lines of poetry cited in later authors, frags. 1–3 West. These constitute the complete works of Socrates.

as well as tears.[4] The comic poets of Athens seized on the rich potentials of the barefoot, ill-dressed, ugly, and tenaciously argumentative Socrates long before the first of the *Sokratikoi logoi* (and the early dialogues of Plato) were published. We have now only Aristophanes' *Clouds* (first produced in 423) as a specimen, but we know of others: Telekleides' *Kallias*, Ameipsias' *Threadbare Cloak*, and Eupolis' much admired *Demesmen*.[5] Socrates is ridiculed later by Aristophanes in both the *Birds* and the *Frogs*, where he shares many of the irritating characteristics of Euripides.[6]

One of the comic poets called him "two formed" (*dimorphos*).[7] It is clear that Socrates had his tragic side as well. The comic poets charged him with contributing to the loquacity of Euripidean tragedy, but it is as a serious object of serious *mimēsis* that Socrates comes to resemble a tragic figure at the very beginning of the fourth century. In the Platonic dialogues, Socrates is a tragic figure in the two senses of this word now familiar: Socrates offered Plato a serious and noble object of representation, a human who contains within his satyr's exterior "images of divinity"; and, as Plato came to adopt the irony of the tragic poet, Socrates emerged as a character whose full career was well known to Plato's audience. Because Plato invested his dialogues in historical settings and because he composed his dialogues after the death of Socrates, the dialogues also resemble Attic tragedies. They represent the serious actions and conversations of a figure whose life was well known in its essential outlines and best known in its end (see I § 4, "The Shadow of Death").

It is tempting to speak of Plato as a dramatist. In his own terms, his style was purely dramatic, or "mimetic." One of his dialogues, at least, cannot be understood without an appreciation of the tragedy that stands in its background. This is the *Gorgias*, which casts Socrates in the role of the musical Amphion in Euripides' *Antiope*. The *Antiope* of Euripides does not survive en-

---

4. *Phaedo* 59A.

5. The fragments of the comic treatments of Socrates are collected in *SSR*, vol. 1, pp. 3–12.

6. *Birds* 1280–84 and 1553–55; *Frogs* 1491–99. In the case of the *Frogs*, these petty concerns are elegantly captured in the translation of Richmond Lattimore (*Aristophanes: The Frogs* [Ann Arbor, Mich., 1958], 198):

> Where oh where are my pitchers gone?
> Where is the maid who hath betrayed
> My heads of fish to the garbage trade?
> Where the garlic of yesterday?
>
> 978–79

7. He is anonymous; *SSR* I.A.17 (vol. 1, p. 7).

tire, but we have enough of it (thanks in part to Plato) to know that it was a dramatization of the contest (*agōn*) between two paths of human life: the musical (represented by Amphion) and the political (represented by his twin brother, Zethos). The drama has as its setting Thebes, and Plato used it as the significant background to his own dramatic presentation, set in Athens, of the contest between the lives represented by the philosopher, Socrates, and the man of the polis, Kallikles. It is Kallikles who claims that power is the source of natural "justice" and that his own power is rhetoric. It is for this reason that we find him in the company of Gorgias. Kallikles casts Socrates in the role of the unpolitical and ineffectual Amphion and recalls a number of the reproaches Zethos casts in Amphion's face in the *Antiope*:

KALLIKLES [ZETHOS]:

Socrates, you are not taking seriously the things you should turn your mind to. Although you have received a soul noble in its birth, you give to all the world the appearance of being a mere boy. You could not contribute a proper speech in the deliberations of the court, or utter a plausible and persuasive argument, or give voice to a fresh and smart piece of advice on behalf of someone else.[8]

There are intimations throughout this bitter dialogue that Socrates, who refuses to practice Kallikles' political rhetoric, will face death because he is not trained to defend himself or others in court and that he will receive the same verdict before a popular judicial assembly as would a doctor forced to debate with a "pastry cook" before a discriminating jury of children.[9] What Plato has done by restaging this debate in the *Gorgias* is to extend the role of the musical man to the role of the philosopher. (Euripides had already cast Zethos as a contemporary sophist.) Plato's audience knew both the *Antiope* and the result of the indictment brought against Socrates in 399. And his readers knew that no god appeared at the end of Socrates' judicial contest to compose his quarrel with Meletos, Kallikles, and the Athenian *demos*, as the god Hermes had composed the strife between Amphion and Zethos in the closing scene of the *Antiope*, commanding Amphion to take his lyre and raise the walls of Thebes. Here we have the most dramatic of Plato's icons of Socrates—Socrates as the musical Amphion, who, unlike his political brother,

8. *Gorgias* 485E–486A; cf. Euripides, *TGF*, frag. 185.
9. *Gorgias* 486A–B and 511A–B, on which, see I §4 ("The Shadow of Death"); and *Gorgias* 464D and 521E.

created a city. Plato's reenactment of the contest between Zethos and Amphion has no happy ending brought about by a *deus ex machina*. After all of Socrates' arguments, Kallikles abandons the role of Zethos and says: "I react as most people react when they speak with you: I am not persuaded."[10]

The *Symposium, Phaedo,* and *Gorgias* are not the only dialogues in which Plato pointed to himself and to his conception of his Socratic dialogues as tragic and yet as uniting and transcending—and, indeed, supplanting—the genres of comedy and tragedy. The *Republic* reveals such a conception as well. Once again, we are involved with the issue of *mimēsis*, but *mimēsis* understood as impersonation. We recall that the first example Socrates gives of the dramatic genre is Homer and his treatment of the priest Chryses (see II § 4, "Mimesis"). Homer first describes Chryses' actions, "but in what follows he speaks as if he were Chryses himself, and, indeed, he attempts as best he can to make us believe that the person speaking is not Homer but the priest, who is an old man."[11] Socrates' description of the dramatic style of poetic discourse is a perfect description of the Platonic dialogues, "in which the poet conceals himself throughout."[12] These words also betray Plato's conception of himself as a purely dramatic and anonymous poet. Adeimantos has no trouble understanding what is meant by the purely dramatic style: it is the style of tragedy. But Socrates has to remind him that it is the style of comedy as well.[13] The dangers of this style are now familiar, but it is the style Adeimantos comes to prefer—so long as it is practiced by "the pure imitator of a decent character."[14]

The illustration of this "decent character" and the question of how poets should depict human beings have been left in suspense at the end of Socrates' discussion of the content of poetry, which had descended from gods to *daimones,* to *hērōes,* to men.[15] This conversation is deferred until Socrates can discover what justice is. Although justice is defined in the next book,[16] the question of how human beings should be represented is never returned to explicitly in the dialogue. But character is a theme implicit in the discussion of the three types of "personality" in book 4,[17] and character is manifest

10. *Gorgias* 513C.
11. *Republic* 3.393A–B.
12. *Republic* 3.393C–D.
13. *Republic* 3.394C.
14. *Republic* 3.397D.
15. *Republic* 3.392C.
16. *Republic* 4.443A.
17. *Republic* 4.435B–445E.

throughout the dialogue in the brilliant characterization of the actors playing
their parts in the house of Kephalos and in the character of Socrates especially. Socrates returns to the theme of *mimēsis* in book 10 and says there in
passing that it is difficult for most people to appreciate

> a character, intelligent and calm, that remains always true to itself. He
> is neither an easy subject of imitation nor easily understood [when de-
> picted], especially in a public gathering and before a motley group of
> people assembled in a theater. This kind of representation is an experi-
> ence that is somehow alien to them.[18]

Socrates is describing himself, which is to say that Plato, who never
competed as a tragedian in the dramatic festivals of Athens, is describing the
subject of his own dramatic imitations. The literary anecdote evoked at the
beginning of this book contains some truth. Socrates turned Plato away from
a career as a tragic poet. But he did not turn him away from every form of
dramatic poetry. He turned him to a career as the most brilliant exponent of
a new genre of dramatic poetry that in its origins had Socrates as the principal
subject of its imitation.

The poetics of the Platonic dialogue are defined in opposition to the
poetry of the polis and its public gatherings in the theater of Dionysos. They
are adumbrated as Socrates recognizes the powerful enchantment of Homer.
So long as an exiled Poetry cannot argue in her defense that she is capable
of benefiting the citizens of a city, Socrates will be forced to use against her
the countercharm of the *Republic* itself: "We will listen to her [Poetry], as we
chant to ourselves this conversation that we are speaking and this countercharm."[19] Socrates' terms are arresting. His conversation (*logos*) with Glaukon
and Adeimantos is literally a countercharm (ἐπῳδή, *epōidē*) and his own
speech a counterpoetry (the participle is ἐπᾴδοντες). The root of Socrates'
term is ἀείδειν (*aeidein*), "to sing"; it is the second word of the *Iliad* (Μῆνιν
ἄειδε, Θεά . . .). Against the spell of Homer and the poetry of the tragedians,
Plato's reader will intone the words of the *Republic*.

But like the epic and dramatic poetry of the Athenian state, the Platonic
dialogues have no place in Socrates' Kallipolis, where only hymns to the gods
and the praise of the brave are to be heard.[20] The poetry of Socrates' Kalli-

---

18. *Republic* 10.604E, cited already in I §7 ("Socrates Eros") and II §4 ("Mimesis").
19. *Republic* 10.608A.
20. *Republic* 10.607A, a stark conclusion prepared for by Socrates' provisions for the honor due
to the heroic guardians of Kallipolis in *Republic* 5.468D.

polis is as rich as that of Saint Thomas More's *Utopia*, Jonathan Swift's Land of the Houyhnhnms, and Aldous Huxley's *Brave New World*. It is not memorable. But Nietzsche was, as often, right when he portrayed the Platonic dialogues as the ark on which the poetry of the polis survived as it was shipwrecked by the assaults of Socrates' unremitting criticism.[21]

Plato's last dialogue, the *Laws*, shows that neither the praise of Socrates nor reverent talk of the divine can fill the void left by the exile of poetry. In the postexilic poetics of the *Laws*, tragedy is no longer seen as the genre of dramatic poetry representing the doings and sufferings of the great and remote figures of Greek myth; it is seen, rather, as a serious kind of *poiēsis* and *mimēsis*. Now a scene from the *Republic* is reenacted—the vivid scene that closes the discussion of poetry in the *Republic*. Here Socrates imagined a virtuoso who can transform himself into all kinds of shapes and mimic all manner of things. Come to Kallipolis, he offers to display his proud art. He is sent away to another city, fragrant with myrrh and his head bound in sacred fillets.[22] To the troupe of tragic actors who appear before the gates of Plato's Cretan city, the founding fathers say:

> Best of strangers, we ourselves are tragic poets—to the best of our ability—and the creators of a tragedy, the fairest and best form of tragedy. Our city has been founded as an imitation of the best and noblest form of life, and it is this we call what is in reality the truest tragedy.[23]

The Greek words *tragōidia* and *mimēsis* remain the same, but they have been extended metaphorically to the society created as the close replica of a divine pattern "laid up in heaven."[24] Plato is less guarded here than he had been earlier in his career. He characterizes his dialogues as a new form of tragedy.

Does Plato reveal in these courteous words his conception not only of the city of the Magnetes in Crete but of his last dialogue, the *Laws*? As a product of a new kind of *mimēsis* and *poiēsis*, the tragic poetry of the *Laws* is the paradigm of the well-ordered life of Plato's imagined Cretan colonists. But perhaps the *Laws* themselves are designed as a kind of *mimēsis* providing the

21. *The Birth of Tragedy* §14: "The Platonic dialogue was the lifeboat in which the shipwrecked older poetry saved itself, with all its numerous offspring. Crowded together in a small space, and timidly obeying their helmsman Socrates, they moved forward into a new era which never tired of looking at this fantastic spectacle." *The Birth of Tragedy* and *The Genealogy of Morals*, trans. Francis Golffing (New York, 1956), 87–88.

22. *Republic* 3.398A.

23. *Laws* 7.817A–B.

24. *Republic* 9.592B.

model for the work of the legislators and the paradigm from which the founders of cities can work. Plato's signature is legible in what the Athenian visitor
to Crete proposes to his two companions as a paradigm for the Keeper of the
Laws to choose in the education of the young citizens of the new colony:

> Fixing my eyes on the conversation we have had from dawn to this
> moment . . . what we have said strikes me as a kind of poetry. My
> reaction to it is perhaps not so extraordinary, for I felt an intense plea-
> sure invade me as I contemplated the topics of our conversation as if
> they had been drawn up in military formation. Of all the speeches that
> I have either heard myself or heard reported by another, either in verse
> or in the prose we have been speaking—of all these—this conversation
> of ours struck me as coming closest to the mark and as the most per-
> fectly suited to the young. For the Keeper of Laws and the Educator I
> could not, I think, point to a model better than this.[25]

We will put these words into their context in another place (see II § 8,
"The Open Dialogue"). The Athenian's qualification "to the young" seems to
reflect Plato's lack of serious commitment to the written word in the last and
longest of his dialogues. The *Laws* reflect a final stage in Plato's conception
of the poetry and "music" of his dialogues and a new form of civic education.
In Greek, the word for laws is νόμοι (*nómoi*)—first, what is sanctioned by
custom and convention and, then, written laws. The word for a musical mode
is the same, with the same accent. In the *Laws*, education is presented as a
form of enchantment for the souls of the young.[26] The preludes to the framing of the actual laws of the *Laws*, including the entire conversation of books
1–4, are *prooimia*, or preliminary songs to introduce the song of the laws.[27]

Something of Plato's conception of philosophy as "music" is captured in
the late anecdotes describing a dream of Socrates'. The day before he met
Plato, Socrates dreamed that a young swan flew from an altar of Eros in the
Academy to settle in his lap. As it suddenly grew and flew from him, it burst
into song—to everyone's amazement. There is a matching anecdote about a
dream of Plato's. Transformed into a swan, he dreamed that he flew from tree
to tree and no fowler could capture him. The dreams are different; their
ancient reading, the same. As a bird sacred to Apollo, Plato delighted gods
and men; but his meaning remained elusive. Unlike the poets who could not

25. *Laws* 7.811C–D.
26. *Epōidai, Laws* 2.659E and 664B.
27. *Laws* 4.722D.

explain the meaning of their poetry, Plato refused to explain the meaning of his song. But this much he did make clear: his dialogues represented a new form of music and a new form of poetry.[28]

ENDNOTE: There are scattered hints of an appreciation of the self-reflecting character of Plato's discussions of poetry and his self-presentation as the poet of tragic and comic dialogues. The passage from Nietzsche's *Birth of Tragedy* quoted in note 21 above reveals such an awareness, as does Hans-Georg Gadamer's "Plato and the Poets," in *Dialogue and Dialectic* (1980). In "The Tragic and Comic Poet of the *Symposium*" (1975), I have made a longer argument for what I briefly suggest in this essay. Andrea Nightingale (1995) explores the *Antiope* as it is reenacted in Plato's *Gorgias*. Highly recommended for the topics of this essay and II § 5, "Plato and the Poets," is G.R.F. Ferrari, "Plato and Poetry" (1989), especially the section "Plato as Poet" (141–48).

28. Anecdotes 4 and 5 in *Platonica*.

Formalities

The printed edition of each Platonic dialogue begins with a title, most often the name of a speaker in the dialogue. Then comes the subtitle, which identifies its subject. Last comes a list of the characters who speak in the dialogue— the *dramatis personae*. After encountering these formalities, the reader attends to the drama of philosophical conversation. Thus, the first dialogue of the Platonic corpus opens:

Euthyphro, or *On Piety*
Socrates and Euthyphro.

This equivalent of a modern title page is remarkable for one reason: we recognize the Platonic dialogues not from their subjects but for the most part from the names of Socrates' contemporaries. These names as titles are not the only names to reckon with in assessing the personal dimensions of philosophy in the Platonic dialogues. The dialogues are filled with the voices of still other speakers, who do not play title roles. Most of these are presented as the voices of Socrates' contemporaries; some few are the voices of characters created by Plato.

A survey of the titles of Plato's dialogues reveals few subjects and only one occasion: the subjects are *Republic, Sophist, Statesman, Laws;* the occasion, the *Symposium.* It is notable that Socrates retreats from the conversation of the *Sophist,* is silent during the *Statesman,* and is absent from the *Laws.* The main speakers of these dialogues, the Eleatic Stranger, the Athenian Stranger, Kleinias, Megillos, all seem to be Platonic fictions.

By contrast, the speakers in the dialogues that bear their names as titles are known to history. Among these are the companions of Socrates' last day, Crito and Phaedo. We note Socrates' young and aristocratic associates: Lysis, Charmides, Theages, Menexenos, Phaedrus, and Theaetetus. To these we should probably add Clitophon (the character who speaks two sentences in his cameo appearance in the *Republic*).[1] We discover the philosophers Cratylus, Parmenides, and possibly Philebus (who might stand for Aristippos); the rhapsode Ion; the sophists Gorgias, Protagoras, and Hippias (whose name stands as the title of two dialogues), as well as Euthydemus and Meno, who, if not a sophist, was a great admirer of the sophists. None of these sophists was an Athenian. We also discover some of the most important political figures of imperial Athens: Laches, Alcibiades (commemorated in two titles of the corpus), and Critias, who must be the oligarch and the head of the Thirty who took control of Athens after its defeat at Aigispotamoi in 405. He was killed in a battle with the democratic exiles led by Thrasyboulos in 403.

Of the other proper names that figure as titles of the Platonic dialogues, only Timaeus of Locri is likely a fiction, and a fiction made the more salient by the fact that the unwritten third dialogue of the *Timaeus* trilogy would have borne the name of Hermocrates, the well-known Syracusan statesman who organized Sicilian resistance to the Athenian invasion in 415. This leaves the two dialogues that were named for figures who were not contemporaries of Socrates, the *Minos* and *Hipparchus*. These are almost certainly not by Plato. In sum, of the thirty-five dialogues collected into the nine tetralogies of the Platonic corpus, a personal name stands as the title of twenty-seven. On first view, Plato's philosophy presents itself as directed *ad hominem*. By this I mean they were directed to the *ēthos* of the people characterized in the dialogues and more directly to their souls: I could, as well, use the term *ad animam*. That is, Plato did not direct his philosophy to an anonymous readership. He creates the impression of having directed it through the character of Socrates to the known contemporaries of Socrates, who represent his audience of "first intent." This is particularly true of the Socratic dialogues. But the *Laws* is also directed to a well-defined set of national types, Kleinas of Crete and Megillos of Sparta (see III § 8, "Magnesia).

"Dilogic" and "Trilogic" Dialogues

The cast of the characters who speak in the Socratic dialogues is extensive, and it is extended in some dialogues by the number of characters named as

---

1. *Republic* 1.340A–B.

present but given nonspeaking parts. In the great variety of the Platonic dialogues, there are two formal patterns that are distinctly reminiscent of the economy of the Greek tragic poet, who, in the development of Greek tragedy, worked first with one, then with two, and finally with three actors. Many of the early dialogues have only two speaking parts: Socrates addresses a friend or acquaintance. The *Euthyphro, Crito, Hippias Maior, Ion, Lysis, Menexenus,* and *Phaedrus* are examples of this pattern, as are all the spurious dialogues in the Platonic corpus and most of the dialogues of the other Socratics. (Aischines' *Alcibiades* is an example of this two-actor rule.) This pattern prevails in dialogues like the *Sophist* and *Statesman,* where the protagonist is the Eleatic Stranger and he speaks either to the young Theaetetus (in the case of the *Sophist*) or to Socrates' young namesake (in the case of the *Statesman*). In these dialogues, the younger speakers play the distinctly inferior role of the deuteragonist, while the others on hand—including Socrates—say virtually nothing. This pattern of two main speaking roles divided either between Socrates (or the Eleatic Stranger) and a younger man or Socrates and an older professional (as in the *Euthyphro, Hippias Maior,* and *Ion*) is important to Plato's dialogue with his reader.

With the obvious exception of the *Sophist* and *Statesman,* these dialogues might be thought of as "dilogic"—dialogues in which Socrates examines the beliefs of a single companion. Take Euthyphro, who gives his name to the dialogue on piety. The *Euthyphro* is usually the first of the "dilogic" dialogues read by the beginning student in philosophy. Piety is not an academic issue either for Socrates or for Euthyphro. Socrates encounters Euthyphro on his way to the office of the king Archon to answer Meletos' indictment against him for impiety, and Euthyphro himself must appear before this magistrate— not as a defendant but as plaintiff. This enthusiast has charged his own father with responsibility for the murder of a slave and is firmly convinced that he is acting piously by avenging this offense to the gods. He also claims that he incurred ridicule by predicting the future to the citizens of Athens.[2] Socrates and Euthyphro are evidently well known to one another, and Euthyphro recognizes in Socrates' religiosity something akin to his own zealous piety. He realizes that Socrates' divine voice (*daimonion*) has given Meletos a handle in his charge that Socrates has introduced new divinities to Athens and thereby corrupted the young.

Euthyphro, full sympathy not for Socrates but for himself, sees his own

---

2. *Euthyphro* 5C and 3C.

prophetic inspiration as something similar to Socrates' *daimonion*.[3] But any similarity ends here, since Euthyphro is incapable of envisaging any concept of piety other than that exemplified by his own conduct. Socrates does not attempt to introduce him to another more elevated (and dangerous) conception of piety, which entails that a human come to resemble the gods insofar as this is possible. Such is the second definition of piety—doing what is dear to (or like) the gods—and indeed we find it so stated by the Athenian in the *Laws*.[4] But Socrates sticks to Euthyphro's opinion that he is acting piously in removing the pollution created by the murder of a slave from his father's estate on Naxos. As Socrates examines Euthyphro's fixed opinions, he merely shows that they cannot stand up under the pressure of examination. Yet they remain firmly fixed.

As a character, Euthyphro is notable for both his pretensions and his limitations. He exemplifies the intellectual vice of conceit so well characterized in the *Philebus*.[5] Socrates calls him a companion,[6] but the word *hetairos*, as always when used by Socrates, is an indication that this "companion" cannot keep Socrates company. Socrates and Euthyphro part, without ever having reached an agreement on what piety consists in and with the prospect of their own trials and the charge of impiety before them, Euthyphro as plaintiff and Socrates as defendant. The zealot is only too eager to escape the questions of his "companion" and part company. The *Euthyphro* is an aporetic dialogue. It comes to a dead end, as it must. Given Euthyphro's straight narrow-mindedness, he could never arrive at a philosophical conception of piety "on another occasion."[7]

There is an interesting development in the "dilogic" pattern of the dialogues we have just reviewed. In the *Cratylus* and *Philebus* there are two main speaking parts: those of Socrates and Hermogenes in the *Cratylus* and Socrates and Protarchos in the *Philebus*. What is interesting about the morphology of these dialogues is the virtual silence of the eponymous characters. In the *Cratylus*, Socrates had come upon a conversation between Hermogenes and Cratylus on "the rightness of names." Cratylus' position is summarized by Hermogenes, but Cratylus has virtually nothing to say in the dialogue until

---

3. *Euthyphro* 2A–3C.
4. *Euthyphro* 6E and 10A and *Laws* 4.716D.
5. In Socrates' analysis of the tragicomedy of life and the pleasure we feel at the comeuppance of friends who do not understand their own limitations, *Philebus* 47B–50E.
6. *Euthyphro* 15E.
7. *Euthyphro* 15E.

Hermogenes asks him a question midway into the discussion.[8] In the other, the *Philebus*, we find a similar pattern, with an important variation. Socrates, the young Philebus, and Protarchos had been arguing about the claims of pleasure as set against those of intelligence, but, as the Platonic dialogue opens, Philebus is ready to cede his argument to Protarchos.[9] The very silence of Cratylus and Philebus is disquieting to Plato's reader. We know only that both entertain strongly held views, but Cratylus has nothing to say for half the *Cratylus*, and Philebus hardly enters the dialogue to defend his view on the superiority of pleasure, intellectual and sensual. Their silence is in some sense a provocation: it does not betoken assent given by their partners.

There are also the dialogues of three main speaking parts, or the "trilogic" dialogues: the *Theaetetus* is an example of this form, as is the *Phaedo*, which, despite its large cast of characters (reviewed in I § 3, "Portrait Frames"), is an argument conducted by three speakers: Socrates, Simmias, and Kebes. The trilogic form is perfected in the two longest dialogues of the Platonic corpus, the *Republic* and the *Laws*, where the protagonists (Socrates and the Athenian Stranger) control the conversation and calibrate the level of discussion to two others who rank as deuteragonist and tritagonist. Thus, we have the parallel distribution of roles. After book 1 of the *Republic*, with Socrates' three successive conversations with Kephalos, Polemarchos, and Thrasymachos, the pattern becomes clear. Glaukon is the more intrepid of Plato's two brothers and more versed in philosophical conversations. In conducting the long conversation of nine books, Socrates adjusts his topics to the capacities and interests of the two brothers. Adeimantos is so agreeable that the implications of Socrates' modest proposal of a community of women and children completely slips by him.[10] And, as Socrates ascends to metaphysical heights in book 6, it is clear that Glaukon cannot follow him. When Socrates describes the Idea of the Good as "beyond being in seniority and power," Glaukon responds, tongue in cheek: "Apollo! This is more than human hyperbole!"[11] The trilogic pattern of the *Laws* confirms the pattern established in the *Republic*: the Athenian Stranger stands to Socrates as the Cretan Kleinias stands to Glaukon as the Spartan Megillos stands to Adeimantos.[12]

8. *Cratylus* 383A–384A. Cratylus returns to the conversation at 427E and has the last word.
9. *Philebus* 11B–C.
10. Socrates makes the proposal in passing in *Republic* 4.423E–424A, and Adeimantos responds: "This would be absolutely the right course." Difficulties are registered only in *Republic* 5.449A–B, when Polemarchos pulls on Adeimantos' sleeve and asks him: "Shall we let him get away with this?"
11. *Republic* 6.509C.
12. I give a further analysis of the three roles in III §8 ("Magnesia").

Aristotle reports that the contributions of Sophocles to the evolution of Attic tragedy were "three [actors] and scene painting."[13] It might be said of Plato that his contributions to philosophical literature can be described in similar terms. As we have seen (II § 1, "Dialogue"), some earlier Greek philosophers were "dilogic" in that the philosopher chose an addressee: Parmenides' goddess (*daimōn*) speaks to the narrator, who (in the proem to his *On Nature*) identifies himself as a "young man"; Empedocles addresses a young man by the name of Pausanias in his *On Nature*. But most pre-Socratic philosophy is a dramatic soliloquy. The Socratics added a second speaking part to Greek philosophical literature, and the dialogues of Xenophon's *Memorabilia* sometimes involve a third speaker, although the "dilogic" pattern is the rule. Plato's contributions to the dialogue form might thus be described in Aristotelian terms: "three and scene painting." Plato added the third interlocutor—and of a cast of speaking parts that went beyond the "three-actor rule" of tragedy— and the historical backdrop he painted for some of his Socratic dialogues.

Polyphony

Some of Plato's dialogues are polyphonic: they involve more than three speakers and three points of view. We have already considered the "dialogue" established among the seven speeches given in the *Symposium* (see I § 7, "Socrates Eros"). The *Protagoras* affords an example of how Plato handles a dialogue with more than three speaking parts and invites the reader to consider the significance of the scene he elaborates for the dialogue. The *Protagoras* is the most dramatic of all the dialogues in its cast of characters and in its combination of speaking and nonspeaking parts. It gives us a vivid illustration of the philosophical motivation behind Plato's choice of actors for a dialogue. In the *Protagoras*, we first encounter a kind of frame dialogue in which Socrates speaks to an unnamed companion in Athens; we then hear Socrates' dramatic account of his conversation with a friend named Hippokrates; and in the innermost dialogue the first voice we hear is that of the eunuch who is the doorkeeper to Kallias' house. He responds to the newcomers with great irritation: "What, more professors from out of town!"[14] Then, in the morning light, Socrates glimpses the infernal figures of Hippias of Elis and Prodikos of Keos. He introduces these great dim figures in the language Odysseus used in de-

13. *Poetics* 4.1449ª18.
14. *Protagoras* 314D.

scribing the shades of the dead he encountered in Hades: "And then I made out Hippias of Elis. . . . and then I beheld Prodikos of Keos."[15]

As he enters the colonnaded courtyard of Kallias' house, Socrates sees Protagoras himself leading a swaying chorus of admirers, who hang on his every word and turn on his every turn. Seated on an armchair is the figure of Hippias; he is treating the admiring crowd he has attracted to an early-morning lecture on science. And Socrates discovers the sophist Prodikos in the bursar's building, which Kallias had converted for the use of his guests—a brilliant touch for lodging and characterizing a sophist who had come to Athens to teach young men for pay.[16] It must be cold, for Prodikos is wrapped up in wool coverlets, and all Socrates can hear of his speech is the booming echo of his voice.[17] Prodikos, Hippias, and Protagoras are staying at one of Athens' best addresses. Kallias, their host, was the generous father who paid Evenos of Paros the sum of three minas for his son's education.[18] Present but silent in the house of Kallias are Pericles' sons, Paralos and Xanthippos, and others, some of whom are familiar from other Platonic dialogues: Charmides, Philippides, Antimoiros, Eryximachos, Phaedrus, Andron, Pausanias, Adeimantos, Agathon, and Critias. Socrates and Protagoras speak at length; Alcibiades, Hippias, Critias, Kallias, and Prodikos, only briefly.

Many of these names are meaningless to a modern reader, but many are familiar to the reader of the *Symposium* (Phaedrus, Pausanias, Eryximachos, Agathon, and Alcibiades). Even though none of the background figures utters a word in the *Protagoras*, the significance of this crowd assembled at daybreak in the great house of Kallias is evident. These are the young Athenians of wealthy and powerful families, who were attracted to the sophists and particularly to Protagoras because they hoped to learn to speak in the political and judicial assemblies of Athens. This was the ambition of Hippokrates, Socrates' young friend we meet at the beginning of the dialogue.[19]

What makes the *Protagoras* a political dialogue is that it involves would-be politicians such as these in the question whether virtue can be taught and whether there is a unity of the virtues. Protagoras promises to teach the virtue of controlling Athenian political assemblies, but he cannot guarantee his pupils or Socrates the understanding that unites the virtues. The presence of

15. *Protagoras* 315B–E. The allusion is to *Odyssey* 11.572 (Orion) and 582 (Tantalos).
16. *Apology* 19E.
17. *Protagoras* 314E–316A.
18. *Apology* 20A–B.
19. *Protagoras* 311A–314C.

even the silent actors in this dialogue reveals the immense power exercised by these foreign professors and their attraction to Athenian aristocrats with political ambitions. No one except Protagoras is concerned with the promising young Athenian sophist Socrates, for whom he holds out a promising career.[20] Nonspeaking roles were permitted on the Attic stage. These silent characters were called "mute masks" (κωφὰ πρόσωπα). In the *Protagoras* the silent presence of these characters is eloquent, for they constitute the political audience that attracted the sophists to Athens.

Both the silent and the speaking parts introduced at the beginning of the *Republic* are eloquent as well, for they too define the audience of "first intent" envisaged in the dialogue. But, unlike the silent characters of the *Protagoras,* Kephalos and his family are not Athenians but resident aliens (*metoikoi*) attracted to Athens by Pericles. The sophist Thrasymachos of Chalkedon is, like Protagoras of Abdera, a visitor. Socrates speaks as narrator throughout, and in sequence we hear the voices of Polemarchos' slave, Glaukon, Polemarchos, Socrates (now as a character), Adeimantos, Kephalos, Thrasymachos, and Clitophon. Each (except the slave) holds a distinct point of view. Silent is the son of the Athenian general Nikias, Nikeratos, and a character known from the *Phaedo* as a companion of Socrates, Charmantides. Silent too are the other sons of Kephalos, the brilliant orator Lysias, and Euthydemos.

The silent presence of Nikeratos serves as a reminder of his father, Nikias, who commanded the Sicilian expedition and was killed on the outskirts of Syracuse at its terrible end. The presence of the two sons of Kephalos reminds the reader of the end of his family's prosperity and the judicial murder of the heir to Kephalos' argument and estate, Polemarchos, who was put to death by the Thirty to gain his property. In his *Against Eratosthenes,* Lysias gives us the narrative of this crime. The setting of this dialogue is the house of Kephalos in the Peiraeus, the port for the fleet that enforced control of Athens' empire; the occasion, the festival of the Thracian goddess Bendis, whose cult had been introduced to the Peiraeus for the first time. The Thracians, much involved with Athenian campaigns to the north, conduct the festival and introduce a note of barbarism to the already barbaric Peiraeus. This is not an implausible setting for a discussion of the nature of justice. Contemporary Athens stands in stark contrast with the ideal city Socrates will describe in words.

In the *Republic,* the problem of understanding the nature of justice is not

---

20. *Protagoras* 361D–E.

posed in a naked question arising from no recognizable context and addressed to no one in particular. "In this introductory chapter I sketch some of the main ideas of the theory of justice I wish to develop."[21] This introductory sentence of the philosopher John Rawls is an example of another and now more familiar kind of philosophical rhetoric. In the *Republic*, the problem of the *Republic* emerges almost unobserved from a question Socrates puts to an old friend in the intimacy of his friend's house. Kephalos is an old man, and he has begun to worry about the afterlife. He wants to have paid his debts to men and gods. His worries prompt Socrates to ask: "Now, at bottom, does justice consist simply in this: returning what you have taken from another?"[22] The entire fabric of Socrates' ideal city is built upon a considered response to this question, and Socrates tacitly returns to Kephalos' fears of the afterlife in the myth of Er at the conclusion of this long conversation. The *Republic* demonstrates not only the three-actor rule in a Platonic dialogue, or the polyphony we occasionally find in some of the dialogues; it illustrates what I have already called the *ad animam* character of the Platonic dialogues, that is, their way of addressing the soul of the interlocutor and conforming to his *ēthos*. Throughout the dialogue, Socrates' conversation is adjusted to and characterizes his interlocutors: Kephalos, Polemarchos, Thrasymachos, Adeimantos, and Glaukon. It is the best example of what Greek theorists of oratory termed *ēthopoiia* (ἠθοποιία): the creation of a character of a speaker and his audience.

What, then, is the significance of a name as a title of a Platonic dialogue, and what is the meaning of its *dramatis personae?* This question returns us to the *ad hominem* character of Platonic philosophy. All Platonic dialogues are *ad hominem*, but not in the current sense of the term. They do not reveal an embarrassing gap between what a person says and what he does. In debate we are trained not to attack an opponent's character or motivation. An *ad hominem* argument does not argue against a position but against the person who defends the position. "Jean-Jacques Rousseau, you profess a great interest in education, but you send your own natural children to foundling homes" is an example of the *ad hominem* argument. It is clear that Platonic philosophy is not *ad hominem* in this sense. In the *Theaetetus*, Socrates claims that he can address only the position of his interlocutor, but not the interlocutor himself.[23] Yet Plato is careful to delineate Theaetetus as a character and even calls

---

21. Rawls 1971, 3.
22. *Republic* 1.331C.
23. *Theaetetus* 161B.

attention to the way he looks. Theaetetus looks like Socrates; he has a becoming modesty; he is sharp, especially when it comes to mathematics; but
he has not yet begun to investigate the world of his own mind. And, as we
know from the frame dialogue, in the end he turns out to be a brave citizen
of Athens.[24]

But at the moment of his meeting with Socrates he is yet a young man.
Young men play a significant role in the Socratic dialogues. One of their
virtues is that they force Socrates to adjust his argument to a level they can
understand. Consequently, the dialogue begins on the level of safe commonplace ground. Theaetetus first defines knowledge as perception. In drawing
out the many difficulties with this intuitive and commonly held view, Socrates attributes the young Theaetetus' view not only to Protagoras, for whom
"man is the measure of all things,"[25] but to Heraclitus, for whom all things are
in flux.[26] By "man" (ἄνθρωπος) Socrates takes Protagoras to mean not mankind (as distinct from the gods) but each individual human being, an interpretation that leads to a deep relativism of judgment and value. In expounding a
theory of the world as flux, Socrates speaks to "my boy" in such portentious
and abstract terms (active as against passive motion and the infinite number
of "twin births" produced by the interaction of active and passive motions)
that Theaetetus confesses that he doesn't have the slightest idea what Socrates is talking about or how it applies to his view that knowledge is perception.
Socrates is then forced to return to common ground and produce an example
of what he has in mind; the example he chooses is the eye's perception of the
color white.[27] Here, as often in the "dilogic" dialogues between Socrates and
a young man, Plato provides two statements of an argument: one abstract,
the other concrete. The reader of the *Philebus* will recognize the same tactic
at work as Socrates, in his last appearance in the Platonic dialogues, adjusts
his account of the limited and unlimited—a story he claims has been passed
down to him by "men of long ago"—to the understanding of the young
Protarchos by means of an illustration drawn from the alphabet.[28] If Plato's
conversations are *ad hominem* in the sense we have described, they are also *ad
lectorem*: they adjusted to the range of their potential readers and, one should
add, readers who are forced to return to a dialogue after first reading.

24. *Theaetetus* 142B; see I §3 ("Portrait Frames").
25. DK 80 B 1 (which includes *Theaetetus* 151E–152A).
26. DK 22 B 12 (and *Cratylus* 402A = KRS 214 and 215 = L and CXIIIB Kahn).
27. *Theaetetus* 156A–157C.
28. *Philebus* 16B–18D; also *Sophist* 263E.

The conversations among the great variety of characters who speak (or are silent) in the Platonic dialogues constitute one form of dialogue—the inner dialogue. This inner dialogue is also the beginning of what can be termed the outer dialogue of the Platonic dialogues. This is between the reader and the dialogue itself. There is another form of inner dialogue envisaged in one Platonic dialogue, the silent dialogue of the soul with itself. It might serve to describe the silent dialogue within the readers of this silent philosopher. In the *Theaetetus*, Socrates presents Theaetetus with the following description of thought:

> It is a conversation (*logos*) the soul pursues by itself concerning any matter for thought. Even though I do not know the truth, I will reveal my thought to you. As the soul thinks in this way, it presents the picture of doing nothing other than conversing, as it asks itself questions and gives answers, and asserts or denies. And, when it has reached some definite conclusion, it springs to it either after some delay or quickly. It then agrees to this conclusion and no longer hesitates. We think of this as the soul's judgment. For this reason I call forming an opinion a "spoken discourse"—not indeed one addressed to another individual or spoken aloud, but one a person voices silently to himself.[29]

This silent and solitary conversation (*logos*) seems far removed from what happens in a Platonic dialogue. But it describes what can be called Plato's outer dialogue. This dialogue is addressed to the soul of Plato's reader. It is a dialogue in which the reader questions the claims made within a dialogue and seeks to understand the structure of the dialogue. Plato prepares us for this outer dialogue in the intimate conversation between Socrates and Phaedrus in the *Phaedrus*. The initial conversation of the *Phaedrus* focuses on a speech written by Lysias and addressed to a young man who never responds to the appeal of a lover who professes to be a nonlover. One of the failures of Lysias' speech is that it contains no characterization either for the young man Lysias is addressing or for himself. His speech lacks *ēthos*. We have seen how Socrates' first speech is capable of developing on interrogation later in the dialogue (see II § 3, "Platonic Writing"). Lysias' speech stands pallid in the shadow cast by the brilliant speech Plato has composed for an erotic Socrates and a young man passionately fond of speeches. There is a powerful erotic bond between Socrates and Phaedrus that is conspicuously absent from

29. *Theaetetus* 189E–190A. Plato returns to a representation of the work of the solitary soul in *Philebus* 38A–39D. Here the soul's inner dialogue is confirmed by conversation with another.

Lysias' anonymous speaker and addressee; this attachment creates in turn a bond between the dialogue and its reader.

When Socrates comes to define the proper art of composing a written speech or a speech meant for dramatic delivery, he reminds us of one deficiency of Lysias' speech.

> Since the power of speech is nothing other than a leading of the soul, the person who intends to be an orator must know how many forms the soul possesses. So, then, there exists this number and these kinds, and because of these some men are of this character and others of that character.[30]

For a variegated soul, a corresponding kind of speech is necessary, as the variegated speech of the *Phaedrus* itself illustrates. For a simple and uniform soul, a uniform mode of speech is necessary.[31] In this prescription of a philosopher who never put his speech in writing, we discover a Platonic signature and a hint of Plato's own conception of his art as a writer. The Platonic dialogue is a written form of speaking that leads the soul. It is a ψυχαγωγία. Plato attempted to reach a various and unknown readership by creating a variety of distinct characters in his dialogues. Most of these characters were known contemporaries of Socrates. It is through these that Plato reaches us, his readers.

The Neoplatonists (as represented by Proclus in his first lecture on the *Republic*) were wiser in one respect than many modern philosophers. They regarded the characters of a dialogue, along with its setting and occasion, as part of the "material" (*hylē*) out of which Plato constructed the dialogue.[32] In his commentary on Socrates' "Great Speech" in the *First Alcibiades* 105A, the Neoplatonist Olympiodorus remarks that, like every proper literary composition, the Platonic dialogues are living, organic wholes. In the plenitude of the characters represented, they imitated that most perfect living organism, the universe.[33] This claim is hyperbolic. We do not find shoemakers in the Platonic dialogues. Plato's characters are young aristocrats, older sophists, and a few philosophers. Many of the *dramatis personae* of the Platonic dialogues re-

---

30. *Phaedrus* 271C–D. Aristotle develops Plato's lead and includes the creation of a character for a speaker as one of the three means to artful persuasion. These are argument (*logos*), character (*ēthos*), and feeling (*pathos*); *Rhetoric* 1.2.3–6 and 2.1.1–4.

31. *Phaedrus* 277B–C.

32. Proclus, *In Platonis Rem Publicam Commentarii*, I.6.7–12 and 16.26–19.25 Kroll (where the rest of the discussion is lost).

33. Olympiodorus, *In Platonis Alcibiadem* 56.14–18 Westerink.

veal the profoundly political character and intent of the dialogues, for they appeal to an audience that is political. But such is the force of Socrates' very unaristocratic personality that one of them (the *Gorgias*) was said to have attracted a farmer from his fields in Corinth to Athens, and another (the *Republic*, naturally) was said to have attracted Axiothea from Phlius to the Academy. This, at least, is the story we find in one of the philosophical speeches of the late-antique orator Themistius. The story was plausible in the fourth century A.D., and the contemporary experience of readers makes it plausible today.[34]

ENDNOTE: Although enormous pains have been expended in determining the syntax, or original sequence, of the Platonic dialogues, there is still no study of their characters and *ēthopoïïa;* nor is there a full study of their formal characteristics. Ruby Blondell's study of character and argument in the Platonic dialogues (to be published by Cambridge University Press) will soon make up for the lack of attention to Plato as the creator of character (*ēthopoiios*). George Grote's *Plato and the Other Companions of Sokrates* (1867) has served as the fullest comprehensive treatment of the characters to be found in the dialogues, but the author does not attend to characterization within the dialogues. The question of character is taken up in the essays included in C.B.R. Pelling, *Characterization and Individuality in Greek Literature* (1990). Mary Witlock Blundell, in "Character and Meaning in Plato's *Hippias Minor*" (1992), provides a promising sample of what attention to characterization within the dialogues can yield. Charles Kahn gives an inspiring example of the relation between character and argument in "Drama and Dialectic in Plato's *Gorgias*" (1983).

---

34. Anecdotes 134 and 135 in *Platonica* (pp. 183–84). Themistius also claims that the *Apology* brought Zeno of Citium to Athens to study not with Plato but Xenokrates and Polemon, his successors, Anecdote 136 in *Platonica* (p. 185).

At the end of a dialogue, characters simply cease speaking. No comic or tragic chorus announces the conclusion of the play. No god appears "from the machine" to wrap things up. In the Socratic dialogues, it is usually Socrates who has the last word. For Plato's reader engaged in the outer dialogue in which he or she questions the meaning of the dialogue just read, one of the peculiarities and frustrations of the dialogues as philosophical writings is that they resist coming to conclusions. In this they are true to the life of most conversations and arguments.

The issue of many of the conversations of the early dialogues is postponed to the next day or for another occasion. Such is the case of the *Euthyphro*, which ends but does not conclude. The nature of piety and the outcome of the trials awaiting Euthyphro and Socrates are left in awkward suspense: "We must postpone this discussion, Socrates. I have another appointment, and I have got to go."[1] The conversations of two programmatic groupings of dialogues seem to promise a sequence of topics but end without completing the program envisaged: these are the conversations of the *Theaetetus*, *Sophist*, and *Statesman*, which do not conclude with the treatment of the philosopher that seems promised,[2] and *Republic*, *Timaeus*, and *Critias*, which ends with a sentence fragment[3] and without the contribution the Sicilian general Hermokrates was scheduled to make to conclude the program of two days of discourse. Last, three dialogues end with a myth of judgment, the *Gorgias*, *Phaedo*, and *Republic*. These myths are not conclusions, since they disorient the reader by opening a startling perspective on human existence.

1. *Euthyphro* 15E.
2. In, e.g., *Sophist* 217A.
3. At, e.g., *Critias* 121C.

Aporia

The *Euthyphro, Lysis, Charmides, Laches, Theaetetus,* and book 1 of the *Republic* all end with a question posed by Socrates but left unresolved. The questions around which four of these dialogues turn are central to Greek values, for in them Plato considers the virtues of piety, self-restraint, courage, and justice and—by implication—the vices and grounds for censure opposed to these virtues. The *Euthyphro* raises the issue of piety; the *Charmides,* self-restraint; the *Laches,* courage; and book 1 of the *Republic,* justice. Only the considerable virtue of intelligence (*phronēsis*) is not included in the overt program of these dialogues. The question of how the virtues relate to one another and whether they can be regarded as a unity is the unresolved question of the *Protagoras,* which begins, like the *Meno,* with the question prompted by sophistic teaching: Can virtue really be taught? At the end of the *Protagoras,* Protagoras praises Socrates for his eager pursuit of wisdom, but excuses himself from further argument by saying, "[N]ow I have to turn to another matter."[4] Such endings to philosophical conversations recall the opening of Bacon's essay "On Truth": "*What is truth,* said jesting Pilate; and would not stay for an answer."

These early Socratic dialogues are usually termed the "aporetic" dialogues. (Because of its similarity to the dialogues of this group, book 1 of the *Republic* is viewed by a few scholars as originally an aporetic dialogue on justice. The name attached to this is the *Thrasymachos.*) The term "aporetic" is, naturally, Greek. Ἀπορία (*aporia*) means that no passage (*poros*) has been discovered to the solution of a problem. The fact that a fuller discussion of the problems raised by these dialogues is postponed to another occasion or that Socrates concludes by confessing his own ignorance does not mean that there are not answers to these questions or that Plato himself did not hold firm and reasoned opinions about them. It only means that Plato's manner of philosophizing was "maieutic," or that of a midwife.

Socrates' description of himself in the *Theaetetus* as the son of a midwife and as a male midwife to men gives us the term for this kind of philosophy, which Socrates calls the *maieutikē technē,* or the art of the midwife.[5] In the impasse reached at its end, the *Theaetetus* looks like an aporetic dialogue of Plato's early period; but perhaps it should be described as a long overdue search for the virtue of intelligence. In the *Theaetetus,* Socrates examines three possible definitions of knowledge, but concludes without confirming any of

---

4. *Protagoras* 361E.
5. *Theaetetus* 161E and 210B.

them. He asks if, at the end of the search, he and his companion are still pregnant and in labor or if they have finally delivered.[6] Early in the dialogue, Socrates had described Theaetetus as being pregnant and in labor and asks if the young Athenian is unaware that he, Socrates, is the son of a brave and strapping midwife by the name of Phainarete (she who makes virtue appear). Socrates practices his mother's occupation, but on men. He reduces them to perplexity (his term connects with *aporia*). This mental state is the equivalent of labor pangs in women: "These pangs my art can awake and bring to an end."[7] The "pangs" are perplexity. There can be no such mental pangs unless the person with whom Socrates chooses to associate has at least a conception of the truth, whether this truth is that knowledge is a perception or a right opinion or a right opinion justified by an argument. The promise of a meeting on the next day is kept in the *Sophist*, but such a promise is also an invitation to the reader to read the dialogue retrospectively and to investigate the problems raised but not solved in the dialogue. Even at the end of the *Statesman* no clear answer to the question What is knowledge? emerges.

Two "Tetralogies"

Theaetetus, Sophist, Statesman, [Philosopher]

The reconsideration of the *Theaetetus* profits from consideration of other Platonic dialogues. As we have seen, the *Theaetetus* ends with the promise that Theaetetus, Theodoros, and Socrates will meet in the same place "tomorrow." Nothing is settled, but three conceptions of knowledge have been set out and their difficulties examined. Nothing has been said about Ideas (*eidē*) as objects of knowledge. This might have offered the possibility of understanding what knowledge is. The *Theaetetus* happens to be the only aporetic dialogue that has a sequel in a renewed conversation on the next day. But the next day seems to belong to a different calendar and another year. The next day introduces a group of connected dialogues to follow the *Theaetetus*: the *Sophist*, the *Statesman*, and the unwritten *Philosopher*.

Things have changed since Socrates left for the King's Stoa to answer to the indictment Meletos had deposed against him.[8] For one, the frame dialogue of the *Theaetetus* in Megara seems to have been forgotten. In the *Sophist*, Theodoros and Theaetetus arrive at the appointed time with a visitor to Ath-

6. *Theaetetus* 210B.
7. *Theaetetus* 150A–151A.
8. *Theaetetus* 210D.

ens from Italy and a silent young man by the name of Socrates, who says nothing during the entire conversation of the *Sophist*. The subject of this new conversation has shifted from the problem of knowledge to the question of how the sophist is to be distinguished from the statesman and the philosopher, clearly a particular version of the general problem of knowledge. In the *Sophist*, as we have seen (II § 2, "Socratic Irony"), the Eleatic Stranger produces an elaborate definition of the sophist, but the *Sophist* is radically unlike the earlier aporetic dialogues in that the definition worked out by the Eleatic Stranger seems to settle the matter once and for all. Socrates, who had conducted the questioning of the aporetic *Theaetetus*, barely says a word, and he is virtually silent throughout the conversation of the *Statesman*, where the young Socrates relieves Theaetetus in a conversation to which he contributes little more than assent. In the *Statesman*, the dialectical Eleatic Stranger defines the statesman by locating him in an elaborate taxonomy of types of rule. It concludes with the young Socrates declaring: "Stranger, you have now very elegantly completed the description of the kingly man for us and the statesman."[9]

The matter seems settled. The fourth dialogue of this philosophic "tetralogy," the *Philosopher*—if we can supply this title—was never written, and it is likely that Plato never intended to write it. It remains possible, as we have seen,[10] that the definition of the philosopher might well be inscribed in the descriptions of the sophist and the statesman. We are alerted to this possibility by Socrates' statement that sometimes philosophers appear as sophists and sometimes as statesmen.[11] The elliptical character of this first "tetralogy" of three connected and one promised dialogue reminds us as readers how difficult it is to arrive at "closure" in reading even dialogues that are as dogmatic as the *Sophist* and *Statesman*. Plato never wrote a Philosopher to conclude the "tetralogy."

Republic, Timaeus, Critias, [Hermokrates]

Sir Karl Popper's sustained attack on Plato's political philosophy, in the first volume of his *Open Society and Its Enemies*, illustrates one reader's response to the appearance of closure in the Platonic dialogues and in the *Republic* in

---

9. *Statesman* 311C. Some editors attribute these concluding remarks to the older Socrates. But his silence would be an indication that the conversation is not yet at its end.

10. In II §2 ("Socratic Irony").

11. *Sophist* 216C–D.

particular.[12] Plato was the first of the enemies of Popper's open society, but Popper ignored the open character of the Platonic dialogue that leaves its reader with problems rather than solutions, unfinished conversations rather than full philosophical treatises, and the stimulus of frustration rather than the comfortable assurance of positive—if objectionable—doctrine. This description holds for the two dialogues Popper relied on to write his account of Plato the "totalitarian"—the *Republic* and *Laws* (whose open ending we will return to in III § 8, "Magnesia"). Despite the closed society of its guardian class, the *Republic* cannot be read as a closed dialogue. The assent that marks the conclusion of books 2 through 9 does not close the open and outer dialogue between Plato and his reader. The first book of the *Republic* ends in an impasse, as do the aporetic dialogues concerned with the virtues. It is a grudging ending with no promise of a renewed conversation "on another occasion." The visiting sophist, Thrasymachos of Chalkedon, has not carried his view that justice is the interest of the stronger, and Socrates confesses that "the result of our conversation is that I know nothing."[13] The first book of the *Republic* merely closes on an episode of *aporia*. It is not in fact aporetic, for Glaukon's challenge, which opens the renewed conversation of book 2, leads to a definition of justice as performing the job for which a citizen is naturally suited.[14] The creation of an ideal state seems complete at the end of book 4, but, unexpectedly, Socrates is forced by the challenge of Polemarchos and Adeimantos to reveal the three "waves of paradox" that occupy books 5 through 7. (We will examine his proposals for a community of wives and children in the guardian class, the equality of the men and women belonging to this class, and his proposal of a philosopher king when we turn to consider the *Republic* as a whole in III § 6, "Kallipolis"). After Socrates' description of states inferior to his proposed state (in books 8 and 9), and the final myth of Er, the *Republic* seems to conclude as decisively as any literary work with a requisite beginning, middle, and end can: "And so, Glaukon, the tale [*mythos*] has been saved and not lost, and it could just save us, if we are persuaded by it."[15] When he adds that "we shall always keep to the upper road," Socrates reminds us that he had begun his narrative of the conversation held in the house of Kephalos the day before with the words: "Yesterday, I

---

12. Popper 1971, *The Spell of Plato*.
13. *Republic* 1.354B.
14. *Republic* 4.433A.
15. *Republic* 10.621D.

descended to the Peiraeus in the company of Glaukon, Ariston's son."[16] This is a classic example of closure by ring composition, by which the end of a narrative links up with its beginning.

But the *Republic*, it appears, is not closed or sufficient unto itself: it comes to be seen as part of the second programmatic grouping of the Platonic corpus: *Republic*, *Timaeus*, *Critias*, [*Hermokrates*]. The grandiose project announced at the opening of the *Timaeus*[17] is as frustrating to the reader's expectations of closure and completeness as the sentence that might have concluded Heraclitus' book: "The fairest arrangement is a heap of random sweepings."[18] The opening of the *Timaeus* forces us to reopen a dialogue that had seemed closed. In Socrates' summary of the topics he had discussed "the day before," the *Republic* or a discourse like that of the *Republic* comes to be seen as Socrates' contribution to a group of four speeches.[19]

There is something missing from the beginning of the *Timaeus*: "One, two, three, but where, my dear Timaeus, is the fourth of yesterday's guests?"[20] This guest was to speak on the next day, but for some reason he could not keep his appointment. Socrates rehearses for Timaeus of Locri a conversation of the day before, when he described to his four guests what he considered the best form of human society. The long speech he gave during the festival of the Panathenaia cannot strictly refer back to the conversation of the *Republic*, which had another cast of characters and was held in Kephalos' house during the new festival of Bendis. But in the *Timaeus*, Plato forges a link with the *Republic* by recalling the main proposals for Socrates' ideal city, with the striking exception of the proposal that philosophers should become kings.[21] Socrates' compares the city he had founded in words to a good-looking animal that stands motionless; he would like to see it in motion and engaged in a contest that would test its mettle.[22] The stationary and fair world of his fair city, Kallipolis, is set in motion as Timaeus describes the creation of a unique universe by a Demiurge, or Master Craftsman. Timaeus' account of *genesis* involves an elaborate account of *kinēsis* (motion); it is motion that makes time and history possible. Critias (the leader of the Thirty) is to follow Timaeus

16. *Republic* 1.327A.
17. *Timaeus* 20A.
18. DK 22 B 124. This is the last fragment in the new ordering of the fragments by Charles H. Kahn in *The Art and Thought of Heraclitus* (1979) (his frag. **CXXV**, p. 287).
19. *Timaeus* 17A–19B.
20. *Timaeus* 17A.
21. *Timaeus* 17C–19B.
22. *Timaeus* 19B–C.

with a speech that would show how Socrates' guardians once lived as a military caste on the acropolis of antediluvian Athens, defended Greece and Europe against an armada from the island of Atlantis, and was overtaken by a catastrophe that overwhelmed the civilizations of both prehistoric Atlantis and Athens. In creating the philosophical fiction of Atlantis in the *Timaeus/ Critias*, "Plato let a djin out of the bottle."[23] And he diverted attention away from the plan of the *Timaeus/Critias* (a single dialogue) to the discovery of the "lost continent" of Atlantis. Critias' speech giving the history of the struggle between Atlantis and Athens breaks of in a sentence fragment. Perhaps it could never have been complete. The document on which it drew for its history depended on Critias' ancestor Solon, who learned of the war of the two prehistoric worlds from an Egyptian priest of the temple of Neith (Egyptian Athena) in Sais. Because of the political turmoil he encountered on his return to Athens, he could not complete his epic of Atlantis.[24] Critias' speech was to be followed by a final contribution to this day of speeches in honor of the goddess Athena by Hermokrates of Syracuse. Hermokrates, however, who speaks only twice in the *Timaeus/Critias*, remains silent.

This last "tetralogic" program in the Platonic dialogues revokes the closure of the *Republic*, even as it sets it in a new temporal sequence, which begins with the creation of the universe and ends implicitly with the Sicilian expedition and the thought of what Hermokrates might have said in honor of Athena and in praise of Athens during the Panathenaia, the quadrennial festival that glorified Athens. This war Thucydides had described as the greatest commotion (*kinēsis*) in Greece and in much of the barbarian world.[25] Hermokrates of Syracuse (as we know from two eloquent speeches in book 6 of Thucydides' history of the war) was the most eloquent and determined opponent of the Athenian imperialism westward and the Athenian expedition to Sicily in the summer of 415. He does not fulfill his promise to deliver a speech after Critias, but, if we read his speeches in Thucydides, we realize what his silent presence means.[26] It is an indictment of imperial Athens on the occasion of the Panathenaia. The speech of Critias, who had confiscated the property of Polemarchos and who died in the civil war of 403, breaks off

---

23. As Harold Cherniss (1947, 252) put it in his review of Ernst Gegenschatz, *Platons Atlantis* (Zurich, 1943).

24. *Timaeus* 23A.

25. *The Peloponnesian War* 1.1.2.

26. He speaks briefly first in *Timaeus* 20C and then in *Critias* 108B–C recognizes his obligation to give a speech; the speeches he did give can be read in Thucydides, *The Peloponnesian War* 6.32.3–34 (his first speech in Syracuse) and 75.3–80 (his speech to the allies in Kamerina).

in midsentence as he is describing Zeus calling a council of the gods to determine how to punish the kings of Atlantis for their fall from divinity and for their material concerns: "He gathered all of the gods together in their most honored dwelling, which, since it stands at the middle of the entire universe, looks down upon all that has a share in becoming. And, when he had gathered them, he said . . ."[27]

Transcendental Meditations

Not every dialogue is as open to the reader's perplexity as the "tetralogy" that has just come under review. Other dialogues seem to observe the reader's expectation of closure. The *Apology* ends with the conclusion of Socrates' speech in his own defense. The *Phaedo* ends with the coming of evening, Socrates' last words to Crito, and Socrates' death, observing the unities of time and place of an Aristotelian tragedy.[28] But it is interesting that both of these conclusive dialogues should end with a myth. As he turns to those of his jurors who have voted to acquit him, Socrates says: "Nothing prevents us from telling stories while this is permitted."[29] He then contemplates his future. If death is, as people say, a journey to another country, he could discover true judges there—Minos, Rhadamanthys, Aiakos, Triptolemos, and the two epic heroes who, like himself, were put to death by an unjust verdict. (The passage is discussed in I § 5, "The Philosopher in Court.") The *Apology* gives us an early hint of the eschatological endings of three major Platonic dialogues: the *Gorgias*, *Phaedo*, and *Republic*. These dialogues all conclude with Socratic myths of judgment. These transcendental meditations are final in that they close a dialogue and contemplate last things, but, in a fundamental way, their project remains open.

In fact, there are a surprising number of myths (μῦθοι, *mythoi*) in the arguments (λόγοι, *logoi*) of the Platonic dialogues. Each of the three myths of judgment that concern us closes a dialogue, but their character is better seen when we first consider the myths placed in the body of other dialogues. Early on in the *Protagoras*, for example, Protagoras tells his Just-So Story of how the gods preserved human society by inculcating into the new human race a sense of justice and respect for others.[30] As an older man speaking to

27. *Critias* 121C.
28. *Phaedo* 116B and 118A. The canon of the unity of time and place has been extrapolated from *Poetics* 5.1449[b]9–16.
29. *Apology* 39E.
30. *Protagoras* 320C–323A.

younger men, Protagoras chooses to show that virtue can be taught by resort-ing to a story (*mythos*) rather than an argument (*logos*). His long unbroken myth is a prelude to the long argument of the *Protagoras,* which has Socrates questioning and Protagoras responding. Still other examples of myths told within a dialogue come quickly to mind. The *Symposium* has Aristophanes' Just-So Story explaining how we human beings have become severed from our original other halves,[31] and Diotima tells the young Socrates the story of how Eros was born of Poros and Penia.[32] The *Phaedrus* has two myths. The first is Socrates' arresting image of the soul as a winged two-horse chariot controlled by a human driver, which Socrates terms a shorter and human depiction of the nature of the soul rather than one that must be lengthy and divine.[33] Toward the end of the dialogue, Socrates tells Phaedrus the caution-ary tale of how Theuth presented his invention of writing to Thamous, the king of upper Egypt, and was repudiated.[34] In the *Statesman,* the Eleatic Stranger tells the young Socrates the myth of alternating cosmic cycles that has its origins in a tradition associated with the house of Atreus.[35] The philo-sophical myth of Atlantis occupies the beginning of the *Timaeus* and the *Critias* up to its abrupt end.

In the *Gorgias, Phaedo,* and *Republic,* we find Socrates concluding long and difficult conversations about the choice of life, the immortality of the soul, and justice with a myth of judgment that discloses a prospect of the fate of the soul in the afterlife. Our short and partial list of the noneschatological myths in the Platonic dialogues attracts our attention to a distinctive feature of the dialogues that employ myth: the noneschatological myths are varied in their themes, but, taken together, they are significantly different from the myths of judgment that conclude the *Gorgias, Phaedo,* and *Republic,* and, in-deed, the *Apology.* The ends of these dialogues illustrate another way in which Plato left his dialogues open. The three myths of judgment are each the occasion for some justification. Socrates addresses these tales to a hostile and impatient Kallikles in the *Gorgias,*[36] the sympathetic Pythagorean, Simmias, in the *Phaedo,*[37] and the urbane Glaukon, who is provoked to quizzical amaze-

---

31. *Symposium* 189C–193D.
32. *Symposium* 203B–204C; see I §7 ("Socrates Eros").
33. *Phaedrus* 246A–256E.
34. *Phaedrus* 274C–275B; see II §3 ("Platonic Writing").
35. *Statesman* 268C–274E.
36. *Gorgias* 523A–527E.
37. *Phaedo* 107C–115A.

ment by Socrates' suggestion that the soul is immortal, in the *Republic*.[38] In each case, Socrates invokes an authority that is either anonymous or a mystery: He has heard the story he will tell from an anonymous informant, perhaps a Greek from Sicily or southern Italy;[39] he has heard about the topography of the "true" earth from someone who has convinced him of its truth;[40] or his tale goes back to Er, the son of Armenios, a Pamphylian.[41]

As he launches into his myth of Er, Socrates says that he will not be giving the "tale told Alkinoos"—by which he means Odysseus' narrative, in *Odyssey* 11, of his descent into the underworld—but the tale told by a brave man, Er. In the *Gorgias*, Socrates is emphatic that what he will tell Kallikles is a serious matter (*logos*), but he knows that Kallikles will regard it as "an old wives' tale."[42] The fact that one and the same account can be described as either *logos* or *mythos*, depending on one's point of view, alerts us to the shift in perspective effected by these Platonic myths. In the *Gorgias*, the shift is from here and now in the city of Athens to the there and then in the underworld. In the *Phaedo*, Socrates tells Simmias that what he has learned about the topography of the earth he owes to a nameless informant. This authority parts company from the natural philosophers whose theories of causation Socrates had just discussed. Simmias is unfamiliar with any such description of the earth, and we never hear from him again. Nor do we hear from Kallikles or Glaukon as Socrates' concludes the myths of judgment of the *Gorgias* and *Republic*. The dialogues concluded by these eschatological myths end in silence. The person they are addressed to does not respond.

These three transcendental meditations have this much in common: they move from a conversation here and now to a future one cannot know until death makes the claims of these myths of judgment true, false, or indifferent. Like the *Apology*, they close by opening a dim prospect of what lies beyond human experience. Socrates, as is his habit, takes credit for none of them. They are hearsay. They are also antagonistic in that they counter and transcend another version of reality: that of Kallikles and his polis-bound commitment to self-interest in the *Gorgias*, that of natural philosophy in the *Phaedo*, and that of Homer's *Nekuia* (or Book of the Dead) in the *Republic*. As such, these myths are correctional, and they extend the arena of the moral

38. *Republic* 10.614B–621D.
39. *Gorgias* 493A and 524A.
40. *Phaedo* 108C.
41. *Republic* 10.614B.
42. *Gorgias* 527A.

agōn[43] to a place and time when the soul, separated from the body, is judged for only its virtue or vice. Socrates speaks of the version of the afterlife he addresses to Simmias in the *Phaedo* as an incantation for the soul.[44] These terminal "incantations" recognize poetic versions of the afterlife and their hold on the Greek soul. They recognize the power of Homer's *Odyssey*, Hesiod's *Works and Days* and its "account" (*logos*) of the destiny of those who lived in the ages of gold, silver, bronze, and *hērōes*,[45] the *Purifications* of the Sicilian Empedocles; Pindar's *Olympian 2*, as well as the Orphic poetry now better known from the Derveni papyrus and other texts discovered in graves from northern Greece and southern Italy.

Plato's eschatology shares this in common with these visions of the afterlife: all are particular about topography. There are places reserved for those who have led pure or virtuous lives and will be rewarded, and places for criminals, who will be tormented. A gold tablet from Hipponion in southern Italy (modern Vibo Valentia) of about 400 B.C. gives hexameter instructions in Greek to a woman in whose grave it was discovered: Do not drink from the spring by the white cypress but from the Lake of Memory; follow the crowd of glorious bacchants and initiates on a holy road.[46] Some versions of the afterlife envisage a cycle of incarnations, and in the *Republic* (and in the central myth of the *Phaedrus*) Plato keeps them company. But it is only in Plato that we discover a truly transcendental perspective. Socrates' geography at the end of the *Phaedo* provokes a drastic dislocation and disorientation. What we take to be the air we breathe is, when viewed from the perspective of the "true earth," gross sea water. The bright sky above us is the surface of the sea. High above it is the "true heaven." And in this scheme of transcendental proportions the infernal hollows of the "true earth" correspond to the earth we live on.

> *Who knows if life is death,*
> *And death life?*

This is the tragic question[47] that Socrates puts to the earth and polis-bound Kallikles in the *Gorgias*.[48] It is, finally, the question Plato leaves open at the conclusion of three of his major dialogues.

43. *Phaedo* 114C.
44. *Phaedo* 114D.
45. *Works and Days* 106–73.
46. A partial text in KRS **29** (pp. 29–30).
47. From Euripides' *Phrixos*, *TGF*, frag. **833**.
48. In *Gorgias* 492E.

ENDNOTE: Just as there has been no full study of the frame dialogues among the Platonic dialogues, there has been no study of the conclusions of the dialogues, or Plato's last words. I offer an approach to the open dialogue in "Gaps in the Universe of the Platonic Dialogues" (1987) and "Reading the *Republic*" (1988). Stimulating for reflection on the endings of the Platonic dialogues are the general remarks of D. P. Fowler, "First Thoughts on Closure: Problems and Prospects" (1989) and "Second Thoughts on Closure" (1997).

An excellent treatment of Plato's "myths of judgment" is that of Julia Annas, "Plato's Myths of Judgment" (1982). For Plato the mythographer in general, we now have in English translation Luc Brisson's, *Plato the Mythmaker* (revised original 1994; translation 1998), in which Brisson is much occupied with Plato's myth of Atlantis. A revealing interpretation of Plato's myth of Atlantis that sees Atlantis as a distant mirror of imperial Athens of the fifth century is Pierre Vidal-Naquet, "Athens and Atlantis: Structure and Meaning of a Platonic Myth" (1986). In Clay 1997 and Clay 2000, I have attempted hesitantly to interpret the fragmentary and inconclusive character of Plato's final programmatic "tetralogy."

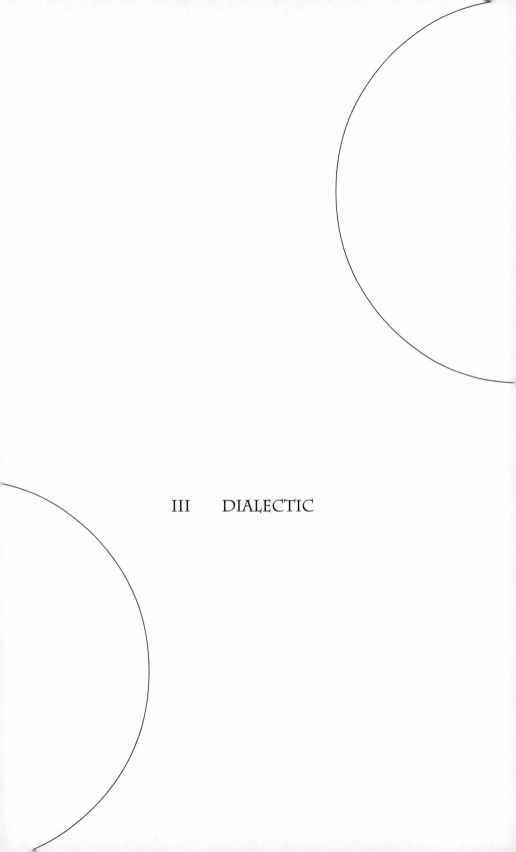

III   DIALECTIC

Vexation

In the *Apology*, Socrates recalls to his jury his way of life: every day finds him engaged in a discussion of virtue and the other topics they have heard him speak of, as he examines himself and others. Anyone who wants is free to listen to him interrogate others in the conviction that for a human being "the unexamined life is not worth living."[1] His questioning of Meletos and the earlier interrogations he recalls in the *Apology* produce surly silence in Meletos, vexation and anger in his earlier interlocutors, and some rancor in his jury.[2] So described, Socrates' method of question and answer strikes Plato's reader as an unrewarding pursuit: rather than understanding, it produces vexation and anger. As he tests himself against the touchstone (*basanos*) of the ignorance of others, he discovers that he is wiser than they on one small point: he knows that he does not know. Yet against his intention, he gives the impression that he knows the answers to the questions he is asking and that he is insincere and condescending. As another unintended result of his examinations, he reproduces versions of himself in the young men who come to imitate him. Some of these turn to write Socratic dialogues.

As he appears to the reader in the pages of Plato and Xenophon (and one can add Aristophanes and the Socratic Aischines), the posthumous and convicted Socrates is not a Socrates "become young and fair" (in the words of Letter II); he is a Socrates who has remained tenacious and—to some— annoying. The young Winston Churchill is one of the readers Plato's Socrates has annoyed. In *My Early Life*, Churchill characterized the Socratic method

1. *Apology* 38A.
2. *Apology* 21E, 22E–23C.

as "a way of giving your friend his head in an argument and progging him into a pit by cunning questions."[3] Similar reactions are recorded within the Platonic dialogues. In the *Republic*, Thrasymachos snarls at Socrates' self-deprecation (*eirōnia*)—something he had warned the company to be on their guard against. He says, as we recall: "I knew . . . you would refuse to answer questions, but would keep up your pretense of ignorance and perform contortions not to have to answer a question, if someone were to ask you one."[4] Thrasymachos' prediction proves right. Socrates asks him questions and submits to the test Thrasymachos' contention that justice is the interest of the stronger. Later in the *Republic*, Adeimantos recalls the philosophical manners of the Socrates known from book 1 of the *Republic* and Plato's early Socratic dialogues. Adeimantos objects to the ineluctable logic that had induced Glaukon to agree that their new state should be turned over to the philosopher:

> Socrates, no one would be able to contradict you and speak against these proposals. Time and time again, those who hear you making this argument have an experience something like this: because of their inexperience in the exercise of asking and answering questions, they think that they are being maneuvered by each question to shift position slightly. But, when all the small concessions are added up at the end of the argument, the opponent is decisively defeated, and his position seems the opposite to what it was at first. They are in a fix, like that of novices at board games who cannot reach the squares opposite them but are blocked and can make no move. Just so, in this version of the board game, the inexperienced players are at a loss, not only in counters but in words. Yet I think that the truth is in no way affected by this game.[5]

The *Elenchos*

The name of Socrates' game is the ἔλεγχος (*elenchos*, or test). The *elenchos* is part of Athenian democratic culture in which many officeholders were subject to an audit (*euthyna*) at the end of their term of office. The difference is that Socrates' scrutiny of his contemporaries was that of a private individual and, by his profession, a daily occurrence. Since examinations are conducted to reveal faults, just as touchstones are used to discover counterfeit metals (and

---

3. *My Early Life* (London, 1959), 116.
4. *Republic* 1.337A; see II §2 ("Socratic Irony").
5. *Republic* 6.487B–C.

provide one analogy for Socratic questioning), the Greek term *elenchos* can mean a refutation and a reproach, just as the word for a touchstone (*basanos*) can mean torture.

In the *Theogony*, for example, the Muses greet Hesiod and all shepherds as *kak' elenchea*, "causes for disgraceful reproaches."[6] Since the Socrates of Xenophon's *Memorabilia* and Aischines' *Alcibiades* closely matches the cagey Socrates who in the early Platonic dialogues examines his contemporaries and never seems to find an adequate answer to his questions, Plato's readers often take these dialogues as directly reflecting the philosophical method of the historical Socrates. Perhaps they are right in this, but when Aristotle refers to the manner of "dialectic" apparently common when he wrote his *Topics* and *Sophistical Refutations*, he refers to the Socratic *elenchos* of the Platonic dialogues.[7] By dialectic he means debating by rule and keeping within the terms of premises that are accepted either by authorities or by the interlocutor. His remarks on "dialectic" in the *Topics* seem to reflect the training given the young in Plato's Academy. The *Topics* remind us that the Socratic *elenchos* was one thing when applied to his contemporaries in the fifth century and something quite different when directed to Plato's students and readers in the fourth century. Plato is testing his readers as he recalls Socrates testing his contemporaries.

The early dialogues sometimes read as a travesty of philosophical dialogue and dialectic as we understand these terms today. One, the *Euthydemus*, is certainly a travesty of philosophical argument. Here Socrates enters the arena of sophistic debate with the sophists Euthydemus and Dionysidoros. What we witness in these early dialogues is a series of speakers who are pressed by Socrates to express their views on some topic—often a topic they are unprepared to discuss. One by one, all are thrown down by this master wrestler, who never allows those he questions to gain a hold on him. As they enter the arena, they are induced by a solicitous and urbane Socrates to state their opinion on some matter. Then, as he fastens onto their statements, they are forced to shift ground and finally are maneuvered into a false position where they contradict their original assertion. In the *Apology*, to take the first example, Meletos' sworn indictment is a claim concerning an individual case (and is virtually unique in this): "Socrates has committed a crime in corrupting

---

6. Or "poor excuses for human beings"; *Theogony* 26.

7. A good example is the procedure of arguing from opposites described in *Topics* 2.9 and 5.6. The advice given in book 8 of the *Topics* comes very close to being a description of the Socratic method in the Socratic dialogues of Plato.

the young and in not worshiping the gods the city worships, but new and strange divinities."[8] As he tests Meletos' claim, charge by charge and in a tactic that will become familiar in the *Gorgias* and *Republic,* Socrates shows that he could have no motive in corrupting the young. To corrupt them is to make them worse and thus to do harm to himself by creating fellow citizens who would by their association harm him in turn.[9] He then turns to the second, related charge of impiety to show that Meletos' charge is self-contradictory, once developed, for the assertion that Socrates introduces "new divinities" shows that he is not a complete atheist. By provoking Meletos into identifying Socrates' own personal voice (*daimonion*) with the "new divinities" of his charge, Socrates can show by implication that he is not a complete atheist but believes in divinities who are the sons of gods and mortals.[10] If Socrates' *elenchos* is a success in that his opponent is entrapped by it, his argument fails to convince his jurors. Success in argument followed by his interlocutor's obdurate refusal to be convinced by his argument seems to be Socrates' fate in the early Platonic dialogues.

In the *Euthyphro,* Euthyphro's successive claims about the nature of piety all fail to satisfy Socrates that he has discovered "that very Form (*eidos*) by which all things holy are holy."[11] He does not find it in the claim that prosecuting a father for the death of a slave is holy, for this is an individual case and not a general definition covering all particular cases; nor is doing what is loved by the gods much better, for Euthyphro's idea of piety leaves unanswered the question Do the gods love the holy because it is holy, or is the holy holy because they love it? As Socrates points out, traditional myths concerning all too human gods show that the sharp and violent disagreements among the gods mean that it is not possible to find agreement even among the gods. What Socrates is seeking, although he does not say so, is some transhuman standard of judgment. And the final possibility—that piety is human tendance of the gods—makes the gods all too needy of human solicitude.

A survey of the results of the Socratic *elenchos* is—at the end of the day—discouraging. First there is the dead end of the aporetic dialogues (see II § 8, "The Open Dialogue"). In the *Lysis,* Lysis is shown to possess no adequate notion of what friendship is; Charmides, modest and reserved as he is in the

---

8. *Apology* 24B.
9. *Apology* 24C–26A.
10. *Apology* 26B–28A; see I §5 ("The Philosopher in Court").
11. *Euthyphro* 6D.

Charmides, can offer no better definition of prudent self-restraint (σωφ-ϱοσύνη) than "minding your own business";[12] the generals Laches and Nikias cannot satisfy the dialectical soldier in Socrates with their understanding of what courage is (either viewed as a kind of endurance or as a kind of wisdom concerning what is to be feared and not to be feared);[13] Meno offers Socrates a "swarm" of definitions of what virtue is (including the ability to rule over a city),[14] and under the pressure of Socrates' examination he recalls the reputation Socrates has gained by this kind of examination:

> And you give me the impression, if it is appropriate to add a note of ridicule, of being the spitting image of the flat stingray—both in your appearance and in other respects as well. This ray numbs whoever gets too close to it and touches it. Now you seem to be having the same effect on me. For, truly, I myself am numb both in soul and tongue, and I cannot find a suitable answer for you.[15]

The other opinions overthrown by the Socratic *elenchos* are the opinions of the major characters of the early dialogues: Alcibiades, who (in *First Alcibiades*) has the conceit that he will one day rule over both Greek and barbarian; Ion, who "understands" Homer and claims that his poet understands the subjects of his epics; Protagoras, who professes that virtue can be taught and that he is a teacher of virtue himself; the young mathematician Theaetetus, who offers in succession three definitions of knowledge: perception, true opinion, and the ability to explain an object of true opinion.[16] To draw this much shortened list to a close, we note Socrates' sustained test of Kallikles in the *Gorgias* and Thrasymachos in *Republic* 1. They both argue that justice is by nature the interest of the stronger. Socrates' testing does not bring about a change of attitude, only a reluctant admission that the interlocutor is no match for Socrates in this contest of wits. We shall soon hear Thrasymachos' surly concession (see III § 6, "Kallipolis"). As for Kallikles in the *Gorgias*, he ends the debate with Socrates over the superiority of the political and philosophical lives with the weary words: "Well, now that you have gotten

---

12. *Charmides* 161B, an early version of the new understanding of justice in the *Republic*, by which every member of Socrates' political community performs the task for which he or she is best suited; see III §6 ("Kallipolis").
13. *Laches* 192B and 194D.
14. *Meno* 73C.
15. *Meno* 80B.
16. *Theaetetus* 151E, 187B, 201C.

this far, why don't you finish this too?"[17] He then listens silently to Socrates'
final myth of judgment (see II § 8, "The Open Dialogue").

This is not what we would consider dialogue. If Socrates' interlocutor
offers a thesis and first moves his counter on the board, Socrates does not
offer his own opposing opinion, or antithesis—or countermove. As Kallikles
says: "If you didn't have someone to answer your questions, you would be
tongue-tied."[18] At the end of the day, Socrates' questioning does not produce
new insight or reform the convictions of the people he argues with; nor does
it produce a synthesis of divergent points of view. His is not a Hegelian
dialectic of thesis, antithesis, and synthesis. Within the dialogues the Socratic
elenchos provokes irritation, weary acquiescence, anger, or an urgent appointment that will remove the interlocutor from the persistent source of his vexation.

Testing the *Elenchos*

The Socratic method of question and answer has long been held up as a
model of teaching, but as philosophical discourse it presents two very dissimilar faces: within the early Socratic dialogues, the contribution and intelligence of Socrates' interlocutor can be very limited; but since the
conversations of these *Sokratikoi logoi* are addressed to Plato's readers, they
have found readers as inquiring and critical as Socrates himself. There are
then two dialogues to engage us: the inner dialogue of Plato's dramatic fiction
and the outer dialogue between the Platonic dialogue and its reader. For
the inner dialogue and the "Socratic method" it is instructive to excerpt the
contributions of Meno to the conversation in a randomly chosen passage
from the *Meno* (a passage immediately following Socrates' demonstration of
the geometrical knowledge of Meno's slave): Meno: "What you say is true";
"Yes"; "It seems so"; "It appears"; "Yes"; "Exactly"; "Yes."[19] In this exchange,
Meno is every bit as servile as his slave.

But Plato's readers have not been so servile, and recently some have become acutely conscious of the fallacies in the arguments of Plato's dialogues,
the early dialogues especially, forgetting perhaps that in none of his dialogues
did Plato ever commit a fallacy, equivocation, or evasion himself. There are
no Platonic arguments, only arguments attributed to others within the dia-

---

17. *Gorgias* 522E.
18. *Gorgias* 519D.
19. *Meno* 85C–D.

logues; and, so far as the *elenchos* is concerned, these arguments are usually attributed to Socrates. Some of the arguments expressed by others in the dialogues are clearly unsound, and Plato tacitly calls attention to their unhealthy state. A modern reader who could be present at one of Socrates' conversations would surely step in to challenge many of his counterarguments.

In testing the *elenchos*, let us first consider the kind of argument that might well have been employed by the historical Socrates. In both the conversation with the young Euthydemos in Xenophon's *Memorabilia* and the conversation with Polemarchos in *Republic* 1, Socrates' method of refutation is to elicit a universal judgment from his interlocutor and then show that it has glaring exceptions. In the conversation recorded in Xenophon, Socrates has recognized the political ambitions of the young Athenian Euthydemos. Once he has gained his confidence, he questions him on the "work" of justice. To test Euthydemos, Socrates asks him to place particular acts under columns headed Justice and Injustice. Enslavement is not just, but Euthydemos agrees that it is just when practiced against an enemy. Euthydemos agrees that stealing is not just, but Socrates points out that stealing a weapon from a suicidal friend is the right thing to do.[20] In the *Republic*, Polemarchos steps into the same dialectical trap. After contending that justice consists in returning what is owed, he must qualify his position by distinguishing between what is owed to friends and what is owed to enemies. But should, Socrates asks, one return a weapon to a friend who is not in his right mind?[21]

A similar mode of argument occurs in the more complex context of the *Gorgias*. Here the *elenchos* takes a more personal turn and is an elegant example of what we have been describing as the *ad animam* argument (see II § 7, "Dramatis Personae"). Kallikles is one of Socrates' most determined opponents. He grapples with Socrates after Socrates has finished with Gorgias and his understudy, Polos. Kallikles realizes that the master Gorgias and his young follower Polos got into difficulties because they were ashamed to say openly what they really thought justice is. For Kallikles, conventional justice is no more than a democratic defensive wall thrown up against the aggrandizement of superior men. Nature's clear bidding is for the superior and more powerful to possess more than the inferior.[22] Kallikles is perfectly capable (as Thrasymachos is not) of spotting Socrates' shifty extension of the term "supe-

20. Xenophon, *Memorabilia* 4.2.10–18.
21. *Republic* 1.331C.
22. *Gorgias* 482C–483C.

rior" (*kreittōn*) to mean "stronger."[23] But, as it turns out, Kallikles is not superior to the political conventions of democratic Athens or to shame. As he faces Socrates' examination of his claim that the superior man will pursue every form of pleasure as his highest good, he balks at Socrates' extension of the range of pleasures to the pleasures of the passive homosexual. Indulgence in such pleasures would, by Athenian convention, debar a male citizen from public life. Kallikles' universal claim collapses with his indignant question: "Have you no shame in dragging the argument down to cases such as these?"[24]

In the *Republic*, the argument with Thrasymachos that follows Socrates' testing Polemarchos' conception of justice involves another kind of refutation, the argument from analogy. The final defeat of the position that justice is "the interest of the stronger" involves getting Thrasymachos to agree to two sets of propositions involving at least fifteen concessions, which lead ineluctably to two adverse conclusions: that, as an expert, the ruler looks not after his own interest but the interest of the ruled; and that the just man is good and intelligent and the unjust man vicious and ignorant.[25] Both results depend on Thrasymachos' accepting the craft analogy Socrates puts before him. He agrees that there is an art to injustice that requires the practical intelligence of the craftsman. Any sharp onlooker—or a Kallikles—could have put up a better argument than Thrasymachos, and the insufficiency of his defenses against Socrates' *elenchos* is indicated by the renewed challenge of Glaukon and Adeimantos at the beginning of book 2. The most interesting result of this argument is that the craft analogy turns positive in Socrates' own defense of justice in the rest of the *Republic* and his own conception that justice is doing what one is naturally suited to do in a well-ordered society, an argument initiated by the inclusion of farmers and artisans in Socrates' first and essential city.

In Socrates' refutation of Thrasymachos' claim, we glimpse how important the craft analogy is not only in the *Republic* but in a series of dialogues culminating in the *Statesman*—a dialogue informed by the analogies of the shepherd in its first part and the weaver in its second. The form this argument usually takes in the Socratic dialogues of *elenchos* is to induce the interlocutor to accept a recognized art (τέχνη, *technē*) as a strict measure of other arts that will, upon examination, prove to be phantom and parasitic—the mere image (*eidōlon*) of a genuine art. The accepted master arts are those of the cobbler

23. A shift he had already made himself; *Gorgias* 489B–C.
24. *Gorgias* 494E.
25. *Republic* 1.341C–344E and 349B–350D.

and builder; the painter and sculptor; the trainer and doctor; and the ship's captain, shepherd, and weaver. This argument is the engine driving Socrates' argument that virtue is knowledge (see III § 2, "The Virtue of Knowledge"). It is used against Ion's claim (in the *Ion*) that there is an art of the rhapsode and that the rhapsode and Homer understand the subjects of the epic (see II § 5, "Plato and the Poets"); it appears in the *Charmides,* where self-restraint is presented as an art, like the art of the builder;[26] it appears in the sparring match of the *Euthydemus;*[27] it is turned against the "art" of rhetoric in the *Protagoras* and *Gorgias;* and in the last conversation of the *Symposium* it was apparently used by Socrates to convince Agathon and Aristophanes of the unity of the arts of the tragic and comic poets. The only important term of this argument that Aristodemos recorded was that the poet who had the know-how (ἐπίστασθαι) to compose a tragedy could also compose a comedy.[28]

When viewed from within the dialogues, the results of the Socratic *elenchos* might seem all negative. Claims are refuted and no counterclaim established. Some of the arguments, especially the initial sophistic maneuvers of the *Euthydemus,* seem frivolous, since they involve the fallacy of the excluded middle. But for the reader interrogating the *elenchos* of the Socratic dialogues, there are within the inner dialogue warnings to be cautious. In the *Euthydemus,* Euthydemus asks the young Kleinias: "Are those who learn wise or ignorant?" Socrates' impulse is to warn him of the trap set for him.[29] The reader is as alert as Socrates. In the *Symposium,* Socrates warns Agathon that, although Love (Eros) lacks (and therefore desires) beauty, Eros is not necessarily ugly.[30] The Platonic dialogues have an inside and an outside, and they wear a Janus face. Viewed from the context of the readers of the dialogues of *elenchos,* the long series of challenges to opinions held by characters within the dialogues constitutes an education in critical thinking and a preparation for the more positive presentation of philosophy that begins in book 2 of the *Republic,* where Socrates defends the claim that the just is superior to the unjust life— 729 times superior.[31] To read critically is to think critically, and, even when it comes to the arguments of the *Republic,* the reader must constantly ask whether Plato should be taken at Socrates' word.

26. *Charmides* 161E.
27. *Euthydemus* 289C.
28. *Symposium* 223D; see II §6 ("Platonic Poetry").
29. *Euthydemus* 275E.
30. *Symposium* 201A–202B.
31. *Republic* 9.587E.

The Virtues of the *Elenchos*

In his *Topics,* Aristotle characterized one of the goals of dialectic conducted in the nonphilosophical guise of the *elenchos:*

> It [the *elenchos*] develops the capacity to discriminate and hold in one view the results of either of two hypotheses, and this is no mean instrument contributing to knowledge and philosophical understanding; for all that remains is for a student to make the correct choice.[32]

Plato had reflected on the same goal long before these words were written by his most gifted pupil. At the end of the *Theaetetus,* Socrates contemplates all that his examination of Theaetetus has achieved:

> If, after this conversation, you try to become pregnant with other conceptions, and if, Theaetetus, you succeed, you will become great with better conceptions, thanks to this examination today. And, if you are empty, you will prove less irksome to your companions and a gentler person, since in your new wisdom you will not think that you know what you do not know. These are the limits of my art.[33]

This conclusion is a reflection on one of the aims of Plato's dialogues of Socratic examination. It also carries a judgment on the question raised in the *Protagoras* and *Meno:* Can virtue be taught? (see III § 2, "The Virtue of Knowledge"). On the next day, which dawns in the *Sophist,* the visitor from Elea mentions the *elenchos* as an alternative to the education boys receive from their fathers. Rather than admonition and encouragement, the stranger recommends the *elenchos:*

> Those who care for the soul proceed in the same manner as those who care for the body. Doctors are of the belief that neither can they administer a proper diet nor the body benefit from it until the internal obstructions have been purged from it. Those who employ the *elenchos* take the same approach to the soul. The soul cannot profit from the knowledge proffered to it before the educator removes the opinions that block its entrance by putting the man who is to be tested to the *elenchos* and performing a purification to leave him in the belief that he knows what he knows and not a whit more.[34]

---

32. *Topics* 8.163^{b}9–14, after the translation of W. A. Pickard-Cambridge, in *The Complete Works of Aristotle,* ed. Jonathan Barnes (Princeton, 1984), 1.276.
33. *Theaetetus* 210B–C.
34. *Sophist* 230C–D.

As it happens, the Eleatic Stranger's method of surgical divisions, so pain-fully evident in the *Sophist* and *Statesman*, is not a philosophical scalpel that bares the distinctions latent in things. Like the *elenchos* it is a method for training the mind that has been purged of all that it has taken for granted, in order to begin another order of philosophical preparation. This is the exercise of making fine distinctions in order to gain an overarching view of the whole in which these distinctions become significant. This is not yet philosophy.[35]

ENDNOTE: The classic study of the Socratic *elenchos* in Plato is Richard Robin-son, *Plato's Earlier Dialectic*, 2d ed. (1953), pt. 1. Gregory Vlastos treats the *elenchos* and fallacy in chapters 4 and 5 of *Socrates: Ironist and Moral Philosopher* (1991) and in chapter 1 of *Socratic Studies* (1994). The appearance of fallacy is one of the major irritants in reading Plato. The extreme case of the *Euthydemus* is treated by Rosamund Kent Sprague, *Plato's Use of Fallacy* (1962), and Thomas H. Chance, *Plato's Euthydemus: Analysis of What Is and What Is Not Philosophy* (1992). It is crucial to recall, with Michael Frede, in "Platonic Argu-ments and the Dialogue Form" (1992), that there are, properly speaking, no Platonic arguments. The detection of fallacy in the Platonic dialogues is an enterprise as engaging as the detection of obscenity in Aristophanes. For the very real difficulties with the argument of the *Republic*, the reader should turn to Bernard Williams, "The Analogy of City and Soul in Plato's *Republic*" (1973), and to the sources listed in the Endnote to III §6, "Kallipolis." Reveal-ing surveys of the dominant craft analogy in Plato are to be found in David Roochnik, *Of Art and Wisdom: Plato's Understanding of Techne* (1996), and Charles Kahn, *Plato and the Socratic Dialogue* (1997), chap. 3.

35. *Statesman* 285D–E.

The Eleatic Stranger's description of the new education of the *elenchos* gives us pause. He had not been present to hear Socrates' concluding words of the day before, and he speaks in the plural of those who employ the *elenchos* as a purgative and a propaedeutic. Despite the plural, this description is one of Plato's many delicate signatures within the dialogues. In pointing to the Socratic testing of Theaetetus in the *Theaetetus*, Plato is also pointing to the philosophical project that had taken him from the *Apology* to the group of middle and late dialogues that advance positive doctrines, often dogmatically (as in the case of the *Sophist, Statesman, Timaeus*). In these dialogues, we seem to see the light of a new day. The *elenchos* has not quite disappeared, for it is transferred from the person Socrates had tested within the dialogue to Plato's reader. If the indications of the *Theaetetus* and *Sophist* reveal a plan, then early on Plato saw his life's work stretch out before him on a clear and distant horizon. In a long series of aporetic dialogues he exercised enormous self-control and reticence, not only in his sustained anonymity but in his caution in revealing any positive philosophical point of view.

Virtue

But a positive point of view does emerge in the means by which Plato's Socrates tests the views of his contemporaries. We have seen this point of view in his deployment of the craft analogy to show that, measured against the knowledge and know-how of real professionals, the parasitic professions of poet, sophist, and democratic politician are phantom arts. Here we encounter a reflection of the Socratic paradox that virtue is knowledge. All genuine craftsmen possess "virtue" (ἀρετή, *aretē*) because of their know-how (ἐπιστήμη, *epistēmē*). In Plato, this is not to be identified with intelligence, which represents a higher order of knowledge. When Socrates speaks of *epistēmē*, we should say skill, but a Greek would say "virtue." Greek virtues are not our virtues, as a reading of Christ's Sermon on the Mount (in Matt. 5.1–12) will make immediately apparent. "Blessed are the poor in spirit" comes to us in Greek and not Aramaic, but Christ's virtues are not pagan virtues, nor do they belong to Plato's tetrad of virtues: courage, self-control, justice, and intelligence. In Greek, the noun *aretē* is connected with the superlative *aristos* (best), and its fundamental meaning is superiority. (It is often associated with the value terms *agathos*, "good at doing something," and *kalos*, "good looking," "noble," "brave.") In the *Iliad*, Sarpedon and Achilles recall the expectation their fathers and elders had instilled in them: "[E]ver show yourself superior (*aristeuein*) and stand out above all the rest."[1] For the Homeric warrior, virtue had two theaters: the battlefield and the political assembly.[2]

Knowledge

The other term of the Socratic equation is *epistēmē*, which translates as "knowledge" in the Socratic equation of virtue and knowledge. But Greek *epistēmē* is not exactly "knowledge," for it does not at first denote abstract or scientific knowledge; it means "know-how." These cardinal Greek terms have to be taken out of their English dress and disguise, for Greek virtues are not our virtues, and knowledge is not theoretical in the early dialogues. A puzzling example of the connection between knowledge and virtue occurs in the *Symposium*. When Alcibiades describes Socrates' words, he says that "he is forever talking of pack asses and tinkers and cobblers and tanners and always seems to be saying the same things by means of the same illustrations."[3] Alcibiades adds that if you open up the hide of his strange conversations you will discover within "images of virtue and everything that is suitable for the person who proposes to become virtuous and honorable."[4] Why should Socrates invoke craftsmen as recurrent illustrations in his strange conversations with aristocrats like Alcibiades? The Greek term that described these artisans (*banausoi*) was a term of upper-class contempt. They could be called "people with

---

1. *Iliad* 6.208 (Sarpedon) and 11.784 (Nestor of Achilles).
2. *Iliad* 1.490–91 and 9.438–42 (Phoenix).
3. *Symposium* 221E, a passage familiar from I §8 ("Socrates Silenus").
4. *Symposium* 222A.

know-how" (*epistēmones*), but our term of praise for them would be "professionals."

Alcibiades does not make the connection, but we can ask: How can illustrations taken from the "mechanic" class of Athens serve as a guide to a person who aspires to virtue? What does the cobbler Simon have to teach us about justice? The answer seems to be that Simon is a "knower" (we would say a professional) and "virtuous" (we would say successful) in putting his knowledge to the test and producing a product that can be judged useful by those who use it and by other experts in his profession. His virtue and true superiority is that he knows how to make proper shoes and sandals. He is a proto-Demiurge in that he works from a pattern and with a purpose. His justice is that he sticks to his last. Socrates could only find fault in a simple Simon if he were to leave his last and meddle in politics, something that requires another kind of art—the royal art.[5]

The Socratic Paradox

The Socratic equation of virtue and knowledge has many consequences now known as the Socratic paradoxes. One is that no one does wrong knowingly—and if not knowingly, not willingly. Its converse is that vice is ignorance; and if so, then chastisement for wrongdoing should have no part in the repertory of punishments known to the Greek states: the only appropriate remedy for ignorance is education. The equation of virtue and knowledge also entails the doctrine that Kallikles finds so incredible in the *Gorgias*: that it is better to be harmed by an act of injustice than to commit an act of injustice, and that the cruel and unusual punishment for injustice is to go without being punished.[6] The Socratic equation also entails the abolition of any conflict between reason and passion and a new moral psychology (explored in III § 3, "Eros and Psyche"). It explains the easy attitude taken toward lack of self-control (*akrasia*) in the Platonic dialogues (and the *Protagoras* especially). There can be no psychomachy between reason and the passions. If moral superiority is know-how, the agent must act on what he or she knows. By contrast, Aristotle regarded lack of self-control as a moral, rather than an intellectual, failing.[7]

If Socrates is right that virtue is knowledge, the question then arises: Can

---

5. *Apology* 22D and *Republic* 4.420E.
6. *Gorgias* 473A–481B.
7. *Nicomachean Ethics* 3.12 and 7.

it be taught? Presumably it can, if it truly resembles the paradigmatic forms of knowledge represented by medicine and sculpture.[8] This is the question that occupies the *Protagoras* and the *Meno*, a dialogue that opens with Meno's question to Socrates: "Can you tell me, Socrates, is virtue something that can be taught?"[9] In the *Protagoras*, one final question arises: Are the separate and conventional virtues—courage, justice, self-restraint, piety—one and uniform, like gold, or are they distinct, yet connected, like the parts of a face?[10]

Plato's concern with these Socratic questions and with what we have been translating as virtue (*aretē*) surfaces in the *Apology*; he returns to it for a last time in the *Laws*. In one of his imagined exchanges with a member of his jury, Socrates says that his divine mission is to urge every one he comes into contact with to care not for their bodies or for possessions but for the perfection of their souls: "Virtue does not derive from possessions, but it is from virtue that possessions and all other things become good for men, both for individuals and for their cities."[11] In the last book of the *Laws*, the unity of the now canonical tetrad of virtues—courage, self-restraint, justice, and intelligence—is held up by the Athenian as one subject the officials (*nomophylakes*) of the new Cretan city must master.[12] Here a verdict is pronounced on the problem of the *Protagoras*. At the end of the day, there is such a thing as education in virtue, and there is a unity to virtues. Just how this is so we do not learn from what the Athenian Stranger prescribes in the *Laws*. But we find in the Athenian's homicide law the most elaborate treatment of the Socratic paradox that no one does wrong knowingly and therefore willingly, which is a corollary to the claim that virtue is knowledge.[13] All evil men are unwillingly evil in their wrongdoing. By this argument, the Athenian annuls the common Greek legal distinction between voluntary and involuntary actions. This view also entails that punishment is education, except in the case of the criminally insane, for whom the only "cure" is death.

If we follow Socrates' procedure in the *Meno* and ask not "Can virtue be taught?" but rather "What is virtue?"[14] we first stir up a "hive" of particular virtues. To Socrates' counterquestion, Meno replies by listing a number of virtues—that of a male and that of a female; that of a child; that of a freeman

8. *Protagoras* 311B–312B.
9. *Meno* 70A.
10. *Protagoras* 329C.
11. *Apology* 30B.
12. *Laws* 12.965C–966B.
13. *Laws* 9.863A–864C.
14. *Meno* 71A.

and that of a slave.[15] We then contemplate Socrates' hypothesis that, if virtue is knowledge, it must be teachable, since what we learn is knowledge, and we are taught what we know.[16] In a sequence of connected propositions, Socrates establishes that, if virtue is something good and we are good and useful because we are virtuous, virtue must be something useful. And, if all possessions and character traits counted good are not good without qualification but only if they are accompanied by intelligence, virtue must be intelligence. By the interlocking of these propositions, virtue is shown to be knowledge.[17] Whether intelligence (*phronēsis*) is the same as knowledge (*epistēmē*) and whether all the virtues (including courage and piety) constitute a unity are questions Socrates leaves in suspense. The apparent conclusion— that virtue is knowledge—is then put to a simple empirical test. If virtue is knowledge and can be taught, it is in fact taught; and if taught, it should be possible to point to professors of virtue and the students they have made better.[18] Here we run into difficulties.

This summary in English disguises two salient features of Socrates' argument and illustrates the difficulty of understanding this argument in English translation. Our word "virtue" cannot convey what is at issue in this discussion. The other disguised feature of this argument is the word *epistēmē*, "knowledge." *Epistēmē* misleads us, in part because it misled Aristotle, who translated it into his own conception of sciences that have universals as their subjects. But *epistēmē* understood as know-how helps us understand Socrates' fascination with cobblers. The knowledge of the cobbler is not theoretical knowledge, on the level of the knowledge of the mathematician and the geometer. It is practical know-how. Socrates recognized this know-how, displayed in the reliable manufacture of some product, in the craftsmen. In his view, the cobbler is intelligent and wise.[19] As we have seen in our discussion of Plato and the poets (II § 5), to "understand" Homer is to know how to recite his poems from memory, not to be able to write *The Discovery of the True Homer*, as did Gianbattista Vico.[20] So it is not just to complain of Socrates, as does Aristotle in the *Eudemian Ethics*, to say that by science Socrates meant something like

15. *Meno* 71E.
16. *Meno* 87C–89A.
17. *Meno* 89C.
18. *Meno* 89C–94E.
19. *Apology* 22C–D, *First Alcibiades* 125C–D.
20. The title of book 3 of his *La scienza nuova* (The new science) of 1725. The language of *Ion* 541E and *Charmides* 159A makes it clear that "knowing Homer" means that a student or a professional rhapsode has memorized his epics and can perform them.

geometry and architecture.[21] The Socratic paradox does not distinguish *theoria* from *praxis;* if there is virtue, there is knowledge. Conversely, if there is knowledge, there is virtue. Virtue is revealed in action.

Most of the individual virtues of Greek popular morality are subjected to the withering light and heat of the Socratic *elenchos.* We have passed them in review: piety in the *Euthyphro,* self-restraint in the *Charmides,* courage in the *Laches,* justice in book 1 of the *Republic.* Some of the early dialogues offer definitions of individual virtues or of virtue in general, but it is not until the *Republic* that the tetrad of Platonic virtues is presented as an associated whole and as a unity.[22] The piety of the *Euthyphro* becomes the orphaned virtue of the *Republic.* Charmides' conception of self-restraint as "minding your own business"[23] and the position taken in the *Protagoras* that courage is the understanding of the things that are to be feared[24] (which resembles the more limited conception of the *Laches*) are not far different from the conceptions of justice and courage in the *Republic,* except that the four virtues of the *Republic* are all political. The virtues of the individual are projected onto the large screen of the polis and (in book 4 of the *Republic*) are relevant to a city that still lacks its ruling class of philosophers.[25] We have not yet arrived at the virtue of intelligence and the heart of the *Republic,* in which Socrates takes up the education of the philosopher in books 6 and 7 (see III § 6, "Kallipolis").

Can Virtue Be Taught?

The treatment of the virtues in the *Republic* suggests that, despite Socrates' refutation of the sophistic advertisement that virtue is something that can be taught (for a fee), Plato himself actually believed that virtue can be taught or inculcated, not in Athens or under the instruction of a foreign professor (*sophistēs*), but in the state education of Kallipolis and Magnesia, the cities he founded in his *Republic* and *Laws.* In response to Meno's question Can virtue be taught? the reader must ask: If Plato was not in fact convinced that virtue could be taught, how could he have devoted his whole career to writing dialogues devoted to the subject of training the young in virtue and, so far as Plato's reader is concerned, to a training to better understand what constitutes virtue?

21. *Eudemian Ethics* 1.5.1216^{b}1–25.
22. *Republic* 4.427C–433C.
23. *Charmides* 161B.
24. *Protagoras* 354A–B.
25. *Republic* 4.429C–430B.

To return to Meno's question: "Can virtue be taught?" By setting it in the form of mutually exclusive—and deceptive—alternatives, Plato might have provided us with a practical and positive answer to this question. In his dialogue with Alcibiades in the *First Alcibiades*, Socrates imagines a conversation between the young and fiercely ambitious politician Alcibiades and himself in the role of a concerned citizen. Alcibiades is imagined as about to mount the speaker's platform to address the Athenian assembly:

SOCRATES:

Alcibiades, on what matter of concern to the city of Athens and on what question for deliberation do you rise to speak and give advice? It must surely be a subject you know better than do the Athenians.

ALCIBIADES:

I would say that it is a subject I understand better than they do.

SOCRATES:

You can, then, give good advice about those subjects you happen to know?

ALCIBIADES:

Why not?

SOCRATES:

Tell me, then, are the subjects you know limited to either what you have learned from others or to what you have discovered by yourself?

ALCIBIADES:

What are the alternatives?[26]

Socrates offers no other alternatives, and Alcibiades accepts the two offered as exhaustive and mutually exclusive. The situation is the same in the *Meno* and in Socrates' conversation with Euthydemos in Xenophon's *Memorabilia*, where the alternatives are that one learns by natural ability or that one learns by education.[27] In the democratic culture in Athens, the decent assumption was that fathers and their fellow citizens transmit their knowledge of virtuous actions to their sons.[28] Evenos of Paros, who offered just such a curriculum for the princely sum of five minas, agreed with the Athenians that

26. *First Alcibiades* 106C–D.
27. *Meno* 89B and Xenophon, *Memorabilia* 4.2.2.
28. *Apology* 24C–25A.

virtue can be taught.[29] And the wealthy Athenian Kallias agreed with the claim of Evenos, for he was the father who paid this fee.

But to return to Plato and the Platonic dialogue: Can Plato be considered—and did he consider himself—a teacher of virtue? One Socratic test of this question is to determine whether he had pupils and whether he made them virtuous. In a way, these strange questions are like that posed by the enemies of Socrates. In the trial of Socrates, their conclusion was that he did have pupils and that he corrupted them. The ready examples in 399 were Alcibiades, Charmides, and Critias. The attitude on which these charges were founded—the view countered by Xenophon in the *Memorabilia*—was that vice, antidemocratic ambition and elitism, can be taught, as can democratic virtue. This same test is applied by Socrates in his criticism of the poets: "Has Homer created a way of life or left pupils to preserve it?" The answer in this case is an emphatic no. Indeed, Homer's close companion, Kreophylos, paid him no attention even when he was still alive.[30]

In fact, Plato established a way of life practiced by his contemporaries in the Academy and maintained (with interruptions) until the age of Proclus, at the end of the fifth century A.D. Socrates left behind him the *Sokratikoi,* some of whom I have already described (see I § 1, "Plato the Socratic"). But *praxis* and the test of action is not a sufficient answer to the question of how the Socratic problem of the teachability of virtue can be answered by the project of the Platonic dialogues (as distinct from the practice of the Academy). Few of Plato's many readers have enjoyed his companionship and conversation on the grounds of the Academy.

If the practice of the Platonic dialogues indicates anything, it indicates that the alternatives Socrates lays out before Alcibiades are not exhaustive. There is still another possibility. It could be that knowledge in its highest form is innate in every human being, that in his or her capacity to learn and understand, every human being is fertile. Rather than a teacher, one needs a midwife who is barren but productive in helping others to bring their own conceptions to birth.[31] A seemingly insignificant incident in the *Symposium* points to Plato's implicit belief that knowledge cannot be imparted by the simple transfer from the wise to the ignorant. When Socrates arrives at Aga-

29. *Apology* 20B.
30. *Republic* 10.599B–600E. The significant comparison is with the way of life established by Pythagoras for the Pythagorean communities of southern Italy and the states established by Charondas in Sicily and Solon in Athens.
31. As Socrates presents himself in *Theaetetus* 148E–151D.

thon's house, he has been delayed by a seizure of meditation in a neighbor's doorway. We do not know what Socrates has discovered there, but Agathon, who wants to be instructed by Socrates, assumes that "it is clear that you have discovered it." Socrates' response is that wisdom (*sophia*) cannot be transferred from a fuller to an emptier vessel—"like cups where a wool thread transfers wine from the fuller drinking cup to the emptier."[32]

Finally, there is in the *Republic* the telling contrast between two forms of education. Socrates has now gone far beyond the education decreed for the guardians earlier in the *Republic*. We have been taken through the Idea of the Good, the sun, the line, and the cave (see III § 5). We leave the cave to address the education of the philosopher. This Socrates contrasts with the education offered by the sophists:

SOCRATES:

Now, I guess, their claim is that they can cram knowledge into the soul in which no knowledge is present, as if they were imparting sight into blind eyes.

GLAUKON:

So they say.

SOCRATES:

But our present argument is that this very power exists in the soul of every human being. The faculty by which every individual learns is like the eye. You cannot see clearly, unless you turn the eye by turning the entire body around from the realm of shadows to a world of brightness. You must do the same with the soul, which learns from its shift in orientation away from the world of change.[33]

Can virtue be taught? Not on either of the alternatives presented by Socrates within the Platonic dialogues: knowledge is neither solely a natural possession nor solely the product of education. But there emerges another possibility presented by the Platonic dialogues. Virtue is innate and, in the words of Letter VII, comes about "from long association," by turning the reader's head around to face the light "flashing from a flame that has darted up."[34] This "turning around" is conversion.

32. *Symposium* 175D–E.
33. *Republic* 7.518B–C.
34. Letter VII 341D, a passage given in fuller form in II §3 ("Platonic Writing").

ENDNOTE: Three studies that illuminate the background of Platonic ethics are A.W.H. Adkins, *Merit and Responsibility: A Study in Greek Values* (1960); Adkins, *From the Many to the One: A Study of Personality and Views of Human Nature in the Context of Ancient Greek Society, Values, and Beliefs* (1970), and K. J. Dover, *Greek Popular Morality in the Time of Plato and Aristotle* (1974). For the educational and social situation in Athens at the time of Plato's youth, Barry S. Strauss provides an important study in *Fathers and Sons in Athens: Ideology and Society in the Era of the Peloponnesian War* (1993). The "Socratic paradoxes" are the subject of M. J. O'Brien, *The Socratic Paradoxes and the Greek Mind* (1967). Pagan virtues are given an analytical treatment by John Casey, *Pagan Virtue: An Essay in Ethics* (1990). Sharp and analytic treatments of Plato's ethical theory are Terence Irwin's *Plato's Moral Theory* (1977) and *Plato's Ethics* (1995). Any reader interested in the fate of *aretē* should read Alasdair MacIntyre, *After Virtue* (1984), especially chaps. 9–12. The argument of the first two paragraphs of this essay is much indebted to Charles Kahn, *Plato and the Socratic Dialogue* (1997).

The adjective "Platonic" is attached to a theory of Ideas; it also describes a form of love. The two, *erōs* and the Ideas, are intimately connected in Plato's conception of *philosophia*, or the desire for wisdom. In Plato, love and the Ideas are inseparable, for the Ideas and the knowledge they impart to their knower are one object of *erōs*. "Platonic love" has had an even more astonishing career than has the Platonic theory of Ideas (which we will take up in sequel in III § 4, "Thinking About Ideas"). The Greek word *idea* has given us our English word for a "thought," a "concept," and the unattainable paradigm of an "ideal"; the adjective "Platonic" as applied to love has provided us with a chaste and fastidious phrase to describe an attachment to another human being that does not involve sexual intercourse—the kind of love known to the Renaissance as *amor Platonicus* or *amor Socraticus* (for it is Socrates who conveys the conception of this kind of love in the *Symposium*). These are the terms employed by Marsilio Ficino in his own version of the *Symposium: Plato's Symposium, or On Love.*[1] It is fitting that Ficino's other great works, *Platonic Theology, or Concerning the Immortality of Souls* and *On Christian Religion,*[2] integrated the pagan with the Christian, for, in the "Academy" of Florence of the fifteenth century, Plato had been converted into a good Christian. These works of Florentine humanism are all connected in associating Christian belief with Platonic arguments for the immortality of the soul, just as they transform Plato's conception of love for an object that transcends any individual into an *amor Dei* far transcending the human object that inspires it.

1. *Convivium Platonis sive de Amore* (1469).
2. *Theologia Platonica sive de Immortalitate Animorum* was written in 1474, as was his *De Christiana Religione*. Ficino's translation of Plato entire into Latin was published in 1484.

But there is this difference: The Platonic concept of *erōs*, when developed, depends upon a conception of the soul as the tripartite seat of three kinds of desires and passions and as a witness to transcendental forms in its discarnate existence. This Platonic conception of the soul is necessarily prior to a concept of *erōs*. In Plato, the word ψυχή (*psychē*) needs an apology, for the traditional and intuitive understanding of the soul is transformed in the Platonic dialogues. *Psychē* in Plato is the closest Greek equivalent to what we call the "self." In Plato we witness a dramatic development in moral psychology and a turning inward that promotes the *psychē*—the invisible intellectual and affective ghost within the machine of the body—to a prominence it did not have before.

The Soul Before Plato

The word *psychē*, long domesticated in English, originally meant for the Greeks the breath of life. (Similarly, the Latin words for soul and spirit, *anima* and *animus*, are cognate with the Greek word for wind, *anemos*.) In the *Iliad*, to give one example, the Lycian warrior Sarpedon faints from the pain of a spear thrust through his thigh. His soul leaves him, but the breath of the north wind Boreas restores him.[3] When we first encounter the word *psychē* in Greek poetry, it has no high status. We see the breath of life transformed into a shade in the underworld, where it is stripped of any intelligence or virtue. In the beginning of the *Iliad*, the anger of Achilles is said to have thrown the mighty souls of many heroes into Hades; "but the heroes themselves it made the spoils for dogs and all the birds."[4] The most important thing about these Homeric heroes is their bodies—"the heroes themselves." In the *Odyssey*, we meet the souls of some of these heroes in Hades. There Odysseus encounters their "heads without strength" and shades with their ghastly wounds and armor somehow visible to the living. Wailing, they gather about the pit dug by Odysseus and filled with blood. Teiresias requires the blood of a black sheep to speak his prophecy to Odysseus. Odysseus tries to embrace the shade (*psychē*) of his mother, but she flits from his arms "like a shadow and like a dream."[5] In the second infernal passage of the *Odyssey*, the murdered suitors follow Hermes down into Hades, whistling shrilly like bats.[6] As for

3. *Iliad* 5.694–98.
4. *Iliad* 1.3–4.
5. *Odyssey* 11.207.
6. *Odyssey* 24.5–10.

the bodies of the heroes who fell at Troy, exquisite care is taken to preserve the corpse of Patroclus. But his soul, as he appears to Achilles, flees from his friend, like smoke, with the shrill twitter of a bat. Achilles is stunned: "Ah, so there really is a soul and wraith in the halls of Hades, but without any organs of thought [*phrenes*]!"[7]

The Soul in Plato

A remarkable shift in the value placed on the *psychē* came about in the sixth and fifth centuries, particularly in the moral thought of Heraclitus and Democritus and among the Pythagoreans and Orphics. But the shift away from the Homeric conception of the soul as the pale, insubstantial shadow of the body and toward our own conception of the inner self does not prepare us fully for what we find in the Platonic dialogues. The *Phaedo* gives us a measure of this shift. The setting of the *Phaedo* is the state prison house in Athens. This is a perfect setting for Socrates' rehearsal of the Pythagorean conception of the body as a prison of the *psychē*,[8] or as a tomb: *sōma sēma* (σῶμα σῆμα). According to the Pythagoreans, the body is a tomb. In Homer, by contrast, *sōma* is a corpse. In this Pythagorean formulation, the living body is the tomb or prison of an immortal soul, and death is not, as it was in Homer, the violent separation of the breath of life from a living body. In the *Phaedo*, death is portrayed as the separation of the refined and intelligent soul from the heavy dull matter that encases it. The work of the philosopher is to prepare his soul for this separation. How far Plato's conception of the soul has moved from Homer's is evident in Socrates' response to Crito's practical question: "How shall we bury you?" The word Socrates reacts to is "you." "However you like, provided you can catch me and I do not get away from you."[9] Socrates' "me" is his soul. The question Crito does not ask is What guarantees Socrates' survival as a distinct individual? Before turning to the soul as a composite of three "parts," we should consider it as a unity of self persisting over time.

There are three serious arguments in the *Phaedo* for the immortality of the soul, but only one guarantees the immortality of an individual soul. This is the doctrine of recollection (*anamnēsis*), which explains our knowledge on this earth by invoking the memory of our having seen the forms in a discar-

7. *Iliad* 23.103–4.
8. *Phaedo* 62B.
9. *Phaedo* 115C.

nate state.[10] By this theory, clearly, *I* cannot know what *I* have never seen myself. There are clear indications that Plato was concerned with the immortality not only of soul but of individual souls. Socrates possessed his own divine monitor (*daimonion*). In the *Phaedo* he states that a *daimōn* receives each human being as his charge and conducts him in death to a place of judgment.[11] In the *Timaeus*, each individual soul is assigned to its own star,[12] a destiny hinted at in the *Phaedo* and book 10 of the *Laws*.[13]

But in the *Republic*, Socrates seems to deny the religious conception he recalls in the *Phaedo*. In his myth of Er, a prophet announces to the disembodied souls of the dead gathered before him: "A guardian spirit [*daimōn*] will not receive you, but you will choose your guardian divinity."[14] This prophet is not only recalling the religious belief that each individual possesses his or her individual guardian spirit; he is recalling the words of Heraclitus: "A man's character is his *daimōn*."[15] That is, the human being and nothing external to him is responsible for his actions. If Plato's myths of judgment (see II § 8, "The Open Dialogue") are to have any force, they must gain it from a conviction that the individual soul, with its intellectual and moral faculties, survives the death of the body.

There are three Platonic dialogues in which arguments are made for the immortality of the soul; there are also a number of confident invocations of the belief. In the *Phaedo*[16] and the *Republic*,[17] these arguments provide a platform for Socrates' myths of judgment (see II § 8). Perhaps the most formally elegant and philosophically impressive argument for the immortality of the soul comes at the center of the *Phaedrus*. It introduces Socrates' image of the soul as a chariot driven by two horses. This argument does not deploy the powerful rhetoric of Platonic myth to persuade us that virtue here and now will be rewarded there and then. It is advanced as an illustration of the nature of *erōs*. It occurs in Socrates' speech in praise of passionate love (*erōs*) and its divine madness, his so-called palinode.[18] Formally, it can be made to look like a categorical syllogism. It begins with its conclusion: "All soul is immortal."

10. *Phaedo* 72B–77A.
11. *Phaedo* 107D.
12. *Timaeus* 41D–42B.
13. *Phaedo* 114C and *Laws* 10.904C, passages discussed further in III §8 ("Magnesia").
14. *Republic* 10.617E.
15. ἦθος ἀνθρώπῳ δαίμων, DK 22 B 119 (= KRS 247 = CLIV Kahn).
16. *Phaedo* 69A–84C.
17. *Republic* 10.608B–614A.
18. *Phaedrus* 245C–257B.

Its demonstration (articulated in twelve steps) depends on establishing the truth of two propositions: (1) what moves itself is immortal; (2) what constitutes a beginning is ungenerated and therefore indestructible. Since the Socratic concept of the soul fulfills the requirements of (1) moving itself and (2) constituting the beginning of movement in something else (the body), the soul is shown to be immortal.

The Eros of Psyche

The fine print of this argument calls for reading glasses and a more careful reading than given here. The most important consequence of this argument is that, even though it has been shown to be immortal, the Platonic soul has desires that contradict a conception of the immortal and divine as self-sufficient and immobile. The divine is motionless, at least in its anthropomorphic form, since any change indicates a lack and some need to attain a better state.[19] In the *Phaedrus*, Socrates' dramatic image of the soul as a chariot drawn by two winged horses and driven by a winged charioteer reveals that the soul, which is not simple but tripartite, has objects of desire that pitch it into violent motion. By its nature of being earthbound and bound to the body, the soul is in constant motion and, like the divided self in Aristophanes' myth in the *Symposium*, desires its complement, the static, and its mirror image in the Ideas. The embodied soul cannot be self-sufficient and divinely immobile. It strives to return to a vision seen in its discarnate state.

As it is described in the Platonic dialogues, the soul is much more complex than "that which moves itself." The self of the *psychē* has three distinct components. These are already visible, if not distinguished, in the *Phaedo*, where Socrates describes philosophers as those "who refrain from all bodily desires and do not surrender themselves to them," as opposed to those who love to acquire possessions and those who love esteem and power.[20] In Greek, all of these three types are described by *philo-* compounds: *philosophoi*, "love wisdom" (*sophia*); *philotimoi*, "love honor" (*timē*); *philochrēmatoi*, "love possessions" (*chrēmata*).

This does not yet amount to a psychology, but it is a portent of the

19. This is the argument of *Republic* 2.380D–E, devised to demonstrate that divinities cannot appear in disguise.

20. *Phaedo* 82C. This distinction prepares for the later distinction of goods into three classes: the physical and personal (goods connected with the body), the external and social (wealth and reputation), and the internal and personal (intellect and character): *Philebus* 48D–E; Aristotle, *Nicomachean Ethics* 1.5.1095^{b}14–1096^{a}10.

psychology that will develop in the *Republic*, *Phaedrus*, and *Timaeus*. For Plato, the soul's energy does not derive from the unconscious, or the "id" (*das Es*), as Freud would later have it. It comes from the perception of a need that translates into desire. We know from the *Symposium* that love (*erōs*) is the symptom of an absence and a desire for what is absent (see I § 7, "Socrates Eros"). When, in his first Lysianic speech, Socrates defines love (*erōs*) for Phaedrus, he defines it as a desire (ἐπιθυμία, *epithymia*).

This treatment of the soul calls for careful attention, since it reflects the bipartite psychology familiar from earlier Greek sources. At this point of the *Phaedrus*, Socrates describes only two objects of desire: one is our natural desire for pleasure; the other is an acquired attitude (*doxa*) that makes the agent strive for what is most noble.[21] The division of the soul is established by the conflict of its parts. Here, the conflict is between reason and passion. Socrates' view of a bipartite soul is commonplace in the fifth century; we find it in Euripides' *Hippolytus*, where Phaedra's reason and passion are locked in conflict,[22] and in the *Medea*, where Medea's anger (*thymos*) is stronger than her reason.[23] Socrates discovers this bipartite psychology already present in Homer, in the passage where Odysseus addresses his heart.[24] In the *Phaedrus* we find it already in Lysias' speech.[25]

In Socrates' "palinode" in praise of love, the soul is seen as more complex: it possesses three distinct personalities represented by the winged human charioteer, the ugly black horse (also winged) who would draw the chariot down to earthly pleasures, and the winged white horse, which is greatly sensitive to the opinion of the charioteer, who is caught in the middle.[26] There is no argument here; only a "myth"[27] set out in a vivid image that has taken a deeper hold on the imagination of Plato's readers than the tripartite psychology argued for in book 4 of the *Republic*.[28] Nor is there any immedi-

---

21. *Phaedrus* 237D.

22. *Hippolytus* 378–90. Phaedra's words "We know and recognize what is good, but we do not carry it out" (380–81) have been taken as a Euripidean comment on the Socratic doctrine that no one does wrong knowingly. I think this is unlikely, since such a sentiment can be found in Sophocles' *Oedipus* 316–18, where Teiresias' knowledge does not control his conduct.

23. *Medea* 1078–80. The *Medea* was a text of great importance for the Stoic Chrysippos. One of his contemporaries quipped that his quotations from the play in one of his ethical treatises constituted "Chrysippos' *Medea*," DL 7.180. Chrysippos does in fact quote exactly these lines from the *Medea* in one of his books.

24. *Odyssey* 20.17, in *Republic* 4.441B.

25. *Phaedrus* 231A and D (Lysias); cf. 237D–238C (Socrates).

26. *Phaedrus* 253C–256E.

27. As Socrates styles it in *Phaedrus* 253C.

28. *Republic* 4.435B–445E.

ately apparent philosophical advantage to be gained in the argument of the *Phaedrus* by adding a third element to the soul, which was usually regarded as a compound of reason and passion. Perhaps we are prompted to reflect on the myth of Boreas and Oreithuia at play with the nymph Pharmakeia, or of Phaedrus caught between the cold Lysias and Socrates.

The *Republic* makes it clear what is to be gained by dividing the soul into three parts: reason, or the calculating part (*to logistikon*); a spirited part (*to thymoeides*), which is the seat of fear, anger, resentment, and ambition; and the lowest level (*to epithymētikon*), which is concerned with satisfying the natural appetites (*epithymiai*) of the body. What emerges from Socrates' analysis of the soul in the *Republic* is a theory of appetite and desire that places the preeminently social part of the soul (*to thymoeides*) at its center. In this psychology, the three parts of the soul are projected onto the three classes of Socrates' theoretical state, where we can view them "writ large":[29] the artisan and farming class is to desires as the guardian class is to the spirited element and the guardians proper (who will develop into philosopher kings) are to reason. In the strict parallelism between the state and the soul, the harmonious working of the three parts of each constitutes "justice."[30]

On the Platonic theory of appetites and desire, as this is articulated in the *Republic*, not all passions of the human soul are social. The passions of the mind are directed to the truth and the divine, and the philosopher who has known these returns to the city only reluctantly.[31] The bodily appetites are social only in that some require a partner for their satisfaction. Only the spirited middle level of the soul is the creation of society. It is for this reason that Socrates spends so much time on provisions for the education of the guardian class (the citizens who combine spirited and gentler qualities of soul) in books 2 and 3 of the *Republic*. Thus, he begins his discussion of education by considering the socializing and traditional lies told to children.[32] The guardians of his city are motivated by what they have been trained to regard as "most honorable." They possess something "philosophical" in their nature, but what this is does not become apparent until they are divided into the guardians of the state and their auxiliaries.[33] The discussion of the training of the philosopher is reached in book 7.[34]

29. *Republic* 2.368D; see III §6 ("Kallipolis").
30. The conclusion arrived at in *Republic* 4.433A.
31. *Republic* 7.519B–D and 539E.
32. *Republic* 2.376E.
33. *Republic* 3.415A and 5.458B–C.
34. *Republic* 7.521C–534E.

In his lesson on psychology in *Republic* 4,[35] Socrates speaks of the parts of the soul as if they were instrumental: we learn with one part; we are angry with another; and we desire with a third. In the element of desire, however, Socrates locates not only an instrument but a force driving the whole human being.[36] Socrates is careful to deprive desire of any element of rationality: when we are thirsty, he argues, we do not want a cup of spring water or Thasian wine; we simply want to drink.[37] By any other account, desire for a cup of Thasian wine, rather than fresh spring water, would involve choice and a hedonistic calculus. Socrates' clear and somewhat implausible tactic is to make the lowest part of the soul purely irrational. By an initial analysis of the soul into two conflicting parts, Socrates demonstrates precisely what he begins by assuming: a divided soul. The part that checks the desire for drink is reason, and a familiar conflict is recognized.

But what of the spirited part? Socrates offers an anecdote to illustrate a conflict between reason and what we might call spirit. He tells the story of Leontios, who, coming up to Athens from the Peiraeus, saw some bodies of executed criminals outside the north wall. (It is likely that they were executed by *tympanismos*; that is, they were clamped by the neck, legs, and arms to a tall plank and left to die of exposure in full view of the public.) Leontios was tempted to look at this grisly sight, but something within him restrained him. When he finally gave in to his base desire, he ran up to the corpses and cried out to his eyes: "You unhappy creatures, feast. Take your fill of this lovely sight!"[38] Socrates' example is a strange one. On the surface, it seems to oppose morbid curiosity, described in terms of appetite, and a sense of shame. But the conflict within Leontios might illustrate more aptly a conflict between the desire to observe and learn (*theōria*) and the feeling of social inhibition and restraint located in the middle part of the soul. The case of Leontios points, I think, to the case of the philosopher and the desires of the philosopher's soul.

Philosophia

Socrates' paradox concerning the necessity for a philosopher king forces him to describe the philosopher to Glaukon. As he does, he returns to the subject

35. *Republic* 4.435E–444E.
36. *Republic* 4.436A–B.
37. *Republic* 4.437D–E.
38. *Republic* 4.439E–440A.

of the soul.[39] He passes from *erōs*, with a single, undifferentiated object, to the love for honor in political life and the love of the philosopher, whose object is wisdom (*sophia*). At this point in the conversation, it is a question no longer of one part of the soul serving as an instrument but of all three parts of the soul possessing their own distinct objects of desire and their distinct sources of energy. The philosopher would "taste" every kind of learning and cannot get enough of it. Glaucon objects that if this were the case, "lovers of spectacles" (*philotheamones*) would qualify as philosophers. Socrates does not disagree: theatergoers are in fact like philosophers, but philosophers are drawn to the spectacle of the truth.[40] One of the functions of the rational soul is to govern the two lower levels, spirit and appetite. But this is not its desire; it desires wisdom. As a theory of desire, Plato's presentation of *erōs* in the *Republic*, *Symposium*, and *Phaedrus* is one of constant human frustration, and on all three of its levels the soul reads like a fable of unrequited love.

There is a strange sequel to the psychology of the *Republic*. In the physiology of the *Timaeus*, reason is described as the immortal part of the soul. From the "citadel" of the head, it controls the spirited and emotional element housed in the chest. In the lower region of the stomach are located the appetites, stirred by bodily needs. This part of the soul can only be controlled by the phantasms and images reflected down onto the smooth surface of the liver.[41]

No appetite or desire on any of these three levels can really be sated. The desires for food, drink, and sex are never satisfied for long; they arise anew like the head of the hydra once severed.[42] Plato does not offer us an analysis of the frustrated desires of the predominantly social part of the soul that yearns for honor and esteem, except as such an analysis is implicit in Socrates' discussion of the "timocratic" type of citizen in *Republic* 8.[43] A need for honor and esteem entails a dependency on one's fellow men, and its satisfaction is in their gift. The superiority of the philosophical life lies in knowing a kind of pleasure untasted by either businessman or politician. The philosopher, who knows the other pleasures, has experienced the pleasure of

39. In *Republic* 5.474C.
40. *Republic* 5.474C–475E.
41. *Timaeus* 69A–72B; this description seems to be a reflection of the "allegory" of the cave. See III §5 ("The Sun, the Line, and the Cave").
42. As Socrates puts it in reflecting on how pleasure has invaded his body after the pain of his fetters, *Phaedo* 60B–C. The *Philebus* entire is the appropriate sequel to these reflections. Here Socrates develops an elaborate analysis of pleasure as belonging to the category of the "unlimited."
43. *Republic* 8.549A–550C.

seeing the truth.[44] But so long as he is a philosopher, he will never possess the truth.

This possession is beyond the reach of humans incorporated in this life. And for this reason the conception of the soul set out in the Platonic dialogues is, like Diotima's demigod Eros, caught "in between" two states. As incarnate, the soul is described as a composite of three elements, and a healthy state of the soul is—like the state of Kallipolis—a harmony of its three parts under the mastery of reason.[45] One description of the soul as a "harmony," or a tuning, is rejected as a misleading metaphor in the *Phaedo*, for the metaphor does not enable us to distinguish between virtuous and vicious soul or to identify any superior element in the tempering of the strings of the soul. It also assumes a soul compounded of reason and the appetites and passions.[46] But the attractive metaphor of the soul as a harmony survives Socrates' refutation of it in the *Phaedo*. In the *Republic*, the terms "virtue" and "vice" attach to the attunement and discord of the soul respectively. Even the distinctions that articulate Socrates' conception of the soul as tripartite involve an ambiguity, for Socrates can speak of a human as being "in control himself" or "superior to himself." Of the two "selves," human rationality is the distinctive self. The concept of the controlling rationality of the soul leads Socrates to a conception of self-control as being the attunement of the three parts of the soul by reason.[47] The world soul of the *Timaeus*, too, has its parts, and these are adjusted to one another in a harmony of progressive, linear ratios.[48]

But human harmony is transient, as the Demiurge of the *Timaeus*, who created these harmonies, knew: everything that has been bound together can one day be loosened.[49] The three elements of the soul can be dissolved in formal analysis, and our inner conflicts show that they are not always in tune. The characterization of appetites, desires, passions, and love in the Platonic dialogues makes it apparent that all the elements of the Platonic soul are motivated by something lacking; they do not receive their energy solely from the power of bodily appetite or sexual desire. Freud, when he sought a respectable authority for his theory of infantile sexuality, reminded his poten-

---

44. *Republic* 9.582C.
45. *Phaedo* 85E–86E.
46. *Phaedo* 91C–95A.
47. *Republic* 4.431E–432A.
48. *Timaeus* 35B–36D.
49. *Timaeus* 41B.

tial critic of "how closely the enlarged sexuality of psycho-analysis coincides with the Eros of the divine Plato."[50] In this, he was mistaken.

But it is true to Plato to say that the most fundamental physical needs and desires of human life provide a model for what is craved by the spirited and intellectual parts of the soul. Leontios' desire (*epithymia*) was to see. The definition of *erōs* as "desire for something, and something [the desiring person] does not possess, and for what he is not himself and what he is in need of"[51] holds for the highest part of the soul. The term "lover" (*erastēs*) is extended metaphorically from the lover of bodies[52] to philosophers, who are "lovers of being and reality."[53]

In the *Symposium*, Diotima initiates the young Socrates into love's mysteries. The initiate first encounters the beautiful object of his passion, then the soul of the beloved, and then noble human activities and social institutions. In the next stage of his initiation, the lover finally transcends the individual and city and arrives at a vision of beauty itself, immutable and absolute.[54] The rapturous conclusion of Diotima's speech almost makes us forget that the vision of beauty is a fleeting experience and that even the highest and most divine part of the soul can never permanently possess what it lacks. Only the gods have wisdom; human beings cannot be wise.[55] But some intelligent men are driven by their awareness of what they lack to seek what they can never possess. These are philosophers. They are like Psyche in Apuleius' allegory of the incarnate human soul passionately in love with a divinity she can never see or possess—a divinity who warns her, "[I]f you see [my face], you will not see it."[56] The difference is that the soul of the philosopher can behold Beauty and the beauty of the Ideas, but not forever. One day it must fall back into the body and renew its longing for what it lacks.

ENDNOTE: Plutarch, in his dialogue *On Love*, and Baldesar Castiglione, in the speech he gives Cardinal Bembo in book 4 of his *Book of the Courtier* (1528, Charles S. Singleton trans. 1959, 349–57), represent two of the most important assimilations of the Platonic conception of *erōs* as love for something

50. "Three Essays on the Theory of Sexuality," in *The Standard Edition of the Psychological Works of Sigmund Freud* (New York, 1976), 7:134, quoted by Bennett Simon (1978), 200.
51. *Symposium* 200E.
52. *Symposium* 210B.
53. *Republic* 6.501D; *Timaeus* 46D.
54. *Symposium* 209E–212A, a passage translated in III §4 ("Thinking About Ideas").
55. *Lysis* 218A and *Symposium* 204B; cf. *Phaedrus* 278D.
56. "Non videbis si videris," *Metamorphoses* 5.11.5.

higher and greater than the human object that first inspired the passion. In strident contrast, Gregory Vlastos' essay "The Individual as an Object of Love in Plato," chapter 1 in *Platonic Studies* (1981), gives an unsympathetic criticism of a view that Cardinal Bembo commended with rapture. Love as unrealizable desire is the focus given *erōs* by David Halperin, "Platonic *Erōs* and What Men Call Love" (1985). Martha Nussbaum's essay, "The Speech of Alcibiades: A Reading of the *Symposium*" (1986, chap. 6), sets out a dramatic conflict between two kinds of love: that of Alcibiades (for the individual) and that of Socrates (for the universal); she (1986, chap. 7) also attempts to show that Plato reformed his thinking about *erōs* in the *Symposium* and recorded this new understanding of *erōs* as intelligent and discriminating in the *Phaedrus*. Thomas Gould's *Platonic Love* (1963) is a study of *erōs* in its manifold appearances in the Platonic corpus. G.R.F. Ferrari, in "Platonic Love" (1992), has an excellent treatment of *erōs* in the *Phaedrus* and especially the *Symposium*.

For the background of Plato's psychology, Jan N. Bremmer's anthropological study, *The Early Greek Concept of the Soul* (1983), is recommended. David B. Claus provides a linguistic history of the word in *Toward the Soul: An Inquiry into the Meaning of* ψυχή *Before Plato* (1981). In *Plato's Psychology* (1970), T. M. Robinson surveys the Platonic dialogues to reconstruct a general theory of the soul. G.M.A. Grube treats both *erōs* and the soul in chapters 3 and 4 of *Plato's Thought* (1935).

In a moment of philosophical daring, Socrates tells Glaukon that the philosopher trained in dialectics can actually *see* the Good itself.[1] This strikes us as the claim of a mystic. And there are, in fact, many mysteries to the theory of Ideas. Indeed, when Diotima describes the final vision of Beauty that awaits the lover, she tells Socrates that he has entered into the final stage of his initiation:

> Even you, Socrates, could be initiated into these [preliminary] mysteries of love. But as for the culminating stage of vision, for the sake of which these mysteries are preliminary—should the initiate approach them properly—I do not know if you are capable of arriving at it.[2]

This final stage brings the initiate to the mystic vision of Beauty itself. Diotima is its hierophant:

> It exists forever. Neither does it come into being, nor does it pass away; nor does it wax or wane; nor is it beautiful in one respect and ugly in another; nor is it beautiful at one moment but not at another; nor is it beautiful in comparison with one thing but ugly in comparison with another; nor beautiful in one place but ugly in another; nor will it appear to the initiate in the guise of a face or hands or anything else that the body partakes of. Nor is it a kind of discourse or knowledge; nor yet does it exist some place in some other thing—in an animal or in the earth or in heaven or in anything else. But it exists in isolation, by itself, with itself, unique of its kind, forever. And all other beautiful things

---

1. *Republic* 7.540A–B. In this treatment I capitalize words for the Platonic Forms (as I do earlier) to set them apart.
2. *Symposium* 209E–210A.

partake of it in such a manner that that Beauty beyond them is in no degree increased or diminished when these other beautiful things come into being and perish; nor does it suffer any change.[3]

Seeing and Knowing

Diotima does not speak of the Form (ἰδέα, *idea*) of Beauty, but her emphasis on sight and vision makes Socrates' talk about seeing the Idea of the Good at once less mysterious and more comprehensible. More comprehensible, that is, to a speaker of Greek. Plato did not invent the word; in Greek the noun *idea* means the look of a thing, an appearance, shape, or form. The word with which it connects is εἶδος (*eidos*). Both derive from the verb "to see" (ἰδεῖν, *idein*), and Plato frequently associates verbs for seeing with the word *idea*[4] to stress its etymology and the connection between sight and knowledge. In Greek "to have seen" is "to know" (οἶδα, *oida*). In the opening sentences of the *Metaphysics* Aristotle makes the connection between sight and knowledge manifest:

> By nature all men have a craving for knowledge. One sign of this is the love they have for their senses, for apart from their usefulness they are loved by themselves, and, more than any other, the sense of sight. For men prefer sight to practically everything else, not only as a means to doing something but even when they intend to do nothing at all. The reason for this love is that, more than the other senses, sight makes it possible to discern reality and reveals many distinctions.[5]

Aristotle's word for knowledge is the perfect infinitive *eidenai* (εἰδέναι), "to have seen," therefore, "to know."

The association between sight and knowledge is compelling in the visual world of the Greek Aegean. Here intense light penetrating a clear atmosphere reveals a stark and simple landscape of water, earth, air, and *aither* (the brilliant, burning vault of heaven). Shapes are sharply delineated in a world of clean profiles. Even man-made objects have the status of clear and distinct "ideas" (in the sense of shape). The profiles of Greek vases declare their type and function over millennia. The paintings of Monet would wither in this world of sere, clear light. A glance at Monet's studies of the cathedral of

---

3. *Symposium* 211A–B.
4. As he does in *Parmenides* 132A and *Republic* 7.517C.
5. *Metaphysics* 1.1.980ª20–27.

Rouen seen at different times of day and Frederick Edwin Church's illuminist painting of the Parthenon silently establishes the contrast.

We find the word *idea* in Herodotus in the sense of appearance and shape (as contrasted with color) and in the extended meaning of type. In the Hippocratic corpus the word is used to indicate types of bile or a type of disease. Thucydides reflects this medical usage when he describes the symptoms of the plague that devastated Athens in 430 as presenting an *idea* of the disease, a disease he describes in clinical detail so that it could be recognized if it ever recurred.[6] The words *idea* and *eidos* did not possess a monopoly on the designation of types and classes. The semantically related *typos* (an impression struck on a receiving surface) and *charaktēr* (an impression etched on a receiving surface) also served, as did words in the semantic field of *genos* (cognate with our word "kind"). In their metaphoric extensions, these words expressed abstract categories. One of these abstractions, recognized with clarity by the mind's eye but invisible to the naked eye, was the atomic shapes that defined and were defined by void. These Democritus called *atomoi ideai*—"shapes of matter that cannot be sectioned."[7]

Recollecting Lost Conversations

In Plato's dialogues, we find the words *idea* and *eidos* used as both the look of a thing and an abstract type. We find too a theory, mainly associated with Socrates, who is fully initiated into its powers. This is not the Socrates of Aristotle (in his history of philosophy), who drew attention down from the heavens to the earthbound problems of ethics as he sought for definitions and universals in this contentious field.[8] In the Platonic dialogues, Socrates' theory is that there exist in the mind's eye "forms" that relate to visible objects, states, relationships, and virtues as archetypes relate to their copies. It seems that in his conception of the relation between an archetype and its copy (or product), Plato owes something to Greek art. The term *paradeigma* is best known from Greek architecture, one of Plato's master arts. It describes the architect's design for a building as well as a model for the profile of the capitals that surmount its columns.

The Platonic theory of Ideas is so well known and, indeed, so notorious that we expect a careful presentation of it somewhere in the dialogues. This,

6. *The Peloponnesian War* 2.48.3 and 2.51.1.
7. DK 68 A 57 and B 141.
8. As Aristotle characterizes his contribution in *Metaphysics* 1.6.987ª29–987ᵇ13.

surprisingly, is not what we find. Socrates refers to the theory in both the *Phaedo* and the *Republic*—two dialogues in which the theory has a crucial role to play—as something long familiar to his interlocutors. In both cases the theory is used as a hypothesis in order to establish something else. In the *Phaedo*, Socrates deploys a theory of Forms in his discussion of causality. He tells Kebes that he has made use of this procedure "on other occasions and in our conversation of just a short time ago."[9] But he adds mysteriously: "Now I will return to those considerations so often dinned into your ears and begin with them. Accordingly, I assume the existence of some Beauty itself that exists in relation to itself and of some Good and of everything else."[10] Socrates provided an example of this kind of entity when he distinguished for Kebes between things that are compounds and things that are simple; the essential nature of what is uncompounded is that it always remains in the same state and never suffers any change. He offers as examples the Equal itself and Beauty itself. "The Equal itself, the Beautiful itself, the essential nature of each thing, its being, is never susceptible to any change, of any kind at all."[11]

In this brief and tantalizing section of the *Phaedo* we have one of the longest treatments of the theory of Ideas in the Platonic dialogues, but Socrates alerts us to the elliptical character of his exposition by referring to conversations that have gone unrecorded. When he refers to his often stated argument that knowledge is recollection, his companion Simmias fails to recollect it from their earlier conversations: "Remind me. I don't have a very clear recollection at present."[12] Just as Simmias has failed to recollect the theory Socrates disclosed to him in their earlier conversations, the human soul is capable of forgetting that it had once seen in the realm of Ideas. Yet the argument from recollection is crucial in explaining how we come to recognize the Forms in this life, and our discarnate knowledge of the Forms is crucial to Socrates' argument that the soul is immortal.

Socrates makes this same curious claim in a conversation with Glaukon in the *Republic*. When he introduces the Idea of the Good as the highest form of knowledge for the philosopher, he recalls his theory to his forgetful companion:

9. Referring to *Phaedo* 78B–80C.
10. *Phaedo* 100B.
11. *Phaedo* 78D.
12. *Phaedo* 73A.

SOCRATES:

I have reminded you of what has been said before and has already been said on many other occasions.

GLAUKON:

What is that?

SOCRATES:

We say of many beautiful things that they exist and of many good things that they exist, and in this manner we say that every individual thing exists, and we define them in our speech.

GLAUKON:

So we say.

SOCRATES:

And we take the position that there is a Beauty quite by itself and a Good itself, and so, for everything that we then posit as many, we in turn speak of each of these under the category of a single form, taking this form to be single, and we name each thing what it is in truth.[13]

This is an opaque conversation, and Glaukon can be forgiven for letting it slip out of memory. Socrates is evidently thinking of his earlier claim to Glaukon that justice and injustice, good and bad, and all the subjects of the conversation of the *Republic* are "each one, when taken by themselves; but, when each is associated with bodies, actions, and with one another on many occasions, it takes on the appearance of a number of different things."[14] Socrates' point in this earlier passage is to distinguish true philosophers from their look-alikes, but it is clear from Socrates' reminder of this method that Glaukon cannot immediately apply this brief lesson in abstraction to the Idea of the Good, to which Socrates introduces him at the end of book 6.

In his final discussion of the status of *mimēsis* in *Republic* 10, Socrates returns to still other earlier conversations about the Ideas—some lost, some briefly recorded. Again, he is speaking to Glaukon: "Do you want us to begin our inquiry from this point and follow our usual method? Now, I take it that we are in the habit of positing a single Form [*eidos*] for each of the many things to which we apply the same name."[15] Socrates goes on to use the single

13. *Republic* 6.507A–B.
14. *Republic* 5.475E–476A.
15. *Republic* 10.596A.

name we apply to the many beds of our experience and argues that there must exist a single Form of Bed.

Even as we attempt to come to terms with the theory of Ideas advanced by Socrates in the Platonic dialogues, we become aware of difficulties, which are compounded by a certain mystery. In the *Phaedo* and *Republic* the theory is not developed at any length, ostensibly because Socrates can refer to what he has said earlier in the dialogue and on "previous occasions." Within these two dialogues we have the briefest and most frustrating sketch not of an argument but of a conclusion, too readily agreed to by Socrates' interlocutors. These arguments made "on previous occasions" remind us of the conversations postponed to "another occasion" in the aporetic dialogues.

There are occasions in the dialogues when we hear of "Beauty itself." We have heard Diotima's mystic description of it in the *Symposium*. In the longer *Hippias* (whose authenticity has been doubted but which is revealing for the discussions surrounding the theory of Ideas) we gain another notion of how the mind arrives at the Idea of the Beautiful. Again, the conversation concerns Beauty. Since we ascribe the adjective "beautiful" to the many sights and sounds that give us pleasure, there must exist some single thing "that makes two objects beautiful and that belongs to both in common and to each separately."[16] Taking the part of a skeptic, Socrates identifies some of the difficulties of such a claim: the number one applies to Socrates and Hippias individually but not in common. Socrates asks Hippias: "You say that both pleasures [of sight and hearing] are beautiful?" By "you," plural, Socrates means Greeks who, he claims, are in the habit of subsuming all the scattered things they praise as beautiful under the abstract concept "beauty." "The beautiful thing" (τὸ καλόν, *to kalon*) is one way Greek forms the abstract concept "beauty"; the neuter article and adjective stand as a substantive.

But Socrates' notion of Beauty goes well beyond the habits of speakers of Greek in the cluster of qualifications that attach to a concept that is elevated to the status of *idea* or *eidos*. By adding "taken by itself, in relation to itself, with itself" (as does Diotima), Plato reveals his motives for advancing a theory of absolute Beauty. Diotima's long speech makes it abundantly clear that Beauty, when taken by itself and isolated from the things we call beautiful, is not relative. It admits comparison with nothing else and excludes judgments like "Socrates is fair when compared to Silenus but ugly when compared to Alcibiades."

16. *Hippias Maior* 300A.

Coming to Recognize the Forms

Before turning to Plato's philosophical motives for advancing a theory of ideas, and the criticisms Plato and others exposed it too, I should try to summarize as simply as I can what Socrates has said about the Forms so far. We begin to become aware of the existence of Forms by reflecting on the way we use the same adjective or noun to describe or name many things. An *idea* is, then, an enabling concept that, taken in isolation and abstracted from its many instances, allows us to speak of things of our experiences as being many yet one. In Greek, our ability to speak of things as "beautiful" (*kala*) would be impossible without a guiding conception of *to kalon*. Our very judgments involving superiority and inferiority involve such an absolute standard.[17] By a process of abstraction from the particular to the universal, we can gain a clear view of Forms like Justice or Beauty or the Good in our mind's eye.

What then do Ideas amount to? And where do they exist? It is clear, I think, that they cannot be innate to the mind, for in a manner of speaking we can "see" them as something external to us. Nor is an Idea in all of its fixity and certainty to be discovered in the visible world, where all things change. An Idea must be an immutable object of human reason. If we ask persistently, How do we come to recognize the existence of such Forms? we seem to hear three answers. The first is familiar from the *Republic*: we recognize Forms such as "the Beautiful itself" by abstracting from the many things we name "beautiful" in our sensuous experience. Or we can say, with Diotima in the *Symposium*, that we know the Form of Beauty by an ascent: Beauty "itself" is known first as it is present in a single beautiful body; it is then seen in all beautiful bodies; and then it is recognized as the soul moves upward (through its two higher levels) to institutions and the culminating vision of Beauty itself. There is a third version of this perplexing account in two dialogues concerned with the immortality of the soul, the *Phaedo* and *Phaedrus*: an idea is known by the discarnate soul in its "free" state and is dimly recognized and recalled by the soul when it is incorporated in the body and is reminded of the Idea by something in its experience in the world.[18] All of these versions of the theory are open to objection, but, before we consider their difficulties and vulnerabilities, we should consider Plato's philosophical motives for advancing such a theory.

17. Most clearly stated in *Phaedo* 74D–E.
18. *Phaedo* 72E–77A and *Phaedrus* 248A–252C.

The Question of Motivation

There are a number of curious features to this theory, so stated. One is that in the dialogues we have considered so far, the theory is employed solely as a hypothesis in order to explain something else, not as a philosophical goal in itself. The theory is employed to demonstrate the immortality or, at least, the preexistence of the soul in the *Meno* and *Phaedo*, and it seems to be latent in Socrates' description of the heavenly vision of the discarnate soul in the *Phaedrus*;[19] In *Republic* 10 it is deployed by Socrates to prepare for his demonstration of the immortality of the soul and to illustrate the degree of reality possessed by the objects depicted by the painter. It is only in book 6 of the *Republic* that the crucial Idea of Ideas—"the Idea of the Good"—is treated independently (see III § 5, "The Sun, the Line, and the Cave"). Another feature of this theory is that it can be invoked without using the terms *idea* or *eidos*. These words are not employed to describe the concept in the passages we have reviewed from the *Phaedo* and *Symposium*. The concept is described rather by the use of the definite article with the neuter singular of an adjective and the isolating pronoun (αὐτὸ τὸ ἴσον, αὐτὸ τὸ καλόν, *auto to ison, auto to kalon*): "the equal thing, the beautiful thing, taken in isolation."

This pronoun is eloquent, for it indicates Plato's philosophical motives for advancing a theory of absolute standards by which we can name, judge, measure, and, as will appear, make. *Eidē*, the Forms, make knowledge possible, since they are neither relative (except in the *Sophist* and *Parmenides*, where they relate to their opposites) nor changing. What is positive and not antagonistic in the theory clearly owes something to Plato's reflections on Parmenides' conception of being, as this is set out as a revelation in the Way of Truth in his poem *On Nature*. For Parmenides, being is single, ungenerated and eternal, indivisible, whole and continuous, and unmoving—like a perfect sphere.[20] It is the object of mental perception. The goddess of the proem directs the narrator of the poem to gaze with his mind's eye: "Even so, gaze steadily at things that are distant yet vividly present to your mind."[21] But the theory also has its antagonistic motivation, which is to counter the sophistic relativism associated with Heraclitus and Protagoras in the dialogues and very much a force both in the age of Socrates and that of Plato. This relativism is exposed

---

19. *Phaedrus* 246A–256E, 249B–C especially.
20. DK 28 B 8.18–23, or as the fragment is further fragmented in KRS 296–98.
21. DK 28 B 4.1 (KRS 313).

in the *Theaetetus*, where Heraclitus is made the originator of a theory of flux and Protagoras is made his disciple. It has clear political implications.

Beauty, the Good, and Equality are secure members in a limited set of Forms. It would seem that the theory of Forms has no particular bearing on the world of judgments made by men in the polis. But this is not the case. In the *Republic*, as we have seen, Socrates speaks of Justice and Injustice, the Good and the Bad, in language that describes the Forms.[22] Later in this same dialogue he asserts that the Form of the Good is the most important thing a ruler should know; and at the end of book 9 the Form of absolute Justice provides the philosopher with the pattern by which to put his own soul in order.[23] The theory of Forms is made political in the *Republic*.

In the *Republic*, Socrates distinguishes sharply between the realms of truth and opinion. In Socrates' image of the cave, the contrast with the flickering play of shadows before the prisoners of the cave makes the possibility of clear and absolute standards of judgment powerfully attractive.[24] Socrates' cave is one version of the world of Athenian democracy, in which opinion (*doxa*) was tyrant. If they are to be identified, the puppeteers of the cave, whose shadow theater engrosses the prisoners of the cave, must be the poets and politicians of Athens. The rhetorical training merchandised by the sophists helped Athenian politicians manipulate the perception of "what seemed best" (in the language introducing the decrees of the state of Athens) to the people.[25]

Protagoras held the view that "man is the measure of all things: of things that are, that they exist; of things that do not exist, that they do not exist."[26] Whatever he meant by this, he certainly meant that human beings and not the gods are the measure of all things that concern humans. In the *Theaetetus*, he is made to hold the view that each individual is the measure of all things.[27] The reason Plato turned to some higher and absolute standard of judgment in political life emerges in the digression in the *Theaetetus* where Socrates

22. *Republic* 5.475E–476A.
23. *Republic* 6.504E–505B, 519C–D, and 9.592B.
24. *Republic* 7.514A–517A, a passage read in III §5 ("The Sun, the Line, the Cave").
25. "It seemed best to the Council and the Assembly." (The verb *edoxe* is cognate with the noun *doxa*.) Socrates makes much of this formula of Attic inscriptions in the *Phaedrus* (258A), where it is presented as the prelude to written praise. In the *Gorgias* (481D), Socrates contrasts his loves with those of Kallikles: Socrates is in love with Alcibiades and Philosophy; Kallikles with the Athenian *demos* and Demos, the son of Pyrilampes.
26. DK 80 B 1.
27. *Theaetetus* 152A.

extends Protagoras' principle of man (the individual, that is) as the measure to political communities.[28] Socrates asks:

Does this not hold for things political? Whatever a city conceives of as noble and disgraceful, just and unjust, holy and not, and establishes as lawful and customary, is such in truth so far as the city is concerned. And in these matters no private individual or city is a whit wiser than any other.[29]

In this same passage, Socrates stirs the "river gods" Heraclitus and his follow-ers into a titanomachy against the stability of Parmenides' conception of real-ity, in a philosophical cartoon many have taken to represent Plato's own position, as he stands in the middle of the two drawn lines and attempts to reconcile fluidity and plurality with the stability and uniformity of the Forms.[30]

Plato returns to Protagoras for a last time in the *Laws* as the Athenian Stranger reflects on who is best qualified to rule a political community and pits individual ambition and electoral rivalries against a higher standard. What qualifications should such a ruler have, if not those that prevail in most cities? The answer the Cretan founding father, Kleinias, gives him is: "He should be one of those who follows the god." To which the Athenian replies:

Well, then, what activity is dear to the god and follows in his footsteps? There is only one, and there is an ancient account of it, that he who is like to a being who is truly moderate and measured would be dear to that being, and that things that have no measure are dear neither to one another nor to those things that have measure. For us, god will be the supreme measure of all things and much higher than the individual human being, who is, as they say, "the measure of all things."[31]

A theory of absolute forms is not required to make this assertion, but the relativism Plato detected in Protagoras explains in part his motives for intro-ducing the hypothesis that there are invariant and absolute Forms that make true knowledge and judgment possible.

28. *Theaetetus* 172A–181B.
29. *Theaetetus* 172A.
30. *Theaetetus* 179C–181B.
31. *Laws* 4.716C. The "ancient account" the Athenian Stranger refers to is that of *Odyssey* 17.218.

Friends and Critics of the Forms

In the *Republic*, Socrates speaks of the "Friends of the Forms."[32] Aristotle was a friend of Plato, but, as he said in his *Nicomachean Ethics*, of two friends, Truth is preferable to Plato. Plato's theory of Forms, which he never advances in his own name (except in Letter VII), has been under constant attack, even among his closest students. Aristotle's criticism of the theory of Forms might have been the decisive event in formulating his own philosophy. But Plato was not himself a friend of "Plato." We can see the first stages of rigorous philosophical criticism of the theory in the Platonic dialogues themselves.

In the *Parmenides*, Parmenides subjects the young Socrates' concept of transcendental Forms to debilitating dialectical criticism. In this dialogue, the young Socrates states his conception of the theory to Parmenides' younger associate, Zeno of Elea, in terms that are now familiar. However, we are then introduced to a new pair of antithetical forms: "Do you not think," Zeno asks, "that there exists a Form of Similarity itself, taken by itself, and that there exists a form opposite to this Form so described, which is dissimilar; and do you not think that you and I and everything we call 'many' come to participate in these Forms, which are two in number?"[33] The new feature in the theory attributed to Socrates[34] is that forms are relational and fall into columns of opposing pairs. In this sense they cannot be "taken by themselves."

After Zeno has urged his criticism of Socrates' conception of Forms, Parmenides steps in and deftly and rapidly exposes the difficulties of any theory stated in these terms. (These are the terms of the *Republic*.) He shows first that, whenever we apply the same name to many things, we do not thereby establish the existence of the thing "itself." In Plato, the population of forms has to this point been severely limited. In the dialogues we have reviewed, the census of forms includes Equality, the Beautiful, the Just (and Unjust), and the Good (and Bad). There is also the Bed (which the philosopher would hesitate to dignify with capitals) of *Republic* 10. This Bed is remarkable for being a noun.

In Letter VII, the Good, the Beautiful, and the Just, along with artificial and natural Bodies, the Elements, animate Life, States of the soul, and Actions and Feelings, are listed in the late census of Forms that Plato names in his own

32. *Sophist* 248A.
33. *Parmenides* 128E–129A.
34. Seen already in *Republic* 5.476A.

voice.[35] But earlier, in the *Parmenides*, Parmenides inquires with true Socratic disingenuousness: Is there a Form of Human Being—or Fire or Water—or Hair or Dirt or Mud?[36] Two arguments against the notion of "participation" of Form and the object it informs seem disabling, if their tacit premises are accepted. First, if there is a Form of Largeness that applies to everything to which the adjective "large" applies, the mind, as it contemplates this form together with each large thing in the set of large things, will then require still another form of Largeness for the Form Large to qualify as large. In the schools of philosophy this argument came to be known as the "third-man" argument.

Parmenides then employs the counterargument that if, as Socrates holds, the forms are to be understood as patterns (*paradeigmata*), their copies must resemble them. If patterns in turn resemble what is copied from them, then they must on this hypothesis have an original to which *they* stand as copies, and so on, in an infinite regress.[37] These arguments are not adequately answered within the *Parmenides*, but the reader might reflect and answer that the Form "the Large itself" is not large, as are the measurable objects of our experience; nor can a Form understood as an archetype resemble its copies, for it stands as a standard. A gallon container is not a gallon, a blueprint is not a Parthenon, and a mother cannot be said to "favor" her daughter.

Speaking in Metaphors

There are still other difficulties in the theory of Forms that attract both its friends and enemies. In the first generation of the theory, Aristotle was right in seeing a metaphor as its driving force.[38] The metaphoric slippage he finds illicit is the concept of Ideas as patterns. There are, in fact, two metaphors in play as the Forms are described in the dialogues. One is drawn from human art, the other from nature. Like all good philosophical metaphors, these metaphors also provide philosophical models. The metaphor of pattern (παρά-δειγμα, *paradeigma*) belongs to the field of human art and production, and architecture especially; the metaphor of family groupings and natural kinds (γένη, *genē*) belongs to the domain of spontaneous nature (*physis*). Socrates' ideal Bed in *Republic* 10 is the most striking example of the Forms as patterns.

---

35. Letter VII 342D. This is a vast extension, which creates serious difficulties for the statements of the theory we have reviewed until now.
36. *Parmenides* 130B–C.
37. *Parmenides* 132C–133A.
38. *Metaphysics* 1.9.991ª20–22.

Let us consider once again the Bed of the *Republic* and its analogue in an earlier dialogue. Socrates' Bed is anticipated in the *Cratylus,* a dialogue on the rightness of names. On one view, names are like tools that accurately distinguish the nature of the thing named.[39] Is there, then, a maker of these tools, who "fixes his eye on the thing itself that is a name?"[40] When a carpenter makes a shuttle for a loom, he trains his mind's eye on the invisible form of the tool. If he breaks the wooden copy of this form, he looks back to the form to create another. This pattern Shuttle is "that which, with perfect justification, we might call a shuttle." This Shuttle is like the Bed of *Republic* 10.[41] There are many beds in the world about us. The bedmaker creates the bed we sleep on by fixing his mind's eye on the single pattern of a bed. To the question Who creates this pattern of a bed? Socrates responds by declaring that god is the maker of the pattern Bed, which exists in the nature of things. He is constrained to create a single pattern, for, if he produced two, a third would appear, so as to stand as the pattern for the plurality of two. (This qualification seems to recognize the force of the "third-man argument" in the *Parmenides.*) Socrates shifts metaphorical ground as he goes on to speak of this creator god as the *begetter* and maker of the Bed.[42] The patterns of natural and artificial production are exploited to the full in the *Timaeus,* where the creator of the universe is called both father and craftsman (see III § 7, "The World of the Demiurge").

The second Platonic metaphor for the forms is that of natural kinds. It makes its dramatic appearance in the *Phaedrus,* in Socrates' description of the philosophical method of division and collection, by which things scattered up and down are collected in a single form and, in turn, things that are composite are "cut" and anatomized into their natural articulations.[43] This method of division and collection of the categories of our thinking marks the end to Socrates' customary procedure of discovering a single form that makes all of its many namesakes intelligible. Love (*erōs*), for example, can be distinguished into two distinct genera (the right- and the left-handed), and these into their species.[44] Socrates appeals to the natural bilateral articulations of the body. Here in the *Phaedrus* we have the first appearance of a dialectical

39. *Cratylus* 388A.
40. *Cratylus* 389D.
41. *Cratylus* 389B; *Republic* 10.597B.
42. φυτουϱγον, *Republic* 10.597B–D, literally "the planter."
43. *Phaedrus* 265D.
44. As they are distinguished in *Phaedrus* 237B–238C.

method that is put on such prominent display in the *Sophist, Statesman,* and *Philebus.* These dialogues of division and collection stand to the creation of categories and the refined parceling of the distinctions of our conceptual world as Carolus Linnaeus (1707–78) stands to our present binomial nomenclature for plants and animals. His *Genera Plantarum* (1737) and *Species Plantarum* (1753) are due, ultimately, to Plato and to the Socrates who now calls himself a "lover of divisions and collections." Yet, as appears from a confession of the Eleatic Stranger, in the *Statesman,* the practice of making these divisions, however strange they may seem, is no more than training in critical thinking.[45]

Both paradigms for the Forms—the artificial and the natural—present their own difficulties. The invention of the computer chip and the publication of Darwin's *Origin of the Species* (1859) point to one: some inventions have come into being where they did not exist before, and species have changed. The Forms can do neither. And those Forms that designate moral concepts (Holiness, Justice, the Good, Beauty) do not fall comfortably under the paradigm of natural kinds. Nor do moral concepts seem, particularly today, fixed in the nature of things as eternal standards for action and moral judgment. But of the two paradigms, the artistic has gained the most eloquent adherents. It is said that Socrates' contemporary, the painter Zeuxis, produced a painting of the ideal Helen for the city of Croton by abstracting his perfect form from the partial perfections of five of the young beauties of that city. The result of this abstraction might be called Helen "herself." In the Renaissance, Leone Battista Alberti retells this notorious anecdote to stress that the study of nature yields "that idea of beauty which even the most experienced mind can hardly perceive."[46] Renaissance painters, who worked from cartoons, were duly impressed by the anecdote they discovered in the elder Pliny concerning the greatest of all Greek painters, Parrhasios. At his death he left dispersed throughout the Greek world not only his paintings but his sketchbooks and panels. In these the aspiring artist could find the outlines of the world of painterly forms.[47] In Greek, the word for a painter (*grapheus*) is the word for an etcher (from the verb *graphein*).

Freed of its philosophical context in Plato and invested in matter, as it

---

45. *Phaedrus* 266B and *Philebus* 16B; *Statesman* 285D–E.

46. Leone Battista Alberti, *On Painting* (*Della Pittura,* 1436), 151, as cited by Erwin Panofsky (see Endnote) and Anthony Blunt (1940, 17). This is the painterly solution to the choice of Paris: not one, but abstracting from all.

47. *Historia Naturalis* 35.68. Parrhasios' conversation with Socrates about ideal types (Xenophon, *Memorabilia* 3.10.1–6) was well remembered in the Renaissance.

was by Aristotle, the conception of ideal Forms is most memorably expressed by Michelangelo, the sculptor who "liberated" Night from Carrara marble:

> *The best of artists possesses no conception*
> *That a single block of marble does not*
> *In its excess of matter*
> *Circumscribe within itself.*
> *And this only the hand*
> *That is obedient to the mind can reach.*[48]

This conception of form is exploited by Aristotle, for whom a bronze ingot is the foremost example of a material cause, and the shape that has taken form in the mind of the sculptor is the best example of the cause he calls *eidos.* Despite his philosophy that invests form in matter, his judgment of the union of material and formal cause is Platonic: "So, the form is prior to the matter and more real."[49]

ENDNOTE: The best approach I know to an appreciation of the Platonic theory of Ideas is not philosophical or linguistic but artistic. Erwin Panofsky's *Idea: A Concept in Art Theory: A Study of the Definition and Conception of the Term "Idea," from Plato to the 17th Century, When the Modern Definition Emerged* (original 1924; translation 1968) is, as its long title suggests, a retrospective study. But, in its emphasis on art, it reveals the importance of ideal shapes in Greek artistic culture. Rhys Carpenter, *The Aesthetic Basis of Greek Art* (1959, esp. 107–8), stresses the importance both of the clarity of the Aegean and of profiles in Greek art. Pierre Devambez, in *Greek Painting* (1962), provides a convenient foldout illustrating the repertory of Greek vase profiles, which represent one form of *eidē.*

The problems of the theory of Ideas are addressed already in Plato's *Parmenides.* Aristotle devoted a treatise to the problem, *On Ideas,* and he touches on the problem in his *On Philosophy.* In many ways the terms of this treatise will be unfamiliar to the reader of the Platonic dialogues. The testimonia for *On Ideas* are collected as frags. 1–5 in Ross (= *The Complete Works of Aristotle,* 2.2435–2441). An excellent guide to Aristotle's criticism of the theory is Gail Fine, *On Ideas: Aristotle's Criticism of Plato's Theory of Forms* (1993).

48. "Non ha l'ottimo artista alcun concetto," poem 151 in James M. Saslow, *The Poetry of Michelangelo* (New Haven and London, 1991), 302 (my translation). On the next page Saslow reproduces a photograph of Michelangelo's *Awakening Slave* (Florence, Galleria dell'Accademia).

49. *Metaphysics* 7.3.1029^{a}1–7.

The principal comprehensive study of Plato's theory of Ideas is that of Aristotle's editor, W.D. Ross, *Plato's Theory of Ideas* (1951). Also noteworthy are G.M.A. Grube's chapter on the subject, in *Plato's Thought* (1935); Harold Cherniss, "The Philosophical Economy of the Theory of Ideas" (1936); and the more analytically acute article of Nicholas P. White, "Plato's Metaphysical Epistemology" (1992). Drew Hyland, "But What About the Ideas," in *Finitude and Transcendence in the Platonic Dialogues* (1995), raises many of the problems that I raise here. The reader who becomes fixed on the "third-man" argument in the *Parmenides* should begin with Gregory Vlastos, "Plato's 'Third Man' Argument" in *Platonic Studies* (1981), and pause with Constance C. Meinewalt, "Good-bye to the Third Man" (1992). The debate, of course, continues.

SOCRATES:

Now form an image of our nature in respect to its education or lack of it that corresponds to the condition I will describe to you. Behold human beings in a subterranean and cavelike dwelling, as it were, with a long entrance opening up to the light that travels the entire length of the cave. These people have lived there since they were children, with their hands, legs, and necks bound so they cannot budge but can only see in front of them and, because of their bonds, are incapable of moving their heads around. Above them, to their backs, and at some distance, burns the light of a fire. See a roadway above, between the light and the prisoners, and a small wall that has been built alongside it, like the parapets puppeteers set in front of their audience, on which they manipulate their puppets.

GLAUKON:

I see.

SOCRATES:

Now see men carrying all sorts of props that are visible above the wall—statues and other creatures fashioned out of stone and wood and of every kind. As you would expect, some of the men carrying these props speak and others remain silent.

GLAUKON:

You are talking of a strange image and strange prisoners.

SOCRATES:

They are like us.[1]

1. *Republic* 7.514A–515A.

No passage in the Platonic dialogues is or should be better known than this. In it Socrates describes a cave with prisoners fixed in front of its back wall. They are the audience to the shadow theater that flickers on the surface of the cave wall before them. This passage in the *Republic* is usually described as Plato's "allegory" of the cave. Its profound influence on later philosophy is one token of the success of Plato's educational enterprise of preparing the reader for philosophical thought by radically alienating him or her from the familiar and trusted. But the wages of Plato's success are that this "allegory" (or, better, comparison) itself is now familiar and trusted. In his early dialogue *On Philosophy*, Aristotle drew on its inspiration to turn his readers to philosophy, and, by his deliberate allusion to Plato's image of the cave, he made it familiar to Cicero, who transmitted it to us. Like all of his early dialogues, Aristotle's *On Philosophy* survives only in later reports. The image he develops for his own introduction to philosophy is not of subterranean prisoners but of humans who had lived their lives underground in refined and elegant dwellings and, without ever having emerged into the light of day and beheld the sight of the heavens of the night. And in such dwellings they thought themselves blessed. Without experience of the beauty and order of the heavens, these subterranean dwellers could have no conception of the gods and therefore no true happiness.[2] Aristotle does not seem to have insisted on the theatrical world of the cave.

In the early modern period Sir Francis Bacon and Descartes attempted "purgative" exercises that have as their aim estrangement from familiar and long-held beliefs. The first such exercise owes an unacknowledged debt to Plato. In his *Great Instauration* of 1620 Bacon attempted to purge our minds of their familiar ways of thinking and opinions by analyzing four "idols"—his idols of the tribe, cave, market, and theater. His term "idols" is his version of the props (or equipment, *skeuē*) manipulated by Plato's puppeteers, which populate the "real world " reflected on the back wall of the cave. It is significant that he chooses to designate the personal yet public world of each individual with the term "idols of the cave."[3] In this he was a careful reader of Plato, for as we shall see, dialogue among the prisoners is impossible in Plato's cave. Descartes, in his *Meditations* (of 1641), seated alone in a room before a fire, attempted to clear his mind of all the "adventitious" baggage of his education and experience in society and could imagine that the world he had

2. Aristotle, *On Philosophy*, frag. 13 Ross (= Cicero, *On the Nature of the Gods* 2.37.94–96; *The Complete Works of Aristotle*, ed. Jonathan Barnes (Princeton, 1984), 2.2392).

3. Francis Bacon, *The Great Instauration*, pt. 2 (*Novum Organum*), aphorism 42.

trusted so well was nothing more than a theatrical illusion some malevolent genie had displayed before his trusting mind.[4] His world is at first public and filled with adventitious ideas; it then becomes personal and concentrated on the objects of his mind.

Our very words "education" and "conversion" go back to Socrates' allegory, which tells how a fettered prisoner is turned around by a philosophical conversion and led out of the cave in which he has spent his life, secure in its flickering and insubstantial reality. For education (*educatio* in Latin) is "leading out," and "conversion" (*conversio* in Latin) is turning around.

The Cave of Athens

Before going deeper into the cave and exploring its hidden depths, we should recognize the terrain in which Plato situates it. In its immediate context it is introduced as an analogue, or image (*eikōn*), that corresponds structurally to the divided line Socrates requires Glaukon to draw at the end of book 6 of the *Republic*. But it should not come as a surprise that the allegory of the cave is anticipated by the discussion of education that begins with the fictions told to children in book 2 and concludes with a discussion of the education of the guardian class of Socrates' city, Kallipolis, in book 3.

At the conclusion of his discussion of education and the educational project of implanting in the souls of young guardians a representation of good character, Socrates turns to Glaukon: "Nowhere should we allow the young to see ugly images in the 'representations' [*eikones*] of animals, or in their buildings, or in any other product of their art."[5] The pure and harmonious environment in which the guardians grow as children can be seen in retrospect as a counterimage of Socrates' "image" of the cave. In one way it resembles the cave. The young guardians live in a world of images that are noble and attractive, but they do not know what the originals of these images are. The judgments of the young guardians are automatic, and their world all-engrossing. But, with the advent of reason, this theatrical world changes, and image is linked to reality. Once he has reason, the child so educated can make the connection between the images of virtue and harmony projected by the purified poetry (and music) of his city and their originals.

Socrates employs an analogy to make his point. When we learn to read, we develop the skill to recognize the limited set of letters of the alphabet as

4. René Descartes, *Meditationes de Prima Philosophia* 1 (1641).
5. *Republic* 3.401B.

they are shifted about in different combinations and in different texts. It is our eagerness to develop this diagnostic ability that makes us literate:

> And is it not true that we will not know the images of letters, when these appear on water or in mirrors, before we come to know the letters themselves? This skill belongs to the same art and discipline. . . . Just so, we must recognize the distinct forms (*eidē*) of self-restraint, courage, high-mindedness, and dignity—and their opposites—as these are shifted about, and we recognize them as being present in the things they are discovered in, both as themselves and as their images.[6]

At this stage of the *Republic*, Socrates' language is somewhat opaque. By the time we have reached the Idea of the Good, it is more understandable.

The Divided Line

It is only in *Republic* 6 that the crucial Idea of Ideas—the Idea of the Good—is argued for independently. Here an Idea is not employed as a hypothesis in an argument to establish some other claim, as it was in the *Meno* and *Phaedo*, but it is argued for itself by the use of an analogy. In order to illustrate the highest form of knowledge the guardian philosopher must attain, Socrates deploys the visual analogue of the sun, which makes vision possible, just as on the level of thought the Idea of the Good makes knowledge possible.[7] He illustrates the distinct domains of sight and understanding and the kinds of knowledge appropriate to each by asking Glaukon to subdivide each of two unequal sections of a line into two further segments, which are to be proportioned one to the other as are the initial sections.[8] Socrates then asks Glaukon to form an image to illustrate not the levels of knowledge he has ranked in four divisions on the line but "our nature in respect to education or the lack of it."[9] This is the "allegory of the cave." Socrates then invites Glaukon to apply this image to what he had said about the two domains of intelligence and sight.

If we, as readers, perform this exercise, we come up with some results that take us deeper into the meaning of Plato's cave. The essential element of the structural comparison between the divided line and the cave has nothing to do with the initial division of the line into two *unequal* segments, which

6. *Republic* 3.402A–C.
7. *Republic* 6.503E–509C.
8. *Republic* 6.509D–511E.
9. *Republic* 7.514A–517A.

provides the grid for the comparison. The line divides the range of human experience into what is seen by the eyes and what is known to the mind. The unnatural light of a fire casting shadows on the wall of the cave from behind a parapet is the analogue to the natural light of the sun; its shadows are the analogue of the images reflected on water and other smooth surfaces at the bottom of the divided line. The world of sunlight outside of the cave is the analogue to the realm of what is known to the mind (Fig. 2).

In one respect, however, Socrates' image of the cave fails to match that of the divided line. This can be appreciated from a study of the diagram given here (Fig. 2). The inconcinnity is interesting because it seems deliberate. On the lowest segment of the divided line, we contemplate *eikones*—images and shadows. On the higher segment of the visible are located the objects that

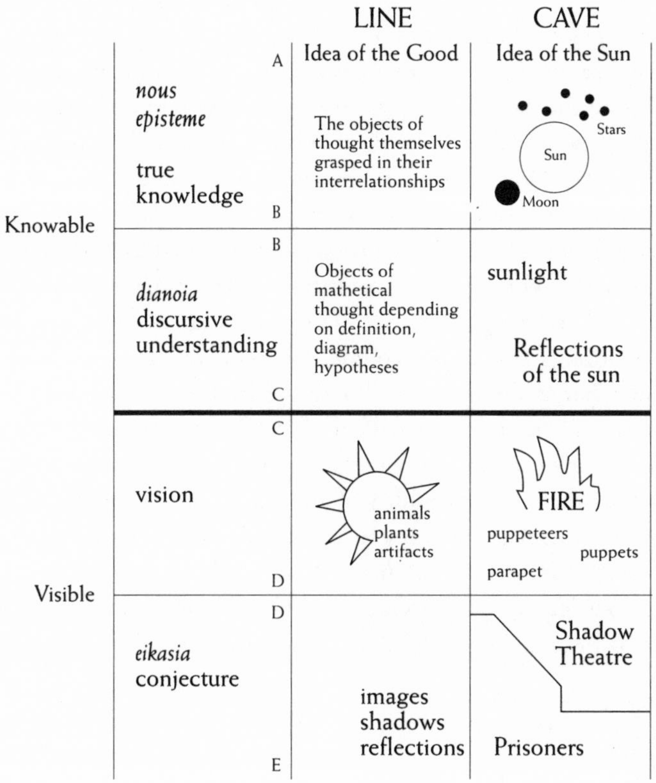

			LINE	CAVE
Knowable	*nous* episteme true knowledge	A B	Idea of the Good The objects of thought themselves grasped in their interrelationships	Idea of the Sun ••• Stars Sun Moon
	dianoia discursive understanding	B C	Objects of mathetical thought depending on definition, diagram, hypotheses	sunlight Reflections of the sun
Visible	vision	C D	animals plants artifacts	FIRE puppeteers puppets parapet
	eikasia conjecture	D E	images shadows reflections	Shadow Theatre Prisoners

FIG. 2

cast these reflections—the objects these reflections resemble.[10] The first striking difference between the lower section of the line and its visual analogue
in the cave is that the movement upward on the line from E–D to D–C is
what I would term transitive. That is, level E–D implies level D–C. If we turn
our heads around, we see what produces these reflections—animals, plants,
artifacts. Artifacts imply a maker. Surprisingly, so do animals and plants. But
in Socrates' "allegory" the prisoners of the cave are bound, limbs and neck.
They are incapable of turning their heads around and recognizing the puppets whose shadows are cast on the wall of the cave.[11] On the line, conjecture
is possible, and one can say of a bed reflected in a mirror: "This is that." In
the cave this linking of reflection and its source is impossible. The reason for
this, as we shall see, is that the cave represents human society; the line does
not. It is our education—or rather the fact that we have not been turned
around and led out of the cave—that constrains us to look only at the shadows on the rock wall in front of us.

So far, we have not looked at the upper section of the divided line or
emerged from the cave into the light of day. The renewed discussion of the
education of the guardian in books 6 and 7 is required by Socrates' proposal
of a philosopher king in book 5, the last of his "three waves" of paradox.[12]
With the new discussion of the education of the guardian philosopher we
arrive at the highest form of knowledge to be grasped by the ruler—the Idea
of the Good, "by which just acts and those other things that depend upon it
become useful and advantageous."[13] The true nature of this Good as separate
from those things commonly counted as good things, such as pleasure or
intelligence, but as the necessary condition to their being good, is not clear
to Socrates, and he does not believe that he can adequately describe it to
Glaukon in conversation. Yet he claims that he has spoken with Glaukon
about it often before.[14] The Idea of the Good, so described, occurs in no
other Platonic dialogue. We only hear at third hand (as retold by Aristoxenos
in his *Elements of Harmony*) that Aristotle was fond of telling the story about
Plato's famous lecture on the Good and how Plato's discussion of geometry
left most of his audience baffled and disappointed.[15] Socrates is reduced to

10. *Republic* 6.509D–510A.
11. *Republic* 7.514A–515A.
12. *Republic* 5.473C.
13. *Republic* 6.505A.
14. *Republic* 6.505A and E. We have already noticed Plato's tantalizing habit of referring to
earlier unrecorded discussions of Ideas in III §4 ("Thinking About Ideas")
15. In *Platonica*, Anecdote 79 (pp. 124–26).

giving his companions a description of the Idea of the Good in terms of "the offspring that resembles it most closely."[16]

Here we have the first of the three analogical images in this illuminating central section of the *Republic*. The sun is proposed as the visible analogue to the Idea of the Good. Unlike the objects of the visible world, "Beauty itself" and "Good itself" are not visible. But the visible will illustrate the intelligible. This connection might not seem remarkable, but it is. We have seen how the distinctness of Greek visual experience created the possibility of the metaphor *idea*: to know is to have seen (see III § 4, "Thinking About Ideas"). But there is a structural and mimetic relation between the seen and the unseen. This relation is evident in the strange question Socrates puts to Glaukon: "Tell me now, have you ever noticed with what great elegance the Demiurge fashioned the power of seeing and being seen?" Naturally, Glaukon responds: "Not really."[17] In the case of sight alone has the Demiurge created a medium, the medium of light, without which the eye is unseeing and its object unseen. As the sun, the god sovereign over the gods of heaven, provides us with light, so the Idea of the Good provides the medium by which the mind can understand the objects of its thought. The full import of this analogy is never fully evident in the Platonic dialogues, but we gain a better sense of what Plato has in mind from the *Timaeus*, where the Demiurge creates the orb of the eye and the roundness of the human head as commensurable to and as imitations of the shape of the sun and the other heavenly bodies and their divine orbits.[18]

Drawing the Line

Socrates stops short of pursuing his claim that the Idea of the Good is "beyond being" to offer Glaukon his second image: "Now conceive, if you will, that these realms are, as we have said, two. One holds sovereignty over the category and place of the intelligible; the other for its part, over the seen." Glaukon is instructed to subdivide a line as indicated above (Fig. 2).[19] The oddness of Socrates' unequally divided line has caused serious Platonists reasonable perplexity, as attested by Plutarch's short essay on the question.[20]

16. *Republic* 6.506E.
17. *Republic* 6.507C.
18. *Timaeus* 44D–56A; see III §7 ("The World of the Demiurge").
19. *Republic* 6.509D.
20. *Platonic Questions* 3, available in the Loeb Classical Library *Plutarch's Moralia* XIII:1 (Cambridge, Mass., 1976).

This is a revealing essay for many reasons; for one, it gives us a test case of the variety of responses readers in antiquity had to this passage. Modern students of Euclidean geometry have demonstrated that one result of the initial unequal division and subsequent proportional subdivision is that segments B–C and C–D of the divided line are equal (this by resort to four theorems from the fifth book of Euclid's *Elements*).[21] What this result means for Socrates' argument is not entirely clear. It is clear that the equal segments B–C and C–D are interdependent. Mathematical thought and the kind of visualization Glaukon is asked to employ depend on visible diagrams. In our world there are no perfect circles or rhomboids. To make the reasoning of geometry apparent, the Greeks—and particularly the Greeks of Plato's Academy—drew figures on smoothed sand. These figures do not relate to geometrical concepts as the images of the lowest segment of the line do to their originals; they relate rather as pattern relates to artifact. At this point, the movement on the line is both upward and downward: upward to the paradigm and downward to its imperfect copy in sand.

Socrates' careful instructions to Glaukon produce one practical result. Every reader of Plato's *Republic* is obliged to produce a diagram of the divided line, and Plato has engaged his reader in a practical task as nowhere else in his dialogues. Any choice the reader makes about the length of the intelligible as compared to the length of the visible is a test. Most Platonic readers, become geometers, give the intelligible section the greatest length, but we know from Plutarch that one reader (the Platonist Brontius) represented the intelligible by the shorter section, reasoning—correctly—that it is impossible for a true Platonist to honor the intelligible by gross visible length. The diagram presented in Figure 2 shows segments B–C and C–D as equal. The reader is left with the responsibility for making the initial section.

The movement up along the higher section of the intelligible resembles the movement from image to original of the lower section, in that the "hypotheses" of geometry are employed as if they were mental images representing a higher reality: "On the first segment the soul is compelled to treat as images those objects which once [moving up the lower section] were the objects of imitation."[22] This passage makes the renewed consideration of *mimē-sis* in book 10 of the *Republic* necessary. When Socrates unexpectedly returns to the question of representation at the end of the *Republic*, he demonstrates

21. The demonstration is given by Klein (1965, 119 n. 27).
22. *Republic* 6.510B.

how the bed depicted by the painter stands at "three removes from reality." The bed manufactured by a bedmaker is an "imitation," or copy, of the pattern Bed he works from. This pattern, or template, Bed is the creation of a higher and divine maker, the Demiurge of patterns.[23] At this point, we are finally in a position to understand the inclusion of artifacts in segment C–D of the divided line.

The relation between B–C and A–B is less clear, but the method of dealing with ideal figures and definitions (the Triangle itself, the Four-Sided Figure itself) is that of geometry; the method of discursive reasoning on the highest section is that of dialectic. Dialectic treats the objects of its thought not as foundational assumptions but as "what can truly be called hypotheses, as rungs and approaches" toward what is not a hypothesis, "when it arrives at the beginning of all." Its discovery is "by Forms themselves, through themselves, to themselves, and ending with Forms."[24] Socrates' language is liturgical and uplifting, but the mind can move downward, just as it can move upward. Socrates' metaphors of "rungs" and "approaches" and his literal use of the term *hypothesis* (what is set under) illustrates the transitive nature of the divided line, on which movement is not only upward but downward. If the Idea of the Good is to be located in the highest segment of the divided line, it must be as "the beginning of all."

In sequel, Glaukon and Socrates assign names to the states of mind and understanding appropriate to each section and segment of the divided line (Fig. 2). When Socrates takes up dialectic as the final stage in the education of the guardian philosopher, he dispenses with visual analogues and reviews the line, correcting some of his earlier terminology and offering a proportional scheme relating two segments on each of the sections: knowledge stands to belief as discursive reasoning to conjecture.[25] The scheme is tidy, static, and clear when reproduced on a page. But, when Socrates illustrates the line by the third and final visual analogue of the cave, it creates problems of interpretation. The line, unlike the cave, is not the product of collective thought. The only witness to the line is the individual soul.

Release from the Cave

We come now to the mysterious moment when a prisoner is somehow liberated from his bondage and the theatrical world that has so totally absorbed

23. *Republic* 10.596E–597E.
24. *Republic* 6.511B–C.
25. *Republic* 7.533E–534A.

his attention. The bondage of Socrates' strange cave dwellers means that they are incapable of turning their heads to converse (his word is *dialegesthai*) with one another. In their rigid orientation toward the shadow theater on the walls of the cave, Socrates' prisoners cannot compare their experiences. I stress Socrates' vague description of how a prisoner comes to be released *by nature*.[26]

SOCRATES:
Now contemplate just how the release and healing of these prisoners from their bonds might come about *by nature*. If ever one of the prisoners were released and suddenly compelled to stand up and turn his neck around and walk and look up to the light, he would feel pain as he did this; and, because of the intense flashing of the light, he would be unable to look directly at the objects whose shadows he once beheld. What do you think he would say if someone were to tell him that everything he had seen before was a gaudy show but that now he had gotten somewhat closer to reality and could see with more clarity as he turned to objects with more reality. And, indeed, this person could point out each of the objects that are paraded around and compel the prisoner to reply when asked what each object is. Do you not think that the freed prisoner would be at a loss and believe that the sights of the past were truer than the objects now shown to him?

GLAUKON:
Very much so.

When Socrates says that a prisoner might somehow be released from the cave *by nature* (φύσει), he must mean by his native inner resources, not by his education or the conventions of his society. Socrates goes on to tell of the prisoner's forced and painful ascent to the entrance of the cave and into the blinding light of day, his encounter with the sun during the day (once his eyes had grown accustomed to seeing its reflection in water) and the moon and stars at night. In time, the cave dweller begins to reason that this sun, in its annual movement, is responsible for the seasons and the year. His new world of light and rhythmic order is now described as "the place that is seen"—the same language that described the section of opinion in segment C–D of the line. But at this point the liberated prisoner returns to the cave as mysteriously as he had left it. He takes his old seat in the shadow theater.

26. *Republic* 7.515B.

His fellow prisoners greet him with ridicule and say that he has ruined his eyes by making the ascent. Although dialogue is impossible among the prisoners of the cave, collective judgment is real and threatening. Socrates concludes his story by asking Glaukon: "If the prisoners could lay their hands on the person who attempted to release them from their bonds and to lead them upward and could put him to death, would they not put him to death?" Glaukon's response is familiar to us: "They certainly would."[27]

Latent within Socrates' allegory is perhaps another allegory. Behind the parapet and among the projectors of illusion we discover a nameless person who enters into dialogue with the prisoner just released and asks him to identify reality and distinguish it from the shadowy reflections it projects on the walls of the cave. This anonymous philosopher operates by question and answer, and the newly freed prisoner is at a loss to answer his questions. Behind the parapet, in the area of the puppeteers, dialogue, it seems, is possible. The anonymous liberator who greets the prisoner forces him to look on the blaze of the fire. He then drags him up to the light of the sun. After that, the prisoner is on his own. When the prisoner is inexplicably forced to return to the cave, he is not the person who attempts to liberate his fellows. If we read this passage carefully, we realize that the liberator has remained within the cave. If we were to give him a name, it would be Socrates.

The cave is returned to one last time in the *Republic*. When Socrates considers with Glaukon how the rulers will force the philosophers trained in Kallipolis to return to the cave and take up responsibility for their fellow citizens, he considers the emergence of philosophers in other cities. In other cities philosophers arise of their own accord, of their own natural gifts. We now begin to understand better what Socrates meant by the qualification *by nature*. In a corrupt city, the only means of release from the cave does not come from the prisoner's society; it comes from his character. In Kallipolis the guardian class is educated. But, when the philosopher of Socrates' city returns to the cave of his youth, "he will distinguish the *images* of virtue—of things fair, just, and good—and this will be a city of waking consciousness and not a dream."[28] So there is a cave even in Kallipolis. Socrates' liberator has not left it for the rapture of contemplating the heavens; nor have his philosophical guardians. Conversion and education are liberating in this parable, but the committed philosopher can never really leave the cave of Athens

---

27. *Republic* 7.514A–517A; see I §4 ("The Shadow of Death").
28. *Republic* 7.519E–521B.

and political life. He can only be aware, as others are not, of what that life really is.

ENDNOTE: The main readings that might be helpful in pursuing the implications of this reading of the sun, the line, and the cave in *Republic* 6 and 7 can be found in the Endnote to III § 6 ("Kallipolis"). Of particular interest for the pairing of line and cave is J. L. Austin, "The Line and the Cave in Plato's *Republic*" (1979), and for the cave itself, J.R.S. Wilson, "The Contents of the Cave" (1976). A new, brilliant, and problematic interpretation (and diagrammatic rendition) of the familiar passages I have discussed here is to be found in part 2 of C.D.C. Reeve's *Philosopher-Kings* (1988). Reeve draws attention (pp. 52–53) to the prelude to Socrates' description of the cave in *Republic* 3.402B–C.

Postscript: A transcendental meditation on Plato's transcendental meditation on the sun, line, and cave is Peter Ackroyd's *The Plato Papers* (1999).

[O]ne and the same city, as it is viewed from different sides, seems completely different and is, as it were, multiplied by the number of views from which it is seen.
—G. W. Leibniz, *Monadologie*, § 57

In the House of Kephalos

Socrates names the city he founds in words Kallipolis, the Fair City.[1] His Kallipolis has been the Gallipoli of attempts to approach Plato's *Republic* as a foundational document in the history of political philosophy. The political philosophy of the dialogue has been the object of harsh criticism and innocuous praise, it would seem, from the moment of its publication some time after 387, when Plato returned to Athens from Syracuse. One ancient critic claimed to discover the *Republic* entire in the sophist Protagoras' *Book of Refutations*—a curious title for a book of political philosophy.[2] In his *Politics*, Aristotle offered a sustained criticism of the conception of the state urged by Socrates in the *Republic* and the utopian ideal that the wonderful variety of Greek states could be reduced to the unit out of which the household was formed, the individual: "It is as if you were to turn harmony into mere unison, or simplify a complex rhythm to a single beat."[3] It was claimed that Plato got his *Republic* from Egypt, where Solon, the founder of Athenian democracy,

1. *Republic* 7.527C.
2. DL 3.37.
3. *Politics* 2.5.1263ᵇ34. In *Republic* 5.462C Socrates expresses his ideal for the unity of his state as that of a single body.

learned of the ancient war between Athens and Atlantis.[4] Zeno, the founder of the Stoic school, wrote a *Republic (Politeia)*, which was both inspired by and written in response to Plato's. In his *Parallel Lives*, the Platonist Plutarch holds the ideal of Socrates' state constantly before him, especially in his Lives of Numa, Lycurgus, and Dion.

Inevitably, the proposals of the *Republic* for an ideal political order have come to assume a new meaning for the reader of the late twentieth century, who knows more than Plato ever could of Communism, fascism, totalitarianism, and who has survived 1984. Sir Karl Popper began his *Open Society and Its Enemies* in March of 1938, when the news of the German annexation of Austria came as a portent of things to come; and in his first volume—*The Spell of Plato*—he argued that "Plato's political programme, far from being morally superior to totalitarianism, is fundamentally identical with it."[5]

It is tempting to regard the *Republic* as the direct expression of Plato's political thought and to read the dialogue with its title foremost in mind. But such a reading of the *Republic* induces us to take Plato at Socrates' word (and at the assent of Socrates' companions). It leads us away from the first and last concern of the dialogue, which is the value of the just life and the "justice" of the individual soul. It also lulls the reader into the complacency of disregarding the philosophically open character of a dialogue in which conclusions and apparent moments of closure are always new beginnings (see II § 8, "The Open Dialogue").

Moreover, there is the misleading signpost of the title in English, *The Republic*. Aristotle knew our *Republic* as the *Politeia* (Πολιτεία), which means literally a form of society and government—presumably the best form of government. Cicero's implicit version of the title in his own *De republica* has created the habit by which we refer to the dialogue by a name that is antithetical to Socrates' arguments for monarchy or "aristocracy" as the best form of government. It also distracts our attention from the question of the "justice" of the individual soul.[6] The traditional subtitle to this dialogue is "concerning justice," but its beginning seems to have nothing to do with either a state or the question of justice, and Plato's reader is hard put to determine just where or how the dialogue proper gets started. Socrates narrates the entire *Republic*

4. According to Proclus in his comments on Krantor's commentary on the *Timaeus*, *Procli Diadochi in Platonis Timaeum Commentarii* (1903), I.76.2–14; cf. I.197.18–24 Diehl.

5. Popper 1971, 87.

6. *Republic* 5.473C (monarchy) and 8.544E ("aristocracy").

to an unidentified audience on the day after he had the conversation. He seems to be able to recall it to its last syllable. He is speaking in Athens:

> I descended to the Peiraeus yesterday in the company of Glaukon, Ariston's son. I wanted to make my prayers to the goddess and also to see how they would conduct the festival, since this was the first time they celebrated it.[7]

As Socrates and his companion were about to return to Athens, they were stopped by a slave, who told them that his master, Polemarchos, wanted them to wait for him. When Polemarchos caught up with them, he invited them to stay in his house to watch the mounted torch race that evening. With him came Glaukon's brother, Adeimantos, and Nikias' son, Nikeratos, and some others. Polemarchos speaks:

POLEMARCHOS:
Socrates, you two seem to be about to set out for the city.

SOCRATES:
That is not a bad guess.

POLEMARCHOS:
Do you see how many of us there are?

SOCRATES:
Of course I do.

POLEMARCHOS:
Very well. I will give you a choice: either become stronger than this company or stay here.

SOCRATES:
Isn't there another alternative—for us to persuade you that we have to leave?

POLEMARCHOS:
Well, tell me, could you manage to persuade people who will not listen to you?[8]

Eventually, the promise of a dinner, the spectacle of the torch race, and conversation with young men induce Glaukon to agree. At the house of Po-

7. *Republic* 1.327A.
8. *Republic* 1.327C.

lemarchos, Socrates finds a number of guests already gathered and Polemarchos' aged father, Kephalos, who was wearing a wreath and had just offered a sacrifice in his courtyard. He and Socrates turn naturally to the topics of old age and of wealth, and touch on one of the consolations of old age— emancipation from the tyranny of sexual passion. This casual exchange seems accidental, but the tyranny of passion is shown to make the tyrant a slave in book 9 of the *Republic*. At Socrates' prompting, Kephalos speaks of one of the advantages of his wealth—he can pay his debts to both gods and men as he prepares for the "beyond." The "beyond" is the subject of the myth of Er that concludes the dialogue. But it is Kephalos' implicit definition of justice that attracts Socrates' attention.

The long conversation concerning justice emerges from this living context, almost unobserved, and the modern reader, expecting philosophy, reasonably asks why he should be delayed by these seemingly extraneous details. At the beginning of the *Republic*, this question is inevitable. But at the end of the dialogue the reader is in a position to consider once again the meaning of the carefully rendered details of its dramatic setting: the Peiraeus, with its new cult to the Thracian goddess Bendis; the Thracians who reside there; and the visitor to Athens, Thrasymachos of Chalkedon. These details can all be read as emblematic of the radical Athenian democracy, with its base in the men who manned its fleet, and the oratory that was needed to move its political assemblies. The Peiraeus is open to the Greek world and to change. It attracted the Thracians, who inaugurate their new festival to Bendis, and, as we know from other sources, it (and Pericles) attracted Kephalos and his family from Syracuse. The choice of a setting in the Peiraeus might seem accidental, but it is not. In the *Laws* we discover the conservative injunction to found a city in the middle of the island, far away from the sea.[9] The cast of characters gathered in the house of Kephalos is right for this port setting: foreigners, Athenians, and metics (the resident aliens). And it seems right as the context for Socrates' conversation on forms of society and government.

Plato chose the first word of the *Republic* with care: Κατέβην (*katebēn*). I translate it with deliberate awkwardness: "I descended." After Socrates' allegory of the cave, his descent into the Peiraeus can be understood as an instance of the philosopher's descending into the cave of political life. "I descended" is precisely the word Odysseus chose to describe his descent into

---

9. *Laws* 5.745B. It is to be located eighty stades, or approximately ten miles, from the sea.

the underworld.[10] It also prepares us for Kephalos' anxieties concerning the afterlife and for the stories of the poets and, finally, for the myth of Er, with which the *Republic* ends. The myth of Er is clearly Plato's philosophical counterpart to Odysseus' account of his descent into Hades,[11] and, as we have seen (II § 8, "The Open Dialogue"), "the path upward" of Socrates' last sentence in the Greek text balances Socrates' first word.[12]

There are other intimations of the seemingly insignificant details of ordinary life that can take on a philosophical significance when examined. Polemarchos' conjecture that Socrates and Glaukon were about to return to Athens, and the verb that denotes that conjecture (*doxazō*), anticipate the philosophical discussion of the visible world of opinion (δόξα, *doxa*) and the reality that lies behind it and is implicated in it.[13] Polemarchos' urbane threat of force, which evokes the power of the majority directed against the persuasion of Socrates, develops into the argument of Thrasymachos that justice is "the interest of the stronger,"[14] just as it prepares for the treatment of the philosopher in his relation to the democratic polis of Athens in book 6. Socrates' interest in the spectacle of the novel festival of Bendis gives us our first inkling of what philosophy will come to mean in the dialogue. The passion for spectacles, or "shows," and the love of the theater is the first illustration of the philosophical passion for contemplation, or *theōria*, in book 5.[15] In Greek, the word θεωρία means both spectacle and contemplation. It is connected with the word *theatron*, theater.

Logographic Necessities

These are small details, but, if the doctrine of "logographic necessity" has an application to the Platonic dialogues, these seemingly insignificant details must function in the whole of which they are parts. The *Phaedrus* (written after the *Republic*) compels us to ask of the *Republic:* How does the principle of logographic necessity apply on a grand scale? Is some part of the meaning of the *Republic* revealed by its organization? We cannot be certain that the

10. *Odyssey* 23.252. The nominal form *katabasis* is the normal term for a descent into the underworld.

11. Plato makes this quite clear when he has Socrates say: "This is no tale for Alkinoos [*apologia Alkinoou*]"—the term by which the episode of Odysseus' descent to Hades in the *Odyssey* was known; *Republic* 10.614B.

12. *Republic* 10.621C.

13. *Republic* 6.508D.

14. *Republic* 1.338C.

15. *Republic* 5.475D; cf. the term *polytheamon* in *Phaedrus* 251A.

ten books into which the dialogue is now divided go back to Plato's own manuscript. Some recent translations of the dialogue divide it differently, but the traditional book divisions are certainly accurate markers of the progress and apparent detours of Socrates' argument. Book 1 appears to be an aporetic search for a proper understanding of the concept of justice (begun with Socrates' question to Kephalos),[16] and it has sometimes been treated as originally an independent early dialogue and entitled "Thrasymachos." As we have seen, this "early dialogue" ends badly, with the defeat of Thrasymachos' passionately held but weakly argued case that justice is the interest of the stronger and Socrates' own admission that his refutation has produced no light: "So far as I am concerned, the result of our present conversation is that I know nothing."[17] We turn the page (or open another papyrus roll). With book 2 we encounter an unexpected reaction to the impasse reached at the end of book 1: "When I had said this, I thought that I was finished with the argument." But the fraternal challenges of Glaukon and Adeimantos reopen an argument that had seemed closed, and the argument begun anew seems to conclude only in book 9 with Socrates' solemn proclamation that the life of the just man is 727 times happier than that of the tyrant.[18]

This seems to be the last judgment pronounced on the central question of the *Republic*, but the last judgment comes finally with the choice of lives offered at the end of the myth of Er and Odysseus' choice of the life of "an ordinary citizen who minds his own business."[19] Books 2–4 and 8–9 have an integrity when taken together, as Socrates indicates they should be. In books 2–4 Socrates founds a perfect state "in discourse," and in 8–9 he reviews in descending order the kinds of states that are inferior to it and the character of the citizens that correspond to them. Socrates treats the argument of books 5–7 of the *Republic* as a "digression" when he returns to where he had left off at the end of book 4.[20] Yet these three seemingly accidental books develop the central paradox of the *Republic*—that of the necessity of a philosopher king. Without them the discussion of *mimēsis* in book 10 and Odysseus' paradoxical choice of life in the myth of Er would be incomprehensible, and the *Republic* would be only the "Republic"—a dialogue concerning the justice of

16. At *Republic* 1.331C.
17. *Republic* 1.354C; see II §8 ("The Open Dialogue").
18. *Republic* 9.587E. This conclusion should satisfy the request made by Glaukon (at *Republic* 2.367E) that Socrates should demonstrate the superiority of justice over injustice and bring the dialogue to a conclusion.
19. *Republic* 10.620C.
20. *Republic* 8.543C, looking back to 5.449A; see II §8 ("The Open Dialogue").

the perfect state. But the *Republic* has another underlying theme, the "justice" of the soul.

An interruption—a gesture and a whispered comment—provokes Socrates to digress from his discussion of inferior states and inferior types of citizens. Polemarchos has taken hold of Adeimantos' cloak, drawn him close, and whispered: "Shall we let him get away with this or not?"[21] Adeimantos has answered aloud: "Absolutely not." What bothers Polemarchos is the comment Socrates had let drop without justification or elaboration that the wives and children of his guardians should conform to the proverb "Common is what belongs to friends."[22] In response to this challenge Socrates develops three paradoxes: that some women are suited to be guardians and share their "philosophical" temperament;[23] that the wives and children of the guardians should be held in common; and the modest proposal Socrates describes as the third "wave" of paradox:

> Unless either philosophers come to rule as kings in our cities or those who now bear the names of kings and magnates become genuine and competent philosophers, . . . there will be no relief, my dear Glaukon, from the calamities that beset our cities, or, in my opinion, for the entire human race.[24]

The proposals concerning women and children are short-lived in the *Republic*. Socrates does not return to them. But the frontal assault they launch on Greek society and Greek values prepares for the elaborate consideration of the antagonism between philosophy and Greek society and between Socrates and Athens, and it introduces the question of the education of the philosopher king. The orientation of these three central books of the *Republic* takes us away from the city Socrates has just founded in discourse, but it is by no means transcendental. Philosophy, as we have just seen (see III § 5, "The Sun, the Line, and the Cave"), remains in the city. In setting out the program of studies for the would-be philosopher king, Socrates is put in the anachronistic position of advertising Plato's newly founded Academy.[25]

Finally, we come to the last book of the *Republic*, which is transcendental in that it takes into its field of vision the fate of the soul after death. It opens

21. *Republic* 5.449B.
22. *Republic* 4.423E.
23. *Republic* 5.456A.
24. *Republic* 5.473C.
25. *Republic* 7.528B.

as Socrates returns, with no apparent motivation, to the question of *mimēsis* that he had covered in two of its main manifestations—the representation of gods and *hērōes*—in books 2–3. As we saw when we turned to consider Plato on poetry (II § 6, "Platonic Poetry"), *mimēsis* is one thing when considered in terms of the education of a guardian class and something significantly different when considered as the representation of reality (see II § 4, "Mimesis"). Socrates also argues, to Glaukon's utter disbelief, for the immortality of the soul, and ends his discussion with the myth of Er and a vision of the fate of souls, just and unjust, after death. With this myth he returns the dialogue to its beginning and Kephalos' anxieties over his fate after death.[26]

The organization of the *Republic* seems both ordered and haphazard. Books 1 and 10 appear to stand to each side of it like pillars that have no structural relation to the two wings of the great stage building of books 2–4 and 8–9. In the center of this scene open the great central doors of the palace of Kallipolis from which the tragic and enigmatic character of the philosopher king enters the stage. Without the remote inner chambers glimpsed through these suddenly opened doors, Plato's *Republic* would be the text we study as the "Republic." But the republic ruled by the philosopher king and Socrates' "digression" lead to another reading of the *Republic* that does not discount Plato's commitment to political philosophy but finds the initial theme of the *Republic* writ small under the text of the "Republic." We turn from the state to the state of the soul.

This reading focuses on the justice to be discovered in the soul of the individual and the pessimism that casts its dark shadow over Kallipolis as Socrates confronts a theme he would rather avoid:[27] that of philosophy in its antagonism to the polis—and, unwittingly, his own fate in democratic Athens, as he remained within the cave and attempted to liberate its prisoners. We recall that in the *Crito* Socrates refused to leave his prison in Athens for the freedom of the plains of Thessaly.[28]

The State Writ Small

The *Republic* is the heavenly city of a fourth-century philosopher; and it is, as Sir Karl Popper described it, the blueprint for a totalitarian state—provided we understand "totalitarian" in terms of an organic unity, like that of a "single

---

26. *Republic* 1.330D.
27. As he confesses in *Republic* 6.497D.
28. *Crito* 45B.

individual."[29] But Kallipolis is also a metaphor and model designed to illustrate the state of the human soul. Socrates introduces this metaphor in response to the challenges put to him as the defender of the cause of justice in book 2:

> Now, we are not very clever, in my opinion, in carrying out a search of this kind. Imagine that someone were to tell people with poor eyesight to read tiny letters at a distance and then someone else were to notice that this same text could be found elsewhere, written in larger letters and in a larger format. This news would come as a godsend, for they could first read these larger letters and then examine the smaller letters in their light to determine if they were identical.[30]

Socrates' model, or metaphor, assumes as a working hypothesis an identity between the state and the individual. He seeks a proportional analogy by which the state is an accurate and legible projection of the human soul. This assumption reflects the common association of the state and the individual in Greek laws linking, as they often do, the public and the private. The entire project of books 2–4 and 8–9 of the *Republic* is to exploit this model.

The model needs development. Socrates describes three states. The first is the product of the basic human needs for food, clothing, and shelter. In such a state "of absolute necessities" each individual has a single occupation and does not meddle in the work of his neighbors. Although it is not recognized as such, we have here the first statement of the Socratic definition of social justice, by which each member of society performs the function he or she is naturally suited to.[31] The first city develops into an unhealthy and distempered city with the importation of unnecessary luxuries. The growing appetite for these leads to the appropriation of neighboring territory and the need for a class of warriors. Out of this class of warrior guardians (*phylakes*) emerges the third city of the *Republic*, Kallipolis. To the first and essential but least important class of this city belong the farmers and artisans, who produce the necessities of life; to the second class belong the "guardians," who become necessary as the state of unbounded desires annexes to itself land belonging to a neighboring state.[32] Although none of the participants in the inner dia-

---

29. So Socrates describes it in *Republic* 5.462C.

30. *Republic* 2.368D.

31. Intimated at *Republic* 2.370A and stated at 4.443D. It is restated for the case of the individual soul at *Republic* 6.496D.

32. *Republic* 2.373D.

logue of the *Republic* sees or states the truth, Kallipolis is founded upon an initial act of injustice. This appropriation of another's land is, as we shall see, the result of an act of injustice within the soul of the inhabitants of Socrates' second city, and it would be matched by the injustice of a neighboring state, if its citizens "let themselves go after an unlimited acquisition of possessions, transgressing the boundary of what is necessary."[33]

This state of two classes, laboring and warrior, becomes a state of three with the addition a third and ruling class as the guardian class divides into guardians proper—guardians against enemies from without—and guarantors of the internal harmony of the state and the self.[34] With this third class the model of the state is complete, and Socrates concludes his proposals for the education of the class to which he had attributed a "philosophic" as well as a spirited nature.[35] He turns to the soul and discovers three elements there as well. The lowest is that of desire, the middle is that of spirit, and the highest and ruling element is that of reason.[36]

Plato's two older brothers and Socrates' companions accept this model, but many of Plato's readers have found it wanting, as do I, and as perhaps did Plato. Can it be that assent within a Platonic dialogue is designed to provoke dissent in its readers? One of the problems Socrates' model of *psyche* < *polis* creates is that each class within Kallipolis must correspond to one of the three levels of the soul, although each member of this society possesses a soul of three elements. On the short Procrustean bed of this model the class of artisans and laborers is truncated to the level of pure desire (*epithymia*) and acquisitiveness. There are mitigating arguments that can make the theoretical consequences of Socrates' model seem less extreme, but they are unnecessary. Socrates' first and last concern is not for the state but for the individual and the state of his soul, especially at his conception of the ruling element of the soul leads to his argument for the philosopher king. The third wave of hostile reaction stirred up by this proposal returns the dialogue decisively to the only state over which the philosopher can truly have control; this is the state of his soul.

Socrates' psychology at the end of book 4 prepares for a return to the individual and the questions of justice on which the *Republic* is grounded. But now the metaphor is reversed. The soul is described for the first time in the

33. *Republic* 2.373E.
34. *Republic* 3.413E–414B.
35. *Republic* 2.375E.
36. *Republic* 4.434D–443C; see III §3 ("Eros and Psyche").

dialogue in terms of the state and its civil war (or *stasis*).[37] The model is now reversed to *polis* < *psyche,* or the state as it is metaphorically projected onto the soul. This internalization of the polity of the *Republic* distracts our attention from the state to the more interesting text of the soul as the state "write small." An entire book (book 9) is devoted to the description of the inner injustice of the soul of the tyrant, who is tyrannized by his desire.[38] We now understand better the initial act of injustice on which Kallipolis is founded, as we comprehend how the tyrant's desires have gained the upper hand in their revolt against reason. And in this context even the humble laborer is redeemed, since he is said to be capable of governance by the best and most divine part of himself.[39]

From Kallipolis to Athens

In some sense, Socrates' philosopher king is responsible for the decline of Kallipolis. He is introduced as the solution to the problems of contemporary Greek states. His presence in the *Republic* draws the attention of the participants in the dialogue and of its readers to contemporary realities and the antagonism between Athens and philosophy. The realities of Athens in the period of her collapse at the end of the fifth century cloud the heavenly city of Kallipolis. A description of the contemporary state of philosophy in Athens and of the education of the philosopher who would be king are the themes of books 5–7. A measure of the distance the dialogue has moved away from the ideal of Kallipolis as founded by the end of book 4 is the fact that the family has mysteriously reappeared in books 8–9,[40] and the guardians, whose education had preoccupied Socrates in books 2 and 3, are nowhere mentioned in Socrates' discussion of poetry in book 10.

The central and most philosophical books of the *Republic* register a greater awareness of the society just outside the house of Kephalos than do the others, and they seem to be more personal to Plato, who leaves his signature on them. They take into their field of vision Aristophanes' caricature of Socrates in the *Clouds,* Alcibiades, Theages, and Socrates, whose divine monitor (*daimonion*) could keep him from political life but not execution.[41] In addi-

---

37. *Republic* 4.440B.
38. *Republic* 9.575A.
39. *Republic* 9.590C.
40. It suddenly reappears in *Republic* 8.549C.
41. *Republic* 6.494A–495A (Alcibiades), 496B (Theages), 496D (Socrates). The description of Alcibiades is quoted below.

tion, a fourth figure is described at length in Socrates' review of the relation between Athens and philosophy, though he is not named. He is the silent philosopher, whose *Republic* engages its reader in an outer dialogue.

Each of these figures deserves attention. Socrates presents Adeimantos with a parable of the relation between the philosopher and his state. It is clear that the state he has in mind can only be a democracy. The philosopher is represented as the captain of his ship of state, taller and stronger than his crew, but hard of hearing and shortsighted. His crew grows mutinous, and each crew member claims that he should be captain of the ship, but none of the crew has any skill in navigation. Such a skill, they assert, is nothing that requires training. They manage to get rid of their captain, either by killing him or throwing him overboard. The demagogue among them they call "captain" and "expert navigator," but for their true captain they reserve the epithets "stargazer," "all talk," and "useless."[42]

These epithets for the captain who would guide his ship by the stars are echoed from Aristophanes' *Clouds*.[43] There is also an echo of the Pnyx, the rocky outcrop above the Agora where the Athenian assembly met: "the rocks and the site itself in which they gather in their hubbub boom out the echo of their blame and praise."[44] This hubbub is also the reaction of the audience and the jury in the open-air theater of Socrates' trial. As for Alcibiades, his career is commemorated in a few paragraphs and in Socrates' hypothetical question:

> If a man of philosophical disposition should appear in a great city, and if he were wealthy and came from one of its great families and were good looking and tall and muscular, don't you think that he would be consumed by ambition in his conceit that he could manage the affairs of both Greeks and barbarians?[45]

Theages' delicate health keeps him a philosopher, and Socrates' divine monitor (*daimonion*) keeps him clear of political life in the assemblies. And, finally, the anonymous philosopher, in the black squall of political life,

> maintains his calm and minds his own business . . . finding shelter under a wall. As he watches the others filled with lawlessness, he is content and more than content to live his life pure and unsullied with the stain

42. *Republic* 6.488E.
43. *Clouds* 228 and 1480, terms recalled in *Apology* 18B.
44. *Republic* 6.492C.
45. *Republic* 6.494C. We have seen this ambition in the *First Alcibiades* (page 183 above).

of injustice and impious deeds in this world and to exchange this world for another with good hope as his companion, joyous and benign.[46]

It is not difficult to recognize in this description still another Platonic signature. Socrates' description of the silent philosopher who pursues the justice of his soul within the polis but despite its prevailing injustice is a milepost to the reader of the *Republic*. It measures the distance we have moved from Kallipolis. It is telling too that when Socrates returns to his paradox of the philosopher king he should speak not of kings but of the sons of kings becoming philosophers.[47] When these words were written, Dionysios I was still tyrant of Syracuse, but his son, Dionysios II, represented Plato's best hope for a better regime in Syracuse and for the realization of his political philosophy. He did not repose his hopes on Athens.

The text of what appears to be the conclusion of the *Republic* requires, and has sometimes been granted, the meditation of the political philosopher, for Plato's *Republic* can be properly considered the founding document of European political philosophy. Socrates' full project of discovering the soul "writ large" in the state seems to come to an end at the end of book 9. Socrates has just spoken of the philosopher and his reluctance to become involved in the political life of his city. He speaks finally not of the state but of a state of soul:

SOCRATES:

By the dog, . . . [he would be involved in] his own city, and deeply involved—but perhaps not in the city of his birth, barring some divine intervention.

GLAUKON:

I understand. You mean the city we have founded in our discourse. I say this because I think that it exists nowhere on earth.

SOCRATES:

But perhaps there is a pattern[48] for it established in heaven on high for the person who can see it and, keeping his eyes fixed upon it, make himself its citizen. It makes no difference whether it exists now or will

46. *Republic* 6.496D.
47. *Republic* 6.499B and 502A.
48. Socrates' word for "pattern" is *paradeigma*.

exist someplace on earth. He will be involved as a citizen of this city and no other.[49]

ENDNOTE: The first critical engagement with the *Republic* as political philosophy is that of Aristotle in his review of utopian states, in *Politics* 2.1–8. The reader of Plato should appreciate his care in referring to Socrates as the author of the proposals for Kallipolis. Aristotle's review takes in the proposals of the *Laws* as well. George Klosko places the project of the *Republic* in the context of Plato's dialogues and the development of the Greek city states, in *The Development of Plato's Political Theory* (1986). An excellent philosophical guide for the reader of the *Republic* is Julia Annas, *An Introduction to Plato's Republic* (1981); C.D.C. Reeve's *Philosopher-Kings: The Argument of Plato's Republic* (1988), has been mentioned (Endnote to III § 5). Among many other things it is an attempt to understand the architecture of the argument of the *Republic*. Karl Popper's *Open Society and Its Enemies*, vol. 1, *The Spell of Plato* (1971), is notable for its lack of any reflection on how to read a dialogue like the *Republic*. More subtle as a reading of the *Republic* and more sympathetic to some of Socrates' proposals is Leo Strauss, "On Plato's Republic," in *The City and Man* (1964), as is Allan Bloom's "Interpretative Essay" to his translation of the *Republic*, *The Republic of Plato* (1968). Serious and, I think, well-founded criticism of Socrates' model for justice in the *Republic* is urged by Bernard Williams, "The Analogy of City and Soul in Plato's *Republic*" (1973). The entire defense of justice is carefully examined by Richard Kraut, "The Defense of Justice in Plato's *Republic*" (1992). I have set out some reflections on the difficulties in coming to a closed interpretation of the *Republic* in "Reading the Republic" (1988).

49. *Republic* 9.592A–B.

FIG. 3
Raphael, *The School of Athens* (detail of left side). Stanza della
Segnatura, Vatican Palace, Vatican State.

In his iconographical program for the Stanza della Segnatura in the Vatican,
Raphael depicted Plato and Aristotle as the central figures of his *School of
Athens* (Fig. 3). They are both defined by the vault of a monumental classical
building. Plato carries a thick book with the title *Timeo* written on its spine;
Aristotle carries a book entitled *Etica*—his *Nicomachean Ethics*. Aristotle's right
hand is vigorously extended toward his viewer; Plato's right hand is directed
upward and points to the center of the vault above him. Even the title of his
book, inscribed on the dark gilded pages, reads upward. By contrast, the title
of Aristotle's *Ethics* reads horizontally.

Plato might be pointing in the right direction, but Socrates is shown in
a very different gesture. He stands below Plato and to his right. He is addressing three figures and counting on the index finger of his left hand. Clearly,
Raphael is recalling the opening of Plato's *Timaeus* and Socrates' address to
Timaeus, who appears in the company of Critias and Hermokrates: "One,

two, three, but where my, dear Timaeus, is the fourth of those who were yesterday guests at our banquet?"[1] On this wall of the Stanza della Segnatura and in Raphael's monumental (and Roman) Athens, Socrates stands below Plato and Aristotle. Neither of these imposing figures confront another individual. Socrates does. Indeed, it was Socrates who, in Cicero's memorable formulation, summoned philosophy down from the heavens.[2] In reading the Platonic dialogues, we pay little attention to the figure of the old Plato in the Vatican who directs our gaze to the heavens.

The *Timaeus* is such an oddity among the dialogues of Plato that from early Hellenistic times it came to represent all that could be said positively and compendiously about Plato's philosophy. It did not matter to Diogenes Laertius (or his source) or to the usually careful Proclus, who in commenting on Plato's *Republic* attributed its social program to Socrates and not to Plato, that a foreigner from Locri on the toe of Italy was responsible for the long speech recorded in the *Timaeus*; Plato himself was held responsible for its doctrines. Timaeus is known only from the Platonic dialogue that bears his name.[3] Socrates describes him as a citizen of the best-governed Greek city of Italy and one who had served in its highest offices. He also describes him as a philosopher.[4] Critias describes him as an astronomer and natural philosopher.[5] Timaeus is presented as one of Socrates' guests on the day of the quadrennial Panathenaia that followed Socrates' long description of a perfect society (sometimes taken as a reference to the *Republic*); his other guests are the Athenian Critias (who can only be Critias of the Thirty "Tyrants"), the Syracusan general Hermokrates, and a mysterious fourth guest who was ill and could not appear on the day reserved for the speeches of Timaeus, Critias, and Hermokrates, and, it would seem, his own contribution.

---

1. *Timaeus* 17A. The fourth guest is just barely visible in profile between the stooped figure of Timaeus and the grand, expansive figure of Critias. He is bearded and archaic. His model is a herm Raphael must have known from the Vatican of Julius II. This herm is best viewed in profile as the last in the sequence of four herms in the Stanza dei Filosofi illustrated in Paul Zanker 1995, fig. 108 (p. 207).

2. Cicero, *Conversations at Tusculum* 5.4.10.

3. His role in the dialogue that bears his name meant that Timaeus was destined to a posthumous career among readers who took him as a historical figure. We have a manuscript attributed to "Timaeus of Locri" written in Doric dialect and entitled "On the Soul of the Universe and on Nature." It is clearly a later invention. The other figures of the dialogue are all historical.

4. *Timaeus* 20A. Socrates' interest in law and order, *eunomia*, surfaces already in his description of his admiration for the well-ordered polities of Sparta and Crete in *Crito* 52E; cf. the similar praise of Locri in *Laws* 1.638B.

5. *Timaeus* 27A.

Socratic Physiology

The gap between Plato and Socrates, who is often and unwisely taken as his mouthpiece, is greatest in the *Timaeus*. Socrates had spoken the day before of his perfect society and its guardian class (but not of its philosopher king), but he is utterly silent as Timaeus delivers his long speech on the origins of the world and of human beings—as he is during Critias' unfinished history of the conflict between prehistoric Athens and Atlantis, which comes as its sequel. It is clear from all we know of Socrates in the Platonic dialogues and from Xenophon—if not from Aristophanes—that Socrates laid no claim to the knowledge of the natural philosopher, or *physiologos*. But Socrates' silence does not mean that he would have disapproved of what Timaeus had to say about a unique universe created by a supremely intelligent artisan, the Demiurge—supremely intelligent because it is supremely intelligible.[6] As we shall see, this equation of intelligible and intelligent recurs in the *Laws*, where it loses none of its mystery.[7]

The Socrates we know from every literary Socratic, with the exception of the author of a Socratic dialogue entitled *The Clouds*, is not a "pre-Socratic"; that is, he is not concerned, as some early Greek philosophers were, with the origins of the universe and the explanations of its present shape and behavior. On trial, Socrates is firm in his denial that he possesses any wisdom concerning the world above his head and below his feet.[8] It is not that Socrates lacked interest in such questions; but he questioned whether any human being could attain wisdom concerning them. In both the *Apology* and the *Phaedo*, he mentions Anaxagoras of Klazomenai, an important figure in Athenian intellectual life in the mid–fifth century, and, in the intellectual autobiography he offers his companions in the *Phaedo*,[9] he sets out the conditions of a new and possibly unattainable natural science.

Socrates' new science of ends and purpose and not beginnings and matter informs Timaeus' description of the universe in the *Timaeus*. Socrates is not interested in explaining the world by isolating the constituents out of which it evolved or explaining its origin (φύσις, *physis*). He asks rather for an explanation that would reveal to him the intelligence and purpose behind the mechanical behavior of the visible world. Anaxagoras' explanatory principle

6. *Timaeus* 34A–B and 90C–D.
7. *Laws* 10.897C and 898A; see III §8 ("Magnesia").
8. *Apology* 18B and 19B; see I §5 ("The Philosopher in Court").
9. *Phaedo* 96A–99D.

of Intelligence (Νοῦς, *Nous*) caught Socrates' attention because it explained the universe as the creation of an intelligence that works for "what is best" in imposing its order upon it.[10] He was disappointed by the fact that Anaxagoras did not put the principle of *Nous* to work. In Anaxagoras' book Socrates could discover only a welter of material causes such as *aither, aer,* and water.[11] It is as if the scientist were to explain Socrates' position in prison by reference to his bones, tendons, and muscles, not the decision of the Athenian jury, to whom "it seemed best" that he should be imprisoned and put to death.[12] In Greek, the word for causation is αἰτία. *Aitia* can mean either cause or responsibility. It is responsibility that Socrates requires in an explanation of the universe and the city of which he is a part, and he discovers this responsibility in Timaeus' cosmology.

The Work of the Demiurge

Timaeus' main explanatory principle for the state of the universe, both visible and unseen, is its maker and father. This principle is expressed by the mixture of metaphors and models familiar from Plato's vocabulary for the Forms (see III § 4, "Thinking About Ideas"). Timaeus does not, however, explain what motivated the Demiurge to create a universe where none had existed before. His entire history of creation is no more than a "plausible tale," told in the manner of Parmenides' Way of Opinion.[13] The motion of human time is linear and is registered by the notations "it is," "it was," "it will be"; the motion of eternity is axial and circular and captured only by the verb "it is."[14] The invariable and nonlinear history of eternity is not congenial to the human mind. Just as Homer refused to describe the shield of Achilles as an artifact already fashioned by Hephaistos but described it in the making, Plato refuses to describe his universe as static. For Plato, the very fact that the universe is visible means that it is something generated.[15] The Demiurge of the *Timaeus* is not, then, as much the cause of the visible frame and order of the world as he is a principle of explanation that makes necessary concessions to human limitations.

Plato incorporates into his *Timaeus* a great deal he found plausible in the

10. *Phaedo* 97C.
11. *Phaedo* 98B–C.
12. *Phaedo* 98C–D.
13. Timaeus 29D; DK 28 B 8.60 (= KRS 302).
14. *Timaeus* 37C–38C.
15. *Timaeus* 27C–28A.

physiologia of the pre-Socratics, and melds Pythagorean cosmology with the elemental theory of Empedocles (and even his conception of the harmonizing force of Friendship, or *Philia*)—theories that come from southern Italy and Sicily, as do Socrates' visitors. But he stands out as a physiologist of the fourth century against the background of pre-Socratic thought in his explanatory metaphor of the *dēmiourgos*. Literally, a *dēmiourgos* (δημιουργός) is an artisan, unattached to a palace or private household, who works for the public. The name is as old as the Linear-B tablets from Pylos. In the work of the pre-Socratics the hints of Nature conceived as a craftsman are very few, and these hints are mainly concentrated in Empedocles' metaphors describing the works of Aphrodite (or *Philia*) in his poem *On Nature*. Indeed, that this world was created by a god is explicitly denied by Heraclitus.[16]

The god of the *Timaeus* is a craftsman, working from a pattern (*paradeigma*), with the perfection of his handiwork clearly before him in his mind's eye. This Demiurge is not a novelty in the *Timaeus;* he was glimpsed in Socrates' discussion of the Idea of the Good in book 6 of the *Republic*[17] and the astronomical section of *Republic* 7.[18] And, in a Platonic signature, we discover him in the divine plastic artist, or "molding [*platton*] god" of the myth of the metals.[19] His works are implicit in Socrates' discussion of the Form of the Good and the objects included in the second lower segment of the divided line;[20] and they are explicitly described in the final discussion of *mimēsis* in book 10 of the *Republic*.[21] The most remote of the artisans of the *Republic* fashions the pattern of a Bed "in the nature of things"; the carpenter in turn makes a material copy of this Bed; and the painter paints this bed of wood and rope in pigment. The Demiurge of the *Timaeus* takes as his paradigm the invisible and eternal fabric of the world known to thought and visible to his mind's eye. From this the Demiurge creates the visible and material world by associating in a progression of geometrical proportions the precise solid figures that form the world masses of earth, water, air, and fire. But as a copyist, his works of *mimēsis*, or reproduction, must be inadequate. He is not himself the demiurge of the pattern from which he works, and, unlike his model, his visible and material copy is not entirely exempt from the laws of human time

---

16. DK 22 B 30 (= KRS 217 = XXXVII Kalin).

17. *Republic* 6.507C, a passage now familiar; see III §4 ("Thinking About Ideas").

18. *Republic* 7.529C–530B.

19. Ὁ θεὸς πλάττων, *Republic* 3.415A.

20. *Republic* 6.507A and 510A, a conception that has perplexed us before; see III §4 ("Thinking About Ideas").

21. *Republic* 10.597A.

and generation. In Greek thinking, it is an axiom that everything that comes into being also passes away—save the Greek gods. The converse of this axiom is also true: what is unborn is eternal. Because they were not born, the cattle of the Sun will never die.[22]

The World of the Demiurge

The *Timaeus* exemplifies the teleology the young Socrates sought in Anaxagoras' book and in Anaxagoras' *Nous*. And at the end of the first of the three sections into which his long speech divides, Timaeus can say: "What we have described up to this point, with a few minor exceptions, has been shown to be the product of an artisan Mind (*Nous*)."[23] The very structure of this dialogue on the structure of the universe reveals the new conception of causality that would eventually find its codification and exploitation in Aristotle's theory of four causes. In the first phase of the argument, the Demiurge fashions the body and soul of the universe in an abstract medium, creating the geometrical figures and proportions that inform matter in motion.[24] In the second phase,[25] his material and the unformed Recipient that holds the forms he impresses on matter are represented as Necessity (*Anankē*). Timaeus' word is well chosen, for *anankē* was Democritus' word for the autonomous laws governing matter in motion: "recoil, motion, the blow of matter."[26] Parmenides before him had invoked Necessity as the force binding his unique spherical heaven, with its sun, moon, constellations, and stars, in the third phase of his poem *On Nature*, which deals with human opinions, the Way of Opinion.[27] But, as Gregory Vlastos has pointed out,[28] *anankē* is also associated in Greek thought with the condition of slavery, and, in some sense, the pre-Socratic causes of the second phase of Timaeus' speech are "slave causes."

In the *Timaeus*, we discover what we do not find elsewhere in the pages of Plato—the Forms (εἴδη, *eidē*) of matter. The mind exerts its control over matter, as the soul controls the body and as the master directs the slave.[29] The section on Necessity is thus the most "pre-Socratic" of the three sections

---

22. *Odyssey* 12.130–31.
23. *Timaeus* 47E.
24. *Timaeus* 29D–47E.
25. *Timaeus* 47E–68E.
26. DK 68 A 66.
27. DK 28 B 10.6 (= KRS 305).
28. Vlastos 1981, chap. 7.
29. *Timaeus* 69E and 70A.

of the *Timaeus*, for it treats of material causes as well as what Aristotle would term the efficient, formal, and final causes. The theory of light and vision expounded here[30] is one of the most brilliant parts of this section, and it is no accident that Theophrastos at the end of the century would discuss Plato's theories of vision and color in the distinguished company of Empedocles and Democritus.[31] The final phase of the *Timaeus*[32] is synthetic and combines the principles of Intelligence and Necessity.

Timaeus ends his speech, according to plan, with a brief and surpassingly strange footnote on the origin of the female of the species and the other species of animals. His peroration is expected and striking:

> The universe is a perfect ordering [*kosmos*] that has acquired living creatures, mortal and immortal, and achieved its plenitude, a visible animal containing things visible, an image of the intelligible, a god perceived by the senses, that has come into being, the greatest, best, and most perfect, this single heaven like unto which there is no other.[33]

His words "god perceived by the senses," "image" (*eikōn*), and "has come into being" are perfect summaries of the themes and artistic paradoxes of the *Timaeus*. The divine and eternal is invisible; it does not come into being or pass away. But the Demiurge creates his universe in human time and in a linear sequence, which will be continued directly by Critias' history of prehistoric Athens and Atlantis, as Critias takes the new human race from Timaeus and the guardian class of Kallipolis from Socrates' speech of the "day before." It should be noted that in Timaeus' account mankind is originally male and becomes female only as cowards born in the next cycle of incarnation become women.

The artisan and poet responsible for the *Timaeus* has created in the divine Demiurge a necessary fiction, for the real world of intelligibility stands outside of time. Timaeus himself offers his companions no more than a "plausible myth" and a "plausible account." Plato can offer no more. As a mimetic artist he produces a likeness (*eikōn*) and at the same time a sense of distance between his original and this likeness. When Timaeus speaks of the Demiurge as fabricating "skin, as we now call it," he describes it as a covering for the human

---

30. *Timaeus* 67C–68D.

31. In the only surviving section of this doxographical treatise, *On the Senses*, which is readily available only in *Doxographi Graeci*, ed. Hermann Diels (1879), pp. 524–25. Theophrastos has no hesitation about ascribing all the doctrines of the *Timaeus* to Plato.

32. *Timaeus* 69A–92C.

33. *Timaeus* 92C.

head. And as Timaeus describes the manufacture of hair on the head by felting and cooling the layer of skin stretched over the skull,[34] Plato produces in his reader a violent alienation from the familiar worthy of Swift's invention of the Lilliputian interpretation of the objects found in Gulliver's pocket. More than any of the Platonic dialogues, the *Timaeus* meets the problem of rendering a likeness by creating a sense of alienation in the reader. A world of teleology and the product of a divine craftsman are made to seem radically unfamiliar. How can any mimetic artist describe a world that is supremely intelligent precisely because it is supremely intelligible and whose divine thought is circular and self-reflecting? All discourse that is divine is mono-logic; it is "about" itself as it contemplates itself and circles itself.[35] This must be why the *Timaeus* is Plato's least dialogic of his dialogues.

Plato's Astral Theology

Timaeus calls his world a "visible god."[36] His world is a divine world of the heavens above, with the moon and sun circling the earth, the stars fixed in the rhythm of their revolutions, and the five planets, whose seemingly errant paths are intelligible only to the celestial mathematician, describing their orbits. If Plato's reader were granted the knowledge of the order in which he wrote his dialogues, it is likely that he would discover that the *Timaeus* was written late in Plato's career. (It is almost universally placed among the late dialogues.) Would the reader be taken aback by the astral theology of the *Timaeus*, coming as it does without any earlier announcement of this new conception of divinity? The shock, I think, would be great. But there are hints that the stars and heavenly bodies are divine from early on. In the *Apology*, Socrates asks Meletos if he thinks that the man he had indicted for atheism does not believe—"as do other men"—that the Sun and Moon are gods.[37] Helios and Selene were not, in the fifth century, important in the cults of the Greek states. Athena, Apollo, Zeus, Hera, Demeter, and Dionysos—the gods Timaeus leaves to the reverence of tradition established by the "sons of the gods"—were of supreme importance. In the *Symposium* we are told that at the end of a long night of meditation under the open sky, Socrates prayed to the Sun.[38] In the *Phaedo*, every human soul is said to be guided by

34. *Timaeus* 75E–76B.
35. *Timaeus* 37B–C and 90C.
36. *Timaeus* 90C.
37. *Timaeus* 26D.
38. *Symposium* 220D.

its tutelary *daimōn* as it meets its judgment in the underworld; the fate of some souls, purified by philosophy, is to ascend to a region of great purity that Socrates does not describe but is clearly in the heavens.[39] Timaeus suggests that, if a person directs his eyes to heaven, his *daimōn* will be well ordered and he himself happy (*eudaimōn*).[40] We will rediscover this astral theology for a last time in Plato when we come to consider the place of philosophy in Plato's Cretan city (see III § 8, "Magnesia").

Except by indirection, in Socrates' questioning of Euthyphro and in his criticism of theological poetry in book 2 of the *Republic*, theology is not a matter of inquiry or discussion in the dialogues of Plato. The reader of the *Timaeus* is encouraged by Socrates' summary of the state, which he had described "the day before," to reflect back on the *Republic*; as he does, he realizes that the gods of Athenian cult are not important to Kallipolis; nor is the virtue of piety, which is conspicuous by its absence from Socrates' discussion of the other virtues. Questions concerning the religion of the new state are left to the authority and ambiguity of the Delphic oracle.[41] In the prehistory related in the *Critias*, the gods of Greek religion return to the prominence they did not have in the *Republic* or *Timaeus*. Poseidon and Athena eclipse Timaeus' astral divinities. It is only in the *Laws* that Timaeus' astral divinities return to the Platonic dialogues. There, the Olympian gods are given their due acknowledgment,[42] but the gods that revolve in the firmament of the *Laws* are the stars and planets. When the Athenian Stranger urges that anyone who has the responsibility of governing men must inquire into "the greatest god and the entire universe," he seems to be making a Platonic confession. Such an argument, he avows, might not be "becoming to old men," but "it is no longer possible to refrain from stating it." This said, he introduces the new form of state religion devoted to the gods of the heavens.[43]

Timaeus leaves it to the sons of the gods to enlighten mankind regarding the genealogies of the gods of the Greek states;[44] the Demiurge addresses his celestial divinities as "gods of gods, of which handiwork I am Maker and Father," assuring them that he will never dissolve what he has bound together.[45] He instructs these gods to produce—with his guidance—the rest of

39. *Phaedo* 113D–114B.
40. Εὐδαίμων, *Timaeus* 90A.
41. *Republic* 4.427C.
42. *Laws* 4.716C; see III §8 ("Magnesia").
43. *Laws* 7.821A–D.
44. *Timaeus* 40D.
45. *Timaeus* 41A–D.

the universe to bring his project to its perfection. When it comes to their creation of human beings, a question arises. It is prompted by Socrates' description of Italian Locri in the *Timaeus* prologue: Can there exist a well-ordered city like Locri (whose demiurge was the legendary lawgiver Zaleukos) in a random and disorderly universe?[46]

The alternative is the threat to society evoked in the *Apology* and in book 10 of the *Laws*—atheism. In the *Laws*, the Athenian Stranger would offer Kleinias' Cretan colonists "the Sun, the Moon, the Stars, and the Earth as proofs that these bodies are gods and divine," but the scientists known to Athens attempt to persuade the Athenians that these divine bodies are nothing more than earth and stone. The danger of their argument is obvious to the Cretan Kleinias, who is to found the city of the *Laws*.[47] Its danger was quite palpable to Meletos, who tried to seize it as a handle in his attempt to convict Socrates of being one of these "pre-Socratics" and teaching, with Anaxagoras, that the sun was a molten stone and the moon earth.[48] Insofar as it confronts the danger of atheism and the pre-Socratic conception of the autonomous laws of nature, the *Timaeus* is a political dialogue. Although it is a monologue throughout the entire speech of Timaeus and, as we have claimed, the least dialogic of Plato's dialogues, the *Timaeus* is a dialogue in that it speaks with other Platonic dialogues, most notably the *Apology*, the *Phaedo*, the *Republic*, the *Critias*, and the *Laws*.

ENDNOTE: In this essay I have knowingly propagated the commonly accepted opinion that the *Timaeus* is a dialogue separate from the *Critias*. The *Timaeus/ Critias* is, in fact, a single unfinished dialogue, and it poses in its extreme form the problem of closure, reviewed in II § 8, "The Open Dialogue." There is no extended treatment of this unique and fragmentary dialogue. Paul Friedländer devoted separate chapters to the *Timaeus* and *Critias* in *Plato* (1958), vol. 1, "Plato as a Physicist" (chap. 14) and "Plato as City Planner" (chap. 17). The *Timaeus/Critias* and Plato's philosophical fiction of Atlantis is central to Luc Brisson's treatment of Plato the mythmaker (1994, trans. 1998).

David Furley provides an elegant and brief introduction to the worldview of the *Timaeus* in *The Greek Cosmologists*, vol. 1, *The Formation of Atomic Theory and Its Earliest Critics* (1987), chap. 1. Gregory Vlastos has written an illuminating essay on Socrates' discussion of causes in the *Phaedo*, "Reasons and Causes in

46. Locri is so described in *Timaeus* 20A and *Laws* 1.638B.
47. *Laws* 10.886B–E.
48. *Apology* 26D; Anaxagoras: DK 59 A 42 (= KRS 502).

the *Phaedo,"* in *Platonic Studies* (1981), chap. 4. An excellent commentary on the *Timaeus* is that of F. M. Cornford, *Plato's Cosmology: The "Timaeus" of Plato* (1937). I have attempted to state the plan adumbrated in the "tetralogy" *Republic, Timaeus/Critias,* and unwritten *Hermokrates* in "The Plan of Plato's *Critias"* (1997) and in the introduction to Clay and Purvis, *Four Island Utopias* (1999).

Corruptissima res publica, plurimae leges.
[The more corrupt the state, the greater the number of its laws.]
—Tacitus, *Annales* 3.27

In the *Laws*, we have lost Socrates, but have gained an Athenian Stranger. He
is a stranger because the *Laws* is set not in Athens, as are all of Plato's other
dialogues (except the *Phaedrus*, which is set just outside the walls of Athens),
but in Crete, where the Athenian has joined a Cretan from the ancient city
of Knossos and a Spartan to make the long trip on foot to the cave of Zeus
on Mount Ida,[1] for reasons we never discover in the dialogue itself. We learn,
almost by accident, that the Cretan will join still other Cretans to found a
new colony on the island.[2] The name of this colony is the city of the Magnetes. Let us call it Magnesia.

The Road to the Laws

The *Laws* is Plato's last dialogue, and, according to a number of ancient traditions,[3] he left it unfinished at his death. In this dialogue, the advanced age of
the three companions is stressed time and again.[4] The Athenian Stranger
speaks to his companions of "the sober play of old men."[5] This is one of

1. *Laws* 1.625B.
2. *Laws* 3.702C–703C. His project is referred to again in *Laws* 6.751E and for a last time in
12.969A–D.
3. DL 3.37, among others. The *Epinomis*, or "Sequel to the *Laws*," is one Academic philosopher's
response to the closing of the *Laws*. The *Epinomis* will be briefly considered in the Epilogue to this
section.
4. *Laws* 1.625A and 635A, 4.712C, 6.752A, 7.799C and 821A.
5. *Laws* 6.769A.

Plato's most visible signatures. It would seem that a discussion of law and the dialogue entitled the *Laws* was the fitting activity for Plato's last years. The character of the discussion is very much unlike the discussions of Plato's earlier dialogues and what we think of as the Socratic method. In the Socratic dialogues, Socrates at seventy is very much what he was as the very young man who met Parmenides on the occasion of the Panathenaia. Socrates spoke both in court and to Parmenides in "his accustomed manner." But as Plato grew older and more remote from the age of Socrates, his manner of writing changed. In the *Laws* we seem to hear his unfamiliar voice projected through the mask of the Athenian Stranger. But this voice is distorted by a mask that, like all tragic masks, is the mask of a character and not an individual.

The first sign of a change in Plato's manner of writing is the disappearance of Socrates as the dominant intellectual personality of a dialogue and his replacement by a fictive character: a visitor from the Greek city of Elea in the *Sophist* and *Statesman* (in which Socrates is present but virtually silent); Timaeus from Locri in the *Timaeus*; and the Athenian in the *Laws*. Only in the case of Critias and Hermokrates are Socrates' surrogates clearly recognizable historical characters. All indications are that the Critias of the *Timaeus* prologue and *Critias* is Critias of the *Charmides* and leader of the Thirty; as we have seen, Hermokrates is well known from the pages of Thucydides.

The second change manifest in the dialogues of Plato's last period is the character of the conversation. Instead of questioning either received or sophistic opinion by the rigorous examination of the *elenchos*, a method we associate inevitably with Socrates (see III § 1, "The Socratic *Elenchos*"), we find long unbroken speeches in the manner of the sophists of the fifth century and the epideictic orators of the fourth, who spoke at length but did not stay for an answer.[6] Book 5 of the *Laws* is an unbroken speech by the Athenian interrupted only at its end by Kleinias' few words of approval. The *Laws* belong to the late Platonic manner of exposition rather than examination.

Even so, it would be a mistake to take the Athenian as no more than the transparent disguise that Plato assumed out of his long habit of silence and anonymity, and his every statement as an unqualified statement of Platonic political philosophy. It is true that the Athenian occasionally returns to arguments made by other dominant personalities in the Platonic dialogues and particularly to arguments made earlier by Socrates. But the stranger of the

---

6. The style of uninterrupted discourse is characterized in both *Protagoras* 338A and *Critias* 106A (in Timaeus' description of his long, unbroken speech).

Laws is first and foremost an Athenian. This Athenian is more informed about the institutions, poetry, and philosophy of the Greek world and of Athens than are his interlocutors. And, as were the Athenians Saint Paul encountered in Athens, he is curious.[7] The range of his conversation is limited by the character of his interlocutors within the dialogue. Kleinias of Knossos and Megillos of Sparta represent traditional and closed military societies. Sparta was notorious for its expulsion of foreigners (*xenelasia*). In a sense, the *Laws* resembles the *Republic*. As Socrates dominated the conversation of the *Republic*, the Athenian dominates the conversation of the *Laws*, both are circumscribed by the limitations of their companions. I can now repeat my earlier assertion with more evidence and some necessary refinement:[8] Socrates is to the Athenian as Glaukon is to Kleinias and Adeimantos to Megillos. Both dialogues have three major characters who stand at three levels of intelligence. But in the *Laws*, the Athenian Stranger does not reach—or even approach—the top of the divided line of the *Republic*.

The similarity of the *Republic* and *Laws*, in the hierarchy of their voices and the limitations of their characters, is offset by a fundamental disparity. In the *Republic* (after book 1), Socrates speaks to fellow Athenians in the port of Athens. In the *Laws*, an anonymous Athenian, whose character is meant to be generic, not individual and historical, addresses two equally generalized representatives of Dorian culture. They speak in the Cretan countryside at a distance from the city of Knossos, and they enjoy the freedom of old men. In this mountainous terrain, even the Athenian is granted the Athenian privilege of free speech.[9] What this means is that the Athenian, whom both the Cretan and the Spartan address as a stranger, can open the closed and guarded borders of two stable, conservative, and martial polities to foreign prospects, even as he articulates the constitution and laws for Kleinias' new colony. It becomes clear too that he will never be able to join in the actual founding of this new Dorian state.[10]

The Legislators of the Laws

It is natural, then, that the *Laws* should open with a question asked by the Athenian. He addresses it to both his companions: "Was it a god, strangers,

---

7. "For all the Athenians and strangers which were there spent their time in nothing else, but either to tell, or to hear, some new thing"; Acts 17.21.

8. See II §7 ("Dramatis Personae").

9. *Laws* 7.806D.

10. *Laws* 6.753A.

or some mortal, who is responsible for the arrangement of your laws?"[11] His word for "laws" is *nomoi* (νόμοι). In no document from Greek civilization do we have a more profound interrogation into the meaning of *nomos* than in Plato's *Laws*. The difficulty in translating the word that stands as its title is that, even before it means positive written law, *nomos* means "custom," "tradition," "culture." For Plato, this "law" is the foundation of all written laws. At the very beginning of this long conversation, the Athenian observes that the wisest law forbids inquiring into law, but older men are permitted to make this inquiry.[12] This law is custom, not a written statute. It is the Athenian who sets this inquiry afoot by inquiring into the origins of the institutions, or "laws," of Crete and Lacedaemon.

Both Crete and Sparta claim divine authority for their institutions. According to their traditions, Zeus legislated for the Cretans through King Minos, and Apollo for the Spartans through the legislator Lykourgos. What emerges from this opening inquiry into Dorian institutions and the military virtue of courage on which they are based is that the Athenian, as a stranger from a country of laws that are given by human legislators such as Solon, has an awareness of other cultures and the possibilities of human society—and human history—that neither of his Dorian companions possesses. He knows Homer and the tradition of the intimate association between Minos, the legendary lawgiver of Knossos, and Zeus. Kleinias confesses that Homer is not well known in Crete, an island that has little use for foreign poetry.[13] The Athenian's interpretation of the Homeric lines "Minos, / who every nine years held intimate conversation with great Zeus"[14] is that of Socrates in the *Minos*—a short Socratic (but probably not Platonic) dialogue on law.[15] The Athenian reads these lines as meaning that every ninth year Minos went to Zeus to receive his education as a lawgiver.[16] The lines he interprets with this twist come from one of Odysseus' lying tales in which he tells his wife, Penelope, that he comes from Crete. The Cretan, who is inclined to accept this interpretation even without the authority of Homer, recalls the tradition that all Cretans are liars, when he later affirms that "truth is a noble thing."[17] It could be that the Athenian is not being entirely straightforward in his claim

11. *Laws* 1.624A.
12. *Laws* 1.634D.
13. *Laws* 3.680C.
14. *Odyssey* 19.178–79.
15. *Minos* 319B–320B, where the lines are quoted.
16. *Laws* 1.624A–B.
17. *Laws* 2.663E.

that the laws of Crete were secretly given to Minos by Zeus. He seems open to questioning the origins of human laws and the traditions dignifying the institutions of Crete and Sparta; and he is the alien and human lawgiver of Plato's Cretan city.

This tradition is only glanced at in the *Laws*, but, in taking the road from Knossos to Mount Ida,[18] the Athenian and his companions are following the footsteps of Minos. In the dialogue, they never reach their destination in the) cave and sanctuary of Zeus on Mount Ida. At the conclusion of the dialogue, a human, an Athenian, has legislated the institutions and laws of a Cretan colony and provided for everything save its permanence and stability. The authority of Zeus is superseded by that of a nameless Athenian Stranger because the *Laws* recognizes, as the *Republic* recognized only by implication, that human societies are created out of human materials by human lawgivers and can finally be no more than second or third best in the hierarchy of possible states. The age of divine legislators giving law unto heroic humans— and the age of the *Republic*—is long past, as is the reign of Kronos, when, according to the central myth of the *Statesman*, humans and the heavens were guided by gods.[19]

Kallipolis and Magnesia

Magnesia takes on its distinctive shape as the Athenian glances back at Socrates' state in the *Republic*. Kallipolis represents the best form of human society, under which Magnesia ranks second. Magnesia is a city founded—or refounded[20]—on institutions that are not to be found in Kallipolis. Nothing makes the contrast between these two cities more apparent than does the term "law" itself. In the *Republic*, Kallipolis is founded as a state without laws or courts of law; its unwritten laws are a matter of custom and acculturation. In Socrates' view, it would be naive for a founding father to legislate the kind of respect the young owe to their elders: silence, standing in their presence, giving way to them. As for such petty details as laws governing business contracts, libel, insult, suits, judges, taxes, and harbor fees, "would," Socrates asks, "we be so foolhardy as to legislate any of these?" In the *Republic*, the

18. As the hypothesis of the dialogue is developed in *Laws* 1.625B.
19. *Laws* 4.713C–D and 9.853C; *Statesman* 271B–272B.
20. As becomes clear only in *Laws* 8.848D and 11.919D, where the Athenian speaks of the Magnesians, "whose city the god is founding again." This "refoundation" might be an oblique reference to the city founded in the *Republic*.

answer is "No, not for gentlemen."[21] One can attempt to formulate the difference between the *Republic* and *Laws* as follows: in the *Republic* the guardians
(*phylakes*) are guardians of a society and an austere way of life—or polity
(*politeia*); in the *Laws* the guardians have become the Guardians of Laws (*nomophylakes*).

Despite the term "law" that appears in English translation, none of the
institutions of Kallipolis possess the formal characteristics of Greek law. They
are not articulated in the formulaic language of Greek laws: they do not do
not begin by invoking "Good Fortune" or "Gods"; they have no prologue;
they state as their authority no decree of a council or assembly; they contain
no proviso ("If anyone should . . . then . . ."); and they stipulate no penalties
for their contravention. By contrast, in the *Laws* the Athenian formulates 115
separate laws and can claim that a city without properly constituted courts of
law is no city at all.[22] One reason for this contrast between Kallipolis and
Magnesia is, of course, that both laws and courts of law are symptoms of
private property.[23]

Other contrasts between these two cities are as instructive. In the *Republic*, Socrates represents himself, Glaukon, and Adeimantos as the founders
(*oikistai*) of a city. Yet we never discover where this city is to be founded, who
its colonists are to be, how its land is to be divided among gods and men,
what its property classes are to be, the nature of its citizenship, political
assemblies, magistrates, courts of law, or the calendar of its religious festivals.
In the *Republic*, piety is an orphaned virtue, strictly segregated from the four
cardinal virtues, as it is in all the Platonic dialogues since the *Euthyphro*. But
piety and the religion of the new state of the *Laws* are two of the most
important themes of the Athenian's discourse. In this dialogue, Zeus of the
Boundaries is the dread guardian of private property,[24] and the worship of
ancestors, which assumes and assures the solidarity of the family, is meticu-
lously provided for.[25]

One of the most striking statements the Athenian makes in this dialogue
concerns the fundamental piety a child owes his aged and bedridden parents.
He brings his point home by a striking comparison. We distinguish between

---

21. *Republic* 4.425C–D.
22. *Laws* 6.766D.
23. One could state this contrast by invoking Tacitus' epigram on the Roman state: "in corrupti-
sima re publica, plurimae leges" (in the most corrupt state are the greatest number of laws); *Annales*
3.27.
24. *Laws* 7.843A in contrast to *Republic* 2.373D.
25. *Laws* 4.716C–718C.

the visible gods of the heavens and the unseen gods we worship in the forms of lifeless statues and images:

> [J]ust so, if someone has a father or mother or grandfather or grand-
> mother in the house, confined to bed and worn away with years, let him
> never think, when he has such a monument as this at his hearth, that
> any statue can ever be more awe-inspiring to him, if he maintains this
> monument in a proper and fitting manner.[26]

This poignant description of the duty we owe to the aged members of our family depends on a tacit proportional scheme, which once again reveals a view of the ideal in art: as the aged features and ravaged bodies of the old are to the persons they were in their prime and youth, so our statues of the gods are to the real gods.[27]

A consciousness of the meaning of history also makes its vivid appearance in the *Laws*, particularly as the Athenian passes in review actual historical states in book 3 and describes the history of Persia and Athens as revealing the "matrix" polities of monarchy and democracy.[28] The striking contrast between the absence of history from the ideal polity of the *Republic* and its appearance in the *Laws* reminds us of Aldous Huxley's profound insight that in utopian societies (like that of his *Brave New World*) a memory of the past cannot cohabit with the new "reality" of the present.[29] The society of the *Republic* has no past; the society of Plato's Cretan city is informed by a knowledge of other historical societies and is, in fact, a city refounded.

The *Republic* and *Laws* stand to one another in a relation of tension, and the polity of the *Republic* (if not the written dialogue itself) is occasionally recalled in the *Laws*, as it is when the Athenian ranks in descending order the polities Kleinias might employ as models for his new colony. The first and best polity is a city in which all are friends and their possessions held in common:

> This arrangement, whether it exists at present or will exist in the future,
> has wives in common and children in common and all possessions in

---

26. *Laws* 11.931A.
27. See II §4 ("Mimesis").
28. *Laws* 3.693D–699D.
29. In this new world there is a campaign against viviparous reproduction, "[a]ccompanied by a campaign against the Past; by the closing of museums, the blowing up of historical monuments (luckily most of them had already been destroyed during the Nine Years' War); by the suppression of all books published before A. F. 150." Aldous Huxley, *Brave New World* and *Brave New World Revisited* (New York, 1960), 39. *Brave New World* was first published in 1932.

common. In it everything termed "private" has been entirely removed from life by every possible measure, and a program has been carried out, so far as is possible, in order to transform what is naturally private into a sort of community. Eyes, ears, and hands will seem to see and hear and treat the selfsame objects, and everyone will praise or blame in unison, feeling joy or distress at the same thing.[30]

Such is Socrates' state in the *Republic,* and such is the state Aristotle criticized in the *Politics.*[31] Evidently, the model constitution the Athenian elaborates for Magnesia comes second to the communism of the *Republic,* and, as for the polity that ranks third, the Athenian can only say: "[W]e shall describe it after this, the god willing."[32]

By the conclusion of the *Laws,* Magnesia is founded in its essential social and civic structure, and, up until the last paragraphs of book 12 of the dialogue, this structure seems to have been described exhaustively. Despite noble assurances that it is not fitting for the legislator to enter into niggling details, the Athenian descends into a thicket of detailed provisions: his law of homicide includes the case of the homicidal mule;[33] provisions against theft cover the case of "alienated" hives of bees;[34] and there is a contract law providing for club dues.[35] *De minimis non curat lex.* The meticulous care Plato devoted to formulating a system of laws at the end of his life should serve as a warning to his critics who regard him, as he feared he might be regarded, as "all theory."[36]

The Fate of Philosophy in Magnesia

Although the Athenian assumes the role of the legislator, the *Laws* possesses a philosophical depth that is hard to make out in the profusion of its surface details and our perplexities over its organization. Plato's understanding of law is impossible to appreciate in any language other than Greek. For Plato, written laws (*nomoi*) cannot take hold in a society without the civic education of a citizen body by custom (*nomos*). And for this reason any consideration of

30. *Laws* 5.739C–D.
31. *Republic* 5.462C; Aristotle, *Politics* 2.1–5; and see III §6 ("Kallipolis").
32. *Laws* 5.739E.
33. *Laws* 9.873E.
34. *Laws* 8.843D–E.
35. *Laws* 11.915E.
36. *Logos,* Letter VII 328C.

written statutes must take into view what the Greeks spoke of as "unwritten laws": "These are the bonds that keep the entire social and political order together . . . as ancestral customs of great antiquity."[37] To such bonds the mind of man runneth not to the contrary. This fundamental insight explains a great deal about Plato's *Laws*. It explains why civic (and not family) education is so crucial to the Athenian in the *Laws* (as it was to Socrates in the *Republic* and to the Dorian states of Crete and Sparta); it explains too why so much of the *Laws* is devoted to *prooimia*, or poetic and musical preludes that introduce the laws by preparing the citizen to understand and accept them; and it explains why force (*bia*) is combined with persuasion (*peithō*) if persuasion and acculturation fail. The preparation of the character of the future citizen of Magnesia begins even before birth, in the prenatal gymnastics of pregnant women.[38]

In Greek music and poetry a *prooimion* πϱοοίμιον) is the overture, or prelude, that introduces and prepares a listener for the "path of song" (*oimos*) that is to follow. The *prooimia* of the laws set the *Laws* apart from any other Greek code of laws. It is only at the end of book 4 (and when the company has come to rest at high noon) that the Athenian, who has been talking most of the way, realizes that all that has been said to that point is in fact a musical prelude to the "music" of his legislation, like the exploration of musical themes in lyric "nome" (*nómos*).[39]

Casual conversation, philosophical preparation, argument—and exhortation—stand as the prelude to specific laws; just as *nómos* (custom) is the foundation of *nómoi* (written laws), the lyric *prooimion* introduces and prepares for the lyric *nómos*. This analogy is not a metaphorical conceit, for the *Laws* as a whole will come to be viewed as a kind of poetry and incantation directed at the citizens of Magnesia. The greatest part of the *Laws* is devoted to acculturation rather than to legislation. All of books 1–4 constitute the "prelude" to the *Laws*; all of book 5 is a prelude in the form of an address by the Athenian to the future colonists of Magnesia;[40] the Athenian's argument for the Socratic conception of punishment as learning and betterment is the prelude to the detailed discussion of law and punishment in book 9,[41] as is the discussion of

37. *Laws* 7.793A–B.
38. *Laws* 7.789D.
39. *Laws* 4.722C–D.
40. *Laws* 5.741A.
41. *Laws* 9.854A.

intention that precedes the Athenian's law of homicide[42] and his treatment of atheism and theology (in book 10) that precedes the law against impiety.[43]

Training, acculturation, education, persuasion, and even enchantment are Plato's means to create the model for a single city of free citizens dedicated to freedom and human excellence out of the 5,040 households of colonists that constitute the city of Magnesia. The reader who has followed the dialogues of Plato from the *Apology* to the *Laws* will realize that the Athenian repeats in the *Laws* many of the suggestions made by Socrates in the educational books of the *Republic* (2–4 and 6–7); but the old Athenian is more generous to poetry than was Socrates. In Magnesia there will be state choruses of Dionysos; musical competitions in the continuous calendar of festivals to honor the twelve gods; theaters; and even comic poets. Only foreign itinerant tragic poets will not gain admission when they come knocking at the doors of the new state the Athenian calls "the truest tragedy." By this he means the highest form of human "making" (or poetry)—the imitation of the highest form of human life.[44]

The Athenian is more explicit than was Socrates in the *Republic* in suggesting what the alternative to the traditional poetry of the polis would be. In the *Republic*, Socrates suggests only that the argument of the *Republic* itself can serve as a "countercharm" to the spell of poetry: "We shall listen to her, chanting to ourselves this conversation we are speaking as a countercharm."[45] In the *Laws* the conversation of the *Laws* itself is offered as the pattern the Guardian of Law (*nomophylax*) should adopt in supervising the education of the young: "This conversation of ours struck me as coming closest to the mark and as the most perfectly suited to the young."[46]

This conclusion seems appropriate. Yet perhaps it is not. The *Laws* is a dialogue the old Athenian characterizes as "the sober play of old men,"[47] and it is situated far below the heavenly city of Kallipolis. A higher form of state and a higher form of education hover above the state the Athenian fashions for Kleinias; and, as we have seen, still a lower form of state lies beyond the frontiers of the conversation recorded in the *Laws*. This the Athenian will describe, "the god willing." At the end of the long uphill journey of the *Laws*

---

42. *Laws* 9.865A.
43. *Laws* 10.887C.
44. *Laws* 7.817B, a passage quoted in II §6 ("Platonic Poetry").
45. *Republic* 10.608A.
46. *Laws* 7.811C, quoted in II §6 ("Platonic Poetry").
47. *Laws* 3.685A.

the Athenian enters into a discussion of the need for the Magnesians to observe other societies. His new colony will send out Magnesian observers over the age of fifty. A new institution is now seen as needed to assure the survival of the new colony—a Nocturnal Council, whose members will assemble long before dawn to consider the reports from these observers and engage in the kinds of research that will assure the stability of their city. In some ways the members of this new society will resemble philosophers. Like the members of Plato's Academy, they assemble at first light, and their function is to acquaint themselves with political institutions other than their own. Perhaps only an Athenian could propose such a council. But the Athenian cannot legislate for them.[48] They are not entirely laws unto themselves, but the Athenian leaves their association autonomous. The Nocturnal Council reminds us of the one glaring omission in this long and seemingly complete dialogue: the Athenian has not provided for the education of the philosopher. By contrast, the education of the philosopher is the most serious theme of the middle books of the *Republic*.

The words "philosopher" and "philosophy" do not appear in the Greek of the *Laws*.[49] The Athenian takes the education of Kleinias' Dorian colonists only as far as mathematics and some acquaintance with geometry and astronomy: "Most citizens do not need to work these subjects out in elaborate detail, but only a select few. Who these are we will declare as we advance to the end."[50] He makes no provision here for the study of dialectic, nor does he ever keep his promise. The conversation of the *Laws* never really reaches this end or the full program of studies of these select few. So far as it goes, it can serve as the model for the education of the young and meet with the approval of elderly and agreeable citizens of Dorian states.

At the end of the dialogue, the Athenian returns to the topic of the virtues and to the "forms" of virtue—the subject with which the dialogue had begun. Kleinias is puzzled by the terms of this concluding conversation,[51] and the Athenian attempts to make his meaning clearer by engaging in a mock exercise in Socratic dialectic. He distinguishes between the virtues of courage and wisdom, yet suggests that the four virtues can also be seen as a unity. This is as far as he advances, and is perhaps as far as he can advance, into the dialectics of the *Republic*. To make divisions is also to view as a unity

48. *Laws* 9.875C.
49. The verb "to philosophize" occurs once, at *Laws* 9.857D.
50. *Laws* 7.818A.
51. *Laws* 12.963C.

that which has been divided, and in this sense the dialectician is synoptic.[52] As a dialectician, the Athenian can view what unites the virtues, which are usually distinguished as four, and can appreciate, as his Dorian companions cannot, virtues other than courage. He can appreciate especially the virtue of intelligence.

If there are no elaborate provisions in the *Laws* for the training of the philosopher-citizen of Magnesia, something is said about the wise men (*sophoi andres*),[53] or "intellectuals," of an open city like that of Athens. The prospect on these remote and alien thinkers is suddenly opened up by the Athenian Stranger in book 10 of the *Laws*. Neither Kleinias nor Megillos have any experience of the atheists the Athenian describes. They are both the poets of theogonies and the authors of works in prose.[54] They offend against the Magnesian law prescribing a belief in the gods and fall into three classes: the true atheist, who sincerely believes that the gods do not exist; the worse sort of thinker, who believes that they exist but does not believe that they care for humans; and the worst sort, who believes that they care for humans to the extent that they can be moved by the gestures of prayer, libation, sacrifice, and other offerings. The Athenian is most concerned with this last group.[55] They are not unlike the pious votaries of the gods in all Greek communities. The Athenian Stranger's elaborate demonstration that soul and purpose are prior to matter and motion takes us back to Socrates' demonstration of the immortality of the soul in the *Phaedrus*; his astral theology is now familiar from the *Timaeus*.[56] It is remarkable that philosophy enters the dialogue from an alien culture of the poets, the sophists, and the materialists so well known to Athens. In addressing the young atheist, the Athenian Stranger seems to be speaking not in the new colony of Magnesia but in his own native city. The atheists of Magnesia will be taken care of by the Nocturnal Council proposed in book 12 of the *Laws*. The members of this council belong, unlike other Magnesians, to the world outside the island of Crete.

We enter no further into the new philosophy glimpsed only at the end of the *Laws*. This new philosophy does not call all into doubt, but it raises serious questions about the stability of Magnesia. The Athenian's companions, who have kept up with him as he has made his way toward the cave of

---

52. *Republic* 7.537C.
53. So described in *Laws* 10.888E, 890A. They are described as sophists in 10.908D. ▬
54. *Laws* 10.890A.
55. *Laws* 10.905C–908D.
56. *Phaedrus* 245C; for the astral theory, see III §7 ("The World of the Demiurge").

Zeus on Mount Ida, agree that in order to guarantee the stability of their new state, they must establish the Nocturnal Council as its "anchor."[57] Megillos, who has not spoken for a long time, sees how crucial this council will be:

> My dear Kleinias, to judge from all that we have now said, we must either abandon our plan to found this state or refuse to let this stranger depart. Rather, we must employ every strategy and every means to persuade him to join in the foundation of our state.[58]

Kleinias asks the Spartan to join him in persuading the Athenian, and Megillos agrees: "You will have my help." The Athenian, who has already announced that he cannot join this Dorian colony,[59] remains silent. The *Laws* does not conclude—not because Plato died before he could give it a proper conclusion and its final touches, but because no human society, no matter how conservative, can be anchored in the stability of philosophy, nor can any human lawgiver commune with Zeus every nine years in a cave on Mount Ida.

Epilogue and *Epinomis*

Not long after Plato's death and the end of a writing career of more than fifty years, one of his associates and a disappointed reader of the *Laws* wrote the *Epinomis*, or "Sequel to the *Laws*." Its subtitle is *On Philosophy*. In Philip of Opus' continuation of the conversation of the *Laws* we have an appointment to keep "on the next day." We rediscover Kleinias, the Athenian Stranger, and Megillos. Kleinias speaks first: "We have kept our engagement and all three of us have come, stranger, as is proper—I, yourself, and Megillos here—to weigh what kind of argument we should make concerning wisdom."[60] Philip's literary model was clearly the opening of the *Sophist*. It is a quirk of fate that Plato's last dialogue, the *Laws*, should have generated two later dialogues written in imitation of Plato—one to introduce it and the other to complete it—the *Minos* and *Epinomis*. Or perhaps it is the result of Plato's elliptical manner of writing that leaves so much for the reader to fill in.

The *Laws* continued to fascinate and hold out the tantalizing possibility that Plato was framing laws for an actual Cretan city. In the late nineteenth century an inscription was discovered in the Greek settlement of Magnesia

---

57. *Laws* 12.961C.
58. *Laws* 12.969C.
59. At *Laws* 6.753A.
60. Philip of Opus, *Epinomis* 973A.

on the Maeander (Menderes) inland of the west coast of what is now Turkey. It comes from an archive established after the epiphany of Artemis to that city in the year 208/207. It recorded the history of the foundation of Magnesia and, for a moment, seemed to transform the dream of Platonic political theory into a reality. The history commemorated by this inscription seemed a wonderful confirmation of the hypothesis of Plato's last dialogue, the *Laws*, the dialogue with which we now must conclude. The settlers of Asiatic Magnesia came originally from Thessaly, but in the inscriptional history of the founding of their city they claimed to come from Magnesia in Crete, a city located in the middle of the island between Gortyn and Phaistos on the plain of the Messara, exactly where it is located in the *Laws*.[61] This inscription opened up the stunning possibility that Plato's *Laws* reflected the actual laws drafted for a new Cretan colony by the name of "The City of the Magnetes." It forces us to ask at the end of this study if at the end of his life Plato could have been concerned with refounding a city in distant Crete that had once been the mother city of Magnesia on the Maeander. The likely answer to this question is that the Magnesians were inventing their own history some 140 years after Plato's death. One of these Magnesians was a careful—and literal—reader of Plato's *Laws*. He had every reason to read the hypothesis of the *Laws* as fact, for the fundamental realities of the life and beliefs of the Greek polis reemerge in the *Laws* in such a powerful epiphany that an actual Greek colony came to regard and advertise Plato's Magnesia in Crete as its mother city.

We come finally to the third century A.D. and Rome. In his *Life of Plotinus*, Porphyry of Tyre records an interesting episode in the life of his subject: Plotinus was on close terms with the emperor Gallienus and his wife, Salonina. Relying on his reputation in court, Plotinus asked Gallienus to grant him a "city of philosophers" in Campania (Cumae?). Like Magnesia, this city had fallen into ruin, and Plotinus evidently saw it as his role late in life to restore the city. Its inhabitants, he proposed, would live according to the laws of Plato. By this, he meant the laws of Plato's *Laws*. The name of this new city was not to be Magnesia, but Platonopolis. Gallienus, however, was no philosopher king. Rival courtiers gained his imperial ear and prevented the refoundation of this philosophic city. Where the ruins of the original city of philosophers lie, we do not know.[62]

---

61. *Laws* 4.704D and 5.745C. The inscription is published by Otto Kern, *Inschriften von Magnesia am Maeander* (Berlin, 1900), no. 17.

62. Porphyry, *Life of Plotinus* 12. Gallienus was co-emperor with Valerian from 253 to 260 and sole emperor from 260 to 268. Plotinus' modest request to the emperor would then have come at the end of the philosopher's life. Plotinus died in 270.

ENDNOTE: For the traditions concerning the divine lawgiver of the Spartan state, Plutarch's *Life of Lycurgus* is an invaluable guide. The outstanding contribution to a historical understanding of the *Laws* is Glenn R. Morrow, *Plato's Cretan City: A Historical Interpretation of the Law* (1960). A useful companion to the *Laws* is R. F. Stalley, *Plato's Laws* (1983). Trevor J. Saunder's translation *Plato: The "Laws"* (1970) is recommended for the virtue of its clarity and for setting out the 115 separate laws of the *Laws* as laws. (I would also recommend the translation of Thomas L. Pangle, *The Laws of Plato* [1980].) Werner Jaeger's treatment of the *Laws* in *Paideia* (1944), vol. 1, chap. 5, should be read only after reading his treatment of "state-education in Sparta" in the same volume. Martin Ostwald's study, *Nomos and the Beginnings of the Athenian Democracy* (1969), provides an excellent analysis of *nomos*. A philosophical reading of the *Laws* is that of Leo Strauss, *The Argument and Action of Plato's Laws* (1975). My own vain and skeptical search for Magnesia on the map of Crete is recorded in "Plato's Magnesia" (1992). The relation between the *Republic* and *Laws* is well set out by André Laks, "Legislation and Demiurgy: On the Relationship Between Plato's *Republic* and *Laws*" (1990).

We will likely never be granted certain knowledge of the sequence in which Plato wrote his dialogues or the dates of their composition. In studying Plato, we do not have the information provided by Porphyry, who in his *Life of Plotinus* gave us the sequence in which Plotinus wrote his discourses to his pupils (*Life of Plotinus* 4–6). So far as chronology is concerned, we have no dates of composition, only allusions to events of the fourth century. These refer to events before the dialogues were written and are *termini ante quem*. In the *Menexenus* Socrates (who lives on) refers to the Peace of Antalkidas of 387 (*Menexenus* 244B–C). In the *Symposium* Aristophanes refers to the partition of Mantinea in 385 (*Symposium* 193A), and the frame dialogue of the *Theaetetus* refers to the Corinthian War of either 369 or, less likely, of 394 (*Theaetetus* 142A). In book 1 of the *Laws* there might be a reference to the defeat of Locri by Dionysios II in 356 (1.638B). If these references are secure, these dialogues were written after these terminal dates; how long after we cannot tell. We find in Diogenes Laertius (3.37) and other sources the tradition that Philip of Opus transcribed the *Laws* from wax tablets, which has led to the conclusion that Plato must have been at work at it until his death in 347. It is likely, I think, that Plato wrote *The Apology of Socrates* "immediately after" Socrates death (cf. *Apology* 39C) and published the *Republic* some considerable time after his return from Sicily in 387.

So far as the sequence of dialogues is concerned, it is clear that Plato wanted some dialogues to be read together as a philosophical program (see II § 8). *Theaetetus, Sophist,* and *Statesman* constitute the first grouping of these programmatic dialogues; *Republic, Timaeus,* and *Critias* constitute the last. The remarkably similar literary form of the aporetic dialogues, taken either individually or as a whole (*Charmides, Lysis, Laches, Protagoras,* and, as some would have it, book 1 of the *Republic*), together with the unifying theme of the virtues, encourages us to read these dialogues as a group. One thing is clear of the relation between the early aporetic dialogues and the *Republic*: the *Republic* is the dialogue toward which all of the early dialogues tend; to use an Aristotelian word, it is their entelechy. Although Plato never refers to one dialogue in another as a written document, except perhaps in *Statesman* 284B, with its reference "as we said in the case of the sophist," there are in some of the dialogues clear backward references that seem to establish a priority of composition. We have seen how the *Laws* refers back to the *Republic* and *Statesman* (see III § 8, "Magnesia"). The *Theaetetus* seems to recall the *Parmenides*, where Socrates recalls his earlier conversation with Parmenides (*Theaetetus* 183E), as does the *Sophist* (213C). The connection between the *Phaedrus* and *Symposium* is obviously their common theme of love, and scholars have taken Phaedrus' statement in the *Symposium* that there had been no proper praise of Eros until Agathon's banquet (177A) to mean that the *Phaedrus* must come after the *Symposium*, since it contains a praise of love. But Phaedrus is speaking of poetic praise, and the inference that the *Symposium* must come before the *Phaedrus* depends on the untested assumption that Plato could not have written these words of Phaedrus if he had already composed Socrates' praise of the lover in the *Phaedrus*.

The sequence implied by these observations is, in fact, confirmed in part by the stylistic method of dating the Platonic dialogues that goes back to Lewis Campbell's *Sophistes and Politicus of Plato* of 1867. What Campbell showed was that the two dialogues he edited were late dialogues. Plato's style in the *Sophist* and *Statesman*, particularly his word order and choice of words, relates these dialogues to the style of the *Parmenides*, *Timaeus*, and *Critias*. Campbell's statistical analysis of the evolution of Plato's style has only been confirmed by more elaborate studies employing different linguistic criteria, aided in the last few years by a concordance to Plato, the *Thesaurus Linguae Graecae*, and the computer. The stylistic study of the late dialogues seems to have produced harmonious results. In his *Plato's Theory of Ideas* (1951), Sir W. D. Ross, on stylistic grounds, gives in parallel columns five reconstructions of the sequence in which Plato wrote his dialogues. What is impressive about this display is the agreement of our authorities on the sequence of dialogues that follow the *Republic* (*Phaedrus*, *Theaetetus*, *Parmenides*, *Sophist*, *Statesman*, *Philebus*, *Timaeus*, *Critias*, *Laws*). (The discordant note in this harmony is that the *Theaetetus* seems to refer back to the *Parmenides*.)

But to know the sequence in which Plato wrote his dialogues does not guarantee an appreciation of Plato's reasons for implicating the argument of one dialogue in the argument of another or for taking up one argument before another. On the purely stylistic model of development, there is no reason why we should read the *Apology* in preparation for reading the *Laws*. Going beyond *lexis* (or style) there is also the consideration of argument, or *logos*. The arguments of the Platonic dialogues give us no clear guidance. It is clear from the stylistic analysis that the six dialogues of the two groups of programmatic dialogues do not fall into place in a chronological sequence and that, on the criteria chosen, even book 1 of the *Republic* can be disassociated from the next nine books. It could be that Plato's bibliography does not correspond to his intellectual biography. We know that when Shakespeare wrote his history plays, he did not follow the sequence of English kings but composed his plays as he had the patronage, resources, actors, and inspiration to produce them. No reader today would read Shakespeare's plays in the chronological sequence of their composition and production. In the sequence of his plays, as this has been reconstructed, three or four years and six plays might well separate *Richard III* from *Richard II*.

I reproduce here the two major attempts in this century to order the dialogues in a meaningful philosophical program. They are proposed in Paul Friedländer's *Plato* and Charles Kahn's *Plato and the Socratic Dialogue*. Both critics are well aware of the results of stylistic study, and both have a coherent conception of Plato's intellectual biography. Friedländer (vol. 3, 447–56) adopted the ordering of the dialogues into three groups, a grouping that had been arrived at by Ritter in 1888. But Friedländer's three groupings and subgroupings are by period and argument, not by style. Kahn's study (see pages 47–48) takes us only as far as the *Phaedrus* and, more than any other presentation of Plato, produces an argument for a *psychagōgia*, or leading of the soul of the reader, that conducts us from one dialogue to another.

Friedländer	Kahn
First Period	**Group I**
Protagoras	1. *Apology, Crito*
Laches	2. *Ion, Hippias Minor*
"Thrasymachus"	3. *Gorgias, Menexenus*
Euthyphro	4. *Laches, Charmides, Euthyphro, Protagoras*
Lysis	5. *Meno, Lysis, Euthydemus*
Hippias Major	6. *Symposium, Phaedo, Cratylus*
Hipparchus	
Ion	
Hippias Minor	
Theages	
Apology	
Crito	
Eythydemus	

Cratylus
Menexenus

First Alcibiades
Gorgias
Meno

Second Period	**Group II**
Symposium	*Republic* (1–10)
Phaedo	*Phaedrus*
Republic (2–10)	*Parmenides*
	Theaetetus

Third Period	**Group III**
Theaetetus	
Parmenides	
Phaedrus	
Sophist	*Sophist*
Statesman	*Statesman*
Philebus	*Philebus*
Timaeus	*Timaeus-Critias*
Critias	
Laws	*Laws*

This introduction to Plato cannot be as ambitious as the monumental presentations of Friedländer and Kahn. It does not proceed in a chronological sequence, and, in its concentration on a small number of dialogues, it resembles the program of study as practiced by the Platonists of the fourth and fifth centuries A.D. As their program can be reconstructed, the student began with ten dialogues, chosen in order of difficulty, and concluded with two dialogues of very great difficulty. In this school we read *First Alcibiades, Gorgias, Phaedo, Cratylus, Theaetetus, Sophist, Statesman, Phaedrus, Symposium,* and *Philebus,* in that order, and then the *Timaeus* and *Parmenides.* My own recommendation of a sequence of readings is *Apology* and *Phaedo, Euthyphro* and *Charmides, Symposium* and *Phaedrus,* and last the *Republic.* These dialogues are central to Plato's conception of the meaning of Socrates; the program of training he created in the aporetic dialogues; and the arguments and reflections on writing of the longer dialogues. Once the reader has reached the *Republic,* which is the acropolis of the Platonic dialogues, the path to the other dialogues lies open.

BIBLIOGRAPHY

Ackroyd, Peter. 1999. *The Plato Papers: A Prophesy.* New York.

Adkins, A.W.H. 1960. *Merit and Responsibility: A Study in Greek Values.* Oxford.

——. 1970. *From the Many to the One: A Study of Personality and Views of Human Nature in the Context of Ancient Greek Society, Values, and Beliefs.* Ithaca, N.Y.

Annas, Julia. 1981. *An Introduction to Plato's Republic.* Oxford.

——. 1982. "Plato's Myths of Judgment." *Phronesis* 27:119–43.

Asmis, Elizabeth. 1992. "Plato on Poetic Creativity." Chapter 11 in Kraut 1992a, 338–64.

Auerbach, Erich. 1953. *Mimesis: The Representation of Reality in Western Literature.* Translated by Willard R. Trask. Princeton. (German original, 1946.)

Ausland, Hayden W. 1997. "On Reading Plato Mimetically," *AJP* 118:371–416.

Austin, J. L. 1979. "The Line and the Cave in Plato's *Republic.*" In *Philosophical Papers.* 3d ed. Edited by J. O. Urmson and G. J. Warnock, 288–303. New York.

Bacon, Helen. 1959. "Socrates Crowned." *Virginia Quarterly Review* 35:415–30.

Bakhtin, Michail M. 1981. *The Dialogic Imagination: Four Essays.* Edited by Michael Holmquist, translated by Caryl Emerson. University of Texas Press Slavic Series, no. 1. Austin.

Bloom, Allan, trans. 1968. *The Republic of Plato.* New York.

Blondell, Ruby. 2000. *In Character: Persona and Argument in Plato.* Cambridge.

Blundell, Mary Witlock. 1992. "Character and Meaning in Plato's *Hippias Minor.*" In Klagge and Smith 1992, 131–72.

Blunt, Anthony. 1940. *Artistic Theory in Italy, 1450–1600.* Oxford.

Booth, Wayne. 1983. *The Rhetoric of Fiction.* 2d ed. Chicago.

Borges, Jorge Luis. 1962. *Ficciones.* Edited, with an introduction, by Anthony Kerrigan. New York.

Bremmer, Jan N. 1983. *The Early Greek Concept of the Soul.* Princeton.

Brickhouse, T. C., and N. D. Smith. 1988. *Socrates on Trial.* Oxford.

Brisson, Luc. 1998. *Plato the Mythmaker.* Translated by Gerald Naddaf. Chicago. (*Platon: Les mots et les mythes: Comment et pourquoi Platon nomma le mythe.* Paris, 1994.)

Burnet, John, ed. 1924. *Plato's Euthyphro, Apology of Socrates, and Crito.* Oxford.

Carpenter, Rhys. 1959. *The Aesthetic Basis of Greek Art.* Bloomington, Ind.

Casey, John. 1990. *Pagan Virtue: An Essay in Ethics.* Oxford.

Castiglione, Baldesar. [1528] 1959. *Book of the Courtier.* Translated by Charles S. Singleton. Garden City, N.Y.

Chance, Thomas H. 1992. *Plato's Euthydemus: Analysis of What Is and What Is Not Philosophy.* Berkeley and Los Angeles.

Cherniss, Harold. 1936. "The Philosophical Economy of the Theory of Ideas." *American Journal of Philology* 57:445–56. (Reprinted in *Harold Cherniss: Selected Papers,* edited by Leonardo Tarán, 121–32. Leiden, 1977.)

——. 1947. "Some War-Time Publications Concerning Plato." *American Journal of Philology* 68:225–65.

Claus, David B. 1981. *Toward the Soul: An Inquiry into the Meaning of Ψυχή before Plato.* New Haven.

Clay, Diskin. 1972. "Socrates' Mulishness and Heroism." *Phronesis* 17:53–60.

———. 1975. "The Tragic and Comic Poet of the *Symposium.*" *Arion*, n.s., 2:238–61. (Reprinted in *Studies in Ancient Greek Philosophy*, edited by J. Anton and A. Preus, 186–202. Albany, N.Y., 1983.)

———. 1979. "Socrates' Prayer to Pan." In *Arktouros: Studies Presented to Bernard M.W. Knox*, edited by G. Bowersock, W. Burkert, and M. Putnam, 345–53. Berlin.

———. 1987. "Gaps in the Universe of the Platonic Dialogues." In *Proceedings of the Boston Area Colloquium in Ancient Philosophy*, vol. 3, edited by John J. Cleary, 71–94. Lanham, Md.

———. 1988. "Reading the *Republic.*" In Griswold 1988a, 19–33.

———. 1992a. "Plato's First Words." In *Beginnings in Greek Literature*, edited by Thomas Cole and Francis M. Dunn, *Yale Classical Studies* 29, 113–29. Cambridge.

———. 1992b. "Plato's Magnesia." In *Nomodeiktes: Greek Studies in Honor of Martin Ostwald*, edited by Joseph Farrell and Ralph M. Rosen, 435–45. Ann Arbor, Mich.

———. 1994. "The Origins of the Socratic Dialogue." In Vander Waerdt 1994, 23–47.

———. 1997. "The Plan of Plato's *Critias.*" In *Interpreting the Timaeus and the Critias: Proceedings of the IV Symposium Platonicum*, edited by Tomás Calvo and Luc Brisson, International Plato Studies 9, 49–54. Sankt Augustin.

———. 2000. "Plato's Atlantis: The Anatomy of a Fiction." In *Proceedings of the XV Boston Area Colloquium in Ancient Philosophy*, 1–19. Leiden.

Clay, Diskin, and Andrea Purvis. 1999. *Four Island Utopias: Being Plato's Atlantis, Euhemeros of Messene's Panchaia, Iamboulos' Island of the Sun, and Sir Francis Bacon's New Atlantis.* Newburyport, Mass.

Clay, Jenny Strauss. 1983. *The Wrath of Athena: Gods and Men in the Odyssey.* Princeton.

Connor, W. R. 1991. "The Other 399: Religion and the Trial of Socrates." *Georgica: Greek Studies in Honor of George Cawkwell* (Institute of Classical Studies, London), bulletin supplement 58:49–56.

Cornford, F. M. 1937. *Plato's Cosmology: The "Timaeus" of Plato.* London.

Coulter, James A. 1976. *The Literary Microcosm: Theories of Interpretation of the Later Neoplatonists.* Columbia Studies in the Classical Tradition 2. Leiden.

Coventry, Lucinda. 1990. "The Role of the Interlocutor in Plato's Dialogues." In Pelling 1990, 174–96.

Derrida, Jacques. 1981. "Plato's Pharmacy." In *Dissemination*, translated by Barbara Johnson, 63–171. Chicago. ("La pharmacie de Platon." In *La dissémination.* Paris 1972.)

Descartes, René. 1641. *Meditationes de prima philosophia.* Paris.

Detienne, Marcel. 1996. *The Masters of the Truth in Archaic Greece.* Translated by Janet Lloyd. Cambridge, Mass. (*Les maîtres de la vérité dans la Grèce archaïque.* Paris, 1967.)

Devambez, Pierre. 1962. *Greek Painting.* New York.

Dover, K. J. 1964. "Eros and Nomos (Plato's *Symposium* 182a–185c)." *Bulletin of the London Institute of Classical Studies* 1:31–42.

———. 1967. "Portrait Masks in Aristophanes." In *KOMOIDOTRAGEMATA: Studia Viri Aristophanei W.J.W. Koster in Honorem*, 16–28. Amsterdam.

———. 1974. *Greek Popular Morality in the Time of Plato and Aristotle.* Berkeley and Los Angeles.

Ferrari, G.R.F. 1987. *Listening to the Cicadas: A Study of Plato's "Phaedrus."* Cambridge.

———. 1989. "Plato and Poetry." In *The Cambridge History of Literary Criticism*, vol. 1, *Classical Criticism*, 92–148. Cambridge.

———. "Platonic Love." Chapter 8 in Kraut 1992a, 248–76.

Fine, Gail. 1993. *On Ideas: Aristotle's Criticism of Plato's Theory of Forms*. Oxford.

Fish, Stanley. 1972. *Self-Consuming Artifacts: The Experience of Seventeenth-Century Literature*. Berkeley and Los Angeles.

Fowler, D. P. 1989. "First Thoughts on Closure: Problems and Perspectives." *Materiali e Discussioni* 22:75–122.

———. 1997. "Second Thoughts on Closure." In *Classical Closure: Reading the End in Greek and Latin Literature*, edited by Deborah H. Roberts, Francis M. Dunn, and Don Fowler, chap. 1. Princeton.

Frede, Michael. 1992. "Platonic Arguments and the Dialogue Form." In Klagge and Smith 1992, 201–20. (Reprinted in Smith 1998, 1:254–69.)

———. "The Literary Form of the *Sophist*." Chapter 5 in Gill and McCabe 1998.

Friedländer, Paul. 1958–69. *Plato: An Introduction*. 3 vols. Translated by Hans Meyerhoff. New York.

Furley, David. 1987. *The Greek Cosmologists*. Vol. 1, *The Formation of Atomic Theory and Its Earliest Critics*. Cambridge.

Gadamer, Hans-Georg. 1980. *Dialogue and Dialectic: Eight Hermeneutical Studies on Plato*. Translated by P. Christopher Smith. New Haven, Conn.

Gagarin, Michael. 1977. "Socrates' *Hybris* and Alcibiades' Failure." *Phoenix* 31:22–37.

Giannantoni, Gabriele. 1990. *Socratis et Socraticorum Reliquiae*. 4 vols. Naples.

Gill, Christopher. 1998. "Afterword: Dialectic and the Dialogue Form in Late Plato." Chapter 10 in Gill and McCabe 1998.

Gill, Christopher, and M. M. McCabe, eds. 1998. *Form and Argument in Late Plato*. Oxford.

Gould, Thomas. 1963. *Platonic Love*. London.

Griswold, Charles L., Jr. 1981. "The Ideas and the Criticism of Poetry in Plato's *Republic*, Book 10." *Journal of the History of Philosophy* 19:135–50.

———. 1986. *Self-Knowledge in Plato's Phaedrus*. New Haven, Conn. (New ed., University Park, Pa., 1996.)

———, ed. 1988a. *Platonic Writings/Platonic Readings*. New York.

———. 1988b. "Plato's Metaphilosophy: Why Plato Wrote Dialogues." In Griswold 1988a, 143–70. (Reprinted in Smith 1998, 1.221–52.)

———. 1999. "E Pluribus Unum? On the Platonic 'Corpus,'" *Ancient Philosophy* 19:361–97.

Grote, George. 1867. *Plato and the Other Companions of Sokrates*. 2d ed. 3 vols. London.

Grube, G.M.A. 1935. *Plato's Thought*. London.

Guthrie, W.K.C. 1962–81. *A History of Greek Philosophy*. 6 vols. Cambridge.

———. 1971a. *Socrates*. Vol. 3, pt. 2, of *HGP*. Cambridge.

———. 1971b. *The Sophists*. Vol. 3, pt. 1, of *HGP*. Cambridge.

Halliwell, Stephen. 1986. *Aristotle's Poetics*. London.

Halperin, David. 1985. "Platonic *Erōs* and What Men Call Love." *Ancient Philosophy* 5:161–204. (Reprinted in Smith 1998, 3:66–121.)

———. 1992. "Plato and the Erotics of Narrativity." In Klagge and Smith 1992, 93–129. (Reprinted in *Plato and Postmodernism*, ed. S. Shankman, 43–75. Glenside, Pa., 1994, and [reprinted] in Smith 1998, 3.41–272.)

Hansen, Mogens Herman. 1995. *The Trial of Socrates from the Athenian Point of View*. Copenhagen.

Havelock, Eric. 1963. *Preface to Plato*. Cambridge, Mass.

Herington, John. 1985. *Poetry into Drama: Early Tragedy and the Greek Poetic Tradition.* Berkeley and Los Angeles.

Hyland, Drew. 1995. *Finitude and Transcendence in the Platonic Dialogues.* Albany, N.Y.

Irwin, Terence H. 1977. *Plato's Moral Theory.* New York.

———. 1988. "Socrates and the Tragic Hero," In *Language and the Tragic Hero: Essays in Greek Tragedy in Honor of Gordon M. Kirkwood,* edited by Pietro Pucci. Atlanta, Ga.

———. 1995. *Plato's Ethics.* New York.

Jaeger, Werner. 1944–46. *Paideia: The Ideals of Greek Culture.* 3 vols. Translated by Gilbert Highet. New York.

Kahn, Charles H. 1979. *The Art and Thought of Heraclitus: An Edition of the Fragments with a Translation and Commentary.* Cambridge.

———. 1983. "Drama and Dialectic in Plato's *Gorgias*." *Oxford Studies in Ancient Philosophy* 1:75–121.

———. 1994. "Aeschines on Socratic Eros." In Vander Waerdt 1994, 87–106.

———. 1997. *Plato and the Socratic Dialogue.* Cambridge.

Kerferd, George B. 1981. *The Sophistic Movement.* Cambridge.

Keuls, Eva C. 1978. *Plato and Greek Painting.* Columbia Studies in the Classical Tradition 5. Leiden.

Kierkegaard, Søren. 1966. *The Concept of Irony with Constant Reference to Socrates.* Translated by Lee M. Capel. London. (Danish original, Copenhagen, 1841.)

Klagge, James C., and Nicholas D. Smith, eds. 1992. *Methods of Interpreting Plato and His Dialogues.* Oxford Studies in Ancient Philosophy, supplement 2.

Klein, Jacob. 1965. *A Commentary on Plato's "Meno."* Chapel Hill, N.C.

Klosko, George. 1986. *The Development of Plato's Political Theory.* London.

Kosman, L. Aryeh. 1976. "Platonic Love." In *Facets of Plato's Philosophy,* edited by W.H. Werkmeister, 53–69. Assen.

———. 1992a. "Acting: Drama as *Mimesis* of *Praxis*." In *Essays on Aristotle's Poetics,* edited by Amélie Oksenberg Rorty, 51–72. Princeton.

———. 1992b. "Silence and Imitation in Plato's Dialogues." In Klagge and Smith 1992, 73–92.

Kraut, Richard. 1984. *Crito, Socrates, and the State.* Princeton.

———, ed. 1992a. *The Cambridge Companion to Plato.* Cambridge.

———. 1992b. "The Defense of Justice in Plato's *Republic.*" Chapter 10 in Kraut 1992a, 311–37.

Laks, André. 1990. "Legislation and Demiurgy: On the Relationship Between Plato's *Republic* and *Laws.*" *Classical Antiquity* 9:209–29.

Lissarrague, François. 1986. "Why Satyrs Are Good to Represent." In Winkler and Zeitlin 1986, 228–36.

MacIntyre, Alasdair. 1984. *After Virtue.* 2d ed. Notre Dame, Ind.

Meinewalt, Constance C. 1992. "Good-bye to the Third Man." Chapter 12 in Kraut 1992a, 365–96.

Miller, Mitchell H., Jr. 1986. *Plato's Parmenides: The Conversion of the Soul.* Princeton.

Morrow, Glenn R. 1962. *Plato's Epistles.* 2d ed. Indianapolis. (Originally published 1935.)

———. 1993. *Plato's Cretan City: A Historical Interpretation of the Laws.* Reprint (of 1960 edition) with a foreword by Charles H. Kahn. Princeton.

Murdock, Iris. 1990. *The Fire and the Sun: Why Plato Banished the Artists.* New York.

Murray, Penelope. 1996. *Plato on Poetry: Ion, Republic 376a–398b, Republic 595–608b*. Cambridge.

Nagy, Gregory. 1979. *The Best of the Achaeans: Concepts of the Hero in Archaic Greek Poetry*. Baltimore. (Rev. ed., Baltimore, 1999.)

Nehamas, Alexander. 1982. "Plato on Imitation and Poetry in Republic 10." In *Plato on Beauty, Wisdom, and the Arts*, edited by J. Moravscik and P. Tempko, 47–78. Totowa, N.J. (Reprinted in Smith 1998, 3:296–323.)

Nightingale, Andrea Wilson. 1992. "Plato's *Gorgias* and Euripides' *Antiope*: A Study in Generic Transformation." *Classical Antiquity* 11:121–41.

———. 1995. *Genres in Dialogue: Plato and the Construct of Philosophy*. Cambridge.

Nussbaum, Martha C. 1986. *The Fragility of Goodness: Luck and Ethics in Greek Tragedy and Philosophy*. Cambridge.

O'Brien, M. J. 1967. *The Socratic Paradoxes and the Greek Mind*. Chapel Hill, N.C.

O'Neill, William, ed. 1985. *Proclus Diadochus: Alcibiades 1: A Translation and Commentary*. The Hague.

Osborne, Catherine. 1987. "The Repudiation of Representation in Plato's *Republic* and Its Repercussions." *Proceedings of the Cambridge Philological Society* 213, n.s., 33:53–73.

Ostwald, Martin. 1969. *Nomos and the Beginnings of the Athenian Democracy*. Oxford.

Pangle, Thomas L., trans. 1980. *The Laws of Plato*. Chicago.

Panofsky, Erwin. 1968. *Idea: A Concept in Art Theory: A Study of the Definition and Conception of the Term "Idea," from Plato to the 17th Century, when the Modern Definition Emerged*. Translated by Joseph J. S. Peake. Columbia, S.C. (German original, 1924.)

Patterson, Richard. 1982. "The Platonic Art of Comedy and Tragedy." *Philosophy and Literature* 6:76–93.

Pelling, C.B.R. 1990. *Characterization and Individuality in Greek Literature*. Oxford.

Popper, Karl. 1971. *The Open Society and Its Enemies*. Vol. 1, *The Spell of Plato*. 5th ed. Princeton.

Prince, Michael. 1996. *Dialogue in the British Enlightenment: Theology, Aesthetics, and the Novel*. Cambridge.

Rawls, John. 1971. *A Theory of Justice*. Cambridge, Mass.

Reeve, C.D.C. 1988. *Philosopher-Kings: The Argument of Plato's Republic*. Princeton.

———. 1989. *Socrates in the "Apology."* Indianapolis.

Reinhard, Karl. 1979. *Sophocles*. Translated by H. Harvey and D. Harvey. Oxford. (German original, 1933.)

Richter, G.M.A. 1965. *The Portraits of the Greeks*. 3 vols. London. (Abridged and revised by R.R.R. Smith. Ithaca, N.Y., 1984.)

Riginos, Alice Swift. 1976. *Platonica: The Anecdotes Concerning the Life and Writings of Plato*. Columbia Studies in the Classical Tradition 3. Leiden.

Robinson, Richard. 1953. *Plato's Earlier Dialectic*. 2d ed. Oxford.

Robinson, T. M. 1970. *Plato's Psychology*. Toronto.

Roochnik, David. 1996. *Of Art and Wisdom: Plato's Understanding of Techne*. University Park, Pa.

Rosen, Stanley. 1988. *The Quarrel Between Philosophy and Poetry: Studies in Ancient Thought*. New York.

Ross, W. D. 1951. *Plato's Theory of Ideas*. Oxford.

Rutherford, R. B. 1995. *The Art of Plato*. Cambridge, Mass.

Ryle, Gilbert. 1966. *Plato's Progress*. Cambridge.

Saunder, Trevor J., trans. 1970. *Plato: The "Laws."* London.

Schein, Seth L. 1984. *The Mortal Hero: An Introduction to Homer's "Iliad."* Berkeley and Los Angeles.

Shorey, Paul. 1930. *Plato, Republic*. Loeb Classical Library. Cambridge, Mass.

———. 1933. *What Plato Said*. Chicago.

Simon, Bennett. 1978. *Mind and Madness in Ancient Greece: The Classical Roots of Modern Psychiatry*. Ithaca, N.Y.

Smith, Nicholas D., ed. 1998. *Plato: Critical Assessments*. 4 vols. London.

Solmsen, Friedrich. 1942. *Plato's Theology*. Ithaca, N.Y. (Reprint, New York, 1967.)

———. 1972. *Intellectual Experiments of the Greek Enlightenment*. Princeton.

Sprague, Rosamund Kent. 1962. *Plato's Use of Fallacy*. New York.

———, ed. 1972. *The Older Sophists: A Complete Translation by Several Hands of the Fragments in "Die Fragmente der Vorsokratiker" Edited by Diels-Kranz, with a New Edition of Antiphon and Euthydemus*. Columbia, S.C.

Stalley, R. F. 1983. *Plato's Laws*. Indianapolis.

Stanford, W. B. 1963. *The Ulysses Theme: A Study in the Adaptability of a Traditional Hero*. 2d ed. Oxford.

Stone, I. F. 1988. *The Trial of Socrates*. Boston.

Strauss, Barry S. 1993. *Fathers and Sons in Athens: Ideology and Society in the Era of the Peloponnesian War*. Princeton.

Strauss, Leo. 1964. *The City and Man*. Charlottesville, Va.

———. 1975. *The Argument and Action of Plato's Laws*. Chicago.

Taylor, Thomas. 1804. "An Apology for the Fables of Homer." In *The Works of Plato*, 1:133–99. London.

Tigerstedt, E. N. 1977. *Interpreting Plato*. Stockholm Studies in the History of Literature 17. Uppsala.

Thomson, J.A.K. 1926. *Irony: An Historical Introduction*. Cambridge.

Vander Waerdt, Paul A., ed. 1994. *The Socratic Movement*. Ithaca, N.Y.

Vidal-Naquet, Pierre. 1986. "Athens and Atlantis: Structure and Meaning of a Platonic Myth." In *The Black Hunter: Forms of Thought and Forms of Society in the Greek World*, translated by A. Szegedy-Maszak. Baltimore, 1986. (Original, Paris, 1981.)

Vlastos, Gregory. 1981. *Platonic Studies*. 2d ed. Princeton.

———. 1991. *Socrates: Ironist and Moral Philosopher*. Ithaca, N.Y.

———. 1994. *Socratic Studies*. Edited by Myles Burnyeat. Cambridge.

von Blanckenhagen, Peter H. 1964. "The Shield of Alcibiades." In *Studies in Memory of Karl Lehmann*, 38–42. Locust Valley, N.Y.

———. 1992. "Stage and Actors in Plato's *Symposium*." *Greek, Roman, and Byzantine Studies* 33:51–68.

West, Thomas G. 1979. *Plato's "Apology" of Socrates: An Interpretation, with a new Translation*. Ithaca, N.Y.

Westerink, L. G. 1962. *Anonymous Prolegomena to Platonic Philosophy*. Amsterdam.

White, Nicholas P. 1992. "Plato's Metaphysical Epistemology." Chapter 9 in Kraut 1992a, 277–310.

Williams, Bernard. 1973. "The Analogy of City and Soul in Plato's *Republic*." In *Exegesis and Argument*, edited by E. N. Lee, A.P.D. Mourelatos, and R. M. Rorty, 196–206. New York.

Wilson, J.R.S. 1976. "The Contents of the Cave." In *New Essays on Plato and the Presocratics* (*Canadian Journal of Philosophy*, supplement 2), edited by R. A. Shiner and J. King-Fellow, 117–27. Calgary, Alta.

Winkler, John J., and Froma I. Zeitlin, eds. 1986. *Nothing to Do with Dionysos? Athenian Drama in Its Social Context*. Princeton.

Zanker, Paul. 1995. *The Mask of Socrates: The Image of the Intellectual in Antiquity*. Translated by Alan Shapiro. Berkeley and Los Angeles.

Zeitlin, Froma I. 1994. "The Artful Eye: Vision and Spectacle in Euripidean Theater." In *Art and Text in Ancient Greek Culture*, edited by Simon Goldhill and Robin Osborne, 138–96. Cambridge.

INDEX OF PASSAGES CITED

GENERAL INDEX